TEACHING READING & STUDY STRATEGIES

AT THE COLLEGE LEVEL

RONA F. FLIPPO
Fitchburg State College

DAVID C. CAVERLY
Southwest Texas State University

Editors

ira
International Reading Association
Newark, Delaware 19714

The International Reading Association attempts, through its publications, to provide a forum for a wide spectrum of opinions on reading. This policy permits divergent viewpoints without assuming the endorsement of the Association.

Copyright 1991 by the
International Reading Association, Inc.

Library of Congress Cataloging in Publication Data

Teaching reading and study strategies at the college level /
  Rona F. Flippo, David C. Caverly, editors.
    p.   cm.
  Includes bibliographical references and index.
  1. Study, Method of.   2. Reading (Higher education)
I. Flippo, Rona F.   II. Caverly, David C.
LB2395.T4   1991   90-45739
428.4'2'0711—dc20   CIP
ISBN 0-87207-359-9

Contents

Foreword

There are two ways to deal with students who show up for college without the requisite skills to benefit fully from their instruction. The first is to ignore their problems and teach them with the attitude that they're on their own: "If they can't make it in my class, that's just too bad!" This attitude prevails too often among college instructors; the results are high student dropout rates and wasted potential. The second option is to recognize the problem and deal with these students in constructive ways: teach them the learning skills and strategies necessary to reap the full benefit of their college learning experiences.

The authors and editors of this volume, of course, advocate the teaching of learning strategies at the college level. Furthermore, they support such instruction among all college students. They have reviewed the evidence carefully in order to provide explicit and valid guidance on how to help college students improve their reading and study skills.

Covering a range of topics from the nature of vocabulary acquisition and instruction to strategies for taking tests, these authors have written a book that is both scholarly and practical. They have—in all respects—thoroughly reviewed the literature on their respective topics and have identified the strategies that work for the teachers *and* for the learners.

If you want to know how to increase student-initiated questions in your classes, this is your book. If your students are overly anxious about tests, this is your book. If you need information about how to help students take notes, or about whether notetaking is even necessary, this is also your book.

If I had the power to do so, I would place a copy of this book into the hands of every community college teacher; indeed, into the hands of every teacher of college freshmen and sophomores. Rona Flippo, David Caverly, and their colleagues are to be commended. This book is excellent.

Alden J. Moe
Lehigh University

Introduction

The field of reading and study strategy improvement at the college level is as old as college itself. However, with the expansion of college enrollment after World War II and the rapid growth of junior and community colleges in the early 1960s, college reading and study strategy instruction has gained new attention. Today, reading and study strategy assistance can be found in medical schools, universities, community and junior colleges, and technical schools around the world.

During the widespread growth of college reading and study strategy instructional programs, we have learned a great deal. Until now, however, no one has made available a comprehensive collection of knowledge about teaching and implementing reading and study strategy programs. This book provides a review of the theoretical, empirical, and instructional issues in the field of college reading and study strategies through a careful and systematic examination of the relevant literature.

We had to make many decisions as we developed this volume. One decision was to limit our scope to college reading and study strategy instruction. While many remedial and developmental college programs include components in adult basic education, English as a second language, writing, mathematics, and counseling, we chose not to discuss these related but separate areas.

Another decision was what to call the programs we did include and the personnel teaching or directing them. These programs have a variety of labels, including college reading and study skills, college reading improvement, learning strategies, special studies, developmental or remedial instruction, basic skills instruction, and compensatory education. Personnel in this field are collectively called reading specialists, reading practitioners, or learning specialists; they can be college reading program directors, administrators, staff, instructors, professors, teachers, or counselors. We chose not to force conformity on our authors, since all these labels and titles are used in the field. We let the authors of each chapter decide on the labels that seemed to fit best with their orientation and experience.

A third decision was the organization of the chapters. We sought comprehensiveness and some organizational conformity. We asked the authors to approach their chapters in a way that seemed appropriate to their topics and writing style, but to include four general components: (1) an introduction and rationale for their topic; (2) a review of the relevant literature; (3) a synthesis of this literature, including a discussion of implications, recommendations, and further avenues of research; and (4) a bibliography of references and suggested readings. We asked the authors to indicate the most relevant works in this list by noting them with an asterisk (*).

In Chapter 1, Simpson and Dwyer begin by reviewing vocabulary instruction and discussing what it means to know a word, how such knowledge can be measured, and the role of the student in learning new words. They follow with a critique of studies that focus on strategies for developing both general and content-specific vocabulary, and conclude with the characteristics of effective vocabulary instruction.

Nist and Mealey review the more teacher-directed comprehension strategies in Chapter 2. Building from a review of current theoretical bases for college reading instruction (e.g., metacognition, schema theory, text structure), they discuss the effect of direct comprehension instruction on college-age readers. Next, they review the research on various comprehension-building techniques. They end with specific recommendations for teaching comprehension strategies.

In Chapter 3, Caverly and Orlando review student-initiated strategies for studying college-level textbooks. As a framework for discussion, they present a historical overview of comprehension theories, moving from the product perspective to the process perspective to our current interactive perspective. Then they review current models of textbook studying and the empirical research in support of such models. The chapter ends with recommendations for teaching textbook study strategies to college-age readers.

Anderson and Armbruster begin Chapter 4 with a review of the literature on taking notes during lectures. Using both the external storage hypothesis and the encoding hypothesis put forth to explain the effects of notetaking, they discuss the implications of research for instruction in notetaking at the college level.

In Chapter 5, Risko, Alvarez, and Fairbanks review the literature on time management, study environment, and library use. They examine the recommendations of study strategy textbooks and the correlation between these recommendations and the empirical literature, concluding with specific implications for teaching study strategies.

Risko, Fairbanks, and Alvarez review what the study strategy textbooks recommend regarding motivation, memory enhancement, and students' attention in Chapter 6. Again, they examine the correlation between these recommendations and the empirical literature and end with implications for instruction.

In Chapter 7, Wark and Flippo discuss study strategies for test preparation and test taking. Specifically, they review the literature on test coaching, test wiseness, and the treatment of test anxiety. They close with suggestions for instruction and future research.

We believe you will find this publication the most comprehensive and up-to-date source available in the field of college reading and study strategies. While several excellent books address similar topics for elementary or secondary school populations, this is one of the first books to thoroughly examine reading and study strategy instruction at the college level. It is intended to provide specific and necessary information to a diverse audience, including practitioners who are looking for ready answers, administrators who are interested in developing relevant and beneficial programs, and professors who are training students in college reading and study strategies without the benefit of a textbook or a compilation of readings. This volume also should be of interest to reading educators, researchers, and librarians who want to add a comprehensive review of the literature in this area to their collections.

RFF

DCC

Acknowledgments

W e wish to thank the International Reading Association for recognizing the need for this book. We are indebted to the individuals in IRA who encouraged and assisted us throughout the various stages of the manuscript's preparation.

The field of reading owes a great debt to those who have devoted so much of their talents, careers, research, and writing to enriching our knowledge base in reading and study strategy instruction at postsecondary levels. We wish to acknowledge their critical contributions. We also wish to thank the professional organizations that have played an important role in advancing knowledge in this field.

We owe our greatest thanks to the excellent researchers and writers who authored the chapters included in this book.

They were invited to contribute because of their expertise in both the specific area covered in their chapter and the field of college reading in general. Thank you for making this book possible.

RFF

DCC

Contributors

Marino C. Alvarez
Tennessee State University
Nashville, Tennessee

Thomas H. Anderson
Center for the Study of Reading
University of Illinois
Champaign, Illinois

Bonnie B. Armbruster
Center for the Study of Reading
University of Illinois
Champaign, Illinois

David C. Caverly
Southwest Texas State University
San Marcos, Texas

Edward J. Dwyer
East Tennessee State University
Johnson City, Tennessee

Marilyn M. Fairbanks
West Virginia University
Morgantown, West Virginia

Rona F. Flippo
Fitchburg State College
Fitchburg, Massachusetts

Donna L. Mealey
Louisiana State University
Baton Rouge, Louisiana

Sherrie L. Nist
University of Georgia
Athens, Georgia

Vincent P. Orlando
Metropolitan State College
Denver, Colorado

Victoria J. Risko
Peabody College
Vanderbilt University
Nashville, Tennessee

Michele L. Simpson
University of Georgia
Athens, Georgia

David M. Wark
University of Minnesota
Minneapolis, Minnesota

1

Vocabulary Acquisition and the College Student

Michele L. Simpson
Edward J. Dwyer

The subject matter to be mastered in most content-oriented college courses includes discipline-specific and often highly technical vocabulary with numerous underlying concepts (Hopper & Wells, 1981; O'Rourke, 1974; Sartain et al., 1982). To guarantee successful independent learning, college students need well-developed receptive vocabularies—that is, words that are known when either heard or read (Manzo & Sherk, 1971-1972). They also need effective and efficient strategies for coping with previously unknown words. Many students, however, possess neither the receptive vocabulary nor the strategies necessary to cope with the demands of independent learning in college.

While this lack is often camouflaged by students who diagnose their difficulties in a course as solely content related, Sartain et al. (1982), in a 2-year study tracing the learning difficulties of college students, found some very intriguing patterns. Students enrolled in four core courses (philosophy, physics, psychology, and English composition) were asked to keep logs and attend weekly seminars conducted by graduate assistants to discuss the problems they were having in their classes. During those 2 years, the most common difficulty reported by students across all four content areas was technical vocabulary. (Hopper and Wells [1981] reached similar conclusions in a study involving 600 college students.) Sartain et al. also reported that inadequate general vocabulary development was a major obstacle to success in the college courses studied. If the vocabulary demands of these four content areas were representative of the demands of other college courses—and if student reports were typical and accurate—it is evident that general and technical vocabulary deficiencies are major causes of difficulty with course content.

Since an extensive vocabulary and a well-developed repertoire of strategies for improving vocabulary are critical for success in content area learning, college reading professionals need to use systematic and effective approaches to vocabulary instruction. Interestingly enough, such approaches have yet to be adequately defined for any age level. Reading teachers must help students learn vocabulary that is directly related to content-oriented material. On the other hand, the long-range goal of a vocabulary program must be to provide students with the means to develop vocabulary on their own—particularly since it is unlikely that college teachers will provide vocabulary instruction along with course content instruction. Thus, the purpose of this chapter is to review current research with the goal of developing practical guidelines for implementing effective vocabulary enhancement approaches and strategies.

Theoretical and Methodological Issues

Several theoretical and methodological issues have been explored through research, either explicitly or implicitly, to determine a superior method of vocabulary instruction. These issues are similar to those that classroom teachers face daily—whether in middle school, high school, or college—when they make decisions concerning the types of instructional activities and forms of assessment to use with students. For example, one troublesome methodological issue for both researchers and classroom teachers is how best to measure whether students have learned the words they were taught. If the teacher/researcher selects a format to measure vocabulary growth that matches the instruction, he or she cannot reliably tell from the test scores whether the students really learned the words that were taught or whether they merely demonstrated effective test-taking skills. Further, such evaluations involve only recognition, which tells nothing about students' ability to use words in course contexts or to generate material of their own using a particular word. Thus, the real impact of vocabulary instruction becomes obscured by the selection of the testing instrument, causing the teacher/researcher to make tenuous conclusions about the effectiveness of the instruction.

While these issues may seem to be somewhat routine, their impact on the results of various vocabulary studies has been significant (Fairbanks, 1977; Mezynski, 1983; Vaughn et al., 1981). Therefore, three of the most critical issues will be discussed in this section: the criteria for knowing a vocabulary word, the type of assessment procedure, and the role of the learner.

What Does It Mean to "Know" a Word?

What factor determines whether a student has learned a new word? That question is difficult to answer because most research supports the conclusion that word meanings become progressively differentiated as learners age and become more experienced. Word knowledge is not a static product but a fluid quality that takes on additional characteristics and attributes as the learner experiences more associations with the word. Several models, however, have attempted to describe the levels of word knowledge through which a learner progresses.

Dale's (1965) continuum-concept model is one such attempt. He suggested that word knowledge follows four stages: (1) I've never seen the word; (2) I've heard of it, but I don't know what it means; (3) I recognize it in context, it has something to do with...; and (4) I know the word in one or several of its meanings. Dixon and Jenkins's (1984) analysis of receptive vocabulary knowledge is similar to Dale's in that a continuum is emphasized. They break down the levels of knowledge into full concept, partial concept, and verbal association knowledge. Most classroom teachers would say that full concept knowledge is their goal for vocabulary instruction.

For the purposes of this chapter, full concept knowledge is defined as being attained when students can recognize examples of the targeted concepts without teacher assistance, and when they can discriminate between the use of a particular concept and similar examples drawn from other concepts. Concepts can be fully defined by a set of critical features (those common to all examples) and variable features (those demonstrated by some examples but not all). When a student's knowledge of a concept consists of any of the various combinations of such features, that student has partial concept knowledge. Obviously, partial knowledge exists in several degrees. A student's verbal association knowledge is not an indication of concept knowledge; rather, it is the pairing of a label to its meaning, a one-dimensional rote activity.

With such a perspective of word knowledge, the issue is not whether students know the word but in what way they know the word. Dale (1965) and Dixon and Jenkins (1984) imply that it is best for students to know a new word as a full concept, especially if knowing the word can have a substantial impact on subsequent understanding and learning.

For whatever reason, researchers rarely strive with their subjects for the full concept dimension of word knowledge. Moreover, only a few researchers have explicitly stated their criteria for word knowledge (Beck, Perfetti, & McKeown, 1982; Stahl, 1983), whereas the majority have depended on their assessment instruments to create that criteria implicitly. Conse-

Simpson and Dwyer

quently, the type of vocabulary assessment used in research or in the classroom becomes critical to the entire process since it can lead to the formation of instructional goals.

How Can Vocabulary Knowledge Be Measured?

The type of instrument used to measure vocabulary acquisition should be closely related to the researcher/teacher's concept of what is involved in knowing a word and sensitive to what is being attempted via the instruction (Kameenui, Carnine, & Freschi, 1982). If this sensitivity is lacking, there is a strong possibility that the measurement will mask or understate the instructional strategy's effectiveness. For example, if a multiple choice test is used to measure the effectiveness of an instructional lesson that emphasized word classification or categorization, some students may do poorly on the test because the instruction did not focus on the strict memorization of definitions. If, however, the researcher selects an analogy test format, the students will be better able to demonstrate what was learned.

Objective and recall assessment procedures have distinct advantages and disadvantages that need to be acknowledged. Earlier studies with college students tended to rely heavily on standardized tests with a multiple choice format (Alexander, 1969). More recent studies (Diekhoff, Brown, & Dansereau, 1982) tend to use free recall assessment measures such as short answer questions or modified cloze procedures. This trend may be indicative of how researchers are defining what it means to "know" a word.

Researchers need to more carefully define which level of word knowledge they wish to stress, select vocabulary strategies that will help students learn at that level, and then create a test that will be sensitive to the effects of that instructional strategy. Unfortunately, researchers have not been consistent in their procedures, thus causing some unwarranted conclusions to be drawn about the effectiveness of certain vocabulary strategies.

What Is the Student's Role in Vocabulary Acquisition?

The third methodological/theoretical issue concerns the role of the learner during vocabulary instruction. This critical area involves efforts to determine whether the learner is seen as a passive recipient of knowledge or an active seeker of information. The activity of the learner has been theoretically defined by Craik (1979) and Craik and Lockhart (1972), who proposed that deeper, more elaborate, and distinctive processing of stimuli results in better performance, all other things being equal. (Deeper processing is typically semantic in nature, whereas superficial processing is acoustic or visual.) Because the levels of processing model has been criticized (Eysenck, 1979), other researchers have suggested modifications. For example, Tyler et al. (1979) proposed that the amount of cognitive effort required by a task is an important determinant of later recall performance, with greater cognitive effort leading to greater recall. Cognitive effort research with college-level learners (Craik & Tulving, 1975; Hyde & Jenkins, 1973; Johnson-Laird, Gibbs, & de Mowbrey, 1978) supports this concept.

Within these theoretical frameworks, which are speculative, vague, and difficult to quantify, Stahl (1985) attempted to describe the tasks of the learner. He suggested that, depending on the instructional methods used, a student learning new vocabulary should be involved in associative processing, comprehension processing, or generative processing. Associative processing requires the learner to make an association or connection between a word and its synonym or definition within a particular context. This level of activity might involve the learners in dictionary study or programmed learning. Associative processing is the lowest level of involvement, requiring the least amount of processing (Craik, 1979; Craik & Lockhart, 1972) and the least amount of effort (Tyler et al., 1979), but it is the basis for the next two levels of processing.

The second level, comprehension processing, requires the learner to apply word associations to a new situation in a meaningful and correct manner. The learner could be asked to complete analogy or categorization exercises, fill in the blanks in cloze exercises, or judge whether a word has been used correctly. For example, in a study by Beck, McCaslin, and McKeown (1980), some of the subjects were asked to answer questions using targeted words rather than simply told the definitions by the teacher.

The third level, generative processing, asks the learner to create or generate a novel context for the targeted word. This task could require the learner to write original sentences, to paraphrase definitions, or to create categories or semantic maps.

When researchers compare different vocabulary strategies to determine which is more effective, they often fail to define adequately or to keep equivalent the processing requirements (or involvement) of the learners (Mezynski, 1983). Consequently, a strategy that actively engages the learner in solving problems, answering questions, or producing applications in new situations may be compared directly with another strategy that asks the learner to fill in blanks or to match words with definitions. Not surprisingly, the more active strategy involving the learner in generative processing appears to be the superior method of vocabulary instruction.

Researchers must thoroughly address the issue of processing levels, as well as issues pertaining to the criteria for determining whether a word is known and the methods of assessing vocabulary instruction, before they draw conclusions about the effectiveness of particular vocabulary strategies. This is absolutely essential if research is to contribute to the improvement of vocabulary instruction in the college classroom.

Review of Empirical Literature

Within the past 5 years, interest in vocabulary study has increased tremendously. Most recent studies have focused on intermediate-aged students, leaving college reading professionals with little direction. Through an extensive survey, Berg, Hess, and Crocker (1983) found that only 14 percent of college reading teachers were able to find relevant research to warrant teaching vocabulary in courses designed to help students improve in reading competence. This finding is not comforting considering the multitude of commercially available vocabulary workbooks and kits, none of which appear to be empirically based (Stahl, Brozo, & Simpson, 1987). There is, however, a small body of recent research on how college students learn words that can provide reading professionals with some guidance. These studies, most of which were conducted within the past decade, can be divided into two categories: general vocabulary development studies and content-specific studies.

General Vocabulary Development Studies

Practitioners and researchers who believe that systematic instruction should focus on general vocabulary improvement probably favor the instrumentalist position outlined by Anderson and Freebody (1981). The instrumentalist hypothesis maintains that word knowledge is a direct causal link affecting text comprehension. Thus, the more individual word meanings taught, the better students will comprehend any new or difficult expository material they read. Anderson and Freebody stressed that the most distinguishing characteristic of the instrumentalist hypothesis is the emphasis on direct vocabulary-building exercises.

Research focusing on the development of general vocabulary among college students reflects a gradual change over time relative to the issues of which words should be taught, how students should be taught the targeted words, and which measures should be used to assess the effectiveness of vocabulary instruction. Studies from the late 1960s and early 1970s tended to emphasize master word lists, with words taught by repetitive associations with synonyms or brief dictionary definitions; standardized reading tests were used to measure vocabulary acquisition. In contrast, studies in the late 1970s and early 1980s emphasized more active and generative strategies, words taught within context, and informal assessment procedures.

Because of the vast methodological differences in earlier and later general vocabulary improvement studies, it is not surprising that the findings tend to be highly equivocal. Neverthe-less, we will make an effort to systematically analyze these general vocabulary improvement studies. These studies were divided into seven subcategories: word list, word part (affix), key-word/imagery, experience-based, contextual analysis, mixed method, and student-initiated learning studies.

Word list studies. Teaching vocabulary from a list is perhaps the oldest and most prevalent instructional method in secondary and postsecondary education. In experimental studies using word lists, subjects receive a list of words and their definitions/synonyms or are told to consult a dictionary for comprehensive definitions. The words to be learned generally come from commercial workbooks, standardized tests, or high-frequency word lists. Both the control group (usually with no instruction) and the experimental group are given a standardized test to measure the effects of the instruction. In general, these types of studies, conducted in the 1950s and 1960s, found no significant differences favoring the subjects who used word lists to improve their general vocabulary (Crump, 1966, Fairbanks, 1977; McNeal, 1973).

Affix studies. Unlike word list instruction, teaching word parts, or affixes, is a generative strategy that allows students to unlock the meaning of at least some of the unknown words they encounter. Teaching affixes has been widely recommended for all ages and levels of students (Cushenberry, 1972; Dale, 1965; Deighton, 1960; O'Rourke, 1974). In fact, this technique might be considered a college reading tradition. Of the 55 vocabulary workbooks analyzed by Stahl, Brozo, and Simpson (1987), 44 (80 percent) heavily emphasized word parts. However, little empirical research exists at any age level to support the teaching of affixes as a method of developing general vocabulary (Graves & Hammond, 1979).

We found only three empirically based studies that focused on using affixes with college students. Albinski (1970) found that the preteaching of affixes was effective with a group of 37 college students. On the other hand, he did not consider the advantages great enough to warrant teaching word stems on a routine basis. Einbecker's (1973) study with junior college freshmen compared three different methodologies for teaching 40 different words. Group one was simply directed to study the words, group two was instructed to note and look up root words, and group three watched an audiovisual presentation of root words and their uses. On the 40-word posttest, the three groups showed no significant differences in their ability to recognize word meanings.

In the third study focusing on college students, Strader and Joy (1980) compared three distinctly different vocabulary teaching methods, one of which involved highly structured lessons on 60 Greek and Latin prefixes, suffixes, and roots. On the vocabulary section of the Nelson-Denny Reading Test (Brown, Nelson, & Denny, 1976), there were no significant differences in performance across the three groups. However, on the other dependent measure—a researcher-made 30-item multiple choice test assessing the ability to combine forms—the group receiving the highly structured affix instruction performed significantly better than the other two groups.

On the theoretical level, student knowledge of affixes as a generative strategy for unlocking the meaning of new words has some appeal. On the other hand, the lack of empirical research supporting this practice invites caution. Future researchers should carefully design their dependent measures to be sensitive to instruction on affixes. They also should build into their instructional paradigm some transfer lessons, as Graves and Hammond (1979) did. Unlike Graves and Hammond, the researchers in the three studies described did not seem to provide students with the guided instruction necessary to transfer their knowledge of affixes to unlock difficult words in their personal reading. Further, it is unlikely that isolated drills on the meanings of affixes will increase a student's general vocabulary, although empirical research has not verified this conclusion.

Keyword/imagery studies. During the past 5 years, considerable interest and research have focused on a mnemonic strategy called the keyword method, which was originally designed for learning a foreign language (Raugh & Atkinson,

1975). In this strategy, students arc trained either to find a keyword or clue within the unknown target word and then develop a mental image of that keyword or to use the keyword and mental image provided by the researcher/trainer. A variation of this method asks the learner to place the keyword and definition in a meaningful sentence. For example, if the target word to be learned was *acrophobia*, a student might focus on the clue of *acro* and then develop the image of an *acro*bat who was afraid of heights walking on a tightrope high in the sky. The learner could then generate a sentence such as: *The acro*bat, who has always been *afraid of high places*, suffered from *acrophobia*.

Paivio (1971) stated that mental imagery is important in facilitating long term retention for adults because of the dual coding of organizational factors. Advocates of the dual-coding theory maintain that two different but interconnected symbolic processing systems exist for encoding information—one verbal and the other nonverbal. They propose that information is encoded in verbal, nonverbal, or both systems depending on the task and the concreteness or abstractness of the words read. Abstract words are more likely to activate verbal codings and concrete words are more likely to activate either nonverbal codings or a combination of both verbal and nonverbal systems. Other researchers have suggested that the associative imagery of the keyword mnemonic operates by linking or relating items so they form unified wholes or higher order units. Thus, when one item is recalled, that item acts as a retrieval cue for the other items to regenerate the whole (Begg, 1972, 1973; Bower, 1970, 1972).

There is some evidence to suggest that when college students invent or discover their own images they retain more than when they are provided with the images (Bobrow & Bower, 1969). It appears that self-induced images are superior to researcher/trainer-induced images because learners are more actively involved when they generate the images and, consequently, are able to relate the images to their own way of thinking and their own experiential backgrounds.

Often the target words in keyword research are words with extremely low frequency (e.g., bolter, cowry, hosel, ratine). In this light, a hypothesis proposed by Eysenck (1979) explains, in part, why students trained in the keyword mnemonic almost always seem to perform significantly better than students in a corresponding control group. Eysenck's experiments demonstrated that rare words (such as those typically utilized in keyword research) are more distinctly encoded than common words and tend to be remembered more easily.

In addition to theoretical explanations supporting the keyword method, several studies with college students demonstrate this method's effectiveness. Pressley, Levin, and Miller (1981) conducted four experiments with college-age students designed to determine how the keyword method affects contextual measures of vocabulary acquisition. These studies were developed in response to criticism that the keyword method overlooks comprehension and usage and focuses only on simple associations between words and definitions. Critics of the method were answered, at least in part, when in these four studies the subjects using the keyword method performed significantly better than the control group on the dependent measure.

Reacting to criticism that the keyword method had never been compared with alternative vocabulary learning strategies, Pressley, Levin, and Miller (1982) conducted a second set of experiments. In these studies, three groups of subjects were instructed in the verbal-contextual approach to vocabulary instruction, while three other groups were instructed in the keyword method. The scores of the keyword groups were superior to those of the three verbal-contextual groups and to those of a control group that received no instruction, regardless of how the definitions were scored. Even more interesting was the finding that none of the contextually based groups scored better than the control group.

While Pressley, Levin, and Miller (1982) conducted their study with regularly enrolled students in college-level introduction to psychology courses, Roberts and Kelly (1985) studied

Simpson and Dwyer

students in college developmental reading classes. Their study compared the keyword method with a treatment condition using dictionary definitions. Roberts and Kelly found only modest differences favoring their keyword method in an immediate recall test; however, they found much greater differences favoring the approach on a measure of delayed recall. In a more recent study, Smith, Stahl, and Neel (1987) reported similar findings.

Although the findings appear impressive, keyword method studies do have some limitations. The most evident is the lack of applicability to actual classrooms. The words that college reading teachers select to teach their students typically are not like those used in the keyword studies. Keyword researchers usually use concrete, three syllable, low-frequency nouns with concise definitions (Pressley, Levin, & Miller, 1981, 1982). Researchers in future studies must use target words that college students need to know in order to understand what they read and hear, not words that are judged to be conducive to the keyword method.

Another limitation to keyword studies is whether college students can and will transfer the keyword system to their own learning tasks. A literature review reveals that only Jones and Hall's (1982) study with eighth graders attempted to answer that question. Furthermore, only Jones and Hall tried to apply the keyword method to an actual classroom setting. College reading researchers need to follow this example and apply the keyword method in a realistic setting to answer the question, "What would happen if college students were given a list of words without the corresponding keywords and asked to learn the words as efficiently as possible for application in a specific task?" Despite limited empirical support, the keyword method holds considerable promise, especially when compared with traditional and passive methods of vocabulary development that require no more of the learner than the memorization of a dictionary definition.

Experience-based studies. The basic assumption in the experience-based approach is that students can best understand

and remember new vocabulary after they have developed or enhanced their background for the concept the word represents. Manzo (1982) suggested that the teacher can enhance a student's background through the provision of on-the-spot experiences with follow-up discussions. Tulving (1983) suggested that this type of experience can become a part of a student's episodic memory—that is, memory for events. Tulving's theory suggests that vocabulary acquisition must begin in the episodic memory. Once additional contexts for a word are learned, the word, with all its related contexts, becomes a part of the semantic memory—the memory for general meanings that can be applied in numerous situations. This is the ultimate goal of most vocabulary instruction.

Petty, Herold, and Stoll (1968) concluded from a review of 50 different vocabulary studies that providing for experience in using a word is extremely important in a learner's vocabulary acquisition. Few researchers, however, have experimentally explored this concept with college learners. In the one study found in this area, Duffelmeyer (1980) reported positive results. Duffelmeyer tested the impact of providing experiences with new vocabulary by requiring 56 college students to act out investigator-prepared skits. The skits were built around words taken from passages in the comprehension section of the Nelson-Denny Reading Test. After each dramatization the investigator asked the class several questions about the targeted word. Then the students were asked to volunteer a personal experience that would convey the meaning of the word. The subjects in the comparative group used a traditional approach that emphasized context clues, structural analysis, and dictionary use. The experience-based group significantly outperformed the traditional group on the exam, supporting Duffelmeyer's hypothesis that college students can benefit from an experience-based approach to general vocabulary growth.

More research on this approach should be conducted with college-age students. Of particular interest would be attempts to validate student-centered approaches like Haggard's (1982) self-collection strategy or Manzo's (1982) subjective approach to vocabulary (SAV) strategy. Both Haggard and Manzo emphasize the role of student involvement in selecting the words to be learned and the importance of strong initial experiences.

Contextual analysis studies. The use of context clues for vocabulary improvement has long been highly recommended because of its purported advantages over other strategies. The theory is that students need not be dependent on a dictionary or glossary; instead, they can independently apply context strategies when confronted with unknown words. Consequently, many secondary and postsecondary reading method textbooks instruct teachers to tell their students to use contextual clues when they come across a word they do not know. Most commercial vocabulary materials for college students emphasize the use of contextual analysis.

Whether contextual analysis can actually help students understand difficult or unknown words and whether contextual analysis has a long term effect on vocabulary acquisition are issues still being researched and debated. For example, the results of Nagy et al.'s (1984) research with eighth graders support the hypothesis that students do increase general vocabulary via contextual analysis. Providing further support for contextual analysis, Stahl and Fairbanks (1986) concluded from a review of 26 studies (25 percent with college students) that emphasis on contextual information is more effective than emphasis on definitions. On the other hand, Schatz and Baldwin's (1986) study with eleventh graders found that the use of context clues with low-frequency words had no significant effect on subjects' performance.

Little research has been undertaken with college-age learners, but the limited research that does exist supports the use of contextual analysis. These studies have attempted either to describe the types of context clues that college students use or to experimentally measure the benefits of learning a word in context as opposed to learning a word and its definition in isolation. Reith (1981) reported that in choosing from among several types of context clues, college freshmen found the linked synonym clue to be the easiest to use and the comparison-contrast clue to be the most difficult.

An extensive review of the research led Carnine, Kameenui, and Coyle (1984) to conclude that instructional strategies for teaching students how to use context clues have not been well defined. However, Ironside's (1960) study with 211 college subjects is noteworthy because this researcher attempted to define an instructional paradigm that could be used effectively when teaching context clues. The Ironside study used three different experimental treatments: (1) deductive lessons—lectures on the types of context clues, (2) inductive lessons—100 practice exercises with no clue names, and (3) combination lessons—100 practice exercises and lectures on clue types. After 7 hours of instruction, the subjects in each group read a 1,000-word article containing 31 nonsense words that had to be defined on the basis of context clues. Each group then retook a standardized reading test to measure gains in reading power. All groups made gains, but there were no significant differences among the treatment groups.

Bobrow and Bower (1969) concluded that semantic encoding could strongly facilitate associative learning. Anderson and Kulhavy (1972) decided to build on this research and determine whether semantic encoding would have a similar effect on conceptual learning. They tested to see whether college students who saw a word and its definition and then created a sentence using the word would learn more than students who saw the word and its definition and then merely read the definition aloud three times. When the groups were compared on a vocabulary measure, the subjects who composed their own sentences did significantly better than those who read the definitions aloud. These findings are not surprising given the difference in the two groups' level of active involvement in the exercise.

Crist and Petrone (1977) conducted a study similar to that of Anderson and Kulhavy (1972), but their subjects did not generate sentences. The researchers found that the context group not only performed significantly better on the context posttest, but also performed as well as the definition group on the definition posttest. Crist (1981) replicated the Crist and Petrone study but used a single subject design. His results confirmed the earlier study's findings.

While the research looks promising for the use of contextual analysis with college students, it has evident limitations. For example, in the studies by Anderson and Kulhavy (1972), Crist and Petrone (1977), and Crist (1981), the subjects were exposed to short, researcher-constructed passages that were different from the naturally occurring expository text that college students read. Thus, the only credible conclusion is that contextual analysis helps college students learn word meanings (as measured by a test shortly following instruction) from researcher-made instructional sentences. Whether it helps them learn the meanings of unknown words found in more typical expository text is a question yet to be answered.

In attempting to answer this question with eleventh grade students, Schatz and Baldwin (1986) found the use of a context clues system ineffective in helping students determine the meanings of low-frequency words in naturally occurring prose. Considering these findings, replication of this study with college students seems advisable.

A second critical limitation is that researchers' criteria for knowing a word generally appear to be less comprehensive than criteria normally set by teachers. Teachers want their students to be able to derive meaning from unfamiliar words in sentences and paragraphs and to be able to use these words in future situations (Jenkins & Dixon, 1983). Researchers tend to be far less specific.

Another limitation is that little attempt has been made to define the instructional methodology involved in teaching students to use context clues effectively. Only Ironside (1960) appears to have addressed this issue directly and comprehensively. Researchers thus far have provided college reading teachers with little direction in the effective instruction of vocabulary using context clues. On the other hand, when Carnine, Kameenui, and Coyle (1984) attempted to address that issue with intermediate grade students, they found that the explicit teaching of a contextual analysis rule (e.g., "when there is a hard word in a sentence, look for other words in the story that tell you more about the word") was not particularly helpful.

Researchers using contextual analysis with college-age students need to examine the use of operational rules, the use of immediate feedback, and the quantity and pacing of practice exercises. Such analysis could lead to the eventual development of effective strategies for teaching students how to use context clues to understand the meaning of unfamiliar words.

Overall, many unanswered questions remain in the area of contextual analysis. As a beginning, researchers should examine four issues:

- the generalizability of contextual analysis to naturally occurring prose across a variety of content areas;
- the effects of contextual analysis on all types of readers, especially poor comprehenders;
- the long term effects of contextual analysis on different levels of word knowledge; and
- the role of the teacher in the instructional process.

Mixed method studies. Several studies with college-age students have used a mixture of methods and have emphasized both definitional and contextual knowledge of targeted words. When Petty, Herold, and Stoll (1968) reviewed existing vocabulary studies they found that methods involving a number of different teaching strategies were more effective than any one of those strategies used alone.

Johnson and Stratton (1966) carefully defined their instructional methods so that four discrete treatments (definitions, sentences, classification, and synonyms) could be compared with a mixed treatment that contained elements of each of the other four. A sixth group, designed as the control, received an irrelevant treatment. The treatment for each of the groups lasted a total of 12 minutes. Nine days later the 200 subjects were given two tests with open-ended and multiple choice questions. The group that received the mixed treatment got higher total scores than any of the groups that received a single kind of training. There were no significant differences among the four groups that received one kind of training. However, all five groups that received relevant treatments did better than the control group.

Like researchers working with younger students (Gipe, 1979; Stahl, 1983), Johnson and Stratton found that when a single method is specifically defined and then compared with a combination of methods, the combined method yields superior results. Several factors explain why Johnson and Stratton found this to be true when other researchers (Alexander, 1969; Baer, 1974) did not. First, Alexander and Baer compared one mixture with another mixture, thus reducing the impact of any one of the methods. Moreover, they used standardized tests to measure the effects of their treatments, while Johnson and Stratton constructed their own more sensitive tests. Further research based on the Johnson and Stratton study is needed; such research should be designed to examine the long term effects of each instructional methodology.

Student-initiated learning studies. Some researchers propose that a learner's general vocabulary increases more when the motivation is intrinsic than when it is extrinsic (Goodman, 1976; Haggard, 1980, 1984; Herber, 1978). Haggard concluded from her research on vocabulary acquisition that during their elementary and secondary years students tended to learn new words because the words had some immediate usefulness or particular significance. She later replicated the study with college-age students to determine if the same motivations for learning new words existed. Over a 6-week period, 42 college sophomores and juniors logged their own vocabulary development in a journal. The most commonly cited reason for learning new words was to be able to use them immediately in order to be more successful in class. The second most commonly reported reason for selecting a particular word was the need to clarify meaning. Of the total number of words learned, 40 percent were related to courses the students were taking—that is, content-specific words. Haggard concluded that the process of collecting words can definitely enhance a college student's interest in expanding vocabulary, in both course content and general use.

We found only one study that experimentally investigated the value of asking college students to select the words they wish to learn. Whereas Haggard's study was descriptive, Gnewuch (1974) conducted a 12-week empirically based study with 407 college students. Those in the experimental groups (students enrolled in reading classes) skimmed their own reading to find words that they knew vaguely but felt they could not define adequately. Then they were asked to write the words in the context in which they were found, make a guess at the meaning, and check that guess against a dictionary definition. Those in the control group (students enrolled in study skills classes) were given no special vocabulary instructions or guidance. The experimental subjects scored significantly higher than the control subjects in vocabulary growth on a standardized reading test. The question remains as to whether the students enrolled in study skills classes were equal in ability to the students in the reading classes. Nevertheless, Gnewuch's findings are sufficiently intriguing to encourage the undertaking of other studies of this type. Future researchers should, however, collect data beyond standardized test scores. For example, it would be informative to interview the students participating in such a project to discover their opinions about this approach and their strategies for learning unknown words.

Content-Specific Vocabulary Development Studies

While most earlier studies focused on how to increase general vocabulary, more recent studies have investigated generative or teacher-directed strategies to teach difficult but important content area words. This latter orientation is similar to the knowledge hypothesis proposed by Anderson and Freebody (1981); both stress that vocabulary should be taught within the context of learning new concepts so that new words can be related to one another and to prior knowledge. Thus, the source for words to be taught or studied is not teacher-made words lists but the difficult or unknown words that are critical for the comprehension of specific content area reading assignments.

Some of the strategies previously discussed—particularly those related to contextual analysis and affixes—could be used by students to understand key vocabulary encountered while learning from text. However, the strategies examined in this section differ from general vocabulary development strategies because the primary concern is for conceptual understanding.

Research focusing on content-specific vocabulary development in college students is limited. Results from studies discussed in this section, however, strongly support the argument that college students can improve vocabulary while learning concepts from reading.

Graphic organizers. Graphic organizers, often called structured overviews, graphically display key vocabulary terms to show the interrelationship of new concepts and previously learned concepts. These organizers can be teacher- or student-generated and can be used before reading, following reading, or at both times.

The graphic organizer is based on Ausubel's (1963) theory of meaningful receptive learning. Ausubel proposed that new meanings in a content area can be more effectively acquired if they are related to a previously learned background of relevant principles and concepts. Ausubel concluded that new learning could be facilitated if the learner's existing knowledge of cognitive structure was well organized and stable. He proposed the advance organizer as one strategy for organizing and strengthening the existing cognitive structure. Barron (1969), Earle (1970), and Estes, Mills, and Barron (1969) adapted Ausubel's idea to the schematic presentation of vocabulary and labeled this strategy the structured overview.

Numerous studies have been conducted to measure the effects of graphic organizers on students' learning from text. Moore and Readence (1980) concluded from their metaanalysis of 16 of these studies that only 2 percent of the variability in text learning could be explained by the use of graphic organizers. The researchers noted, however, that the advantages of graphic organizers were stronger when they were used as a postreading activity and when vocabulary was included as the criterion variable.

Barron and Schwartz (1984) concluded from their review of research that the potential usefulness of graphic organizers might have been camouflaged in past studies because teachers and researchers provided the graphic organizers as readiness activities for the students. Barron and Schwartz suggested that it might be more beneficial to have students construct their own graphic organizers. Thus, the active involvement of the learner in the use of the graphic organizer (before or after reading) seems to be a critical factor to consider when examining the effects of graphic organizers on vocabulary acquisition. Of the four studies reviewed below, two required students to construct graphic organizers after reading, another provided students with graphic organizers before reading, and one required subjects to rate the effectiveness of different organizers.

Bean, Wells, and Yopp (1981) asked two classes of freshmen—one in a philosophy course and the other in a history course—to rate the effectiveness of three models for using guide materials: (1) instructor-prepared guides, (2) graphic postorganizers, and (3) vocabulary concept guides. History students rated all the guides highly, whereas philosophy students rated the graphic postorganizer as superior. Overall evaluation of student responses led the researchers to conclude that use of the graphic postorganizer with accompanying small group discussion among students "appears to increase deep semantic processing" (p. 9).

Carr (1985) examined the effectiveness of a vocabulary overview guide (a graphic organizer) and self-monitoring instruction on vocabulary retention with 50 community college students. The students in the treatment group completed a vocabulary organizer after reading a set of messages. Then they were asked to write self-generated clues on the organizer itself to relate the words to their own schemata. These students were also given a four-step procedure for studying the targeted words. Students in the control group read the same messages the experimental group did, but they were required to define the target terms without using a vocabulary organizer. A vocab-

Simpson and Dwyer

ulary posttest and an unannounced delayed test (4 weeks later) were administered to measure retention of the targeted words. The experimental group scored significantly higher on both the immediate and the delayed vocabulary tests.

Carr's (1985) study used the graphic organizer on a post-learning basis and involved the students in the active completion of their own organizers. This design was made even more potent by the inclusion of several critical treatment conditions:

- Students were asked to record a personal reaction/clue for each of the target words, thus ensuring personal involvement.
- Students were asked to survey and skim for important unknown words and underline them before they read.
- Students were given a four-step procedure to study the words.
- Students received training and guidance with eight practice passages before they participated in the study.

Through careful and extensive utilization of the graphic organizer strategy, Carr has provided the strongest evidence of the efficacy of this approach. She concluded that the graphic organizer can be an effective and efficient vocabulary learning strategy. Further research is needed to examine the effectiveness of the graphic organizer approach using students' textbooks and other forms of naturally occurring prose since Carr authored the passages used in the study. Although the passages appear to be representative of text encountered by students in everyday reading, the fact that the material was artificially constructed for research purposes remains a limitation.

Barron and Schwartz (1984) examined the effects of graphic postorganizers on the learning of vocabulary relationships in a learning task undertaken with 64 graduate students. The experimental group was given four partially completed graphic postorganizers and asked to complete each organizer by inserting terms from an attached list of words. They were assigned in pairs to complete the organization in 1 hour. At the end of the hour the instructor displayed the completed organizers using an overhead projector. The control group was presented with the same word list, but this time the instructor defined and elaborated on the definitions of the words. One week after treatment all the subjects took a vocabulary relationship test consisting of 30 multiple choice items. The students who had completed the graphic postorganizer performed significantly better on the test than the control group. This finding is particularly impressive in light of the fact that the treatment condition lasted only 90 minutes.

Barron and Schwartz (1984) referred to Ausubel's concept of learning sets to partially explain the strong positive effects of the graphic postorganizer treatment. The experimental subjects were involved in a meaningful learning set because they were consciously and actively attempting to relate and incorporate less familiar concepts into their cognitive structure. In contrast, the control subjects were involved in a rote learning set where information was processed on an arbitrary basis, thus increasing the rate of memory loss since the new learning was not directly linked to existing knowledge.

Pyros (1980) investigated the relationship between the use of advance graphic organizers and the learning and retention of vocabulary relationships from the content areas of psychology and economics. Subjects in the experimental group were given 1 hour of training on the purpose and function of the graphic organizer. During the study the experimental group received both a verbal and a visual presentation of an advance graphic organizer from a unit in psychology. The control group received a list of technical terms with definitions that related to the same psychology unit. Both groups then read a 2,500-word selection from a college textbook. Half of each group was tested with a vocabulary relationship test immediately following the reading of the textbook passage. All subjects were given the same test 5 weeks later. This procedure was repeated with a unit in economics. Analysis of the data revealed no significant differences between the groups on either the immediate or the delayed test in either content area.

Simpson and Dwyer

The results of the Pyros (1980) study using advance organizers contrast with the results of Barron and Schwartz (1980) and Carr (1985). However, an important difference must be noted. Barron and Schwartz and Carr actively involved students in developing organizers, whereas in the Pyros study the organizers were provided for the subjects. Apparently, the more actively involved students are in the construction, manipulation, discussion, and independent study of the organizer, the more they seem to benefit. This is not surprising considering the similar general findings in vocabulary research. In future research, efforts should be made to build on Carr's promising findings and to study more comprehensively the issues examined by Barron and Schwartz. Further, researchers are advised to undertake investigations to answer the following critical questions, at least in part:

1. Is the graphic postorganizer more advantageous to use in some content area tasks or reading situations than in others?

2. How long does it take to train college students to independently construct, employ, and transfer a graphic postorganizer to their own learning situations?

3. How much control, regulation, and guidance are required from an instructor to facilitate student development and ultimate practical application of a graphic organizer?

NAIT. The Node Acquisition and Integration Technique, or NAIT (Diekhoff, Brown, & Dansereau, 1982), is based primarily on network models of long term memory structure (Collins & Loftus, 1975; Rumelhart, Lindsay, & Norman, 1972) and the depths of processing approach described by Craik and Tulving (1975). The NAIT strategy was designed to help students systematically select and define key concepts, consider examples and applications, and identify existing relationships among the concepts.

This strategy has four basic stages. In stage one the students are asked to identify key concepts or important terms they need to learn within a text. The second stage involves using relationship-guided definitions to construct a semantic network around each of the selected key concepts. This is done by finding six different kinds of relationships linked to each targeted concept. The authors suggest using a definition worksheet to facilitate this information-gathering process. In stage three, the elaboration stage, students are asked to think of examples or potential applications of the key concept and to record these examples on the definition worksheet. The final stage involves making relationship-guided comparisons. In this step the students discover meaningful similarities and differences among the different concepts being studied.

Diekhoff, Brown, and Dansereau (1982) tested NAIT for effectiveness with 35 undergraduate students. The 16 students in the experimental group received 3 hours of NAIT training that utilized prose passages from biology, physics, geography, and geology. Two days after the training, both the experimental and the control group received two passages from an introductory psychology textbook to study for 60 minutes. The experimental group was told to use NAIT in studying the passages, while students in the control group were told to use any of their own learning techniques. Following the study period, all passages and worksheets were collected from both groups. One week later both groups were given a 30-minute essay test on the passages. The test required the students to define and discuss five experimenter-selected key concepts in as much depth and detail as possible and to make comparisons among pairs of words selected by the researchers. The experimental subjects performed significantly better than the untrained control group on both measures, supporting the effectiveness of the NAIT approach. However, as the researchers pointed out, the testing format was obviously biased in favor of NAIT since the subjects were asked to recall the same information on the test that they had to recall in their NAIT training sessions.

Regardless of this research limitation, the NAIT strategy appears to be promising in that it actively involves the students in the selection of key vocabulary terms and then provides a systematic format to help them determine the definitions of these words, thus creating a stronger understanding than would ordinarily be gained without such intensive involvement. As the authors suggested, research should be undertaken to determine the effectiveness of the approach where the test format differs from NAIT's format. In addition, future studies should examine the impact of NAIT with differing types of material to determine how effectively this strategy can be used in a variety of content areas.

Effective Vocabulary Instruction

Overall review and analysis of the literature suggest that relatively little is known about vocabulary instruction at the college level. More research must be undertaken to provide the means for college reading teachers to have at hand effective strategies for vocabulary instruction. Although the present research cannot conclusively recommend one vocabulary approach over another or even accurately describe a comprehensive program of vocabulary instruction, there is enough evidence to describe some characteristics of effective vocabulary instruction (Simpson, Nist, & Kirby, 1987). Five highly interrelated characteristics will be examined in this section: (1) the use of mixed methods, (2) the active role of the learner, (3) the use of vocabulary in context, (4) capitalization on student interests, and (5) the intensity of instruction.

Mixed Methods

From reviews of research on vocabulary acquisition, Stahl (1983, 1985) suggested that a student who really *knows* a word has both definitional and contextual knowledge about that word. Stahl described definitional knowledge as knowledge of the relationships between a word and other known words, such as those that appear in a dictionary definition or a network model of semantic memory (Collins & Loftus, 1975). Since most readers do not break words into their definitional parts during comprehension, Stahl maintains that another type of information, contextual knowledge, is necessary to account for a reader's full knowledge of words. Contextual knowledge is the knowledge of a core concept, first acquired in a specific context, that becomes generalized or decontextualized through a number of exposures in different situations.

When a method of vocabulary instruction involves the student in both the definitional and contextual information of the word, it can be termed a "mixed method." An important point to note is that a mixed method model does not necessarily give equal emphasis to each strategy employed. Several studies with college students (Anderson & Kulhavy, 1972; Carr, 1985; Crist, 1981; Crist & Petrone, 1977) support the mixed method approach.

What does the research on mixed methods suggest for the college reading teacher? Most important, instruction that emphasizes only memorization and pairing of labels to synonyms (e.g., *arduous* means *difficult* or *hard*) imparts only definitional knowledge. Such knowledge is likely to have a negligible impact on a student's subsequent reading comprehension and learning (Kameenui, Dixon, & Carnine, 1987). Students can easily memorize definitions of words from lists (they have done it all through the elementary and secondary grades), but they quickly forget those verbal associations. Thus, the college reading teacher who uses materials or strategies that focus primarily on definitional knowledge needs to move beyond that point with additional strategies, including use of relevant teacher-made materials, to emphasize contextual understanding.

Active Role of the Learner

Researchers who required subjects to be actively involved in their own vocabulary development (Anderson & Kulhavy, 1972; Bobrow & Bower, 1969; Carr, 1985; Diekhoff,

Brown, & Dansereau, 1982; Duffelmeyer, 1980; Pressley, Levin, & Miller, 1981, 1982) found that they performed significantly better than other subjects on measures designed to evaluate vocabulary knowledge. From their reviews, Stahl (1983, 1985), Stahl and Fairbanks (1986), and Mezynski (1983) likewise concluded that active processing is critical for vocabulary acquisition. Stahl (1985) labeled active involvement of the learner "generative processing." Generative processing engages students in activities such as restating formal definitions in their own words, creating semantic maps, studying definitional aspects of a word, and writing sentences using targeted words. In contrast, passive associational tasks related to vocabulary instruction are characterized by worksheet-type activities asking students to match words with definitions or by instructional methods such as asking students to repeat words and definitions aloud several times.

It seems, then, that college reading teachers should use instructional materials and strategies that stimulate students to engage in active thinking. Unfortunately, it appears that most commercial materials do not actively engage students in their own learning; rather, they tend to treat learners as passive recipients of knowledge. In a content analysis of 60 college-level vocabulary texts, Stahl, Brozo, and Simpson (1987) found that sentence completion and sentence fill-in exercises predominated in 82 percent of the books, while matching exercises appeared in 70 percent of the texts. Further, these exercises are typically used in individualized or self-paced learning environments where little or no interaction occurs between student and teacher or between students. Research by Stahl and Fairbanks (1986) suggests that group discussions are more effective than individualized assignments.

The college reading professional, however, can make commercial materials more effective by modifying or supplementing them in several ways. For example, students could be invited to discuss workbook answers in small or large group settings. Such discussion might engage the students in generative processing by encouraging them to justify their answers. Another approach would be to ask students to write their own sentences. Such activities would ensure that both definitional and contextual knowledge of a word is emphasized. The college reading teacher could also experiment with the strategies previously discussed. These strategies actively involve students in deeper and more elaborate processing through such activities as imagining, finding examples, applying words to new contexts, comparing and contrasting, and determining interrelationships among words. The keyword, NAIT, and graphic postorganizer strategies could be easily integrated within an existing college reading program whether supplementary vocabulary workbook exercises were used or not. Lists of critical vocabulary terms, for use as target words, could be obtained from professors in various courses. Thus, students would have a practical reason for studying such word lists.

Manzo's (1982) subjective approach to vocabulary (SAV), though not empirically tested with college students, holds promise for the college reading teacher since it requires students to make some personal images and active associations. The four-step SAV approach requires no special materials or preparation. In the first step the teacher explicitly presents a target word with a definition and several contexts. In the second step the teacher invites active involvement by asking students what experiences, thoughts, or images they associate with the target word. To justify this step the teacher might mention that words are easier to remember when personal images or experiences can be associated with them. If students offer no associations, the teacher can start by offering his or her own associations with the target word. Once several personal associations have been offered, the students move on to the third step, in which they write the word in vocabulary notebooks. The notebook entry includes a dictionary-type definition along with a brief note about the student's personal associations, mental pictures, or experiences with the word. During the fourth step the students silently read a selection where the target word occurs in relevant context.

SAV, the keyword method, NAIT, and the graphic postorganizer invite the learner to engage in distinctive and elabo-

Simpson and Dwyer

rate levels of processing by providing the opportunity to gain both definitional and contextual information about a word.

Vocabulary in Context

The main instructional approach in earlier vocabulary research involved giving students a list of words and requiring them to manipulate and memorize appropriate definitions. The long term benefits of such an approach on a student's expressive and receptive vocabulary, and on reading comprehension, appear very limited. While there are numerous reasons for this lack of effectiveness, one important explanation needs to be emphasized: vocabulary should be taught from a unifying context (Jenkins & Dixon, 1983; Mezynski, 1983). Words taught in the context of a subject area will be learned more effectively than words in isolation or from unrelated lists because context allows words to become integrated with previously acquired knowledge. As Mezynski (1983) points out, "when a student encounters the word during reading, an organized schema can be activated, providing a large 'chunk' of information (as opposed to a single definition) that can aid the construction of meaning" (p. 267).

Thus, a college reading teacher needs to select or have the students select target words from textbooks, newspapers, magazines, or novels. For example, if students are reading a short selection from a speech textbook on words and their meaning, words such as *arbitrary, connotation, denotation,* or *syntax* could be intensely studied. Another alternative is to group target words into semantic categories (Beck, Perfetti, & McKeown, 1982). One such category could be adjectives that negatively describe a person's actions: *lax, infantile, obsequious, narcissistic.* Whatever approach is used to provide the context and organizing schema, college reading teachers need to remember that long term vocabulary learning occurs within realistic school-related or life-coping tasks, not within artificially contrived word lists. This is true whether such words come from locally produced or commercially prepared materials.

Student Interest

The idea that students can more efficiently and effectively learn concepts that interest them personally seems obvious. However, the history of vocabulary instruction at the elementary, secondary, and postsecondary levels does not seem to acknowledge this obvious fact. The common routine of asking students to look up words in a dictionary and write a sentence using the words is neither interesting nor beneficial to the typical college student.

One reason student interest may be lacking with current approaches or materials is that someone else (the teacher or the producer of commercial materials) has made an *a priori* decision concerning the words students are to study and learn. When college students are encouraged to select their own words, greater interest is ensured. Consequently, they not only make significant gains on standardized measures (Gnewuch, 1974) but also show more intrinsic interest in vocabulary development (Haggard, 1984).

College reading teachers therefore are advised to incorporate strategies and approaches that encourage and reward students for learning new words of personal interest to them. Haggard's (1982) vocabulary self-collection strategy (VSS) is one approach to student-initiated vocabulary study that can be easily incorporated into virtually any existing program. During Haggard's research on the conditions that expedite word learning, she found that peer group usage and immediate usefulness were the most frequently cited reasons for learning new words during adolescence.

VSS capitalizes on these conditions by asking students to bring to class two words from their own environments (television, peers, reading) that they believe the whole class could benefit from learning. The teacher also selects two words. When the students enter the classroom, they immediately write the words on the chalkboard. Once the class officially begins, the students identify their words and tell what they mean (with a formal and/or informal definition), where they found the words, and why they feel the class should learn them. After all the words on the board (including the teacher's) have been explained, the class narrows the list to a predetermined number of words. During the next phase, the students who introduced the words selected for study again define their words. The teacher facilitates the discussion by clarifying, redefining, and extending student definitions. At this point, all the students record in their vocabulary journals the selected words and their definitions. By the end of the session, each student has a class list of words in addition to the two words he or she brought in.

Haggard (1982) suggested several activities for reinforcing vocabulary from the class list. Among the activities are writing sentences, composing stories, and developing dialogues, all tasks emphasizing contextual information and generative processing. At the end of the week, all students are tested on the class list and on their own two words.

Even though VSS has not been empirically researched, it has several virtues to recommend it: it is sensible, it requires little or no advance preparation, and it can be easily modified to fit different environments (Simpson, Nist, & Kirby, 1987). Strategies such as VSS that encourage and motivate students to be independent word learners should be an integral part of any comprehensive college reading program.

Intensity of Instruction

Research reviews by Jenkins and Dixon (1983), Mezynski (1983), and Stahl and Fairbanks (1986) have consistently concluded that for vocabulary instruction to be effective it should be intense. Intense instruction is characterized by the use of multiple examples, repetition, and review in differing contexts over a long period of time. An example of intense instruction is the frequently cited study with intermediate grade students by Beck, McCaslin, and McKeown (1980). In this study, 30 minutes a day were devoted to vocabulary instruction over a 5-month period; a total of 104 words were taught, with each word receiving between 16 and 22 different exposures.

While brief practices can have some effect on an immediate vocabulary test, there is considerable memory loss over time. However, researchers who have used a more intense approach (Beck, McCaslin, & McKeown, 1980; Stahl, 1983) have noted little or no decline in the number of words learned even after delayed testing. Stahl and Fairbanks (1986) suggested that there is little decline in words learned through intense instruction because multiple repetition leads to decontextualized knowledge of word meanings. Moreover, they concluded that students involved in intense vocabulary study tend to have fewer comprehension difficulties caused by slowness in lexical access. Nevertheless, by itself, intensity is not the critical characteristic of vocabulary instruction. Mere repetition of a word and its definition over time will not be beneficial unless the student is actively involved in processing.

The implication of this research for the college reading professional is obvious. Fewer words should be taught, and more instruction time should be provided for meaningful reinforcement activities and cumulative reviews in order to promote the breadth of word knowledge necessary for long term retention and the ability to use target words successfully in independent learning.

These five characteristics of instruction can assist the college reading professional in developing a systematic and comprehensive vocabulary program. Materials and instructional approaches in such a program not only emphasize the definitional and contextual information of a word but also involve students in the deeper or more elaborative processing levels. The words to be studied would come from what the students were reading or learning, not from commercial workbooks or lists. And, most important, such a comprehensive program would emphasize a wide variety of instructional and evaluative approaches since no one commercial program or strategy completely addresses these research-based characteristics of effective vocabulary instruction.

Future Directions

College reading professionals face three major challenges. The first, and perhaps most important, requires that they objectively scrutinize their present programs with the following questions in mind:

1. Does the present vocabulary program offer a balance between more global strategies designed to encourage general vocabulary development and more specific strategies designed to encourage student-initiated, often content-oriented, vocabulary growth?

2. Does the present program contain materials and employ instructional strategies that require students to be involved in more elaborative levels of processing?

3. Do the evaluation instruments used require students to demonstrate long term conceptual knowledge of the targeted words?

4. Are the instructional strategies and evaluation procedures used supported by research conducted with students representative of those in the program?

5. Does the present program rest on a sound theoretical base?

A second major challenge for college reading professionals is to provide ongoing feedback to the editors and writers of commercial materials concerning the relevance and quality of their products. College reading teachers must not accept without question what publishers present. They need to examine materials in light of their own specific needs, keeping in mind what research has said about effective vocabulary instruction. As Stahl, Brozo, and Simpson (1987) discovered in their content analysis of 55 vocabulary workbooks, the materials on the market today tend to be based on tradition rather than on research-supported principles. The critical link between researchers and publishers is the teacher; consequently, it is vital that college reading professionals offer their objective and constructive opinions on commercial materials.

The final challenge for college reading professionals is to conduct with their own students action-oriented, applied, and empirical research. The process could begin with valuable descriptive studies, such as Haggard's (1980, 1984), that ask students to share their perceptions of how they learn new words and what strategies they use. A fruitful step is to conduct single-subject research, as Crist (1981) did, or to utilize a quasiexperimental design in an actual classroom setting, like that of Beck, McCaslin, and McKeown (1980). Regardless of the approach or design, more grassroots level research is needed with students enrolled in college reading programs.

If the research is to be of value, it needs to focus on important questions that are unanswered. Although not all encompassing, the following questions exemplify major issues that are still unresolved concerning college level vocabulary instruction:

1. What long term effect does knowledge of affixes have on a student's subsequent vocabulary acquisition? What type of training is necessary to ensure that students will transfer this knowledge to unknown words encountered in their reading?

2. Can the key word method be readily implemented in actual classroom settings with the types of words college students encounter in their assigned reading?

3. Can research on the use of context clues with naturally occurring text demonstrate the effectiveness of this approach?

4. What is the long range impact of having students select their own words for vocabulary study?

5. Is the graphic postorganizer equally useful with all content area reading? What specific procedures will help train college students to independently construct these strategies and transfer them to their own learning?

Researchers need to be sensitive to several conditions to add to the research base on vocabulary instruction at the college level. Further studies should include several types of expository text and subjects with differing levels of reading competency rather than testing a strategy with only one type of

Simpson and Dwyer

text and one type of reader. Attempts should be made to describe the levels of processing required of the learner and, if comparing different strategies, to keep those processing requirements equivalent. Finally, with any research, whether quasiexperimental or empirical, the college reading professional should be careful to design evaluation instruments that not only reflect the breadth of knowledge desired about word meaning but also measure long term recall. Once these questions have been adequately answered, the more critical issue of defining a comprehensive vocabulary program for college students can be addressed.

References and Suggested Readings

Albinski, E.E. (1970). Part, whole, and added parts learning of same-stem words and the effect of stem learning on acquisition and retention of vocabulary. *Dissertation Abstracts International, 31*, 1609A.

Alexander, J.E. (1969). A programmed versus a conventional approach to vocabulary development in college remedial classes. *Dissertation Abstracts International, 30*, 1425A.

*Anderson, R.C., & Freebody, P. (1981). Vocabulary knowledge. In J.T. Guthrie (Ed.), *Comprehension and teaching: Research reviews* (pp. 77-117). Newark, DE: International Reading Association.

Anderson, R.C., & Kulhavy, R.W. (1972). Imagery and prose learning. *Journal of Educational Psychology, 63*, 242-243.

Ausubel, D.P. (1963). *The psychology of meaningful verbal learning*. New York: Grune & Stratton.

Baer, F.B. (1974). A comparison of the effects of the two methods on the reading vocabulary, comprehension, accuracy, and rate of selected students at George Washington University. *Dissertation Abstracts International, 35*, 7668A-7669A.

Barron, R.F. (1969). The use of vocabulary as an advance organizer. In H.L. Herber & P.L. Sanders (Eds.), *Research on reading in the content areas: First year report* (pp. 29-39). Syracuse, NY: Syracuse University Press.

Barron, R.F., & Schwartz, R.N. (1984). *Spatial learning strategies: Techniques, applications and related issues*. San Diego, CA: Academic Press.

Bean, T.L., Wells, J., & Yopp, H. (1981). *University students' perceptions of critical reading guides in history and philosophy*. (ED 211 956)

Beck, I.L., Perfetti, C.A., & McKeown, M.G. (1982). The effects of long term vocabulary instruction on lexical access and reading comprehension. *Journal of Educational Psychology, 74*, 506-521.

Beck, J., McCaslin, E., & McKeown, M. (1980). *The rationale and design of a program to teach vocabulary to fourth-grade students*. Pittsburgh, PA: University of Pittsburgh, Learning Research Center.

Begg, I. (1972). Recall of meaningful phrases. *Journal of Verbal Learning and Verbal Behavior, 11*, 431-439.

Begg, I. (1973). Imagery and integration in the recall of words. *Canadian Journal of Psychology, 27*, 159-167.

Berg, P.C., Hess, R.K., & Crocker, A. (1983). The contribution of reading research to college reading programs. *Forum for Reading, 14,* 17-29.

Bobrow, S.A., & Bower, G.H. (1969). Comprehension and recall of sentences. *Journal of Experimental Psychology, 80,* 455-461.

Bower, G.H. (1970). Imagery as a relational organizer in associative learning. *Journal of Verbal Learning and Verbal Behavior, 9,* 529-533.

Bower, G.H. (1972). Mental imagery and associative learning. In L.W. Gregg (Ed.), *Cognition in learning and memory* (pp. 51-87). New York: Wiley.

Brown, J.I., Nelson, M.J., & Denny, E.C. (1976). *Nelson-Denny Reading Test.* Boston, MA: Houghton Mifflin.

*Carnine, D., Kameenui, E.J., & Coyle, G. (1984). Utilization of contextual information in determining the meaning of unfamiliar words. *Reading Research Quarterly, 19,* 188-204.

Carr, E. (1985). The vocabulary overview guide: A metacognitive strategy to improve vocabulary comprehension and retention. *Journal of Reading, 21,* 684-689.

Collins, A.M., & Loftus, E.A. (1975). A spreading-activation theory of semantic processing. *Psychological Review, 82,* 407-428.

Craik, F.I.M. (1979). Levels of processing: Overview and closing comments. In L.S. Cermak & F.I.M. Craik (Eds.), *Levels of processing in human memory* (pp. 447-461). Hillsdale, NJ: Erlbaum.

Craik, F.I.M., & Lockhart, R.S. (1972). Levels of processing: A framework for memory research. *Journal of Verbal Learning and Verbal Behavior, 11,* 671-684.

Craik, F.I.M., & Tulving, E. (1975). Depth of processing and the retention of words in episodic memory. *Journal of Experimental Psychology: General, 104,* 268-294.

Crist, R.L. (1981). Learning concepts from contexts and definitions: A single subject replication. *Journal of Reading Behavior, 13,* 271-277.

Crist, R.L., & Petrone, J. (1977). Learning concepts from contexts and definitions. *Journal of Reading Behavior, 9,* 301-303.

Crump, B.M. (1966). Relative merits of teaching vocabulary by a direct and an incidental method. *Dissertation Abstracts International, 26,* 901A-902A.

Cushenberry, D.C. (1972). *Remedial reading in the secondary school.* West Nyack, NY: Parker.

Dale, E. (1965). Vocabulary measurement: Techniques and major findings. *Elementary English, 42,* 895-901.

Deighton, L.D. (1960). Developing vocabulary: Another look at the problem. *English Journal, 49,* 82-88.

Diekhoff, G.M., Brown, P.J., & Dansereau, D.F. (1982). A prose learning strategy training program based on network and depth-of-processing models. *Journal of Experimental Education, 50,* 180-184.

*Dixon, R.C., & Jenkins, J.R. (1984). *An outcome analysis of receptive vocabulary knowledge.* Unpublished manuscript, University of Illinois, Champaign.

Duffelmeyer, F.A. (1980). The influence of experience-based vocabulary instruction on learning word meanings. *Journal of Reading, 24,* 35-40.

Earle, R.A. (1970). Reading and mathematics: Research in the classroom. In H.A. Robinson & E.L. Thomas (Eds.), *Fusing reading skills and content* (pp. 162-170). Newark, DE: International Reading Association.

Einbecker, P.G. (1973). *Development of an audiovisual program based upon the acquisition of perceptual knowledge to increase college students' vocabulary.* (ED 101 303)

Estes, T.H., Mills, D.N., & Barron, R.F. (1969). Three methods of introducing students to a reading-learning task in two content subjects. In H.L. Herber & D.L. Sanders (Eds.), *Research on reading in the content areas: First year report* (pp. 40-48). Syracuse, NY: Syracuse University Press.

Eysenck, M.W. (1979). Depth, elaboration, and distinctiveness. In L.S. Cermak & F.I.M. Craik (Eds.), *Levels of processing in human memory* (pp. 89-118). Hillsdale, NJ: Erlbaum.

Fairbanks, M.M. (1977, March). *Vocabulary instruction at the college/adult levels: A research review.* (ED 134 979)

Gipe, J. (1979). Investigating techniques for teaching word meanings. *Reading Research Quarterly, 14,* 624-645.

Gnewuch, M.M. (1974). The effect of vocabulary training upon the development of vocabulary, comprehension, total reading, and rate of reading of college students. *Dissertation Abstracts International, 34,* 6254A.

Goodman, K.S. (1976). Behind the eye: What happens in reading. In H. Singer & R. Ruddell (Eds.), *Theoretical models and processes of reading* (2nd ed.) (pp. 470-496). Newark, DE: International Reading Association.

Graves, M.F., & Hammond, H.K. (1979). A validated procedure for teaching prefixes and its effect on students' ability to assign meaning to novel words. In M.L. Kamil and A.J. Moe (Eds.), *Perspectives on reading research and instruction* (pp. 184-188). Washington, DC: National Reading Conference.

*Haggard, M.R. (1980). Vocabulary acquisition during elementary and post-elementary years: A preliminary report. *Reading Horizons, 21,* 61-69.

Haggard, M.R. (1982). The vocabulary self-collection strategy: An active approach to word learning. *Journal of Reading, 26,* 203-207.

Haggard, M.R. (1984, December). *A study of university student vocabulary acquisition: Motivation, sources, and strategies.* Paper presented at the National Reading Conference, St. Petersburg, FL.

Herber, H.L. (1978). *Teaching reading in the content areas* (2nd ed.). Englewood Cliffs, NJ: Prentice Hall.

Hopper, J., & Wells, J.C. (1981, April). *The specific vocabulary needs of academic disciplines.* (ED 207-000)

Hyde, T.S., & Jenkins, J.J. (1973). Recall for words as a function of semantic, graphic, and syntactic orienting tasks. *Journal of Verbal Learning and Verbal Behavior, 12,* 471-480.

Ironside, R.A. (1960). A study of directed concept formation: The teaching of context clues for vocabulary development. *Dissertation Abstracts International, 20,* 1691A.

*Jenkins, J.R., & Dixon, R. (1983). Vocabulary learning. *Contemporary Educational Psychology, 8,* 237-260.

Johnson, D.M., & Stratton, R.P. (1966). Evaluation of five methods of teaching concepts. *Journal of Educational Psychology, 57,* 48-53.

Johnson-Laird, P.N., Gibbs, G., & de Mowbrey, J. (1978). Meaning, amount of processing, and memory for words. *Memory and Cognition, 6,* 372-375.

Jones, B.F., & Hall, J.W. (1982). School application of the mnemonic keyword method as a study strategy by eighth graders. *Journal of Educational Psychology, 74,* 230-237.

*Kameenui, E.J., Carnine, D.W., & Freschi, R. (1982). Effects of text construction and instruction procedures for teaching word meanings on comprehension and recall. *Reading Research Quarterly, 17,* 367-388.

Kameenui, E.J., Dixon, R.C., & Carnine, D.W. (1987). Issues in the design of vocabulary instruction. In M.G. McKeown & M.B. Curtis (Eds.), *The nature of vocabulary acquisition* (pp. 129-145). Hillsdale, NJ: Erlbaum.

Manzo, A.V. (1982). Subjective approach to vocabulary acquisition. *Reading Psychology, 3,* 155-160.

Manzo, A.V., & Sherk, J.K. (1971-1972). Some generalizations and strategies for guiding vocabulary learning. *Journal of Reading Behavior, 4,* 78-89.

McNeal, L.D. (1973). Recall and recognition of vocabulary word learning in college students using mnemonic and repetitive methods. *Dissertation Abstracts International*, *33*, 3394A.

*Mezynski, K. (1983). Issues concerning the acquisition of knowledge: Effects of vocabulary training on reading comprehension. *Review of Educational Research*, *53*, 253-279.

Moore, D.W., & Readence, J.E. (1980). Meta-analysis of the effect of graphic organizers on learning from text. In M.L. Kamil & A.J. Moe (Eds.), *Perspectives on reading research and instruction* (pp. 213-218). Washington, DC: National Reading Conference.

*Nagy, W.E., Herman, P.A., Anderson, R.C., & Pearson, P.D. (1984). *Learning words from context* (Tech. Rep. No. 319). Champaign, IL: University of Illinois.

O'Rourke, J.P. (1974). *Toward a science of vocabulary development*. The Hague: Mouton.

Paivio, A. (1971). *Imagery and verbal process*. New York: Holt, Rinehart & Winston.

Petty, W.T., Herold, C.P., & Stoll, E. (1968). *The state of knowledge about the teaching of vocabulary*. Champaign, IL: National Council of Teachers of English.

Pressley, M., Levin, J.R., & Miller, G.E. (1981). How does the keyword method affect vocabulary, comprehension, and usage? *Reading Research Quarterly*, *16*, 213-225.

Pressley, M., Levin, J.R., & Miller, G.E. (1982). The keyword method compared to alternative vocabulary-learning strategies. *Contemporary Educational Psychology*, *7*, 50-60.

Pyros, S.W. (1980). Graphic advance organizers and the learning of vocabulary relationships. *Dissertation Abstracts International*, *41*, 3509A.

Raugh, M.R., & Atkinson, R.C. (1975). A mnemonic method for learning a second-language vocabulary. *Journal of Educational Psychology*, *67*, 1-16.

Reith, R.K. (1981). The ability of high risk college freshmen to use specific context clues to derive word meanings. *Dissertation Abstracts International*, *41*, 2038A.

Roberts, J., & Kelly, N. (1985). The keyword method: An alternative strategy for developmental college readers. *Reading World*, *24*, 34-39.

Rumelhart, D.E., Lindsey, P.H., & Norman, D.A. (1972). A process model of long term memory, In E. Tulving and W. Donaldson (Eds.), *Organization of memory* (pp. 198-246). San Diego, CA: Academic Press.

Sartain, H.W., Stahl, N., Ani, U.N., Bohn, S., Holly, B., Smolenski, C.S., & Stein, D.W. (1982). *Teaching techniques for the languages of the disciplines*. Pittsburgh, PA: University of Pittsburgh.

Schatz, E.K., & Baldwin, R.S. (1986). Context clues are unreliable predictors of word meaning. *Reading Research Quarterly*, *21*, 439-453.

Simpson, M.L., Nist, S.L., & Kirby, K. (1987). Ideas in practice: Vocabulary strategies designed for college students. *Journal of Developmental Education*, *11*(2), 20-24.

Smith, B.D., Stahl, N.A., & Neel, J.H. (1987). The effect of imagery instruction on vocabulary development. *Journal of College Reading and Learning*, *22*, 131-137.

Stahl, N.A., Brozo, W.G., & Simpson, M.L. (1987). A content analysis of college vocabulary textbooks. *Reading Research and Instruction*, *26*(4), 203-221.

*Stahl, S.A. (1983). Differential word knowledge and reading comprehension. *Journal of Reading Behavior*, *15*, 33-50.

*Stahl, S.A. (1985). To teach a word well: A framework for vocabulary instruction. *Reading World*, *24*, 16-27.

*Stahl, S.A., & Fairbanks, M.M. (1986). The effects of vocabulary instruction: A model-based meta-analysis. *Journal of Educational Research, 56,* 72-110.

Strader, S.G., & Joy, F. (1980, November). *A contrast of three approaches to vocabulary study for college students.* (ED 197 330)

Tulving, E. (1983). *Elements of episodic memory.* New York: Oxford University Press.

Tyler, S.W., Hertel, P.T., McCallum, M.C., & Ellis, H.C. (1979). Cognitive effort and memory. *Journal of Experimental Psychology: Human Learning and Memory, 5,* 607-617.

Vaughn, J.L., Castle, G., Gilbert, K., & Love, M. (1981). Varied approaches to pre-teaching vocabulary. In J.A. Niles & L.A. Harris (Eds.), *New inquiries in reading research and instruction* (pp. 94-98). Rochester, NY: National Reading Conference.

2

Teacher-Directed Comprehension Strategies

Sherrie L. Nist
Donna L. Mealey

Although conducted primarily in elementary and middle school classrooms, Durkin's (1978-1979) research opened the floodgates for studies in the area of reading comprehension. Durkin's findings, along with those of Armbruster and Gudbrandsen (1986) and Neilsen, Rennie, and Connell (1982), suggest that little direct comprehension instruction occurs in the classroom. The overriding questions that emerge from this research are: Is comprehension being taught? Are instructors using teaching techniques that not only increase comprehension but also offer students strategies they will eventually be able to use independently? More germane to this chapter is whether the teacher-directed comprehension strategies being used in college reading programs are helping students learn to deal with text.

Some college reading instructors insist that they are teaching comprehension by assigning repetitive skill-oriented workbook activities. These activities (which usually consist of reading brief passages and then answering the multiple choice questions about them) provide no teacher direction except perhaps to tell students how many of these activities they are to carry out. Simply because students are engaged in some type of comprehension activity does not mean that the activity is either teacher-directed or strategic.

To help determine the relationship between theory, research, and practice in this area, we examine each of three theoretical bases that directly influence college level reading: metacognition, schema theory, and text structure. Metacognition generally is seen as the foundation on which comprehension is built. The instructor's role, therefore, is to create metacognitive awareness by teaching strategies that enable students to realize when their comprehension is breaking down. Schema theory is important to teacher-directed comprehension because of the role the organization of prior knowledge plays in understanding. Finally, text structure (difficulty and organization) obviously affects comprehension.

To link theory to research, we discuss studies that relate to each theoretical perspective. We tie in practice by discussing direct instruction and providing a generic model appropriate for use in college reading classrooms. Next, we address the specific teacher-directed comprehension strategies that are most appropriate for college students, whenever possible presenting related research. (We define strategies here as methods or techniques instructors choose to use with students on the basis of text, task, and student characteristics.) Finally, we draw conclusions from the research and offer suggestions for future lines of research.

Theoretical Foundations

Teacher-directed comprehension strategies appear to be grounded in the three theoretical bases mentioned earlier: metacognition, schema theory, and text structure. While variations exist within each theory, each contributes to our understanding of why certain strategies work well with readers and others do not.

Metacognition is important because unless students are aware of when their comprehension is breaking down and know what to do about it, teacher-directed strategies will fail. This is particularly true for at-risk populations since research indicates that poor readers tend to possess weak metacognitive abilities. Schema theory helps students organize, store, and retrieve information. Text structure approaches help students comprehend what they read to the fullest.

Metacognition

Although some aspects of how we currently define metacognition are anything but new (Dewey, 1910; Thorndike, 1917), the term was not directly related to reading comprehension until the late 1970s. At that time, Flavell (1978) defined metacognition as "knowledge that takes as its object or regulates any aspect of any cognitive endeavor" (p. 8). More recently, Baker and Brown (1984), Brown, Armbruster, and Baker (1986), and Garner (1987a) have defined metacognition in more precise terms. These theorists delineate two (not necessarily independent) aspects of metacognition: knowledge about cognition and self-regulation of cognition.

Knowledge about cognition concerns what readers know about both their cognitive resources and the regulation of those resources. Regulation includes the ability to detect errors or contradictions in text, knowledge of different strategies to use with different kinds of texts, and the ability to separate important from unimportant information. According to Baker and Brown (1984), knowledge about cognition is both stable and statable in that if readers know how to learn information, they can explain what they do when asked.

The second key aspect of metacognition is readers' ability to control or self-regulate their actions during reading. Self-regulation includes planning and monitoring, testing, revising, and evaluating the strategies employed when reading and learning text (Baker & Brown, 1984).

In short, metacognition involves the regulation and control of learning. It is a complex process that depends on several interrelated factors: the text, the required criterion task, the strategies readers know and use, and the readers' learning styles (Garner, 1987b). Because of its relevance, metacognition has become an integral part of models of learning and comprehension (Paris, Lipson, & Wixson, 1983; Weinstein & Mayer, 1986).

Some might think that metacognitive theory relates primarily to student-centered comprehension strategies, but we believe that it is also tightly tied to teacher-directed strategies. In fact, we view metacognition as the foundation of understanding. Students must be able to judge whether they understand the information presented by the instructor and also the manner in which it is presented.

For those reading this article, the process of metacognition may be automatic. Mature readers recognize when a comprehension failure occurs and know what to do about it. Such individuals are metacognitively aware. In a nation of readers, however, they are in the minority. Research indicates that there are major differences between the metacognitive abilities of poor readers and those of good readers (Schommer & Surber, 1986). Nowhere is this discrepancy more clearly seen than in college reading programs. In an environment where 85 percent of all learning comes from independent reading (Baker, 1974), college students who are metacognitively unaware probably will experience major academic problems.

There also are differences between the metacognitive abilities of older readers and those of younger readers. Older students seem better able to regulate and control their understanding than do younger children. Younger readers, even those identified as "good" readers in relation to their peers, have difficulty with monitoring and self-regulation. Markham's (1977) classic study indicated that when given directions for a card game, young children were unable to recognize that the directions were incomplete and that it would be impossible to continue with the game. Additional studies (Meyers & Paris, 1978) have indicated that even older grade school and high school students have similar problems with metacognitive awareness.

But there also appears to be something of a developmental trend: as children become older, their capacity to use metacognitive skills increases, and their reasons for not using these skills change.

By the time students go to college, they are expected to possess metacognitive skills. Professors have little sympathy for students who say they did poorly because they thought they understood the material but did not, studied the wrong information, or felt ready for a test when they really were not. Yet research indicates that among well-meaning college students, particularly those who are less skilled readers, failures in self-regulation are common (Schommer & Surber, 1986).

Although considerable research has been conducted in the area of metacognition, much of it has focused on younger children. Studies carried out with either high school or college students are difficult to synthesize because of their small numbers and diverse nature. What's more, the college-age subjects in these studies were enrolled in regular undergraduate courses (generally introductory psychology), and therefore did not necessarily typify students who would be enrolled in a college developmental reading program. Thus, generalizability is something of a problem. Given this caveat, however, we can still draw some useful conclusions.

Metacognitive studies involving older students and adults seem to break down into three main classifications: (1) those that compare the metacognitive abilities of skilled readers with those of unskilled readers (Baker, 1985; Gambrell & Heathington, 1981); (2) those that examine the effects of inserted text contradictions on the "illusion of knowing" (Epstein, Glenberg, & Bradley, 1984; Glenberg, Wilkinson, & Epstein, 1982; Schommer & Surber, 1986); and (3) those that attempt to improve metacognitive abilities with some sort of strategic intervention (Larson et al., 1985; Pressley et al., 1987).

In the comparison studies, differences surfaced in the metacognitive abilities of skilled and unskilled readers at all age levels. Poor readers generally lacked knowledge of comprehension strategies, had misconceptions about the reading process, and did not know what to do about comprehension failures (Gambrell & Heathington, 1981). In addition, poor readers used different standards by which to judge their understanding (Baker, 1985).

The text contradiction studies found that when subjects were informed that a piece of text contained contradictions, they generally not only failed to detect the contradictions but also experienced a high "false alarm" rate, frequently identifying noncontradictions as contradictions (Epstein, Glenberg, & Bradley, 1984). In other contradiction studies, subjects experienced greater illusions of knowing (i.e., believing falsely that they understood what they read) with passages that researchers had rated as difficult, even though these passages required only shallow processing (Schommer & Surber, 1986). Results were consistent for both good and poor readers.

Although research indicates that even college students lack needed metacognitive skills (Baker, 1985), the results of the intervention studies suggest that college students can better monitor their level of text understanding and test preparedness by employing a variety of strategies. Pressley et al. (1987) found that when adjunct questions were inserted into reading passages on which subjects were to be tested, the students' perceived readiness for examination improved. Elaborative devices such as cooperative learning pairs (Larson et al., 1985) were also found to improve metacognition. Any of these strategies should begin as teacher-directed activities and then be modified to become part of students' repertoire of comprehension activities.

Schema Theory

The second theoretical perspective that affects teacher-directed reading comprehension strategies—particularly at the college level—is schema theory. Schema theory relates to the effect of prior knowledge on a new learning situation. Like metacognition, the concept of schema theory is not new. It emerged in the early 1930s with Bartlett's (1932) somewhat ambiguous definition of schema, although it has been suggested that Bartlett was at least partially influenced by Gestalt psychologists (Anderson & Pearson, 1984).

Recently, theorists have defined schema theory more specifically as an abstract framework that organizes knowledge in memory by putting information into the correct "slots," each of which contains related parts (Anderson & Pearson, 1984; Just & Carpenter, 1987; Wilson & Anderson, 1986). When new information enters memory, it not only must be compatible with one of the slots, but it must actually be entered into the proper slot before comprehension can occur. Some researchers (Ausubel, 1963) believe that this knowledge is structured hierarchically, with the most abstract features of a concept at the top and the most concrete features at the bottom.

According to schema theory, comprehension is an interactive process between the text and the reader. Wilson and Anderson (1986) compare this interaction with putting together a jigsaw puzzle. If each piece of incoming information fits perfectly into a slot, if each slot contains important information, and if the text is coherently interpreted (much like the pieces of a puzzle fitting snugly together), the text has been satisfactorily comprehended. The puzzle analogy breaks down after this, however, because even with a well-written text, the author expects readers to make inferences, and therefore does not provide information for every slot in a schema.

The importance of schema theory as it relates to reading comprehension can be seen in the six functions a schema performs. These functions affect both the learning and the remembering of textual information (Anderson, 1978; Anderson & Pichert, 1978; Anderson, Spiro, & Anderson, 1978):

1. A schema provides ideational scaffolding. Schemata provide a framework for organizing incoming information and retrieving stored information. Text information fits into slots within each schema. For example, if readers have been exposed to World War II in high school, they already possess an initial framework into which new information can be in-

Nist and Mealey

corporated when they read about the war again in college.

2. A schema permits selective attention. Schemata help readers select the important information from the text. Good readers attend more to important information and to material that is unfamiliar to them.

3. A schema permits inference making. As noted earlier, no text is completely explicit; a reader will always need to make inferences, no matter how well written the text is. Schemata permit such inferences by enabling readers to fill in the gaps with preexisting knowledge. The publisher of a college history text containing a chapter on World War II, for example, may assume that students already possess some information about the war and thus not include that material.

4. A schema allows orderly memory searches. Since schemata have slots for certain pieces of information, the reader can be guided to the kinds of information that need to be retrieved. If readers can follow the schema the author used to structure the text, later they will be able to retrieve information learned during text reading. Remembering the key headings, for example, allows students to limit a memory search to information that pertains to the desired heading rather than searching all information.

5. A schema facilitates editing and summarizing. This function also relates to readers' abilities to determine key ideas. Since a schema allows readers to distinguish important from unimportant information, it also facilitates the formulation of graphic organizers or questions containing important information. For example, after reading the World War II chapter, students should be able to state or make a map of the key ideas presented.

6. A schema permits inferential reconstruction. Readers

often have gaps in their memory; a schema helps them generate hypotheses about the missing information. Remembering a key battle, for example, might help a learner remember the general who fought in the battle.

While a considerable amount of research supports the various theoretical aspects of schema theory (Bartlett, 1932; Just & Carpenter, 1980; Sanford & Garrod, 1981), recent studies also have focused on the practical classroom applications and implications of schemata and prior knowledge. These studies can be grouped into three main categories: (1) manipulation studies, in which subjects call up schemata based on manipulated texts or purposes; (2) cross-cultural studies, which examine how students' cultural familiarity with a subject affects the way they learn and interpret information about that subject; and (3) expert-novice studies, which present a topic and then compare the learning strategies of subjects who have little knowledge about that topic with the strategies of knowledgeable subjects.

Currently schema activation is being incorporated as a regular part of teacher-directed reading instruction in the public schools (Just & Carpenter, 1987), but comprehension instruction in college reading programs often fails to address the importance of schema theory and prior knowledge in text comprehension. Thus, schema activation often does not occur.

Manipulation studies. Much of the research on schema theory has focused on manipulation studies, often employing contrived passages and situations to induce a particular scenario. For instance, Pichert and Anderson (1977) told subjects to read an ambiguous passage about a house from the viewpoint of either a prospective burglar or a prospective homebuyer. Subjects tended to remember more of the information that was pertinent to their assigned group: those in the homebuyer group were more likely to remember that the house had a leaky roof, whereas those in the burglar group were more likely to remember that the house had a color TV and a valuable coin collection. Additional research using these same scenarios (Anderson & Pichert, 1978; Anderson, Pichert, & Shirey, 1983) has extended the initial research by having subjects switch perspectives after the first reading. Subjects in these studies were often able to recall previously unrecalled information after the perspective shift. These findings also held true for a 2-week delayed recall period. As a result of these studies, Anderson, Pichert, and Shirey concluded that schema influenced not only the activation but also the retrieval of knowledge.

Numerous other studies have found similar results (Anderson et al., 1977; Henk & Helfeldt, 1985; Sjogren & Timpson, 1979). However, a more recent study by Henk and Helfeldt (1987) produced different findings. In this study, three different groups of students—music majors, physical education majors, and elementary education majors—read an ambiguous text that could have been interpreted as being about either playing cards of playing music. The students' perspectives (as indicated by their majors) had little effect on their reading of the text.

The key difference between this study and previous studies seems to be the methodology used; this difference may account for the variance in results. Henk and Helfeldt (1985) presented the sentences one at a time rather than in paragraph form, as had been the case in past studies. The subjects noted when there was a change in what they thought the passage was about. Virtually all subjects changed their ideas, and 70 percent of the subjects indicated an awareness of alternative explanations of the paragraph. According to the authors, these data suggest that accommodation and assimilation may play larger roles in interpreting ambiguous text than was once believed. The results also indicate that even if the "wrong" schema is activated, additional information could correct misconceptions. While the Henk and Helfeldt research has yet to be replicated, it offers a new and interesting perspective to the schema literature that certainly deserves further exploration.

The overall results of the manipulation research indicate that it is important for college readers to activate the proper schema and that instructors should teach students how to identify and deal with ambiguous text. While it probably is safe to say that no text will be as ambiguous as the contrived passages used in many of the studies, it is still important for college reading instructors to teach students ways to identify and handle ambiguous information.

Cross-cultural studies. Although cross-cultural studies number the fewest, their results have considerable implications for college reading instructors. Two studies—one examining two totally different cultures, and the second examining cultural differences between blacks and whites within the United States—offer strong support not only for the notion of schema theory but also for the idea that it is important for instructors to help students activate the proper schema.

In many ways, cross-cultural studies are similar to the manipulation studies of Bransford and McCarrell (1974) and Anderson et al. (1977). These two studies compared individuals majoring in or expected to be familiar with particular areas of an ambiguous topic. Depending on their backgrounds, the groups interpreted the passages differently. Similarly, cross-cultural studies have compared students from different cultures or subcultures in terms of their ability to read, comprehend, and interpret culturally related passages. Steffensen, Joag-dev, and Anderson (1979) had natives of India and the United States read two passages, one dealing with an American wedding and the other with an Indian wedding. The results of the study provided strong evidence for the role that schemata play in reading comprehension. Subjects spent more reading time on the culturally unfamiliar passage and made more distortions when recalling that passage. In addition, subjects recalled more culturally important propositions from the culturally familiar passage.

In a study exploring how blacks and whites interpreted the idea of "sounding"—an inner city term—Labov (1972) and Reynolds et al. (1982) again found that culture played a key role in schema formation. Both groups read a passage that described sounding as a fun, one-up-manship, give-and-take form of play

Nist and Mealey

with words. While white teenagers tended to view the passage as violent and confrontational, blacks understood the passage for what it was. These results have strong implications for selecting the kinds of materials that should be used in college reading classrooms. Obviously, college reading instructors must be sensitive to the responses of cultural groups when selecting material to read.

Expert-novice studies. Simply stated, expert-novice studies examine the learning differences between subjects who are knowledgeable about a specific topic and those who lack knowledge about that topic but are equal in terms of intelligence, verbal ability, and reading ability. Spilich et al. (1979) and Chiesi, Spilich, and Voss (1979) used subjects' knowledge of baseball to determine the role schema plays in learning new information and in designating what is important. Spilich et al. (1979) found that when subjects listened to a passage about baseball, those who knew a lot about the sport were better able to remember and synthesize important information than were those with little knowledge, who tended to include unimportant information in their recalls.

These studies indicate that learning new information is easier if one already has a considerable amount of knowledge about the topic (Chiesi, Spilich, & Voss, 1979). This facility presumably results from the preexistence of knowledge structures or slots, which can be expanded and organized to include the new information. Mean and Voss (1985) corroborated these findings in addition to noting developmental trends in the complexity and levels of schema.

In college reading programs, which cater to students with widely varying degrees of background knowledge, the implications of the expert-novice research are obvious. Instructors must be sensitive to the fact that some students will learn and understand the material more readily, depending on the amount of prior knowledge they possess. Instructors also must devise teaching methods that incorporate and build upon students' backgrounds.

Text Structure

The third factor that influences teacher-directed college level comprehension instruction is text structure. Until recently, researchers and practitioners alike have relied on readability formulas to determine text difficulty. Most formulas, however, fail to provide an accurate picture of text difficulty because they measure only vocabulary frequency, word length, and sentence length. Hence, readability formulas have long been criticized for being primarily concerned with surface factors and failing to consider the text's conceptual level or structure (Meyer & Rice, 1984). However, some researchers have included text structure in their theories (Kintsch & van Dijk, 1978; Kintsch & Vipond, 1979; Klare, 1984), and others have examined text difficulty solely from the perspective of text structure (Anderson & Armbruster, 1986; Meyer, 1977, 1979, 1983, 1985). These studies examine text through three types of structure: micropropositions, macropropositions, and top-level structure (Meyer, 1981; van Dijk, 1979).

Micropropositions. Micropropositions, or microstructures, are the lowest level of text structure, dealing with linguistic analysis at the sentence level. Research at this level is often associated with connectives such as "because," "although," or "rather" (Marshall & Glock, 1978; Walmsley, 1977), or with cohesive ties (Halliday & Hasan, 1976). These links help text flow or hang together.

Instruction in micropropositions generally takes the form of asking students to combine information from one sentence with that of another. When researchers examined this activity, they found that it had a positive effect on reading comprehension (Combs, 1975; Straw, 1979). Other microstructure research has found that the greater the number of concepts presented in brief, easy-reading paragraphs, the longer it takes subjects to read the paragraphs and the less they recall (Kintsch et al., 1975). The same patterns emerged with more difficult and unfamiliar passages, as well as when subjects listened to passages rather than reading them.

Macropropositions. Rather than focusing on the linguistic or syntactic level, macropropositions, or macrostructures (van Dijk, 1977), tend to focus on the logical relationships among the ideas presented in the text. Several classifications of macrostructures exist (Fredericksen, 1975; Grimes, 1975; Halliday & Hasan, 1976; Meyer, 1975). We will focus on Meyer's system because it is representative and because it allows practical application. Meyer examines five groups of logical relationships:

1. antecedent/consequent (cause/effect) relationships, showing a causal relationship between ideas;
2. response relationships, including problem/solution, question/answer, and remark/reply;
3. comparison relationships, dealing with likenesses and differences among ideas;
4. collection relationships, showing that ideas are linked by one or more common factors; and
5. description relationships, giving information by presenting attributes or explanations about a topic.

Meyer's system is valuable for classroom use since students need to be taught only a limited number of classifications, which they can then apply to their own texts. While van Dijk's (1977) system may be more closely tied with schema theory in that it asks students to call up "frames" or "slots" to help them organize reading, it fails to provide a set of relationships that can be taught and then applied. Much of the more recent macroproposition research has focused on Meyer's work; in fact, a considerable amount of the research in this area has been conducted by Meyer and her colleagues. These studies have focused on determining which type of structure tends to produce the highest level of immediate and delayed recall. In general, this research has indicated that subjects can recall more information from the compare/contrast structure (Meyer & Freedle, 1984; Richgels et al , 1987), but that even with this structure, recall is higher on the delayed measure (Meyer & Freedle, 1984).

Other findings appear to indicate that better students use text structure to a greater extent than do poorer students, but that even good readers are inconsistent in their use of structure. Often, good readers use the same structure as that of the target passage to organize their free recall, while poor readers do not (Meyer, Brandt, & Bluth, 1980). Without training, however, even college-age students tend not to be aware of the differences among text structures (Heibert, Englert, & Brennen, 1983).

Top-level structure. The final factor in both of these text structure systems is that of top-level structure, or the overall organizing principles of a text. Most of the work to date in this area has been done with narrative materials, most often in the form of story grammars (Mandler & Johnson, 1977; Rumelhart, 1975; Stein & Glenn, 1979). Like macrostructures, story grammars are closely related to schemata. According to the story grammar theory, every story has six elements that together typify story structure: setting, initiating event, internal response, attempt, consequence, and reaction (Stein & Glenn). Hence, when students know these elements, their story schema is immediately activated, making understanding both easier and better.

Other research has focused primarily on training subjects to identify the top-level structure used in various disciplines. Brooks and Dansereau (1983) found that subjects could be taught to use a structural schema to improve recall of science texts. However, they also found that even with training, subjects often failed to employ the target text's organization in their free recalls.

In another series of experiments, Barnett (1984) found similar results. His subjects were assigned to one of six conditions in which they read a passage structured in either a journalistic or a scientific style. In some conditions the passage organization was described and in others it was not; the description was given either before or after subjects read the pas-

Nist and Mealey

sage. Barnett found that while subjects who received the organizational patterns before reading performed statistically better than those who received the descriptions afterwards or not at all, the text structure had no major effect on recall. However, Barnett's study seems flawed for two reasons. First, although Barnett called this a training study, subjects actually received no direct training. Second, all subjects performed poorly on the dependent measure—the highest score was only 58 percent. Hence, even those who received the organizational patterns before reading "failed" the criterion measure.

Textual coherence. Anderson and Armbruster (1986) take a somewhat different—and perhaps for college reading instructors, a more practical—approach to examining text structure. They examine text in terms of local and global coherence, working under the logical assumption that the more coherent the text, the more likely it is that readers will construct a clear understanding.

The first element of Anderson and Armbruster's (1986) system is local coherence. According to Tierney and Mosenthal (1982), local coherence functions like linguistic mortar to hold ideas together in text. It is similar to microstructures and micropropositions in that it is achieved through the correct use of pronoun referents, substitutions, connectives, or conjunctions. If texts are to cohere locally, the relationships among ideas should be explicitly stated and connectives should not be missing or merely implied. In addition, if appropriate, events should be arranged in causal or temporal sequence. Finally, referents should be clear.

The second element, global coherence, is similar to van Dijk's (1977) macrostructures. When texts cohere globally, they are structured so that the ideas are arranged logically and connected in such a way that they are easily understood. Content also plays a part, since the significance and accuracy of what the author writes affect global coherence. For example, the author may paint a colorful picture for the reader but fail to offer pertinent information about the key concepts presented. Accuracy may also present a problem—particularly since instructors and students alike often take the printed word as law and therefore fail to detect inaccuracies in text. Thus, Anderson and Armbruster (1986) assert that in looking at coherence, content as well as structure must be examined. In all, texts that are globally coherent should be predictable; chapters should be arranged logically and fit into an overall plan or structure.

Text coherence is particularly important to developmental college readers for three reasons. First, the students enrolled in college reading programs have reading deficiencies and need all the assistance they can get from text. Second, because a cohesive text can be read more quickly and is more easily understood, it enables developmental students to infer more when they read. Third, since developmental students often enter college with insufficient background knowledge, coherent texts help because they provide students with information in a logical and predictable order without requiring quantum leaps in understanding.

Direct Instruction

A discussion of teacher-directed comprehension strategies would certainly be incomplete without a review of the importance and elements of direct instruction. The relevance of direct instruction emerged from the teacher effectiveness research that received attention in the late 1970s and early 1980s (Berliner, 1981; Berliner & Rosenshine, 1977; Rosenshine, 1979). The emergence in the early 1970s of cognitive psychology, which emphasized the reading process rather than the product, also has contributed to recognition of the important role direct instruction plays in the reading process. As a result, reading educators have realized that when students get 5 out of 10 items correct it does not necessarily mean that they know only 50 percent of the information. It means that instructors should consider the kinds of items students are missing and why they are missing them. These ideas are slowly beginning to penetrate college reading programs.

More recently, the importance of direct instruction in learning transfer has been addressed. If we as college reading educators expect students to map key text concepts on their own or to generate questions during reading, we need to teach them how to carry out these tasks. For example, Hare and Borchardt (1984) found that subjects who received direct instruction employed summarization rules more effectively and improved the quality of their summaries. Garner (1987a) reiterated the importance of learning strategic rules through direct instruction. Still others (Nist, 1987a; Weinstein & Mayer, 1986) suggest that direct instruction is necessary if we expect students to transfer the strategies learned in a college reading class to regular college courses.

We believe that the two most valuable types of direct instruction models for college reading instructors to use are the self-control training model (Brown, Campione, & Day, 1981) and the teacher-to-learner model (Nist & Kirby, 1986). The self-control model relies heavily on student monitoring as a way of encouraging transfer, while the teacher-to-learner model focuses on gradually weaning students from reliance on instructor guidance and assistance.

The Brown, Campione, and Day model was derived from Jenkins's (1979) tetrahedral model. It includes four overlapping and interacting components: the characteristics of the learner, the criterion tasks that must be carried out, the nature of the materials, and the learning activities employed. Student monitoring enters into each of these four components; based on the text, the task, and their own personal characteristics, students must be able to select the proper learning activity and monitor their understanding during learning. While the authors stress that instructors must teach students how to extract and learn important information from text, they fail to suggest how to do so. In addition, the instruction discussed in the article focuses more on training subjects in experimental research studies than it does on training subjects in traditional classroom settings.

The Nist and Kirby (1986) model, which has been used successfully in college reading and study strategy classes, moves students away from teacher dependence and toward carrying out strategies on their own. The model also includes a metacognitive component to help students get a feel for their level of understanding once teacher guidance is limited or withdrawn. Transfer results from direct instruction based on the concept of observational learning through modeling (Bandura, 1969) and thinking aloud. Following the Nist and Kirby model, instructors guide learners through a complex series of interrelated steps:

1. *Focus attention.* The instructor must initiate an activity or make a statement as a way of preparing students to learn.

2. *Give a general overview.* The instructor should inform students what they are going to do. This step helps students understand where they will begin and end and puts them in the proper learning mindset.

3. *Introduce any new terms.* The instructor needs to point out new terms, particularly content-specific or frequently occurring words with which the students may not be familiar.

4. *Go through the procedure step by step.* During this phase, the instructor gives students a ''cookbook'' procedure to follow. The message here is watch and listen. At this point, students assume that the instructor's way is the most efficient and effective. Unfortunately, many instructors begin and end their instruction with this step.

5. *Model the process.* Next, the instructor must show the ''how'' of learning. Instructors think aloud, showing students how a mature learner thinks through an idea or solves a problem. They also show students metacognitive devices by indicating not only when and where they are having problems understanding text but also what they do about their comprehension failures.

6. *Guide practice.* Students now repeat the instructor's strategy using new situations or problems. Instruc-

tors should be available to help students and to guide them in modifying ineffective processes and thinking. This activity is best undertaken at the end of the class during which the instructor presented and modeled the strategy.

7. *Encourage independent practice.* Students should also practice this strategy on their own outside the classroom. This practice will allow teachers to give students additional process and product feedback regarding their use of the strategy.

8. *Redemonstrate if necessary.* Rarely will students acquire the correct behaviors the first time through. Instructors need to remodel processes, while helping students learn how to better monitor their own learning.

As these steps progress, the responsibility for learning moves from the teacher to the student. While the steps cannot be neatly categorized, the model as a whole is a three-phase process: in the first stage, the responsibility falls totally on the teacher; in the second stage, the responsibility is shared as teacher and student work together; and in the third stage, students become responsible for their own learning. It is not until this third stage that transfer occurs.

Every college reading instructor strives to get students to the point of transfer, but this is a difficult goal to accomplish. The next section discusses strategies that can be used to get students on the road to taking charge of their own learning and eventually to being able to transfer information to new learning situations.

Strategies

Strategies for teaching comprehension abound in the literature on reading and studying. But while many of these strategies are popular and accepted, few are grounded in a solid research base. Fewer still have been examined using at-risk students enrolled in college reading courses. Where possible, we will cite research that has been used with high school and college students as subjects; in the absence of such research, other studies will be discussed.

Most of the vast number of strategies recommended can be placed into one of three classifications: organizers, questioning techniques, and guides. Some of these strategies can be used before, during, or after reading, and some are appropriate at all three times. We have noted within the discussion of each strategy when it may optimally be used.

Organizers

The purpose of organizers is to build and activate students' background knowledge, cue awareness of the quality and quantity of that knowledge, and focus attention before reading. Many kinds of organizers exist, and their effectiveness differs across situations. College reading instructors must select the appropriate organizer by carefully considering the difficulty of the text and, even more important, the ability and prior knowledge of the learners.

Advance organizers. The advance organizer, developed by Ausubel (1963, 1968), is probably the best known prereading strategy. It consists of prefatory material that is written at a higher level of abstraction than the target text. Tightly tied to present-day schema theory, its purpose is to prepare students for reading by drawing on their prior knowledge and providing ideational, or intellectual, scaffolding to help build comprehension of new information. Ideational scaffolding is the basic cognitive structure on which pieces of new, related information may be hung (Ausubel, 1968).

Two problems are apparent with the research on advance organizers. First, although advance organizers have been the subject of countless studies, research reviews (Barnes & Clawson, 1975; Hartley & Davies, 1976; Lawton & Wanska, 1977; Mayer, 1979), and the more recent metaanalyses (Luiten, Ames, & Ackerson, 1980; Moore & Readence, 1980), conclusive evidence of their effectiveness has not been found. To compound the problem, Ausubel (1968) has given no specifics about the actual development and writing of advance organizers. Thus researchers who test these organizers' effectiveness may each be devising very different materials for use in their studies. The materials may not be true advance organizers; therefore, results of both individual studies and advance organizer research as a whole may be questionable.

The research suggests that students exposed to advance organizers tend to improve in problem solving and in recalling conceptual information from science text, but that they perform less well when attempting to recall details and technical information (Mayer, 1983). It is important to note that students may need to paraphrase or otherwise encode organizer material in addition to attending to its presentation in order to reap any benefit from it (Dinnel & Glover, 1985).

Another finding is that while advance organizers may be more effective with older students, they may not work well for poorer readers (Luiten, Ames, & Ackerson, 1980). This is a serious point for consideration by college reading instructors, since only Smith and Hesse (1969) report benefits for poor readers. However, Vacca and Vacca's (1986) guidelines for the use of advance organizers may increase the usefulness of these tools for poor readers. According to these researchers, instructors should use advance organizers only with difficult material, and should supplement them with analogies and questions. In addition, the organizers should consist of the text's superordinate ideas and include examples with which students are familiar. (See Weil & Joyce, 1978, for advance organizer development guidelines.)

Although Ausubel (1968) maintains that advance organizers should be written at a higher level of abstraction, generality, and inclusiveness than the text to be presented, Anderson (1985) suggests that more concrete, familiar language may better facilitate students' learning. This recommendation may be especially pertinent when dealing with college reading students.

Graphic organizers. Graphic organizers (Barron, 1969), also called structured overviews, are hierarchically arranged tree diagrams of a text's key terms and concepts. In a revealing metaanalysis, Moore and Readence (1984) found that graphic organizers were more effective than the advance organizers from which they derive (Dean-Guilford, 1981; Kelleher, 1982; Moore & Readence, 1980). Graphic organizers have an advantage over advance organizers in that their construction is defined clearly and concretely, which makes them easier for teachers and students to design.

Interestingly, the effectiveness of graphic organizers tends to be more pronounced when students devise them as a postreading strategy, although graphic organizers were originally meant to be used as a teacher-directed *prereading* activity (Moore & Readence, 1984). Indeed, there is some evidence from this metaanalysis to suggest that construction of graphic organizers enhances the teacher's feeling of preparation. Moore and Readence also posit that student involvement may be the reason for graphic organizers' reported effectiveness. This idea supports Dinnel and Glover's (1985) finding that student encoding of graphic organizers may be a key factor in their effectiveness.

In addition to helping instructors teach new content vocabulary before reading (Moore & Readence, 1984), graphic organizers can be useful in indicating text structure by outlining cause/effect, problem/solution, compare/contrast, chronology, and other patterns. (For guidance in developing text structure graphic organizers, see Readence, Bean, & Baldwin, 1985.) Hence, graphic organizers are grounded not only in schema theory but also in text structure theory. Students should be made aware of the text structure (Bartlett, 1978), or organizational patterns, in order to benefit from both the graphic organizer and the material to be learned. Visual representations of key concepts often enable students to see these organizational patterns. Thus, the graphic organizer should make the text's structure explicit. Graphic organizers that go beyond the simple presentation of terms and develop the relationships between concepts will be more effective.

When deciding whether to use this strategy with college students in developmental or remedial reading programs, the instructor should take note that students may need strong verbal skills for the graphic organizer to be effective, especially as a prereading strategy (Tierney & Cunningham, 1984). Development and use of well-honed metacognitive skills may also be in order. Therefore, the graphic organizer may be more effective with at-risk populations if instructors emphasize the vocabulary of the content area being studied and help students construct graphic organizers *after* reading. This endeavor will be difficult for college reading students without a great deal of direct instruction, practice, and teacher feedback, followed by gradual tapering of instruction over the course of a quarter or semester. As noted in the discussion of direct instruction models, this tapering of teacher guidance and eventual assumption of student responsibility are difficult to achieve. Instructors can alleviate this problem, as well as make the strategy more relevant to students, if they use graphic organizers with content area material—especially since the students will need to grapple with lengthy texts, become familiar with various organizational patterns, and detect key concepts and their interrelationships.

A positive feature of the graphic organizer, from the teacher's point of view, is that its form can be varied according to its desired purpose. In addition, training in this strategy may indeed facilitate transfer to new text (Dansereau, Holley, & Collins, 1980). Mapping (Armbruster & Anderson, 1980) can be considered a variation of the graphic organizer, but again its effectiveness is optimal during the postreading, elaboration stage.

Previews. Another organizer used as a prereading strategy is the oral or story preview (Graves & Cooke, 1980). The preview is more than just a few introductory statements; it is a somewhat lengthy description that provides considerable information about an upcoming expository or narrative text. The instructor attempts to link students' prior knowledge with the new information that will be encountered; thus, previews are related to schema theory. Instead of simply assigning a selection (e.g., "read to page 130 for Wednesday"), the instructor builds anticipation and interest in the content, directs students' attention, and reminds them, through discussion, of what they already know about the topic at hand. In addition, the preview allows instructors to "plant" purpose-setting questions and thoughts in order to give students direction when they read. If the instructor carries it out properly, this process can also lead to increased metacognitive awareness. (See Vacca & Vacca, 1986, for a thorough description of preview construction.)

The effectiveness of previews, especially with difficult materials, is well substantiated for use with students at all levels (Alvarez, 1983; Graves & Cooke, 1980; Graves, Cooke, & LaBerge, 1983; Graves & Prenn, 1984; Hood, 1981; Risko & Alvarez, 1986). This research indicates that previews help students understand, remember, and make inferences about narrative or expository content.

Analogies. An analogy is "an expositional method of comparing sets of information that are similar enough in essential respects to permit transposition of attributes across sets, usually from familiar to unfamiliar information" (Tierney & Cunningham, 1984, p. 613). Analogies are often suggested as a prereading organizing strategy, but research findings on their effectiveness are far from conclusive. Extant studies show that if instructors fail to make explicit the comparison between a familiar and an unfamiliar concept, the effectiveness of the analogy decreases considerably (Perfetti, Bransford, & Franks, 1983).

Glynn et al. (1990) suggest the following model for teaching analogies: (1) introduce target; (2) cue retrieval of analog, (3) identify relevant features of target and analog, (4) map similarities, (5) draw conclusions about target, and (6) indicate where analogy breaks down. Note the similarities between this model and the direct instruction model. It is particularly important to realize that misunderstanding may occur if the instructor neglects the last step, telling students in what way the analog and the target are dissimilar (comparisons are never identical). Teachers should make a special point of leading students to examine all comparisons between the analog and target in order to find where the analogy breaks down (Glynn et al.).

Summary of organizer findings. While not conclusive, the research on organizers appears to cautiously support their use. Advance organizers, the most controversial in terms of support, are probably beneficial in providing ideational scaffolding as long as they are written in a concrete way and presented before students read difficult material. Graphic organizers may best be used as a postreading activity, with emphasis on the previously taught content vocabulary. This strategy may also be used with the aim of teaching students how to construct their own organizers, but success will depend on the amount of training, practice, and feedback students receive over several weeks. In addition, graphic organizers can help students increase their knowledge of text structure. Research supports the use of previews before reading expository or narrative material and suggests that these organizers are effective with students of all ages. The use of analogies is certainly not unequivocally supported, but they may be a good way to link a familiar concept with an unfamiliar one, as long as the instructor indicates where the analogy fails to correspond.

Overall, organizers are certainly tied to schema theory, and some also relate to text structure theory. While all organizers improve metacognitive awareness in some way, those constructed by students contribute more to building strong monitoring abilities.

Questioning

Questioning has many purposes, from prompting the retrieval of prior knowledge and focusing attention to checking literal, inferential, and applied comprehension of information and predicting possible test items. Questioning also improves comprehension (Hamilton, 1985; Klauer, 1984; Tierney & Cunningham, 1984), and it holds an important place in the college reading classroom. Research in this area has much to offer instructors. It can help them understand how different types of questions and their placement affect students' level of comprehension as well as how to evaluate questioning strategies for use with college reading students. (For a comprehensive review of questioning, see Graesser & Black, 1985.)

Types of questions. The questioning frameworks suggested by Herber (1978), who looks solely at questions themselves, and Pearson and Johnson (1978), whose model also takes into account answers to questions, offer instructors guidance in formulating inquiries that tap different levels of students' understanding of text. Teachers can become aware of these levels and use them with students to activate prior knowledge, focus attention, and evaluate comprehension.

Textually explicit questions (Pearson & Johnson, 1978) are based on the text, and their wording is similar or even identical to that of the text. Since students retrieve facts directly from the text, these questions require only an understanding of what the author explicitly states. *Textually implicit* questions demand the interweaving of text information and students' prior knowledge. Readers must make reasonable inferences from the facts at hand and from what they already know about a particular topic. Both Meyer's (1975) and van Dijk's (1977) systems of text analysis note the comprehension problems caused by text that requires excessive inferencing. This problem may be eased by using a third type of question, *scriptually implicit* questions, which go beyond textual information by asking readers to give plausible answers based on their experiences as they relate to the text.

Placement of questions. The placement of questions— whether they are asked before, during, or after reading—can greatly affect students' comprehension. Such effects are evidenced in the theoretical schema studies discussed earlier as well as in more practical studies.

Prereading questions activate schema and cue important information (i.e., intentional learning), so students tend to learn that material better, but perhaps at the expense of information they need to extract from text on their own (Anderson & Biddle, 1975). Prereading questions also facilitate comprehension of more difficult material (Levin & Pressley, 1981). Therefore, if instructors want students to focus only on very specific parts of the text or if they want to help students understand difficult text, prereading questions are an option. However, college reading students may be better served by other prereading aids, such as organizers. The temptation for at-risk students to focus solely on the information requested in prereading questions (which are usually text-explicit) may be too great, and a fuller understanding of the content text may be sacrificed.

Postreading questions are more effective if incidental comprehension is the objective because these questions help students learn information of both greater and lesser importance (Anderson & Biddle, 1975). Alvermann (1987) suggests that this effect occurs because students probably anticipate tests covering the majority of the material rather than a few specific pieces of information. A major problem with many of the studies in this area, however, is that the questions on the test to measure intentional learning are the same as those asked in the postreading questioning session. This situation does not occur in actual classroom settings. In the few studies examining performance on tests using different questions, the effect of postreading questions was quite small (Anderson & Biddle, 1975). The value of questioning at this stage, therefore, may depend on the nature and level of the questions as well as on students' participation in the questioning process and the quality of their responses.

Taking into consideration the effect of the levels of questions also is important. Many studies suggest that asking higher level textually and scriptually implicit questions prompts better performance than asking factual, textually explicit questions (Denner, 1982; Rickards, 1976; Yost, Avila, & Vexler, 1977). But while higher level questions are important, we are not suggesting that factual questions should be omitted. In a college reading course, it is frequently necessary to check comprehension of content area material by asking textually explicit as well as textually and scriptually implicit questions.

Questions supplied during reading, or inserted questions, tend to focus students' attention and improve their performance on the targeted information (Reynolds & Anderson, 1984). In a delayed test, however, Duchastel and Nungester (1984) found no statistical differences in performance between students who answered postreading questions and those who answered inserted questions, although both treatments were more effective than the control condition.

Teacher-provided questions appear to enhance recall of main ideas and details more than student-generated questions (André & Anderson, 1979; Denner & Rickards, 1987). Unless students are trained to generate different levels of questions, their tendency is to devise literal questions that focus on less important details. If the instructor chooses not to teach students how to generate questions, providing conceptual questions is an adequate alternative.

ReQuest. ReQuest (Manzo, 1969), or reciprocal questioning, places much of the responsibility for generating questions on the students. First, both the students and the instructor silently read the same segment of text; next, students ask the instructor a number of questions about the target information; and then the instructor asks questions of the class. If many of the students' questions are textually explicit, the teacher can model higher level questioning. Finally, the teacher asks the students to predict further information or occurrences. After the entire selection is read, discussion centers around the accuracy of the predictions.

This strategy differs from traditional teacher-centered questioning in that it prompts students to become more active and involved with the text. It is also an alternative to the questioning stage of SQ3R-type activities. ReQuest will work well with college reading students as long as the instructor is careful about choosing the kind and amount of text read. Text structure comes into play here: if the text is difficult, smaller sections, even individual sentences, should be selected for the ReQuest procedure; with easier text, longer passages may be used. While it is important not to overuse a strategy and thus possibly dampen motivation, students need repeated exposure to the ReQuest procedure to improve their questioning behavior and increase their autonomy with text.

Question-answer relationship (QAR). QAR (Raphael, 1982, 1984) builds on Pearson and Johnson's (1978) three-tier model of questioning and takes into account both the level of the question and the location of the answer. The QAR strategy alerts students to the differences between higher and lower level question types, called "Right There" (textually explicit), "Think and Search" (textually implicit), and "On Your Own" (scriptually implicit). The instructor provides passages and questions as well as answers from each QAR category. Discussion focuses on the questions and on the location of their answers. Students may work in groups or alone to determine both answers and QAR categories. Eventually, students generate questions, either for their own use or for class discussion, making sure that each QAR category is tapped.

QAR requires a substantial amount of direct instruction before student questioning improves. Also, depending on students' attitudes, it may be advisable to substitute Herber's (1978) framework of *literal*, *inferential*, and *applied* for Raphael's terms. Many college reading students are sensitive to being in a strategies course; using terms they perceive as childish or high schoolish may undermine the benefits of the strategy. Also, the instructor needs to guard against the tendency to focus too much on levels of questions and not enough on actual content.

Directed reading-thinking activity (DRTA). The DRTA (Stauffer, 1969), can be modified for use in college reading or content area classes. Presetting purposes for reading and eliciting student prediction and speculation about the material are the keys to this strategy. First, students survey the title, subheadings, and graphs, and predict orally or in writing what the material will be about. Once they have read a segment of the text, the instructor asks them to refine their predictions, clarify information, and define unfamiliar vocabulary. More speculation ensues, after which students read the next segment and discuss or refine the predictions already made. This cycle is continued until the text is finished. The instructor should ask higher level questions to stimulate thinking and speculation. Students' opinions must be reinforced with information from the text or from experience.

The DRTA probably is most effective with at-risk students who have great difficulty learning from text. Short reading segments and discussion will help them verbalize main ideas and supporting details, give them opportunities to learn specialized content vocabulary, and improve their understanding of important signal words such as *however, therefore*, and *nevertheless*. It might be advisable to use this strategy in the beginning of the quarter or semester for the first few pieces of assigned text, gradually fading out the stop-start aspect of reading (Hansen, 1981) and moving into strategies that require more autonomous learning behavior.

Summary of questioning findings. Questioning positively influences comprehension, but in unexpected ways. Instructors need to be aware of the effects of different levels of questions, the placement of questions, and different teacher-directed questioning strategies. Questioning is influenced by both text structure and schema theory, and it helps students grow metacognitively by calling attention to areas of text with which they may be experiencing difficulty.

In order to ensure that they are not simply asking students to regurgitate facts from text, teachers can rely on guidance from comprehension frameworks, such as Herber's (1978) and Pearson and Johnson's (1978), to tap higher levels of student understanding. Asking more textually and scriptually implicit questions will enrich comprehension and prompt students to engage the text more actively, using their own experience to connect with new information.

Placement of questions can seriously influence the quality and quantity of comprehension. Prereading questions cue important information that probably will be learned well, but at the expense of other main ideas and details. Postreading questions, on the other hand, may be more effective for broader understanding of text; however, the quality and level of questions need to be assessed, as does the degree of student participation in the questioning process. Inserted questions are as effective as postreading questions and may serve to focus student attention during reading. Often, providing questions is a more effective strategy than having students generate their own questions unless they are carefully trained to emphasize main ideas and tap into different levels of comprehension.

Instructors must select from a variety of questioning strategies on the basis of students' ability and prior knowledge, whether training is feasible, and the desired performance. With the student-centered ReQuest strategy, teachers model desired questioning behavior without explicitly stating the differences among literal, inferential, and applied questions. The purpose of QAR, on the other hand, is to make students more aware of the different types of questions and sources of answers; therefore, if provoking that awareness is the instructor's goal, QAR is an excellent strategy. The key to DRTA is prediction and reading short segments of text for preset purposes. This goal gives students specified reading goals and tends to engender a great deal of discussion based on experience and inference. DRTA is especially suitable for use with poor readers.

Guides

Guides are used while the material is read to provide students with questions directed at different levels of comprehension, as well as with warnings, signals, and other directions. The purpose of guides is to lead students through difficult text by questioning and distinguishing important from less important information. Some guides may not be as beneficial as other teacher-directed strategies for college reading students, since the hand-holding features inherent in guides might give students mixed signals regarding what independent learning is all about.

Anticipation guides. Herber (1978) devised this type of study guide to aid students in predicting text concepts. The anticipation guide consists of a list of statements to which students respond prior to reading a text. The statements may or may not support facts or the author's point of view. The students mark the statements true/false or agree/disagree. Their answers reflect their level of background knowledge; thus, these guides draw heavily from schema theory. (See Readence, Bean,

& Baldwin, 1985, for suggestions on constructing anticipation guides.)

After discussing each statement, students read to see if their predictions and prior knowledge are accurate or in accord with the author's point of view. Students may refine or change their prior knowledge. In addition, instructors can get a good idea of the depth and breadth of students' prior knowledge and take any necessary compensatory measures. Instructors may also ask students to return to the original statements after reading and use them as a reaction guide and a basis for discussion to see how or if their perceptions and knowledge have changed as a result of reading.

This strategy appears to be effective with college reading students, who perceive it as a type of advance organizer and a chance to bring prior knowledge to bear on content. When their prior knowledge is incorrect, the reaction aspect of the guide lets them see for themselves that they were wrong and have learned as a result of reading.

Marginal glosses. The marginal gloss (Richgels & Mateja, 1984) operates as an in-text study guide with the eventual purpose of showing students how to annotate text. The instructor provides notations of interesting points in the text, prompting the student to extract specific main ideas, lists, and examples. In this sense, the marginal gloss can help students see the top-level structure of text. This strategy may be particularly useful if the instructor plans on teaching students how to mark text. Initially providing the glosses for students is similar to modeling an annotation marking system (Nist, 1987b). It is important to remember, however, that the goal is independent learning. Thus, phasing out the marginal gloss technique and training students to write their own glosses or annotations is the preferred route.

Study guides. Although listing literal-level questions is usually the norm with study guides, Readence, Bean, and Baldwin (1985) recommend that instructors develop guides with Herber's (1978) or Pearson and Johnson's (1978) questioning framework in mind. Vacca and Vacca (1986) recommend the similar three-level guide, which uses the anticipation-reaction format, using statements reflecting the three levels of comprehension rather than questions. Students respond to the statements before, during, or after reading.

Selective Reading Guide-O-Rama. The Selective Reading Guide-O-Rama (Cunningham & Shablak, 1975) points out only the most important information in the text so that students do not need to read an entire selection. Obviously, the Guide-O-Rama should be used only for certain purposes, such as reading for main ideas and perhaps skimming. If it is used frequently, students may get the idea that reading entire texts is not often necessary.

Pattern guides. These guides elucidate the patterns of text structure, such as compare/contrast, cause/effect, and chronology. As noted earlier, when text patterns are made explicit to students, comprehension increases (Bartlett, 1978; Meyer, Brandt, & Bluth, 1980). Vacca and Vacca (1986) suggest that pattern guides be designed in such a way that students must respond to text structure by examining the relationships between concepts in the material. For instance, for a text with a predominantly cause/effect structure, the instructor can list either the cause or the effect and have the students supply the missing element of the pair; for a chronology pattern, the instructor can list certain events from the text and ask students to supply the missing occurrences.

Summary of guide findings. While very little research focuses on the effectiveness of guides, what does exist indicates a modest positive effect on comprehension. However, college reading instructors should proceed with care when choosing which to use. Keeping in mind the goal of helping students become independent learners, instructors need to judge how much assistance students require with different texts at different times during the quarter or semester. In addition, they must take into account the desired levels of comprehension and the types of text structure used in order to choose the prereading, during, and postreading strategies that offer the best opportunities for successful learning.

Different types of guides serve different purposes. Anticipation guides are generally useful as both prereading and post-reading organizers since they encompass prediction, use of prior knowledge, and a check of comprehension. The marginal gloss is probably best used in teaching text marking systems, especially annotation. Study guides, such as the three-level guide, should be approached with considerable caution since they may not benefit college reading students who need to be shown strategies for achieving academic autonomy. Finally, pattern guides may be an appropriate and effective way of getting students to grapple with the link between text structure and comprehension.

Conclusions and Recommendations

For Instruction

The varying populations, methods, and quality of studies can leave well-meaning instructors feeling overwhelmed and possibly confused about the extant research and its lack of conclusive findings. While it is difficult to recommend the use of certain strategies when research fails to solidly support their effectiveness, we have attempted to determine which strategies are more solidly supported than others, which strategies may be effective with developmental students, and where trouble spots may emerge.

Of the many kinds of organizers available, graphic organizers, previews, and (if judiciously selected and used) analogies are best supported. Graphic organizers in particular are quick and easy to construct and very helpful, although they are even more effective as a student-centered activity. The use of oral and story previews is advocated, but these organizers require considerable preparation on the instructor's part. Analogies can be very effective, but only when the analog and the target concept correspond closely and when any dissimilarities are pointed out by the instructor. Advance organizers that are devised as Ausubel (1963, 1968) recommends may not be effective with developmental students. Instead, instructors should use advance organizers to introduce new concepts and materials through concrete ideas and familiar language.

Questioning is an excellent instructional tactic as long as teachers are aware of the different levels of questions, the effects of question placement, and the various recommended strategies. Questioning frameworks can guide teachers in their attempts to enhance student comprehension. Asking more textually and scriptually implicit questions will prompt students to draw on previous experience and knowledge to connect with new concepts. Prereading, inserted, and postreading questions have different effects, which instructors should be aware of in order to direct students' attention to the material targeted for learning. Guides have yet to be the object of much research, but the few relevant studies point to some benefits for students. Guides may be useful for at-risk populations if they are used only for the first two or three assigned texts, and only with difficult texts. Ultimately, guides should be replaced with strong prereading organizers and questioning strategies that gradually pass the responsibility for learning to the students, as a group and individually.

For Research

Our review of the theory and research related to teacher-directed comprehension strategies at the college level points to several conclusions and recommendations. Most evident is the lack of research conducted with at-risk students at the college level. Although most of the strategies discussed have been examined in studies using college students, the subjects were generally enrolled in introductory psychology or education classes, not in developmental reading classes. This problem calls into question the generalizability of the results to at-risk college students and casts doubt on the suggestions made in numerous pedagogical articles directed at college reading teachers.

Many of these strategies are not grounded in solid research bases, yet practitioners appear to view them as such. So great is the problem that, for some strategies, we could find no empirically based studies that demonstrated effectiveness or ineffectiveness. Therefore, we recommend that future research begin to focus on developmental populations in order to determine which teacher-directed comprehension strategies lead to the greatest increase in learning and to the creation of autonomous learners.

A second observation concerns the methodology employed in the empirical studies using college students as subjects. Although the strategies in question are classified as teacher-directed, few empirical studies involved any training component. As a result, such investigations fail to reveal what could happen with instructor intervention and suggest only what happens when subjects are told to use a certain strategy or technique. Another methodology concern is that most of the studies were short in duration, some collecting data for only 15 minutes at a time. We found these data collection procedures very disturbing, particularly since in order to gain any statistical results when testing strategies the treatment must be powerful and training must occur over an extended period of time. We recommend that future empirical studies incorporate a training component that occurs over a reasonable amount of time.

A third positive point is that, for the most part, the research that has been conducted on teacher-directed comprehension strategies appears to be solidly grounded in theory. All of the strategies, particularly questioning, improve metacognitive awareness and thus also improve comprehension. Both guides and organizers are firmly grounded in schema theory. In particular, advance organizers help students call up prior knowledge and provide for ideational scaffolding as a means of accommodating new information. Guides that are constructed to help students better understand how texts are organized also aid in comprehension.

Fourth, seriously lacking in the literature are studies indicating that teacher-directed strategies eventually lead to transfer. Unless college students can move beyond teacher dependence and apply strategies on their own, they will have a difficult time being academically successful in college. Studies must be de-

Nist and Mealey

vised that indicate alternative methods instructors can employ to move students toward becoming independent learners with strong comprehending abilities. For example, anticipation guides push students to call up prior knowledge and perhaps to begin thinking differently about a topic. As instructors, we know that once students leave the confines of college reading classes they are not going to sit down and construct their own guides; we hope they will begin to think about what they are going to read before beginning an assignment. Studies that would indicate the value of teacher-directed comprehension strategies as a springboard to transfer are needed.

References and Suggested Readings

Alvarez, M.C. (1983). Using a thematic preorganizer and guided instruction as aids to concept learning. *Reading Horizons, 24,* 51-58.

*Alvermann, D.E. (1987). Comprehension/thinking skills. In D.E. Alvermann, D.W. Moore, & M.W. Conley (Eds.), *Research within reach: Secondary school reading.* Newark, DE: International Reading Association.

Anderson, R.C. (1978). Schema directed processes in language comprehension. In A. Lesgold, J. Pelligreno, S. Fokkema, & R. Glaser (Eds.), *Cognitive psychology and instruction.* New York: Plenum.

*Anderson, R.C. (1985). Role of the reader's schema in comprehension, learning, and memory. In H. Singer & R.B. Ruddell (Eds.), *Theoretical models and processes of reading* (3rd ed.). Newark, DE: International Reading Association.

*Anderson, R.C., & Biddle, W. B. (1975). On asking people questions about what they are reading. In G. Bower (Ed.), *The psychology of learning and motivation* (Vol. 9). San Diego, CA: Academic Press.

*Anderson, R.C., & Pearson, P.D. (1984). A schema-theoretic view of basic processes in reading. In P.D. Pearson (Ed.), *Handbook of reading research.* New York: Longman.

Anderson, R.C., & Pichert, J.W. (1978). Recall of previously unrecallable information following a shift in perspective. *Journal of Verbal Learning and Verbal Behavior, 17,* 1-13.

Anderson, R.C., Pichert, J.W., & Shirey, L.L. (1983). Role of reader's schema at different points in time. *Journal of Educational Psychology, 75,* 271-279.

*Anderson, R.C., Reynolds, R.E., Schallert, D.L., & Goetz, E.T. (1977). Frameworks for comprehending discourse. *American Educational Research Journal, 14,* 367-381.

Anderson, R.C., Spiro, R., & Anderson, M.C. (1978). Schemata as scaffolding for the representation of information in connected discourse. *American Educational Research Journal, 15,* 433-440.

*Anderson, T.H., & Armbruster, B.B. (1986). Readable textbooks, or selecting a textbook is not like buying a pair of shoes. In J. Orasanu (Ed.), *Reading comprehension: From research to practice.* Hillsdale, NJ: Erlbaum.

André, M.E.D.A., & Anderson, T.H. (1979). The development and evaluation of a self-questioning study technique. *Reading Research Quarterly, 14,* 605-623.

*Armbruster, B.B., & Anderson, T.H. (1980). *The effect of mapping on the free recall of expository text* (Tech. Rep. No. 160). Champaign, IL: University of Illinois, Center for the Study of Reading.

*Armbruster, B.B., & Gudbrandsen, B. (1986). Reading comprehension instruction in social studies. *Reading Research Quarterly, 21*, 36-48.

Ausubel, D.P. (1963). *The psychology of meaningful verbal learning.* New York: Grune & Stratton.

Ausubel, D.P. (1968). *Educational psychology: A cognitive view.* New York: Holt, Rinehart & Winston.

*Baker, L. (1985). Differences in the standards used by college students to evaluate their comprehension of expository prose. *Reading Research Quarterly, 20*, 297-313.

*Baker, L., & Brown, A.L. (1984). Metacognitive skills and reading. In P.D. Pearson (Ed.), *Handbook of reading research.* New York: Longman.

Baker, W.E. (1974). *Reading skills* (2nd ed.). Englewood Cliffs, NJ: Prentice Hall.

Bandura, A. (1969). *Principles of behavior modification.* New York: Holt, Rinehart & Winston.

*Barnes, B.R., & Clawson, E.W. (1975). Do advance organizers facilitate learning? *Review of Educational Research, 45,* 637-660.

Barnett, J.E. (1984). Facilitating retention through instruction about text structure. *Journal of Reading Behavior, 16*, 1-13.

Barron, R.F. (1969). The use of vocabulary as an advance organizer. In H.L. Herber & P.L. Sanders (Eds.), *Research on reading in the content areas: First-year report.* Syracuse, NY: Syracuse University, Reading and Language Arts Center.

Bartlett, B.J. (1978). *Top-level structure as an organizational strategy for recall of classroom text.* Unpublished doctoral dissertation, Arizona State University, Tempe.

Bartlett, F.C. (1932). *Remembering: A study in experimental and social psychology.* New York: Cambridge University Press.

*Berliner, D.C. (1981). Academic learning time and reading achievement. In J.T. Guthrie (Ed.), *Comprehension and teaching: Research reviews.* Newark, DE: International Reading Association.

Berliner, D.C., & Rosenshine, B. (1977). The acquisition of knowledge in the classroom. In R.C. Anderson, R.J. Spiro, & W.E. Montague (Eds.), *Schooling and the acquisition of knowledge.* Hillsdale, NJ: Erlbaum.

*Bransford, J.D., & McCarrell, N.S. (1974). A sketch of a cognitive approach to comprehension. In W.B. Weimer & D.S. Palermo (Eds.), *Cognition and the symbolic processes.* Hillsdale, NJ: Erlbaum.

Brooks, L.W., & Dansereau, D.F. (1983). Effects of structural schema training and text organization on expository prose processing. *Journal of Educational Psychology, 75*, 811-820.

*Brown, A.L., Armbruster, B.B., & Baker, L. (1986). The role of metacognition in reading and studying. In J. Orasanu (Ed.), *Reading comprehension: From research to practice.* Hillsdale, NJ: Erlbaum.

Brown, A.L., Campione, J.C., & Day, J.C. (1981). Learning to learn: On training students to learn from texts. *Educational Researcher, 10*, 14-21.

Chiesi, H.L., Spilich, G.J., & Voss, J.F. (1979). Acquisition of domain-related information in relation to high and low domain knowledge. *Journal of Verbal Learning and Verbal Behavior, 254-274*.

Combs, W.E. (1975). *Some further effects and implications of sentence-combining exercises for the secondary language arts curriculum.* Unpublished doctoral dissertation, University of Minnesota, Minneapolis.

Cunningham, D., & Shablak, S. (1975). Selective Reading Guide-O-Rama: The content teacher's best friend. *Journal of Reading, 18*, 380-382.

Dansereau, D.F., Holley, C.D., & Collins, K.W. (1980, April). *Effects of learning strat-*

egy training on text processing. Paper presented at the annual meeting of the American Educational Research Association, Boston, MA.

Dean-Guilford, M.E. (1981). An investigation of the use of three prereading strategies on the comprehension of junior high school students. *Dissertation Abstracts International*, *42*, 1576A-1577A.

Denner, P.R. (1982). The influence of spontaneous strategy use on the development of provided and generated self-test questioning. *Dissertation Abstracts International*, *42*, 4778-A.

Denner, P.R., & Rickards, J.P. (1987). A developmental comparison of the effects of provided and generated questions on text recall. *Contemporary Educational Psychology*, *12*, 135-146.

Dewey, J. (1910). *How we think*. Lexington, MA: D.C. Heath.

*Dinnel, D., & Glover, J.H. (1985). Advance organizers: Encoding manipulations. *Journal of Educational Psychology*, 77, 514-521.

*Duchastel, P.C., & Nungester, R.J. (1984). Adjunct question effects with review. *Contemporary Educational Psychology*, *9*, 97-103.

Durkin, D. (1979). What classroom observations reveal about reading comprehension instruction. *Reading Research Quarterly*, *14*, 481-533.

Epstein, W., Glenberg, A.M., & Bradley, M.M. (1984). Coactivation and comprehension: Contribution of text variables to the illusion of knowing. *Memory and Cognition*, *12*, 355-360.

Flavell, J.H. (1978). Metacognitve development. In J.M. Scandura & C.J. Brainerd (Eds.), *Structural/process theories of complex human behavior*. Alphen ad. Rijn, The Netherlands: Sijthoff and Noordhoff.

Fredericksen, C.H. (1975). Representing logical and semantic structure of knowledge acquired for discourse. *Cognitive Psychology*, 7, 371-458.

*Gambrell, L.D., & Heathington, B.S. (1981). Adult disabled readers' metacognitive awareness about reading tasks and strategies. *Journal of Reading Behavior*, *13*, 215-222.

*Garner, R. (1987a). *Metacognition and reading comprehension*. Norwood, NJ: Ablex.

*Garner, R. (1987b). Strategies for reading and studying expository text. *Education Psychologist*, *22*, 313-332.

Glenberg, A.M., Wilkinson, A.C., & Epstein, W. (1982). The illusion of knowing: Failure in the self-assessment of comprehension. *Memory and Cognition*, *10*, 597-602.

*Glynn, S.M., Britton, B.K., Semrud-Clikeman, M., & Muth, K.D. (1990). Analogical reasoning and problem solving in science textbooks. In J.A. Glover, R.R. Ronning, & C.R. Reynolds (Eds.), *Handbook of creativity: Assessment, research, & theory*. New York: Plenum.

*Graesser, A.C., & Black, J.B. (Eds.) (1985). *The psychology of questions*. Hillsdale, NJ: Erlbaum.

*Graves, M.F., & Cooke, C.L. (1980). Effects of previewing difficult short stories for high school students. *Research on Reading in Secondary Schools*, *6*, 38-54.

Graves, M.F., Cooke, C.L., & LaBerge, M.J. (1983). Effects of previewing difficult short stories on low ability junior high school students' comprehension, recall, and attitudes. *Reading Research Quarterly*, *18*, 262-276.

Graves, M.F., & Prenn, M.C. (1984). Effects of previewing expository passages on junior high school students' comprehension and attitudes. In J.A. Niles & L.A. Harris (Eds.), *Changing perspectives on research in reading/language processing and instruction*. Rochester, NY: National Reading Conference.

Grimes, J.E. (1975). *The thread of discourse*. The Hague: Mouton.

Halliday, M.A.K., & Hasan, R. (1976). *Cohesion in English*. White Plains, NY: Longman.

Hamilton, R.J. (1985). A framework for the evaluation of the effectiveness of adjunct questions and objectives. *Review of Educational Research*, *55*, 47-86.

Teacher-Directed Comprehension Strategies   81

Hansen, J. (1981). The effects of inference training and practice on young children's comprehension. *Reading Research Quarterly, 16,* 391-417.

*Hare, V.C., & Borchardt, K.M. (1984). Direct instruction of summarization skills. *Reading Research Quarterly, 20,* 62-78.

*Hartley, J., & Davies, I.K. (1976). Preinstructional strategies: The role of pretests, behavioral objectives, overviews, and advance organizers. *Review of Educational Research, 46,* 239-265.

Heibert, E.H., Englert, C.S., & Brennen, S. (1983). Awareness of text structure in recognition and production of expository discourse. *Journal of Reading Behavior, 15,* 63-79.

Henk, W.A., & Helfeldt, J.P. (1985, October). *In-process measures of ambiguous text interpretation: A test of the prior knowledge hypothesis.* Paper presented at the annual meeting of the College Reading Association, Pittsburgh, PA.

Henk, W.A., & Helfeldt, J.P. (1987). In-process measures of ambiguous text interpretations: Another look at the influence of prior knowledge. In J.E. Readence & R.S. Baldwin (Eds.), *Research in literacy: Merging perspectives.* New York: National Reading Conference.

Herber, H.L. (1978). *Teaching reading in content areas* (2nd ed.). Englewood Cliffs, NJ: Prentice Hall.

Hood, M. (1981). *The effect of previewing on the recall of high school students.* Unpublished master's thesis, University of Minnesota, Minneapolis.

Jenkins, J.J. (1979). Four points to remember: A tetrahedral model and memory experiments. In L.S. Cermak & F.I.M. Craik (Eds.), *Levels and processing in human memory.* Hillsdale, NJ: Erlbaum.

Just, M.A., & Carpenter, P.A. (1980). A theory of reading: From eye fixations to comprehension. *Psychological Review, 87,* 329-354.

*Just, M.A., & Carpenter, P.A. (1987). *The psychology of reading and language comprehension.* Boston, MA: Allyn & Bacon.

Kelleher, A. (1982). The effect of prereading strategies on comprehension. *Dissertation Abstracts International, 43,* 707A.

Kintsch, W., Kozminsky, E., Streby, W.J., McKoon, G., & Keenan, J.M. (1975). Comprehension and recall of text as a function of context variables. *Journal of Verbal Learning and Verbal Behavior, 14,* 196-214.

Kintsch, W., & van Dijk, T.A. (1978). Toward a model of text comprehension and production. *Psychological Review, 85,* 363-394.

Kintsch, W., & Vipond, D. (1979). Reading comprehension and readability in educational practice and theory. In L.G. Nillson (Ed.), *Perspectives on memory research.* Hillsdale, NJ: Erlbaum.

Klare, G.R. (1984). Readability. In P.D. Pearson, (Ed.), *Handbook of reading research.* New York: Longman.

Klauer, K.J. (1984). Intentional and incidental learning with instructional texts: A metaanalysis for 1970-1980. *American Educational Research Journal, 21,* 323-340.

Labov, W. (1972). *Language of the inner city.* Philadelphia, PA: University of Pennsylvania Press.

Larson, C.O., Dansereau, D.F., O'Donnell, A.M., Hythecker, V.I., Lambiotte, J.G., & Rocklin, T.R. (1985). Effects of metacognition and elaborative activity on cooperative learning and transfer. *Contemporary Educational Psychology, 10,* 342-348.

Levin, J.R., & Pressley, M. (1981). Improving children's prose comprehension: Selected strategies that seem to succeed. In C.M. Santa & B.L. Hayes (Eds.), *Children's prose comprehension: Research and practice.* Newark, DE: International Reading Association.

*Luiten, J., Ames, W., & Ackerson, G. (1980). A metaanalysis of the effects of advance organizers on learning and retention. *American Educational Research Journal*, *17*, 211-218.

Mandler, J.M., & Johnson, N.S. (1977). Remembrance of things parsed: Story structure and recall. *Cognitive Psychology*, *9*, 111-151.

*Manzo, A.V. (1969). The ReQuest procedure. *Journal of Reading*, *13*, 123-126.

Markham, E.M. (1977). Realizing that you don't understand: A preliminary investigation. *Child Development*, *46*, 986-992.

*Marshall, N., & Glock, M.D. (1978). Comprehension of connected discourse: A study into the relationship between the structure of text and information recalled. *Reading Research Quarterly*, *16*, 10-56.

*Mayer, R.E. (1979). Advance organizers that compensate for the organization of text. *Journal of Educational Psychology*, *70*, 880-886.

Mayer, R.E. (1983). Can you repeat that? Qualitative effects of repetition and advance organizers on learning from science prose. *Journal of Educational Psychology*, *75*, 40-49.

Mean, M.L., & Voss, J.F. (1985). Star Wars: A developmental study of expert and novice knowledge structures. *Journal of Memory and Language*, *24*, 746-757.

Meyer, B.J.F. (1975). *The organization of prose and its effect on recall*. Amsterdam, Netherlands: North Holland Press.

Meyer, B.J.F. (1977). The structure of prose: Effects on learning and memory and implications for educational practice. In R.C. Anderson, R. Spiro, & W. Montague (Eds.), *Schooling and the acquisition of knowledge*. Hillsdale, NJ: Erlbaum.

*Meyer, B.J.F. (1979). Organizational patterns in prose and their use in reading. In M.L. Kamil & A.J. Moe (Eds.), *Reading research: Studies and applications*. Clemson, SC: National Reading Conference.

Meyer, B.J.F. (1981). Basic research on prose comprehension: A critical review. In D.F. Fisher & C.W. Peters (Eds.), *Comprehension and the competent reader: Interspecialty perspectives*. New York: Praeger.

Meyer, B.J.F. (1983). Text dimensions and cognitive processing. In H. Mandle, N. Stein, & T. Tabasso (Eds.), *Language and comprehension of text*. Hillsdale, NJ: Erlbaum.

Meyer, B.J.F. (1985). Prose analysis: Purposes, procedures, and problems. In B.K. Britton & J.B. Black (Eds.), *Understanding expository text*. Hillsdale, NJ: Erlbaum.

*Meyer, B.J.F., Brandt, D.M., & Bluth, G.J. (1980). Use of top-level structure in text: Key for reading comprehension of ninth-grade students. *Reading Research Quarterly*, *16*, 72-103.

*Meyer, B.J.F., & Freedle, R.O. (1984). Effects of discourse type on recall. *American Educational Research Journal*, *21*, 121-143.

*Meyer, B.J.F., & Rice, G.E. (1984). The structure of text. In P.D. Pearson (Ed.), *Handbook of reading research*. New York: Longman.

Meyers, M., & Paris, S.G. (1978). Children's metacognitive knowledge about reading. *Journal of Educational Psychology*, *70*, 680-690.

*Moore, D.W., & Readence, J.E. (1980). A metaanalysis of the effect of graphic organizers on learning from text. In M.L. Kamil & A.J. Moe (Eds.), *Perspectives on reading research and instruction*. Washington, DC: National Reading Conference.

*Moore, D.W., & Readence, J.E. (1984). A quantitative and qualitative review of graphic organizer research. *Journal of Educational Research*, *78*, 11-17.

Neilsen, A.R., Rennie, B., & Connell, B.J. (1982). Allocation of instructional time to reading comprehension and study skills in intermediate grade social studies classrooms. In J.A. Niles & L.A. Harris (Eds.), *New inquiries in reading research and instruction* (pp. 81-84). Rochester, NY: National Reading Conference.

Nist, S.L. (1987a). The problem of transfer. In D. Lumpkin, M. Harshbarger, & P.

Ransom (Eds.), *Changing conceptions of reading: Literacy learning instruction.* Muncie, IN: Ball State University.

*Nist, S.L. (1987b). Teaching students to annotate and underline text effectively: Guidelines and procedures. *Georgia Journal of Reading, 12,* 16-22.

*Nist, S.L., & Kirby, K. (1986). Teaching comprehension and study strategies through modeling and thinking aloud. *Reading Research and Instruction, 24,* 254-264.

*Paris, S.G., Lipson, M.Y., & Wixson, K.K. (1983). Becoming a strategic reader. *Contemporary Educational Psychology, 8,* 193-216.

Pearson, P.D., & Johnson, D.D. (1978). *Teaching reading comprehension.* New York: Holt, Rinehart & Winston.

Perfetti, G.A., Bransford, J.D., & Franks, J.J. (1983). Constraints on access in a problem-solving contest. *Memory and Cognition, 11,* 24-31.

Pichert, J.W., & Anderson, R.C. (1977). Different perspectives on a story. *Journal of Educational Psychology, 69,* 309-315.

Pressley, M., Snyder, B.L., Levin, J.R., Murry, H.G., & Ghatala, E.S. (1987). Perceived readiness for examination performance (PREP) produced by initial reading of text and text containing adjunct questions. *Reading Research Quarterly, 22,* 219-236.

Raphael, T.E. (1982). Question-answering strategies for children. *The Reading Teacher, 36,* 186-191.

Raphael, T.E. (1984). Teaching learners about sources of information for answering comprehension questions. *Journal of Reading, 27,* 303-311.

*Readence, J.E., Bean, T.W., & Baldwin, R.S. (1985). *Content area reading: An integrated approach* (2nd ed.). Dubuque, IA: Kendall/Hunt.

*Reynolds, R.E., & Anderson, R.C. (1984). Influence of questions on the allocation of attention during reading. *Journal of Educational Psychology, 74,* 623-632.

*Reynolds, R.E., Taylor, M.A., Steffensen, M.S., Shirey, L.L., & Anderson, R.C. (1982). Cultural schemata and reading comprehension. *Reading Research Quarterly, 17,* 353-366.

Richgels, D.J., & Mateja, J.A. (1984). Gloss II: Integrating content and process for independence. *Journal of Reading, 27,* 424-431.

Richgels, D.J., McGee, L.M., Lomax, R.G., & Sheard, C. (1987). Awareness of four text structures: Effect on recall of expository text. *Reading Research Quarterly, 22,* 177-196.

Rickards, J.P. (1976). Type of verbatim question interspersed in text: A new look at the position effect. *Journal of Reading Behavior, 8,* 37-45.

*Risko, V., & Alvarez, M.C. (1986). An investigation of poor readers' use of a thematic strategy to comprehend text. *Reading Research Quarterly, 21,* 298-316.

*Rosenshine, B.V. (1979). Content, time and direct instruction. In P.L. Peterson & H.J. Walberg (Eds.), *Research on teaching: Concepts, findings, and implications.* Berkeley, CA: McCutchan.

Rumelhart, D.E. (1975). Notes on a schema for stories. In D.G. Bower & A. Collins (Eds.), *Representation and understanding: Studies for cognitive science.* San Diego, CA: Academic Press.

Sanford, A.J., & Garrod, S.C. (1981). *Understanding written language: Explorations in comprehension beyond the sentence.* New York: John Wiley & Sons.

Schommer, M., & Surber, J.R. (1986). Comprehension-monitoring failures in skilled adult readers. *Journal of Educational Psychology, 78,* 353-357.

Smith, R.J., & Hesse, K.D. (1969). The effects of prereading assistance in the comprehension of good and poor readers. *Research in the Teaching of English, 3,* 166-177.

Spilich, G.J., Vesonder, G.T., Chiesi, H.L., & Voss, J.F. (1979). Text processing of domain-related information for individuals with high and low domain knowledge. *Journal of Verbal Learning and Verbal Behavior, 18,* 275-290.

Stauffer, R. (1969). *Directing reading maturity as a cognitive process*. New York: Harper & Row.

*Steffensen, M.S., Joag-dev, C., & Anderson, R.C. (1979). A cross-cultural perspective on reading comprehension. *Reading Research Quarterly, 15*, 10-29.

Stein, N., & Glenn, C.G. (1979). An analysis of story comprehension in elementary school children. In R.O. Freedle (Ed.), *New directions in discourse processing*. Norwood, NJ: Ablex.

Thorndike, E.L. (1917). Reading as reasoning: A study of mistakes in paragraph reading. *Journal of Educational Psychology, 8*, 323-332.

*Tierney, R.J., & Cunningham, J.S. (1984). Research on teaching reading comprehension. In P.D. Pearson (Ed.), *Handbook of reading research*, New York: Longman.

Tierney, R.J., & Mosenthal, P.J. (1982). Discourse comprehension and production: Analyzing text structure and cohesion. In J. Langer & M.T. Smith-Burke (Eds.), *Reader meets author/bridging the gap: A psycholinguistic and sociolinguistic perspective*. Newark, DE: International Reading Association.

*Vacca, R.T., & Vacca, J.L. (1986). *Content area reading* (2nd ed.). Boston, MA: Little, Brown.

van Dijk, T.A. (1977). Semantic macrostructures and knowledge frames in discourse comprehension. In M.A. Just & P.A. Carpenter (Eds.), *Cognitive processes in comprehension*. Hillsdale, NJ: Erlbaum.

van Dijk, T.A. (1979). Relevance assignment in discourse comprehension. *Discourse Processes, 2*, 113-126.

Walmsley, S. (1977). Children's understanding of linguistic connectives: A review of selected literature and implications for reading research. In P.D. Pearson (Ed.), *Reading: Theory, research, and practice*. Clemson, SC: National Reading Conference.

*Weil, M., & Joyce, B. (1978). *Information processing models of teaching*. Englewood Cliffs, NJ: Prentice Hall.

*Weinstein, C.F., & Mayer, R.F. (1986). The teaching of learning strategies. In M.C. Wittrock (Ed.), *Handbook of research on teaching* (3rd ed.). New York: Macmillan.

*Wilson, P.T., & Anderson, R.C. (1986). What they don't know will hurt them: The role of prior knowledge in comprehension. In J. Orasanu (Ed.), *Reading comprehension: From research to practice*. Hillsdale, NJ: Erlbaum.

*Yost, M., Avila, L., & Vexler, E.B. (1977). Effect on learning of postinstructional responses to questions of differing degrees of complexity. *Journal of Educational Psychology, 69*, 399-408.

3

Textbook Study Strategies

David C. Caverly
Vincent P. Orlando

M any students come to reading and learning centers at the college level to seek help in reading or studying their textbooks. Within these centers, the focus of reading instruction may range from basic literacy to critical reading of graduate-level textbooks. Instruction in studying, on the other hand, is usually directed toward strategies for learning from textbooks; that is, learning how to learn when reading. The first two chapters of this book review the teaching of reading at the college level. This chapter discusses teaching students the strategies for studying a textbook. While this distinction is subtle, it will become clear as we proceed.

At the outset, let us posit our definition of textbook studying. Textbook studying is a strategic approach to reading in which students adjust their comprehending behavior before, during, and after reading much as they do in general reading, but with the purpose of satisfying a specific task that comes from either an internal or an external need. Thus it differs from general reading in that comprehension is strategically directed toward a specific task, such as gaining knowledge for a future career or passing a course test. This definition evolved from our review of the literature on reading comprehension and studying and is consistent with other definitions of studying (Anderson & Armbruster, 1984; McKeachie, 1988; Rohwer, 1984; Thomas & Rohwer, 1986; Wade & Reynolds, 1989).

Reviews on studying textbooks from the past two decades conclude that most study strategies are successful given certain conditions. First, a given study strategy's success will vary with the student's prior knowledge, reading ability, and motivation (Anderson, 1978; Breuker, 1984; Cook & Mayer, 1983; Dansereau, 1980, 1985; Levin, 1986; Rigney, 1978; Simpson, 1984; Weinstein & Mayer, 1985; Weinstein & Underwood, 1985; Wittrock, Marks, & Doctorow, 1975). Second, a given study strategy will vary in effectiveness depending on the difficulty, organization, and content of the material (Baker & Brown, 1984; Breuker, 1984; Jonassen, 1985; McConkie, 1977). Third, a given study strategy must be *taught* to be effective (Dansereau et al., 1974; Goetz, 1984; Orlando, 1978; Rigney, 1978; Simpson, 1984; Weinstein & Mayer, 1985). Fourth, a given study strategy can be effective if it is chosen to fit a particular type of criterion task (Anderson, 1980; Baker & Brown, 1984; Cook & Mayer, 1983; Gibbs, Morgan, & Taylor, 1982; Levin, 1986; Wade & Reynolds, 1989; Weinstein & Mayer, 1985). Recently, a spate of reviews have suggested that a combination of these four variables best explains the effectiveness of a particular study strategy (Anderson & Armbruster, 1984; Campione & Armbruster, 1985; McKeachie, 1988; Paris, 1988; Rohwer, 1984; Schumacher, 1987; Tessmer & Jonassen, 1988; Thomas & Rohwer, 1986; Wittrock, 1988).

Our analysis of the literature leads us to favor the view of these more recent reviews. Specifically, we believe that the interaction among these four variables (student, material, orienting task, and criterion task) is crucial for understanding the effectiveness of study strategies. The question, therefore, is not whether study strategies are successful, but rather where, when, and under what conditions they are successful. In this review we explore these questions, as well as determine what empirical research still needs to be completed and what should be taught to our students when they select a strategy for textbook studying.

To explore these questions, we first review how our understanding of cognition has evolved over the past century into our current ideas about how learning takes place and how study strategies can foster learning from textbooks. Then, we review the empirical literature on five study strategies for textbooks—underlining, notetaking, outlining, mapping, and SQ3R (Survey, Question, Read, Recite, Review)—in light of the four variables identified above and the interactions among them. Next, we suggest avenues of future research on these study strategies. Finally, we draw conclusions and implications for teaching these study strategies to a college-level population.

An Evolving Theoretical Foundation

Current concepts of studying derive from the knowledge about cognition that has been garnered over the past century. This transmutation of knowledge has resulted in the sequential evolution of three perspectives about the studying process: product, process, and intent. The first perspective defined studying as a *product* enhanced by overt manipulations after reading a textbook. The second perspective stressed the need to improve the product by controlling the overt *process* of studying during and after reading. A third perspective has recently emerged that emphasizes teaching students to select a study strategy on the basis of the resources they bring to the text, the material they are reading, and the purpose for which they are studying. This third perspective stresses the *intent* of studying before, during, and after reading.

Figure 1
Broadening Perspectives of Studying Theory

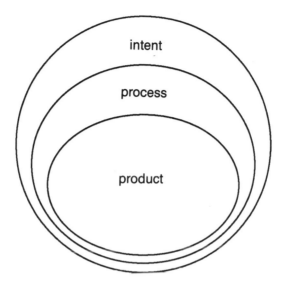

Note that these perspectives are not mutually exclusive, nor do they represent distinct alternative choices. They simply differ in the degree of comprehensiveness with which they embrace our collective knowledge about cognition. They should be seen as one embedded within another, like concentric circles, each encompassing and going beyond the perspective within (Figure 1).

Understanding the evolution of these three perspectives, and the major empirical findings giving rise to this evolution, is an important first step in understanding textbook study strategies at the college level.

A Product Perspective

The overriding concept of studying, until recently, stressed the gathering of information from the text. Studying was viewed as transferring information from the printed page into the student's memory. It was usually defined as an improved product—the outcome of overt manipulations by the student after reading.

The major theoretical foundation for this perspective came from the nineteenth century *storehouse* theory of memory. James (1890) argued that memory has two storehouses: a primary memory, with information an individual is conscious of at any given time; and a secondary memory, with information that is unconscious or that has been absent from consciousness for some time.

Waugh and Norman (1965) and Atkinson and Shiffrin (1968) extended this storehouse theory to include perception, a filter for primary memory. They reasoned that if information could be kept active in short term memory (James's [1890] notion of primary memory), a comparable trace of information would be formed in long term memory (James's notion of secondary memory). They held that for this to occur there must be an *a priori* sensory buffer (i.e., perception) that would briefly store the variety of stimuli that impinge upon the organism. This sensory buffer would allow short term memory (STM) to act as a rehearsal buffer in which information could be maintained through recycling while awaiting transfer into long term memory (LTM). This model resulted in a rather simple theory of cognition: the longer a piece of information is active in STM, the greater chance it has of being transferred to LTM and thus remembered.

Instruction in studying was molded to accommodate this cognitive product view. The idea was that if students could be taught to read well, to perceive the correct information (usually the main idea and details of the paragraph or passage), and to review what they read, information would enter the sensory buffer, be transferred to STM, become strengthened through review, and eventually be stored in LTM. Simply put, if students understood and reviewed what they read, they would tend to remember it. Studying was thus defined as locating information in the text and, through review, transferring that information into memory.

An important component of this model of studying was the need to rehearse or review the information in STM to increase its chances of being transferred into LTM. Several studying theorists therefore argued for the need to rehearse information after reading. This need has been discussed for several centuries in the studying literature. One of the earliest published works giving instruction in rehearsal types of studying was *The Improvement of the Mind, or a Supplement to the Art of Logic* (Watts, 1741). Watts argued for a particular study strategy that has remarkable similarities to present day study systems. Later, Todd (1854) and Porter (1876) began what has become a series of student manuals and workbooks that advocate surveying a chapter, setting purposes, becoming an active reader, and, after reading, summarizing or discussing the chapter in order to facilitate retention

Little has changed within this theoretical perspective, from Watts's ideas in the eighteenth century to Todd's and Porter's ideas in the nineteenth century to Robinson's (1946) notions of SQ3R in the twentieth century. In more than 200 years of advice, the only change has been the argument that review can be more effective if it is spaced or distributed rather than massed (Ebbinghaus, 1913; Spitzer, 1939). More recently, other theorists have argued in favor of postreading rehearsal strategies, such as underlining, notetaking, or summarizing (Rickards, 1980). The basic theory, however, has remained the same. Thus the primary study strategy promoted in reading and study skills classes and textbooks over the past century has been to identify what the student must know and then have the student review that information to remember it.

A continuing problem with this product perspective and with the dual storehouse theory of memory was that the effects of rehearsal dissipated after several recall attempts (Weist, 1972). Also, simple maintenance types of rehearsal were not sufficient to ensure encoding into LTM (Jacoby & Bartz, 1972; Wickelgren, 1973). It seemed that review was necessary but not sufficient to guarantee recall. To address these problems, a new theory evolved in the second half of this century. This new view is called an information processing theory of cognition as it applies to studying (Mayer, 1988b; Schumacher, 1987).

A Process Perspective

In the 1950s and 1960s, a well-documented change occurred in the psychology of learning; the focus shifted away from behavioral psychology, or a concern with external stimuli, and toward cognitive psychology, or the analysis of what has been labeled the "black box" of the brain (Mayer, 1988b). Theorists posited a four-stage information processing model of cognition, including acquisition (selective attention in the sensory register), encoding (processing in STM and transferring information into LTM), integration (processing in LTM), and retrieval (recall from LTM). This model became the foundation for a second perspective on studying. From this model came two theories to explain cognitive processing: levels of processing theory and schema theory.

Levels of processing theory. Through a series of articles, Craik and his associates (Craik & Lockhart, 1972; Craik & Tulving, 1975; Lockhart, Craik, & Jacoby, 1976) stressed that deeper, more elaborative processing of information in STM during encoding (beyond maintenance types of rehearsal) allowed a stronger trace in LTM and a better chance for retrieval. Through elaborate rehearsal techniques, they argued, information gathered from the textbook could be identified, organized, and encoded in STM to be stored in LTM.

In a series of studies using a list learning paradigm, several researchers demonstrated that deeper levels of rehearsal acted to enhance the chances of recall from LTM (Postman, 1975). Moreover, they demonstrated that the amount of time a person rehearsed information had little bearing on encoding. What one did during that rehearsal time was the critical factor.

Several studying theorists used this levels of processing theory as the basis for elaborative study strategies. Marton and colleagues in Sweden (Marton & Saljo, 1976a, 1976b; Saljo, 1981), as well as Entwistle and colleagues in England (Entwistle, Hanley, & Hounsell, 1978; Entwistle, Hanley, & Ratcliffe, 1979) demonstrated a high correlation between depth of processing and depth of understanding when studying. Others used the levels of processing theory to explain the effectiveness of certain study strategies, such as outlining, mapping, networking, and schematizing (Anderson & Armbuster, 1980; Breuker, 1984; Dansereau et al., 1979b; Weinstein & Mayer, 1985), or SQ3R (Jacobowitz, 1988; Tadlock, 1978). It was reasoned that if students could focus attention on the structure of the concepts being presented in the text (a deeper level of processing), they could use that structure as an encoding cue for enhancing storage and retrieval. This process has been labeled the encoding specificity principle (Tulving & Thompson, 1973).

While the levels of processing theory is intuitively acceptable, criticisms emerged regarding whether students were really engaged in deeper levels of rehearsal during *encoding*, or whether this deeper processing actually occurred during *retrieval*. Several studies demonstrated that the level of processing assumed to be used by the reader during encoding was often an artifact of the level of processing required by the criterion task (Craik & Tulving, 1975; Dark & Loftus, 1976; Morris, Bransford, & Franks, 1977). In these studies, students who knew that the criterion task required deeper levels of processing tended to process the information more deeply at the time of retrieval, not at the time of encoding. Processing to fit the criterion task was labeled the transfer-appropriate processing principle (Morris, Bransford, & Franks, 1977). This principle, in combination with the encoding specificity principle, became a catalyst for a further evolution in the theory, as shall be seen next.

A second group of studies questioned whether a certain level of processing was necessary for effective retrieval. Several studies concluded that retrieval improved only when processing reached the semantic level (Hyde, 1973; Hyde & Jenkins, 1969, 1973; Johnson & Jenkins, 1971; Till & Jenkins, 1973; Walsh & Jenkins, 1973). Nelson (1977) and Kohlers (1975, 1976), on the other hand, demonstrated that retrieval could be improved even with shallow processing of connected prose. Baddeley (1978) summarized the evidence against the levels of processing theory as being threefold: (1) no independent means exist for measuring whether a student is actually engaged in deeper levels of processing; (2) the level of processing needed for retrieval is often inconsistent (sometimes a shallow level is sufficient while at other times a deeper level is necessary); and (3) the hierarchy of processing does not hold up outside the paradigm of list-learning experiments.

These well-founded criticisms lead one to question the existence of quantifiably distinct levels of cognitive processing. Still, the nature of cognitive processing does suggest that different types of processing seem to be taking place and that these different types are controlled by the individual (Gibbs, Morgan, & Taylor, 1982; Rigney, 1978). This conclusion is vital, since it suggests that study strategies can be taught to help students control their level of cognitive processing during text studying in order to foster information acquisition, encoding, integration, and retrieval.

This inability to verify the levels of processing theory, along with recent evidence on the contribution made by the reader's background knowledge in the orchestration of constructing meaning, caused theorists to consider yet another factor in information processing theory. This factor has been labeled schema theory.

Schema theory. This theory is built on evidence that students' background knowledge is used to anticipate and direct the processing of print during and after reading. Within this theory, textbook studying is defined as an interaction between students and the text as students accommodate or assimilate their knowledge base to fit their understanding of the text.

An important first consideration schema theorists tackled was the form and function of background knowledge. Tulving (1972) reasoned that knowledge consists of two separate but interdependent functions: a semantic memory and an episodic memory. Semantic memory was defined as what is known about a particular concept—for instance, vocabulary instruction. Episodic memory was defined as the sum total of contexts (episodes) in which individuals have experienced that same concept—for instance, learning vocabulary, reading about how to teach it, or actually teaching it. Each context is unique to each individual, and together they form the individual's idiosyncratic definition of a given concept (in this case, vocabulary instruction).

Tulving further argued that semantic memory is abstracted from episodic memory. Semantic memory has been described in a variety of forms, ranging from frames to scripts and from goals to schemata (de Beaugrand, 1981). Perhaps the best known of these forms are schemata, which often are depicted as three-dimensional webs consisting of nodes of information and links between these nodes (Anderson, 1983).

Several lines of cognitive research have investigated the effect of engaging schemata before, during, and after reading. One early line of research was pursued by Bartlett (1932). He had subjects read a culturally unconventional passage entitled *The War of the Ghosts* and then attempt to recall the passage over varying time periods ranging up to 5 years. The delayed recall protocols reflected several distortions from the original story; eventually, a culturally conventional story line emerged. Bartlett concluded that this construction of a culturally more acceptable story line was the result of the impact of the subjects' schemata for stories and their cultural view of the world.

In a more recent second line of cognitive research, Chiesi, Spilich, and Voss (1979) and Spilich et al. (1979) indirectly demonstrated how a schema for a given topic might be stronger than a schema for another topic. This finding implies the presence of some mechanism for strengthening or developing schemata that would explain how learning occurs. If a schema strengthening mechanism does exist, understanding how it functions can help us understand the role of background knowledge in directing the acquisition, encoding, integration, and retrieval processes during studying.

One interpretation of this schema strengthening mechanism was provided by Anderson (1976, 1983) in his network model of artificial intelligence. He argued that the nodes and links that make up schemata are formed through experience and are probability based. Specifically, the more experiences one has with a given concept, the stronger the probability that the concept will be activated (linked) when episodes relevant to those experiences occur.

For example, if students were to read a passage on the concept of *slump*, they might have a certain probability (say around 70 percent) of engaging their background knowledge about *emotion* (i.e., activating their schemata to link their semantic knowledge of slump with their semantic knowledge of emotion), a higher probability (say around 80 percent) of engaging their background knowledge of baseball, and so forth. However, most of us would predict a rather low probability of students constructing a link between the schemata of concrete and slump. Creating such a link would be useful only, if, say, students in a civil engineering class were studying a manual on testing concrete. As the students studied, they would come to learn that one test for unhardened concrete is a slump test; thus the probability would increase that these students would link the concepts slump and concrete. Once these links are made, we might say learning has occurred.

This example demonstrates the role of schemata in an information processing theory of studying. For learning to occur during studying, existing schemata in the students' knowledge base must be accommodated or assimilated to fit incoming information during encoding. This development of schemata during encoding strengthens the links of activation and increases the probability of recall during retrieval.

Caverly and Orlando

Several studying theorists recently began incorporating schema theory into their descriptions of how students study and learn through print. Pask (1976a, 1976b) in England; Biggs (1976, 1979, 1980) in Australia; Elshout-Mohr (1983) and Breuker (1984) in the Netherlands; and Anderson and Armbruster (1984), Dansereau (1978, 1980), Kintsch and van Dijk (1978), Rigney (1978), Weinstein (1977), and Weinstein and Underwood (1985) in the United States began discussing how background knowledge is used to drive deep processing during encoding. Pask, Biggs, Breuker, as well as Kintsch and van Dijk argued that by identifying similarities and differences between knowledge in the mind (presumably schemata) and knowledge on the page, students engage deep processing that fosters acquisition and retention. Such processing allows the student to identify the superordinate structure (i.e., higher order ideas) and then use this structure to evaluate incoming information. When this occurs, ideas seem to remain active in the short term store longer, thus enhancing their chance of transferring to the long term store and strengthening the link between the pathways in the schema (Kintsch & van Dijk, 1978).

While several other studies over the past decade demonstrated the preeminence of schemata in studying and learning, two studies questioned this line of research. These studies showed that students consistently adjusted their processing and engaged new schemata to fit the criterion task. Bower, Black, and Turner (1979) and Spiro (1977) found that as time passed, understanding became less dependent on the text passage and more dependent on background knowledge. This was particularly evident when the title cue was switched at the time of recall. Spiro demonstrated that students reconstructed their recall to fit this new title even if it presented a different perspective.

This consistent presence of the encoding specificity principle (Tulving & Thompson, 1973) and the transfer-appropriate processing principle (Morris, Bransford, & Franks, 1977) in reading has been argued to be a major factor in interpreting the effectiveness of study strategies (Anderson & Armbruster,

1984). The encoding specificity principle suggests that how a student encodes information can act as a cue for recall. Intuitively and theoretically, this idea makes sense. However, this encoding cue can be overridden by a change in the recall task demands (transfer-appropriate processing), and then the encoding cue becomes less important. So it seems that while the specificity of encoding may determine how a student acquires and retains information when studying, the intent of satisfying the criterion task at retrieval also affects what that student recalls (O'Neil, 1978). It seems that the information processing theory of studying is not sufficient to explain all recall situations.

Another line of research supported the need to modify this information processing notion of studying. Dooling and his colleagues (Dooling & Christiansen, 1977; Dooling & Lachman, 1971; Dooling & Mullet, 1973; Sulin & Dooling, 1974) demonstrated that when students recall, they construct an interpretation consistent with their existing schemata. However, they also found that students' schemata actually biased their studying, pushing them to attend to certain concepts and ignore others. This bias is particularly prevalent when students are given a title cue that acts as a catalyst for accessing background knowledge about a given topic (Pichert & Anderson, 1977). Of particular concern was how this biasing effect might be present in other variables of the studying situation besides the schemata of the student. This incomplete explanation resulted in the need for yet another evolution in study strategy theory.

An Intent Perspective

This latest evolution resulted in an expanded theory of studying that attempted to explain how students adjust their processing with the variables of the study situation. Current theorists are consistent in listing four variables: (1) the attitudes and semantic knowledge students bring to studying; (2) the material students must study; (3) how well students like and use a given study strategy; and (4) the purpose for which students are studying.

Caverly and Orlando

During the past decade or so, theorists and researchers began exploring these variables (Anderson, 1978; Brown, 1982; Cook & Mayer, 1983; Dansereau, 1980, 1985; Rigney, 1978; Simpson, 1984; Smith, 1982; Weinstein & Mayer, 1985; Weinstein & Underwood, 1985; Wittrock, Marks, & Doctorow, 1975). Background knowledge was divided into four areas: declarative knowledge (Ryle, 1949), or knowledge of the content; procedural knowledge, or knowledge of various study strategies; conditional knowledge, or knowledge of when and where to apply the strategies; and volitional knowledge of the study environment, or knowledge of one's own interests and motivations. One explanation of the connection between these types of knowledge and the criterion task was offered by Dansereau (1985), who categorized study strategies as either primary or support strategies. Primary study strategies were defined as the specific comprehension and retention approaches to studying (e.g., declarative and procedural knowledge). Support study strategies were defined as the utilization strategies (e.g., conditional and volitional knowledge) designed to provide a suitable cognitive climate for studying.

Another explanation was put forth by Weinstein & Mayer (1985), who arranged study strategies into eight categories. The first six categories (basic and complex rehearsal, basic and complex elaboration, and basic and complex organization strategies) reflect increasing levels of processing—that is, procedural knowledge. The seventh and eight categories (comprehension monitoring strategies and affective/motivational strategies) manage processing in light of the demands of the material and the criterion task—that is, conditional and volitional knowledge. Weinstein and Mayer argued that students use these two groups of strategies during studying as they construct an interpretation from the text and then match this construction with existing declarative knowledge. This two-way interaction, they said, explains studying processes.

However, Dansereau's (1985) and Weinstein and Mayer's (1985) theoretical explanation fell short when confronted with empirical research demonstrating that the interaction can occur only if the student has learned how to evaluate study strategy effectiveness in a variety of material and criterion task demands. Studying has been shown to be developmental, with older, mature studiers more likely to adjust their strategies to the material and criterion task than younger, immature studiers (Biggs, 1979; Brown, 1982). This finding suggested that students can be taught how to use study strategies. Therefore, an instructional variable needed to be added to form a three-way interaction between the student, the material, and the instruction (or orienting task).

During this same period, other theorists and researchers explored a different three-way interaction between the student, the material, and the criterion task. Meyer, Brandt, and Bluth (1980), Smith (1982), Baker and Brown (1984), and Breuker (1984) demonstrated that both the quality of the material and the type of criterion test used affected students' success with a given study strategy. Meyer, Brandt, and Bluth pointed out differences between good and poor readers' ability to recognize structural patterns in the text as well as their ability to use these patterns to adjust processing and facilitate recall. Smith found that when graduate students were faced with difficult material outside their background knowledge, they employed five sets of activities as they developed a study plan. This plan varied among students depending on their individual characteristics. It was controlled by self-imposed goals based on students' interpretation of the criterion task's context and their own needs, and it changed as decisions were made regarding their progress toward reaching their goals. Baker and Brown demonstrated that students metacognitively adjust their processing to fit the text before, during, and after reading. This metacognitive knowledge includes students' ability to attend to important ideas and ignore trivial ideas, as determined by the criterion task. Breuker argued that students must identify the underlying spatial relationships (schema) of the text in order to match this structure with their prior knowledge during encoding.

Still, this new three-way interaction did not seem to fully explain the effect of studying. For example, some students did not succeed during experiments in which their background knowledge was engaged, the material was deemed easy, and they knew the demands of the criterion task (Davis & Annis, 1976). Ford (1981) argued that part of the reason for this inconsistency was that the criterion task variable of the studying situation was defined in a limited sense—often, simply as the test the student must face. Ford extended this definition to include the affective values a student places on what is to be learned, including the reasons for learning (beyond the immediate need to pass a test or a course). Students, for example, often evaluate certain information they are learning according to how it helps them satisfy some of their life's values, or how they think the information will fit into their lives beyond school. Ford argued that such values should be taken into account when considering the processing strategies students should use.

Because theory and research argue for the need to include all variables of the study situation in a complete theory of studying, most theorists currently are suggesting that the intent perspective should include a four-way interaction between the student, the material, the orienting task, and the criterion task variables (Anderson & Armbruster, 1984; Campione & Armbruster, 1985; Levin, 1986; McKeachie, 1988; Paris, 1988; Rohwer, 1984; Schumacher, 1987; Tessmer & Jonassen, 1988; Thomas & Rohwer, 1986; Wade & Reynolds, 1989; Wittrock, 1988). This intent perspective suggests that it is no longer necessary to explore whether a given study strategy works when all the study variables are controlled in an empirical setting. Rather, what must be determined is how to teach students to perceive all the variables that will affect the study situation, how to select a study strategy or orienting task to fit that perception, and how to monitor their progress toward satisfying that perception. To do so, it is necessary to understand how the individual and combined study variables affect study strategies.

Conclusions from the Theory

A definition of studying from a product or process perspective limits the investigation of studying to learning *from* studying. The intent perspective provides a more productive definition of studying that includes learning *through* studying. To do this, students must intentionally select a study strategy that uses the text as a tool for thinking and for expanding their background knowledge as they attempt to satisfy their perceptions of the criterion task. If we examine the literature on textbook studying from this intent perspective, we can draw sound conclusions about when and where study strategies will work.

Methodology for This Review

As chronicled earlier, several authors have attempted to evaluate the empirical literature on study strategies. These authors' efforts give us a foundation for verifying this intent perspective of study. This theory is generally visually represented by a tetrahedral model proposed by Jenkins (1979) and by Bransford (1979) to examine the literature in cognitive psychology. Later, Brown (1980) used this same model to illustrate the reading literature in general. Recently, Brown, Campione, and Day (1981), McKeachie (1988), and Nist (1985) have adapted the model to illustrate the work in college reading and study strategies. We interpret the tetrahedral model as depicting the four sets of variables that affect the choice of study strategy: the student, the material, the orienting task, and the criterion task (Figure 2).

Each of the four vertices of this figure represents a cluster of variables students must consider when choosing a study strategy for any study situation. Sometimes, however, only one edge of this figure is taught, thus representing to students a simple two-way interaction that leaves out two of these variables. For instance, we imply that studying involves interaction only between the student and the material when we teach poor readers to select one study strategy to study a biology textbook and a different strategy to study a novel.

Other times, one plane of this figure is taught, thus representing a three-way interaction between variables. For instance, we imply that studying involves interaction only

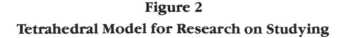

Figure 2
Tetrahedral Model for Research on Studying

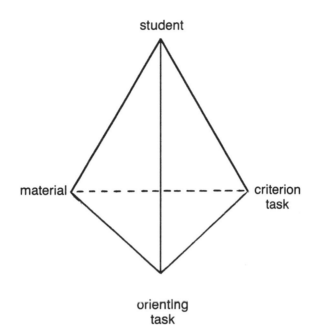

between the student, the material, and the criterion task when we teach poor readers to select one study strategy to prepare for an essay exam on a novel and a different study strategy to prepare for a multiple choice exam on a biology textbook.

Seldom do we teach students to be aware of the interaction among all four edges and all four planes of this model— that is, the four-way interaction, or metacognitive awareness (Wade & Reynolds, 1989) present when we teach poor readers to metacognitively evaluate the success of their strategy choice when studying a biology textbook and a novel for the different types of examinations.

Framework for Discussion

We used the four clusters of variables in the tetrahedral model as a framework for reviewing the empirical literature surrounding study strategies. Once the research results were evident, we were able to identify the results of the two-way, three-way, and four-way interactions of these clusters of variables.

We begin with a discussion of how student variables were manipulated or controlled in the experiments discussed in the literature. That is, what skills and abilities did students bring with them to the experimental study situation, and how did these variables affect what they learned? Although students bring a variety of attributes to any study situation, two variables have been singled out in the theoretical literature as important to studying: (1) the students' reading ability, and (2) whether the students' background knowledge was taken into account. (Other student variables are reviewed in Chapter 5 of this volume.)

The second cluster of variables to be considered involves how the material was manipulated or controlled in the experiments. Can it be determined if a given study strategy would be equally effective in all types of material students must study? Four important material variables are highlighted in the theoretical literature on studying: (1) the content or subject matter, (2) the readability or difficulty of the text, (3) the length of the material, and (4) the explicitness of the structure.

A third cluster of variables is the extent to which the orienting task was manipulated or controlled. That is, how did the means by which the strategy was taught affect how students performed? Three variables emphasized in the theoretical literature on studying are: (1) whether students were taught to review the material after study but before the criterion task, (2) whether they received any instruction in the use of the study strategy, and (3) whether students had criterion task knowledge before they studied.

Finally, this model suggests that how the criterion task was manipulated or controlled must be evaluated. Was performance measured after students used a study strategy? Two important variables indicated by the theoretical literature on studying are: (1) the *test type*—whether the test measured recognition, recall, or both, and (2) the *test administration delay*, or the amount of time that elapsed between use of the study strategy and administration of the test.

It is our premise that this tetrahedral model, with four clusters of 11 variables, provides an initial set of criteria for reviewing empirical research, drawing conclusions, and determining implications for additional research and sound instruction. In order to bring some semblance of order to this process, an integrative review (Jackson, 1980) using the tetrahedral model was completed. Our primary research question for this integrative review was how effective and efficient specific study strategies are in light of individual and interactive effects of the four clusters of variables. In order to answer this question, we examined standard primary sources as well as secondary sources such as *Current Index to Journals in Education*, *Dissertation Abstracts International*, and *Resources in Education*. We also made use of individual literature reviews within specific studies.

Note that no study was included in the review if the subjects in the study were younger than high school age. We had several reasons for imposing this limitation. Brown's (1982) research suggests that most older students perform better than younger students because they have a higher level of cognitive development. Moreover, Perry (1970) argues that the demands of college are different from those of earlier grades, causing significant cognitive growth on the part of the student. Finally, our intent is to draw conclusions and implications only for college-age populations, and we do not believe that doing so with research completed on younger populations is appropriate. Within these limitations, we were able to find more than 500 empirical studies and reviews from which to draw conclusions.

Study Strategies Examined

A casual review of the literature indicates that students can use many strategies when studying. However, in a theoretical analysis, Weinstein & Mayer (1985) contend that the parameters of these study strategies are limited. They outline eight major categories of study strategies that are available to students:

- basic rehearsal strategies—techniques for repeating a list of items, such as common memorizing;
- complex rehearsal strategies—techniques for highlighting material to be learned, such as underlining;
- basic elaboration stategies—techniques for generating mental images to remember, such as imaging;
- complex elaboration strategies—techniques for describing how new information fits into old knowledge, such as generative notetaking;
- basic organizational strategies—techniques for grouping lists of items, such as mnemonics;
- complex organizational strategies—techniques for recognizing and recalling the structure of the information, such as outlining or mapping;
- comprehension monitoring strategies—techniques for establishing a learning goal and monitoring one's progress toward that goal, such as SQ3R;
- affective and motivation strategies—techniques for controlling volitional strategies, such as attention, concentration, anxiety, and time management.

Surveys of materials and student usage at the college level confirm that these eight categories of study strategies are indeed the most commonly used (Annis & Annis, 1982; Fairbanks, 1973; Risko, Alvarez, & Fairbanks, this volume; Sanders, 1979).

To focus this review on study strategies for textbooks, we will use the tetrahedral model and an integrative review procedure to examine five strategies in four of these categories: underlining as indicative of complex rehearsal strategies, generative notetaking as indicative of complex elaboration strategies, outlining and mapping as indicative of complex organizational strategies, and sq3r as indicative of comprehension monitoring strategies. (Other comprehension monitoring strategies are reviewed in Chapter 2 of this volume; affective and motivation strategies are reviewed in Chapter 6.) The following sections first review previous findings surrounding these strategies as they relate to the variables of the tetrahedral model. Next they discuss what new evidence was uncovered in this review. Finally, they offer conclusions and implications for instruction.

Complex Rehearsal Strategy: Underlining

Underlining or highlighting (hereafter called simply underlining) is representative of what Weinstein and Mayer (1985) call complex rehearsal strategies. This type of study strategy involves selecting important material and encoding it through subsequent rehearsal.

Underlining has grown in popularity to become one of the most ubiquitous strategies used in postsecondary schools. In the early part of this century, only 4 percent of college students underlined their textbooks (Charters, 1925). More recently, surveys have shown varying levels of underlining use among college students, ranging from 97 percent (Adams, 1969), to 92 percent (Fowler & Barker, 1974), to 63 percent (Annis & Annis, 1982). Such a proliferation in the use of underlining runs counter to the arguments made in past decades against this strategy both by theorists (Berg & Rentle, 1966; Crawford, 1938) and by study skill textbook authors (Browning, 1976; Laycock & Russell, 1941). More recent study skill text authors have begun again to argue in favor of underlining (Radencich & Schumm, 1984).

A summary of the conclusions made by those who have reviewed the underlining literature (Anderson & Armbruster, 1984; Brown, 1982; Browning, 1976; Cook & Mayer, 1983; Rickards, 1980; Simpson, 1984; Tessmer & Jonassen, 1988; Weinstein & Mayer, 1985) provides support for using the tetrahedral model in our review. In applying the model to the underlining strategy, one student variable, two material variables, and three orienting task variables can be identified from these reviews.

The student variable that these literature reviews seemed to emphasize was that there seems to be a distinct developmental trend in students' ability to use underlining to select relevant parts of the chapter. Younger students (or, for our purposes, less able studiers) do not spontaneously underline high structural concepts (i.e., main ideas). Rather, they tend to underline sentences at random. These reviewers conclude that students must be able to recognize the hierarchical structure inherent in a passage before underlining can be an effective strategy for recall.

The first material variable identified in these reviews relates to the structure of the material. It seems that the more explicit the structure of a passage, the greater success students will have with underlining. If the material provides clues to high structural concepts—for instance, with subtitles, subheadings, or italics—and the student is developmentally mature enough to recognize such clues, underlining seems to foster recall not only of the high structural ideas but also of low structural ideas (i.e., ideas that are not emphasized explicitly). In other words, the student need not underline the lower order ideas to facilitate recall of them. This success, however, may be more an artifact of recognizing that certain ideas are inclusive of others than of the act of marking the text. Previous research has shown similar benefits of recognizing high structural ideas in the recall of low structural ideas when underlining was not allowed (Meyer, 1977, 1979). Nevertheless, this is an example of an interaction between two variables on the tetrahedral model—the student and the material.

The second material variable relates to the difficulty of the passage. Passage difficulty (typically determined by a readability formula) also is a factor in the use and success of underlining. When students are given a choice of study strategies to use, they are more likely to use underlining with a harder passage than with easier material, regardless of their ability. When students perceive a passage to be easy, they do not feel they need to perform any study strategy to remember it. When they perceive it to be difficult, underlining is one of the first strategies they will spontaneously select, often irrespective of its benefit. Here, the previous reviews suggest an interaction in the tetrahedral model on the plane between orienting task, material, and criterion task. If students perceive a passage to be difficult and the criterion task to require recall, they will select underlining as a strategy. If they perceive the passage to be easy, they will not choose to use underlining or any other overt study strategy—whether or not the criterion task requires recall.

Some orienting task variables have also been identified, although they have not been thoroughly verified. First, if underlining is to be effective, only one idea in each paragraph should be underlined. These reviews argue that instructing students to underline one idea per paragraph fosters deeper processing since the student must select the most important concept to underline. The second variable is that the success of underlining (as measured by subsequent criterion tests) seems to depend on the quality and extent of instruction on how to underline the most important concept. Finally, it has been suggested that if the material is encoded (underlined) to fit the criterion task, both intentional and incidental recall may be fostered. This is an example of an interaction on the tetrahedral model's edge between the orienting task and the criterion task variables.

We will now take a closer look at the empirical literature using the variables indicated by the tetrahedral model. In our review of the literature, we found 30 publications that reported 31 separate experiments exploring the effect of student-generated underlining: Adams (1969), Annis & Davis (1978), Arnold (1942), Blanchard & Mikkelson (1987), Brady & Rickards (1979), Brown & Smiley (1977), Craik & Martin (1980), Crewe (1968), Davis & Annis (1976), Earp (1959), Fairbanks & Costello (1977), Fass & Schumacher (1978), Fowler & Barker (1974), Friedman & Wilson (1975), Glynn (1978), Hakstain (1971), Holmes (1972), Idstein & Jenkins (1972), Kulhavy, Dyer, & Silver (1975), Mathews (1938), McKune (1958), Nist & Hogrebe

(1987), Rickards & August (1975), Schnell & Rocchio (1978), Smart & Bruning (1973), Snyder (1984), Stordahl & Christensen (1956), Todd & Kessler, (1971), Weatherly (1978), and Willmore (1966).

We found many other studies on underlining in the literature in which students received experimenter-generated underlined text or in which students completed surveys on their use of study strategies. We did not include the survey reports in our analysis because they do not address strategy effectiveness. And we felt that the studies using experimenter-generated marks, while exploring the effect of underlining on recall in general, had little relationship to what we might teach students to do themselves. Moreover, student-generated underlining has consistently proved more effective than experimenter-generated underlining (Browning, 1976). Therefore, we chose to look only at those experiments in which students marked the material themselves.

Student Variables

Although several student variables are addressed in the underlining literature, we will focus on reading ability and background knowledge. One clear finding is that teaching the use of underlining to students below a certain level of reading ability is not appropriate. This conclusion is evident in the research of Brown and Smiley (1977) and Schnell and Rocchio (1978), who examined immature readers. Their evidence suggests that underlining is effective with younger or less able students only if they spontaneously selected that strategy by themselves. Spontaneous use of underlining is indicative of students' belief in the strategy's effectiveness and of the students' level of metacognitive development. For our purposes, this suggests that students should reach a certain level of development in reading before underlining can be an effective study strategy.

Further evidence of the importance of this variable has emerged from the research of those who have looked directly at reading ability. This research suggests that reading ability correlates highly with success with underlining (Holmes, 1972;

Todd & Kessler, 1971; Weatherly, 1978). This relationship seems to be curvilinear, however; in all but one study (McKune, 1958), underlining was found to hinder better readers, as it tended to interfere with existing strategies. Underlining also tended to hinder poorer readers, since it was not sufficient to overcome lack of reading ability (Arnold, 1942; Blanchard & Mikkelson, 1987; Crewe, 1968; Holmes, 1972; Nist & Hogrebe, 1987; Todd & Kessler, 1971; Schnell & Rocchio, 1978; Snyder, 1984; Stordahl & Christensen, 1956; Weatherly, 1978; Willmore, 1966).

Conclusions regarding the effect of reading ability on underlining must be tempered, since less than a third of the studies reviewed considered reading ability. Still, evidence from an examination of students' academic aptitude (as measured by college entrance tests) supports these conclusions: students who scored higher on academic aptitude tests tended to perform better on reading tests regardless of the study strategy they were asked to use (Hakstain, 1971; McKune, 1958; Stordahl & Christensen, 1956). While this is not a variable we will examine throughout this review, the evidence suggests that the level of students' ability (whether it be exhibited in reading ability or in academic aptitude) is an important factor to consider when teaching the use of underlining as a study strategy.

The effect of background knowledge on underlining generally seems to be positive, although the evidence is scanty. Four studies chose to control for the variable of background knowledge by using it as a covariate (Arnold, 1942; Crewe, 1968; Fass & Schumacher, 1978; Stordahl & Christensen, 1956). This technique, however, serves to factor out the variance explained by background knowledge and consequently reduces the chances that students using underlining will show any increase in performance scores. This factor may have been the reason for the lack of improvement in performance found in the Arnold or the Stordahl and Christensen studies.

Three other experiments (Davis & Annis, 1976; Nist & Hogrebe, 1987; Snyder, 1984) actually manipulated background knowledge within their studies and found that strong background knowledge can facilitate underlining, lack of background knowledge cannot be overcome by underlining, and inducing students to engage their background knowledge does not necessarily foster recall. These seemingly contradictory results might be explained by the lack of adequate strategies for inducing students to engage background knowledge (Caverly, 1982; Paris, 1988; Schumacher, 1987). If background knowledge is engaged effectively, it might serve to reduce the amount of text underlined by improving the students' ability to select only high structural ideas, and thus facilitate recall.

In summary, we can draw three conclusions about the effect of student variables on underlining:

1. Teaching the use of underlining to students who have a low level of reading ability is not appropriate.

2. The relationship between reading ability and underlining is curvilinear, hindering both better and poorer readers and assisting only average readers.

3. The effect of engaging background knowledge is unclear. If background knowledge is engaged before or during reading, underlining may facilitate recall by directing the students' attention to high structural ideas.

Material Variables

The material variables surrounding the underlining strategy have not been as thoroughly researched as the student variables. In the studies we reviewed, nine different content areas were used, with the large majority covering social science topics. These researchers' emphasis on social science topics may be appropriate, given that the largest quantity of reading required by students at the college level is often in the social sciences (Caverly & Orlando, 1985). Still, the research reviewed presents no evidence that the underlining strategy is more effective with any particular type of expository material. The studies that manipulated this material variable (Hakstain, 1971; Idstein

& Jenkins, 1972; Stordahl & Christensen, 1956) found no consistent effect for content area on students' performance with underlining.

It has been hypothesized (Rohwer, 1984; Schumacher, 1987) that the demands of the material (i.e., readability/difficulty level, length of the passage, explicitness of the structure, and relevance for the student) should affect how well underlining works, particularly since reading ability seems to be a factor in the effectiveness of underlining. It has been reasoned that if the demands of the material are great, underlining should allow external storage of the ideas gathered, thus facilitating later review and reducing the processing demands (Rickards, 1980). Therefore, it would be prudent to manipulate the interaction between the subject and the material variables when attempting to determine the effectiveness of the underlining strategy.

Only a third of the studies we reviewed discussed the difficulty of the material used. In those studies, the large majority of passages were below the reading level of the students. Only one experiment (Fass & Schumacher, 1978) actually manipulated the difficulty of the material; this study found that underlining was more helpful with material deemed harder than with material deemed easy. This difference, however, may be due more to the interaction between the ability of the student and the explicit structure of the material than to the success of the strategy. With the paucity of research exploring this subject/material interaction, no definitive conclusions can be drawn.

In terms of the length of the material, the passages in the studies reviewed ranged from 44 words (Todd & Kessler, 1971) to more than 6,000 words (Idstein & Jenkins, 1972). Our review indicates that when the material is longer, the effectiveness of underlining diminishes. Todd and Kessler as well as Brown and Smiley (1977) reported underlining to be more effective in shorter material, while Idstein and Jenkins demonstrated underlining to be less effective in longer passages. Still, questions must be raised regarding the generalizability of research in which passages of fewer than 500 words were used when it is unlikely that students will have to study material that short.

Further evidence still needs to be garnered to support the effect of the length of the material being underlined.

Finally, only seven studies considered the explicitness of the material's structure. Of these, only the Rickards and August (1975) study found that explicit structure interfered with the effectiveness of underlining. Several other studies (Brady & Rickards, 1979; Brown & Smiley, 1977; Earp, 1959; Weatherly, 1978) found no such detrimental effect. This inconsistency might be explained by exploring the student/material/orienting task plane of interactions on the tetrahedral model. None of these seven studies spent more than 1 hour teaching students how to underline—how to select the major concepts and mark them. This knowledge could result in students' processing the information at a deeper level (Wark & Mogen, 1970). According to the intent theory of studying, students need to be able to impose an implicit structure onto the material as an encoding device for later recall if no explicit structure is available. The reasoning behind this argument is that the imposition of an implicit structure leads to deeper processing and creates an encoding-specific device for enhancing recall. This idea has not been tested in the literature on underlining.

In summary, four conclusions can be drawn about the effect of material variables on underlining:

1. Since most studies used social science material, and few manipulated content area, the effect of content on the effectiveness of underlining cannot be determined.

2. Underlining may be more effective with harder passages; however, little research has manipulated this variable.

3. Underlining seems to be less effective in longer material (more than 500 words).

4. Contradictory results with structurally explicit material may be due to researchers' failure to provide sufficient instruction in underlining (a material/orienting task interaction).

Orienting Task Variables

An analysis of the orienting task variables verifies that these variables have some distinct effects on underlining. For example, strong evidence supports the notion that underlining provides students with an effective means of reviewing material either after reading or before the test (Annis & Davis, 1978; Brown & Smiley, 1977; Crewe, 1968; Davis & Annis, 1976; Fowler & Barker, 1974; Holmes, 1972; Idstein & Jenkins, 1972; Todd & Kessler, 1971; Willmore, 1966). In those studies that actually manipulated the review factor (Brown & Smiley; Crewe; Idstein & Jenkins), the longer and more thorough the review, the better the performance. A simple review does not seem adequate even with older students, as illustrated in the Brown and Smiley study.

Further evidence makes clear the need to teach underlining as a strategy. The 16 studies that taught underlining showed either statistical significance or a distinct trend favoring underlining over other study strategies. In only 6 of these studies were more than 2 hours spent on teaching underlining. The amount of time spent on instruction may not make much difference; for example, Holmes (1972) taught his students for up to 8 hours, but this still was not enough to bring about improved performance. However, if we look at the interaction in his study between the subject and orienting task variables, we realize that he controlled for reading ability, thus reducing the chance that any variance would surface showing the impact of instruction on the underlining strategy's effectiveness. Moreover, the passage used in this study was approximately 5,000 words long, which also could have reduced the effectiveness of underlining, particularly since students were not allowed to review the passage. After considering these studies, it is apparent that just teaching underlining as a study strategy for a given amount of time is not sufficient to give an accurate understanding of its role in enhancing students' performance.

An additional instructional variable that has been identified is the need to teach students to alter processing to fit the criterion task. The interaction between orienting task and criterion task that came to light in our review suggests that underlining can foster intentional recall (Fowler & Barker, 1974; McKune, 1958; Smart & Bruning, 1973) but hinder incidental recall (Kulhavy, Dyer, & Silver, 1975; Rickards & August, 1975). Only Brady and Rickards (1979) found a positive incidental effect with underlining. Therefore, it is important that students know what type of criterion test they will have to pass before selecting underlining as a study strategy.

In summary, we can draw three conclusions about the effect of orienting task variables on underlining:

1. Teaching students to review what they have underlined before giving them a test markedly improves their performance.

2. Providing students with even a limited amount of instruction in underlining covering the selection of high structural ideas and the need to review is important for enhanced performance.

3. Students should be taught how to alter their underlining strategy on the basis of their knowledge of the criterion task.

Criterion Task Variables

In this review, we found a strong orienting task/criterion task interaction. Out of the 31 studies we reviewed, 21 found improvement on either a recognition or a recall type of test following underlining. A closer examination reveals that much of this success may be due to review, since 14 of the 21 studies allowed an opportunity for review. Conversely, only 3 of the 10 studies that found no improvement provided students with an opportunity to review. In the 7 studies that found improved criterion task performance following underlining but that did not allow students to review what they underlined, success may have resulted from instruction, the students' reading ability and motivation levels, and the explicit structure of the material. These studies suggest a student/material/orienting task/criterion task interaction that should be explored further.

In terms of the time lag between studying and test administration, 24 tests were delayed, with the gap ranging from 5 minutes (Brown & Smiley, 1977) to 47 days (Crewe, 1968). No clear pattern emerged from these studies. However, a meta-analysis of the data (Caverly, 1985) suggests a slight increase in positive effect for underlining when compared with no underlining as the delay in testing becomes longer. This meta-analysis also suggests that underlining seems to be more effective for intentional recall tasks than for incidental recall; the effect scores were +0.25 and +0.05, respectively. Here, again, we see a potential interaction between orienting task and criterion task variables.

In summary, we can draw these conclusions about the effect of criterion task variables on underlining:

1. Underlining seems to be effective for either recognition or recall tests if review is allowed.
2. The tendency is that the greater the delay in testing, the greater the effect of underlining as compared with no underlining.

Summary

Based on this review, underlining may be considered an effective strategy if students find success with it and consequently prefer to use it over other strategies. Underlining should not be taught to students who are not developmentally ready to use it (i.e., those who are unable to recognize high structural ideas); underlining cannot overcome poor reading ability. For those students ready to use underlining, instruction emphasizing a strategic approach is important. Students must be taught how to underline only the most important concepts based on the explicit or implicit structure of the text and on the criterion demands. They must also be taught to process information on a deeper level to satisfy their intent; only then can the encoding function of underlining emerge. Finally, students must be taught to regularly review what they have underlined if remembering is a goal.

Complex Elaboration Strategy: Notetaking

Another major group of study strategies are what Weinstein and Mayer (1985) call complex elaboration strategies. This type of strategy allows students to monitor their understanding during and after reading by fostering recognition and elaboration of the material. Several such strategies are available to college-level students; perhaps the most commonly used is notetaking, in which students rewrite either in the margin of the textbook or on separate sheets of paper what they learn from reading. These notes can take several forms, ranging from verbatim accounts to notations that represent the structure of the information (Eanet & Manzo, 1976).

Most analyses of notetaking (Carrier & Titus, 1979; Hartley & Davies, 1978) have drawn conclusions from research that has examined both notetaking from lectures and notetaking from textbooks; that is, notetaking while listening and notetaking while reading. We believe that while listening and reading are reciprocal processes, they are not identical. Conclusions drawn from a transitory process such as listening are not necessarily adaptable to a protracted process such as reading. For example, with listening it is difficult (if not impossible) to stop the input in order to consider what is being learned. With reading, the input can be halted at any point to review the message and think about what is being learned. Therefore, the process and the intent of notetaking while listening to a lecture are different from those of notetaking while reading a text. The analysis presented here examines only research dealing with notetaking from text. (For a discussion of notetaking from lectures, see Chapter 4 of this volume.)

Previous analyses (Anderson & Armbruster, 1982; Cook & Mayer, 1983; Rickards, 1980) support the use of the tetrahedral model for exploring the research on notetaking. Two interactions between variables on the tetrahedral model have been discovered: one between the orienting task and the criterion task variables and a second among the subject, the orienting task, and the criterion task variables.

Rickards (1980), in analyzing the literature on notetaking from textbooks and lectures, found an orienting task/criterion task interaction. He concluded that success on recognition types of criterion tasks following notetaking was a factor of encoding the information during processing. However, when recall types of criterion tasks were used, having the material available for review seemed to be necessary. He also found that a factor he called "test mode expectancy" affected success, concluding that students' quality of notes differed depending on whether they expected a recognition or a recall test. Those expecting a recall test tended to take notes on high structural information (i.e., information important to the overall meaning of the material), while those expecting a recognition test did not. Finally, Rickards suggests a student/orienting task/criterion task interaction. He found that students' notes varied in quantity and in level of structural importance, depending on the types of criterion task expected. He also found that students' success with notetaking depended on whether they demonstrated high or low ability and on whether they would spontaneously use notetaking when given the opportunity.

Anderson and Armbruster (1982) concluded that an orienting task/criterion task interaction may explain notetaking's lack of effectiveness when compared with study strategies such as rereading or underlining. Students in the studies analyzed may not have been encoding the information to fit the criterion task. These researchers found that in most studies, students were given a limited amount of time to read the text and develop notes. This limit was often imposed by researchers in an effort to keep constant the amount of time-on-task spent on notetaking, rereading, and underlining. Because of this limited study time, many of the students who used notetaking may have decided to allocate their attention to processing the main ideas at the expense of the details. (This idea is based on Anderson and Armbruster's assumption that notetaking takes more time than rereading or underlining.) In these studies, the students who used rereading or underlining may have distributed their study time and effort over the entire passage. This difference in orienting task may have given those students using re-reading or underlining an unfair advantage on criterion tasks that measured details. Moreover, if the criterion task was a free recall task, students using a notetaking study strategy would tend to produce fewer ideas (without respect to the level of idea) than students who processed the entire passage through a rereading or underlining study strategy.

Anderson and Armbruster (1982) also reasoned that if the students chose to process the information at a deeper level through notes that reflected the structure of the text (Eanet & Manzo, 1976), a test measuring recall accuracy may not show any positive effect for notetaking, since deeper processing would accentuate distortions and intrusions in the recall proto-col. This interaction between the orienting task and criterion task variables caused Anderson and Armbruster to conclude that notetaking can be an effective study strategy if it entails se-lective attention and encoding that is compatible with the crite-rion task.

Cook and Mayer (1983) also found an interaction be-tween the orienting task and criterion task variables. They con-cluded from their analysis that notetaking tended to foster selective attention during text processing and thus encouraged intentional learning. When students were contained in their processing by the rate of presentation or by the information density of the material (hinting at a three-way interaction be-tween the orienting task, material, and criterion task variables), notetaking could focus attention only on main ideas. Subse-quent criterion tasks in the studies they analyzed may not have been sensitive enough to measure this factor. In studies that re-duced the strain on students' processing capacity, and in those that allowed review before the criterion task, the performance of students using notetaking improved.

Cook and Mayer (1983) also found another two-way in-teraction between the orienting task and criterion task varia-bles. They found that under some conditions, notetaking could help students organize the material, enhancing what they call "construction" (integration of new knowledge with existing schemata). If the information was constructed into a student's memory, the criterion task reflected increased inferencing and an improved ability to apply the information. The researchers concluded that if students took structural notes (notes that reflected the structure between the ideas), they had a greater chance of constructing information during processing and of improving their performance on criterion tasks measuring inferencing and application.

We will now focus on the literature on taking notes from textbooks. Our analysis identified 27 reports with 30 experiments examining this study strategy: Annis (1979), Annis & Davis (1978), Arnold (1942), Bretzing & Kulhavy (1979, 1981), Brown & Smiley (1977), Caverly (1982), Davis & Annis (1976), Dyer, Riley, & Yenkovich (1979), Fox & Siedow (1985), Hakstain (1971), Hale (1983), Hannah (1946), Hoon (1974), Kulhavy, Dyer, & Silver (1975), Mathews (1938), McKune (1958), Noall (1962), Okey (1979), Orlando (1979, 1980a), Orlando & Hayward (1978), Rickards & Friedman (1978), Santa, Abrams, & Santa (1979), Schultz & DiVesta (1972), Shimmerlik & Nolan (1976), and Todd & Kessler (1971).

Student Variables

As indicated earlier, many student variables are evident in this literature. Two are specifically analyzed here: reading ability and prior knowledge. Our analysis shows that teaching notetaking to students below a certain level of reading ability is not recommended. This conclusion is evident in the research that has identified differences in performance due to students' reading ability (Fox & Siedow, 1985; McKune, 1958; Santa, Abrams, & Santa, 1979; Shimmerlik & Nolan, 1976; Todd & Kessler, 1971). It seems that students must be able to recognize important information in the material before notetaking can help. Otherwise, they will tend to take verbatim notes of irrelevant concepts. As with underlining, notetaking cannot overcome lack of ability to find the main idea.

No definite conclusions can be drawn regarding the role of students' background knowledge in their use of notetaking as a study strategy. In only eight of the studies (Arnold, 1942; Bretzing & Kulhavy, 1979, 1981; Caverly, 1982; Davis & Annis, 1976; Dyer, Riley, & Yenkovich, 1979; Okey, 1979; Orlando, 1980a) was any consideration of students' background knowledge even reported. In five of the eight studies, background knowledge was controlled by pretesting for it and then either using it as a covariate, removing students who possessed it from the study, or selecting material on which the students were likely to have background knowledge.

Initial evidence from the three studies that manipulated background knowledge (Bretzing & Kulhavy, 1981; Caverly, 1982; Davis & Annis, 1976) suggests that if students engage their background knowledge, they are better able to recognize an implicit structure present in the material and to use that structure to organize their notes. On the other hand, if the structure is explicit in the material, students are less likely to impose their own structure when taking notes and will use the author's structure instead. When an explicit structure is present, students tend to use this shallower level of processing, causing a concomitant reduction in performance. This result seems to indicate an interaction between the student and material variables. With only three studies pointing to this interaction, no valid conclusions can be drawn. However, this trend is supported by the intent theoretical perspective and should be considered in both instruction and in future research.

In summary, two conclusions can be drawn about the effect of subject variables on notetaking:

1. Teaching notetaking from textbooks to students who are unable to recognize main ideas is inappropriate.
2. The effect of engaging background knowledge is unclear because of the small number of studies that have addressed this issue. If background knowledge is engaged before or during reading, notetaking may facilitate recall, either by directing students' attention to the structure of the material if their knowledge is weak or by causing students to impose their own structure onto the material in lieu of the author's.

Material Variables

The studies under review manipulated many material variables. The four most important of these are content, readability, length, and explicit structure. Researchers have not used any particular content area when analyzing the effectiveness of notetaking. Our analysis found that notetaking was used in six different content areas, with a large majority in the social sciences. This choice of material by experimenters seems well founded. As noted earlier, social sciences seem to make up the bulk of the reading load in college (Caverly & Orlando, 1985).

A second material variable is readability level. Schumacher (1987) hypothesized that material's level of difficulty can affect notetaking by affecting students' ability to identify the main idea for subsequent encoding. If the material is exceptionally difficult, students will have trouble recognizing the ideas important enough for notetaking. This is particularly true for poor readers, indicating a student/material interaction. In the literature reviewed, only half of the studies reported the material's level of difficulty. Of those studies, only three (Caverly, 1982; Mathews, 1983; McKune, 1958) used college-level material; the other studies used material that was deemed "easy." Results from these studies do not allow us to draw conclusions about the effectiveness of notetaking in real life study situations, in which the processing demands are often great. Most of these studies manipulated only one variable (usually the orienting task) and attempted to control the other three variables (student, material, and criterion task). Because of this empirical approach, it is difficult to draw any conclusions regarding the value of notetaking from college-level material.

A third material variable is length. Schumacher (1987) hypothesized that if the material is longer, notetaking should help reduce the number of ideas needing retrieval. Research seems to support this view. In 13 of the 30 studies in our analysis, the material used was short (fewer than 1,000 words). The other 17 studies used longer material. Our analysis found that the 13 studies using shorter material had equivocal results when comparing performance after taking notes with performance after using other study strategies. On the other hand, in all but 1 of the 17 studies using longer material, performance improved after notetaking. Only 1 study (Todd & Kessler, 1971) directly manipulated length of the material when examining the effect of notetaking. No differences were found in performance with different lengths of material, but the length of the passages ranged only from 44 words to 256 words. Because the material was so short, caution must be used when drawing conclusions.

From our overall analysis, it seems that length of material is a factor in the effectiveness of notetaking as a study strategy. This conclusion must be qualified, however, because in many of these studies, the effect of length on performance was obscured by other variables—for instance, the use of easy material. It seems that notetaking may not be a beneficial study strategy to recommend when students are faced with short material. The effort required by notetaking may be unnecessary with this material, given its light processing demands. When faced with longer material, however, students might select notetaking as a viable strategy. The impact of the material's length on the effectiveness of notetaking should be explored further.

A final factor that may influence the effectiveness of notetaking is the explicit structure of the text. Several theorists (Baker & Brown, 1984; Breuker, 1984; Jonassen, 1985; McConkie, 1977) have hypothesized that if the structure of the passage is explicit, students will use it to identify main ideas and to create verbatim notes at a shallow level of processing. If the structure is implicit, students are forced to parse out the structure, thus processing the material at a deeper level and presumably enhancing performance. Our analysis identified only 6 studies out of 31 that reported the structure of the material, and only 2 of these actually manipulated structure during the study (Shimmerlik & Nolan, 1976; Schultz & DiVesta, 1972). The trend in these 2 studies was that when the text did not have an explicit structure, better students imposed their own organization. This imposed structure resulted in improved performance, particularly when the criterion task required recognition or recall of high structural ideas (this indicating a student/material/

criterion task interaction). The hypothesis regarding the effect of implicit structure can be tentatively supported, but this three-way interaction should be examined further.

In summary, we can draw the following conclusions about the effect of material variables on notetaking:

1. Notetaking should improve performance in any content area, although it has been explored primarily in the social sciences.

2. Notetaking is productive for "easy" material, but not enough data are available to recommend it for college-level material (particularly for poor readers).

3. Notetaking is more productive with longer material. This may be a product of students' decisions not to use the strategy with shorter material.

4. Notetaking tends to be verbatim when the material has an explicit structure; when the structure of the material is implicit, notetaking tends to help students (particularly better readers) impose a structure.

Orienting Task Variables

Several distinct orienting task variables have also been identified in this review. First, if notetaking is to be effective in most situations, we must teach students to review their notes (Annis, 1976; Annis & Davis, 1978; Bretzing & Kulhavy, 1979; Davis & Annis, 1976; Dyer, Riley, & Yenkovich, 1979; Orlando, 1979; Santa, Abrams, & Santa, 1979). The encoding effect of notetaking seems to hold up for immediate recall whether students review or not; however, only through review will students realize a benefit for any type of delayed test. In those studies that manipulated the review variable, significant improvement in delayed recall was found only if students reviewed their notes before the test. Indeed, some evidence in this literature suggests an orienting task/criterion task interaction, with students taking fewer notes when expecting an immediate test and more notes when expecting a delayed test.

A second variable that arises is the apparent need to teach students how to take notes. Most students in these studies were told or induced to use notetaking without being taught how to take notes. In only three studies (Arnold, 1942; Hannah, 1946; Okey, 1979) were students actually taught how to take notes. Students in all of these studies showed improvement in comprehension after notetaking. In three other studies (Annis & Davis, 1978; Brown & Smiley, 1977; Davis & Annis, 1976), students were allowed to use any study strategy they preferred. Those students who spontaneously used notetaking showed better performance than those who opted for other study strategies. If notetaking is taught properly, it might become the strategy of choice for students faced with a study task.

Our review suggests that this instruction needs to involve several features. First, students should be taught to take notes on the superordinate structure rather than on the subordinate details. Second, students need to be aware of how notetaking can direct them to process the information on a deeper level, thus improving their recall. Third, students need to understand that what matters is not the quantity but the quality of notes they take (Hakstain, 1971; Orlando & Hayward, 1978). Finally, instruction should include teaching students how to recognize the main idea of each paragraph and how to relate each main idea to the underlying structure of the passage (Bretzing & Kulhavy, 1979, 1981; Fox & Siedow, 1985; Kulhavy, Dyer, & Silver, 1975; Orlando, 1980a; Rickards & Friedman, 1978; Santa, Abrams, & Santa, 1979; Shimmerlik & Nolan, 1976).

A third orientating task variable analyzed was the role of criterion task knowledge, or whether students' knowledge of the criterion task caused them to adjust their processing during encoding. Several theorists (Anderson, 1980; Baker & Brown, 1984; Cook & Mayer, 1983; Gibbs, Morgan, & Taylor, 1982; Levin, 1986; Weinstein & Mayer, 1985) have concluded that this variable is an important factor in the success of notetaking as a study strategy. Researchers in only half the studies under review told students that they were going to be tested after studying or gave them an idea of what the test would cover. In only three studies—two by Hakstain (1971) and one by Kulhavy, Dyer, and Silver (1975)—was knowledge of the type of test to be manipulated. In these three studies, specific knowledge of the test content did not benefit students. In the other studies, it is difficult to determine whether students adjusted their processing to fit their knowledge of what the test would cover or whether they adjusted their processing because they knew they were going to have a test (Anderson & Armbruster, 1982).

On the surface, our analysis seems to suggest that criterion task knowledge is not a cogent factor in the effectiveness of notetaking, contrary to the conclusions reached by other researchers. However, if the student/orienting task/criterion task interaction is explored, support for the encoding specificity principle is found. Presumably, in any empirical environment, most college students would expect to be tested in the orienting task whether or not the researcher told them they would be. Some of these students would choose to adjust their processing accordingly. When asked only to read or reread material, they would mentally rehearse the information, counter to the orienting task instructions given before reading. These students would be intentionally encoding information to match what they perceive the criterion task to be; therefore, the encoding specificity principle would be activated whether or not it was part of the orienting task. Other students would follow the orienting task directions religiously to satisfy their perception of the criterion task. In either situation, if the actual criterion task reflects either the students' perceptions of the criterion task or the specific orienting task requested of the students, notetaking will probably improve performance. When the criterion task measures knowledge other than what was encoded, performance probably will drop.

A question arises as to whether performance is linked to criterion task knowledge and the consequent adjustment in processing, or whether it results from the criterion task fortuitously matching the information that was encoded. This may be a "chicken or egg" type of argument. Both correct knowledge of the criterion task and appropriate processing strategies are necessary for successful performance following notetaking (Kulhavy, Dyer, & Silver, 1975). Therefore, previous analyses were correct when the importance of the encoding specificity principle was noted. We suggest that the larger interaction between the student, the orienting task, and the criterion task must also be considered when determining the effectiveness of a study strategy like notetaking.

In summary, three conclusions can be drawn about the effect of the orienting task variables on notetaking:

1. Review is necessary for notetaking to be beneficial in delayed recall tasks.

2. Instruction in notetaking is necessary for those who have not spontaneously developed the strategy (generally average and poor readers).

3. Notetaking is effective if students have knowledge of the criterion task and adjust their processing to fit this task.

Criterion Task Variables

The role of the previous three variables in notetaking becomes particularly evident when we examine the criterion task variable. A surface analysis suggests that notetaking is equally effective on recognition and recall types of tests. This test type variable was manipulated in only three studies—two by Hakstain (1971) and one by Kulhavy, Dyer, and Silver (1975). In the Hakstain studies, performance did not differ significantly between students who received a recognition test and those who received a recall test, even though they were oriented toward expecting a certain type of test. On the other hand, in the Kulhavy et al. study, performance did differ depending on the type of test students expected to receive. This seemingly contradictory result might be explained by the encoding specificity principle discussed above, as well as by the fact that the test happened to match students' encoding behavior. Knowledge that a test will be given and knowledge of the type of test are not the important variables. What seems to be important in explaining the effectiveness of notetaking is the combined effect of these two variables and the students' ability to adjust processing at the time of encoding and/or retrieval.

Similarly, whether the test was administered immediately or after a delay is not an important variable on its own. What seems to influence the effectiveness of notetaking is the interactive effect of the time of the test with either a conscious choice or an induced decision to review. Notetaking seems to improve immediate recall with or without review. However, delayed recall was generally not enhanced unless students reviewed their notes before the test. In the two studies in which performance improved on the delayed test without review (Dyer, Riley, & Yenkovich, 1979; Fox & Siedow, 1985), other variables may have intervened. For example, in the Fox and Siedow study, the material was shorter than 200 words. In the Dyer et al. study, the material was deemed very easy. There may not have been a need to review such short or simple information.

In summary, these conclusions can be drawn about the effect of the criterion task variables on notetaking:

1. Students should be taught to identify the type of test they will be required to take and then adjust their notetaking accordingly.
2. If the test is to be delayed beyond immediate recall, review is necessary.

Summary

We can conclude from this research that notetaking while studying a textbook helps students improve performance. Given an appropriate orienting task, students can produce a set of notes after engaging in deeper encoding processes. Then, if a delayed criterion task requires recall, they can review those notes to help them boost performance. However, students generally must be taught how to take notes that are appropriate to the demands being placed on them.

Complex Organizational Strategies: Outlining and Mapping

A third major group of study strategies categorized by Weinstein and Mayer (1985) are complex organizational strategies. Here, students are directed to recognize and summarize the organization of the material in a structured way in order to facilitate encoding and recall. Perhaps the most common of these strategies is outlining, in which students reconstruct the explicit or implicit structure of concepts presented by the author. Students are taught to use formal outlining notation to list the main ideas and supporting details, as well as the superordinate and subordinate connections between these ideas.

More recently, a type of outline strategy known as mapping (and its many variations, which include the ConStruct procedure, networking, Node Acquisition Integration Technique, and schematizing) has been promoted as a replacement for the older style of outlining. This group of study strategies directs students to construct a diagram, or spatial image, of the text's structure, using nodes to represent the main ideas and supporting details, and links to represent the relationships between the ideas in the text. In the mapping type of study strategy (hereafter simply called mapping), students are often taught to label the connections using common pattern structures, such as problem-solution, cause-effect, and time-order (Armbruster, 1979; Slater, Graves, & Piche, 1985).

Outlining emerged from the product theoretical perspective of the studying process. Mapping is based on the process and intent perspectives. Mapping differs from outlining in that it encourages students to match their background knowledge to the text and to generate spatial images representing this interaction. Neither of these study strategies has a robust research heritage; we found only 10 studies examining the use of outlining among a college-level population and only 11 studies examining the use of mapping. To improve our integrative analysis of this group of study strategies, we combined the literature on outlining and mapping as we reviewed the variables of the tetrahedral model.

Several previous reviewers who have analyzed the literature on outlining and mapping strategies have identified interactions among the variables of the tetrahedral model. Dansereau et al. (1974) found a student/orienting task/criterion task interaction in the outlining research. They found several factors that influenced students' choice and use of a particular strategy to fit their study environment. These student factors included intellectual ability, personality, cognitive style, learning style, motivation, gender, and prior knowledge of the content. From this review, Dansereau (1978) fashioned his notion of the interaction between primary strategies (general and specific textbook study strategies) and secondary strategies (the students' statement of goals, concentration management, and monitoring of progress toward their goals). Dansereau (1980) also reported a student/orienting task interaction in his review of the research on networking (his version of mapping). He found a need for instruction in the study strategy, as well as greater success following instruction among students of middle-level reading ability.

Anderson and Armbruster (1980, 1982, 1984) found an orienting task/criterion task interaction for the outlining study strategy. They concluded that in those studies in which outlining was not taught, it was ineffective with certain types of criterion tasks. When the students were induced to use the outlining strategy, they processed information on a shallow level. Anderson and Armbruster argued that this finding may have been the result of the experiments' design. In attempting to control for the time-on-task of different study strategy treatments, the researchers may actually have made shallow processing inevitable; because outlining is a time-consuming activity, students may have been forced to process the information on a shallow level to finish in the allotted time. They concluded that outlining should be a more effective study strategy than the literature has shown. It could foster deeper processing if the orienting task provides enough time for instruction and if the criterion task allows time for deeper processing.

Dansereau and Holley (1981), in reviewing the networking research, confirmed the student/orienting task interaction that Dansereau (1980) found earlier. Mapping strategies were more effective for students with low grade point averages (GPAs) if support strategies were taught along with the primary strategy. They found a two-way interaction between the material and the criterion task variables of the tetrahedral model. The mapping strategy was more effective in longer material if the links on the map were labeled, and labeling links in longer material was more effective if the criterion task measured recall of main ideas rather than of details. They acknowledge, however, that these interactions are based on relatively sparse research.

Two reviews were completed on another type of mapping called schematizing (Camstra & van Bruggen, 1984; Elshout-Mohr, 1983). These reviewers identified a student/material/orienting task interaction. Schematizing helped students with low verbal ability improve their performance with material that was explicitly structured, but it hindered them with material that was implicitly structured. After instruction in schematizing, low-ability students were able to use schematizing successfully in implicitly structured material as well. This finding confirmed that instruction was necessary for success to be demonstrated with a particular type of textbook.

McKeachie's (1984) review of the outlining and mapping research confirmed the student/orienting task interaction. In the studies he reviewed, medical students needed only 4 hours of instruction, adolescents needed up to 20 hours, and college students with low verbal ability needed 22 hours. McKeachie also identified a student/criterion task interaction. On recall types of tasks, or recall of main ideas, no differences in performance emerged between students with lower GPAs and those with higher GPAs. However, on recognition types of tasks, or tasks that measure mostly details, students with lower GPAs performed better. McKeachie also corroborated a student/material interaction, finding that students with low reading ability needed more structure in the text than did students with high reading ability. Also, mapping study strategies were not as beneficial to students with strong background knowledge about the content as they were to students with weak background knowledge, particularly if the material was poorly structured.

Caverly and Orlando

Holley and Dansereau (1984) reviewed the outlining and mapping literature and identified a material/criterion task interaction. Use of mapping with narrative material facilitated delayed recall but not immediate recall.

Our review of the empirical literature, using the variables of the tetrahedral model, furthers these analyses of outlining and mapping study strategies. In our integrative review, we found 21 studies of these strategies with college-age students presented in 20 reports: Arkes, Schumacher, & Gardner (1976), Arnold (1942), Castaneda, Lopez, & Romero (1987), Dansereau et al. (1979a, 1983), Diekhoff, Brown, & Dansereau (1982), Good (1926), Holley et al. (1979), Long (1977), Long & Aldersley (1982), Mathews (1938), McClusky & Dolch (1924), McKune (1958), Salisbury (1935), Pugh-Smith (1985), Smith & Standahl (1981), Snyder (1984), Stordahl & Christensen (1956), Vaughn, Stillman, & Sabers (1978), and Willmore (1966). Several other studies examined outlining or mapping with younger populations, but we chose not to include these studies in this review.

Student Variables

From our review of the outlining and mapping literature, we found a strong student/orienting task interaction. Among those studies that reported students' reading ability and taught the study strategy, subjects in all except two (Arnold, 1942; Willmore, 1966) demonstrated increased performance following outlining or mapping (Holley et al., 1979; Long & Aldersley, 1982; Salisbury, 1935; Pugh-Smith, 1985; Snyder, 1984; Vaughn, Stillman, & Sabers, 1978). Initially, one might assume that this finding was an artifact of instruction and not of the interaction between instruction and reading ability. However, when we examined those experiments that did not teach the study strategy, only the high-ability students showed improved performance (Arkes, Schumacher, & Gardner, 1976; Castaneda, Lopez, & Romero, 1987; Good, 1926). So it seems that simply advising students to use outlining or mapping is not warranted unless they are able readers; instruction must be provided, particularly for the poor readers.

Another finding was that background knowledge may affect a four-way student/material/orienting task/criterion task interaction, though only eight of the experiments reported examining students' background knowledge. Six of those studies removed the effect of background knowledge from the experiment by controlling it or matching students in the design (Castaneda, Lopez, & Romero, 1987; Dansereau et al., 1983; Diekhoff, Brown, & Dansereau, 1982; Stordahl & Christensen, 1956; Vaughn, Stillman, & Sabers, 1978; Willmore, 1966). Two other studies used material in which the students demonstrated either strong or weak background knowledge (Arnold, 1942; Pugh-Smith, 1985). Arnold found no consistent effect for superior background knowledge, although students who used an outlining study strategy tended to have the poorest performance of students using various study strategies.

Pugh-Smith (1985) argued that superior students with weak background knowledge are often forced by the criterion task to generate a product and to depend on what she calls "bootstrapping" techniques. She suggested that these techniques, which include mapping, annotating, and summarizing, implicitly limit students to the textbook as the only source of information, and that if the students selected several sources to build background knowledge and understanding (a process she calls "scaffolding"), comprehension of difficult texts might be improved.

Pugh-Smith (1985) observed that the students in her ethnographic experiment did not attempt this strategy even though they had 3 weeks to complete the task. They depended only on bootstrapping strategies and used no sources other than the test material in an attempt to understand. These strategies did not seem to help the students understand difficult text. Pugh-Smith argued that students chose these strategies because they perceived their task as generating a product for someone else, not as developing understanding for their own satisfaction. She further argued that this lack of "ownership" on the part of the students and the subsequent reliance on bootstrapping techniques occurs when the material and the criterion task are de-

Caverly and Orlando

termined by external agents. Giving ownership of the study situation to the students, she contended, would affect their choice of study strategy and their eventual comprehension.

These interactions documented by Pugh-Smith seem to substantiate the intent perspective. If these interactions can be verified in other research, it will be clear that how students are taught to perceive the criterion task and its ownership will determine the study strategy they select.

In summary, these conclusions can be drawn about the effect of the student variables on outlining and mapping:

1. Students with low reading ability need instruction to use outlining or mapping effectively.

2. Evidence from our review confirms the arguments of previous reviews that students select a strategy to fit their perceptions of the criterion task.

3. Initial evidence suggests that ownership of the student/orienting task/material/criterion task interaction might affect which study strategy a student selects, particularly if the student has little background knowledge about the material.

Material Variables

The effects of material variables on mapping are not as easily identified in the research reviewed. In terms of content, the majority of the 40 pieces of text used in the studies were from the social sciences. This is consistent with the findings reported for underlining and notetaking. Still, no experiment manipulated the content variable to measure its effect on outlining or mapping.

For those nine studies that reported the readability of the material, all but one (Castaneda, Lopez, & Romero, 1987) selected material deemed at or above reading level of the students. Implicit in this research is a student/material interaction. Unlike underlining or notetaking, it is assumed that outlining and mapping are strategies intended for use with material deemed more difficult for students.

In terms of the length of the material, there seems to be a material/orienting task interaction. When shorter material (fewer than 1,000 words) was used, instruction did not seem as necessary as when longer material (more than 1,000 words) was used. With shorter material, the research is equivocal. Two studies (Long & Aldersley, 1982; Smith & Standahl, 1981) found a significant improvement with shorter material following instruction in and use of outlining or mapping. Three studies (Arkes, Schumacher, & Gardner, 1976; Castaneda, Lopez, & Romero, 1987; Good, 1926) demonstrated improvement when using shorter material without instruction. When using longer material, on the other hand, six studies demonstrated improvement following instruction in outlining or mapping (Dansereau et al., 1979a, 1983; Diekhoff, Brown, & Dansereau, 1982; Holley et al., 1979; Snyder, 1984; Vaughn, Stillman, & Sabers, 1978), while only two demonstrated improvement without instruction (Mathews, 1938; Pugh-Smith, 1985).

The structure of the material seems to be basic to the evaluation of the effectiveness of outlining and mapping study strategies. The structure is what these strategies emphasize, and its reproduction is often the criterion task. Previous research had identified a student/material/orienting task interaction: students with low reading ability performed better if the material was explicitly structured and if they were taught how to outline or map.

Our review found only five experiments that reported identifying or manipulating the structure of the material (Castaneda, Lopez, & Romero, 1987; Good, 1926; Long, 1977; Long & Aldersley, 1982; McClusky & Dolch, 1924). In three of these studies, the structure of the material was manipulated, ranging from explicit to implicit. McClusky and Dolch provided one passage and varied the explicitness of the structure from using no signal words (implicit structure), to providing transitions (vague structure), to numbering the sentences (explicit structure). Good used the same passage that McClusky and Dolch did and manipulated the complexity of the structure by obscuring or not obscuring the main idea with explanatory supporting ideas. Castaneda et al. made the structure more implicit by selecting three passages of increasing length as well as increasing lexical and syntactic difficulty. Although the sample of research is fairly small, these five studies confirm the student/material/orienting task interaction. Students with low reading ability were not able to recognize implicit or embedded structure without instruction.

In summary, we can draw the following conclusions about the effect of material variables on outlining and mapping:

1. Since none of the research manipulated content, the influence of this variable on the effectiveness of outlining and mapping cannot be determined.

2. Outlining and mapping were generally more successful with material that was deemed at or above the reading level of the student.

3. The effectiveness of outlining and mapping is more dependent on instruction with longer material than it is with shorter material.

4. With implicitly structured material, outlining and mapping are effective study strategies for students with low reading ability only if they receive instruction.

Orienting Task Variables

Some potential effects of orienting task variables can be identified in the outlining and mapping literature. We found a possible material/orienting task/criterion task interaction in that reviewing the outline or map made a difference, particularly in studies that used longer material and that required students to produce verbatim recall. This conclusion must be tempered, however, as only three studies reported allowing for review before the criterion task (Castaneda, Lopez, & Romero, 1987; Pugh-Smith, 1985; Willmore, 1966). In the Castaneda et al. study in which review was manipulated, the researchers found that verbatim recall of shorter material was significantly hindered following the use of mapping without review.

The effect of teaching on outlining and mapping is much more obvious. In 13 studies, either outlining or mapping was taught to students, with instruction ranging from 1 hour to 30 hours (Arnold, 1942; Dansereau et al., 1983, 1979a; Diekhoff, Brown, & Dansereau, 1982; Holley et al., 1979; Long, 1977; Long & Aldersley, 1982; Salisbury, 1935; Smith & Standahl, 1981; Snyder, 1984; Stordahl & Christensen, 1956; Vaughn, Stillman & Sabers, 1978; Willmore, 1966). Students in only 4 of these studies demonstrated no improvement in recall after instruction (Arnold; Smith & Standahl; Stordahl & Christensen; Willmore), indicating a material/orienting task interaction, since 3 of these studies did not allow for review prior to the criterion task. In addition, as noted earlier, a student/material/orienting task interaction exists; students with lower reading ability who were given instruction performed better than those not given instruction, particularly with longer or implicitly structured material.

The effect of criterion task knowledge is less obvious in this literature. In 12 of the studies, criterion task knowledge was directly or indirectly influenced. In some the students were told what to expect on the test (two experiments in Arkes, Schumacher, & Gardner, 1976); in some they performed the study strategy while completing the test (Good, 1926; McClusky & Dolch, 1924; Pugh-Smith, 1985); and in others they took several practice tests similar to the criterion test before the experiment (Arnold, 1942; Dansereau et al., 1983, Holley et al., 1979; Long, 1977; Stordahl & Christensen, 1956; Willmore, 1966). In 5 of these studies, knowledge of test demands did not help improve performance following outlining or mapping. A closer examination of these studies reveals that this lack of improvement might have been caused by the students' inability to review prior to the criterion task (Arnold; Long; McClusky & Dolch; Stordahl & Christensen), or by low reading ability among the students (Arnold; Long; Stordahl & Christensen; Willmore). Conversely, the improved performance demonstrated in the other studies may be attributed to variation in the ability of the students (Arkes et al.; Good; Holley et al.;

Pugh-Smith) or to the amount of instruction they received (Dansereau et al., 1983, 1979a; Holley et al.). Within our review, a student/orienting task interaction seems to be masking the variable of criterion task knowledge.

In summary, we can draw three conclusions about the effect of orienting task variables on outlining and mapping:

1. Review before a verbatim recall criterion task tends to be necessary for successful performance.

2. The effectiveness of outlining and mapping is dependent on instruction, particularly for poorer readers.

3. Criterion task knowledge seems to be embedded in a student/orienting task interaction in which students' ability and opportunity for review must also be considered.

Criterion Task Variables

Test type had a distinct influence on the effectiveness of outlining and mapping. Eighteen studies used experimenter-designed recognition and/or recall tests after students studied a text passage. Three other studies used either standardized tests that did not allow mapping or outlining to be used (Salisbury, 1935; Smith & Standahl, 1981) or ethnographic measures that observed spontaneous use of mapping or outlining (Pugh-Smith, 1985). Improved performance was not demonstrated on any recognition-type tests following outlining or mapping (Arnold, 1942; Dansereau et al., 1983, 1979a; Long, 1977; Mathews, 1938; McKune, 1958; Snyder, 1984; Stordahl & Christensen, 1956; Willmore, 1966). Improved performance was found on recall measures in seven of the nine studies that used these measures.

It seems that recognition criterion tasks were not sensitive enough to measure the benefits of outlining and mapping. This may be due to the nature of the outlining and mapping task, which directs students to attend to main ideas and the relationships among them, while de-emphasizing details. It is difficult to tell what ratio of main ideas to details was present on these recognition tests. Students using an outlining or mapping strategy are less likely to demonstrate improved performance on a criterion task that focuses on detail than on a criterion task that focuses on main ideas. This conclusion is consistent with those of previous reviews (Anderson, 1978; Holley & Dansereau, 1984; McKeachie, 1988).

When considering the delay between using outlining or mapping and taking the test, no clear pattern emerged. However, when the orienting task/criterion task interaction is examined, a strong effect emerges. In the seven studies in which students showed no improvement on an immediate test (Arnold, 1942; Long, 1977; Mathews, 1938; McClusky & Dolch, 1924; McKune, 1958; Stordahl & Christensen, 1956; Willmore, 1966), review was not allowed before the test. In the six studies (all but the McClusky & Dolch study) in which students showed no improvement on a delayed test, again review was not allowed before the test. It seems that review is a critical variable in the success of outlining or mapping over both the short and the long run.

In summary, these conclusions about the effect of the criterion task variables on outlining or mapping can be drawn:

1. Outlining and mapping seem to improve students' performance when the criterion task focuses more on main ideas than on details; thus, they seem to favor the encoding and recall of main ideas over the encoding and recall of details.

2. Review seems to be important for outlining and mapping to improve performance on either immediate or delayed tests.

Summary

Based on this review, we conclude that students must be taught how to use the outlining and mapping study strategies. This is particularly true for students with low reading ability and students working with longer material (more than 1,000 words). There is some evidence that students must be taught not only how to use these study strategies but also how to assess the interaction between their purpose for reading (i.e., their knowledge of the criterion task) and how well their background knowledge matches the material. If students can assess their abilities, the text, and the context, outlining and mapping seem to be effective strategies for improving the recall of main ideas, although not necessarily of details.

Comprehension Monitoring Strategy: SQ3R

A fourth group of study strategies posited by Weinstein and Mayer (1985) are comprehension monitoring strategies. Study strategies within this group are often labeled metacognitive strategies. They direct students to establish goals for the study situation, to assess progress toward these goals, and to modify processing if progress is unsatisfactory. (The theoretical foundation for metacognitive strategies is discussed in Chapter 2, this volume.)

One common study strategy that leads students to monitor their comprehension is SQ3R, developed by Robinson (1946, 1961, 1970). This strategy directs the students to complete activities before reading (**S**urvey the material by skimming it for organizing information and formulate **Q**uestions or goals by converting the subheadings into questions), during reading (**R**ead to answer the questions, monitor progress in answering the questions, and modify processing if progress is unsatisfactory), and after reading (**R**ecite the answers to the questions and **R**eview the answers). Of all the independent strategies available to the college reading teacher, SQ3R and its variations (Stahl, 1983) are perhaps the most often taught. Nevertheless, anyone with a passing exposure to the literature realizes that such strategies also are the most maligned (Adams, Carnine, & Gersten, 1982).

Several researchers have reviewed the theoretical and/or empirical foundations used to support the use of SQ3R (Anderson & Armbruster, 1982; Crewe & Hultgren, 1969; Gustafson &

Pederson, 1985; Jacobowitz, 1988; Johns & McNamara, 1980; Kopfstein, 1982; Orlando, 1978, 1984; Pathberg, 1972; Spencer, 1978; Stahl, 1983; Tadlock, 1978; Walker, 1982; Wark, 1965). The majority of these reviewers concluded that while some of the individual steps may have merit, little evidence validates the use of the entire system as designed by Robinson (1946). Further, these analyses found little or no empirical evidence to suggest that SQ3R is more effective than reading or rereading. Finally, they concluded that many intervening variables may help or hinder SQ3R's effectiveness.

These researchers have found evidence to support the effect of two student variables and two orienting task variables on SQ3R's effectiveness. For example, reviewers have concluded that the student's level of cognitive development is a factor that must be considered (Niles, 1963; Orlando, 1984; Trillin & Associates, 1980). These reviewers argue that students must reach an advanced level of cognitive performance before they can understand the SQ3R system. Bean, Smith, and Searfoss (1980) explored another student variable, background knowledge, and found that it can interfere with the effectiveness of SQ3R's question step.

Several reviewers speculated that a major reason for the lack of evidence supporting SQ3R is that the orienting task variables interfere. In their reviews, it was found that SQ3R often was poorly taught (Bahe, 1969; Basile, 1978; Entwistle, 1960; Fox, 1962; Orlando, 1978; Palmatier, 1971) or that success was due to time-on-task rather than on the processing inherent in the strategy's use (Alessi, Anderson, & Goetz, 1979).

In addition to the effect of these individual variables, one two-way interaction and one three-way interaction were found. Anderson and Armbruster (1982) found a two-way interaction between the orienting task and the criterion task variables that may explain the inability of the experiments they reviewed to demonstrate SQ3R's effectiveness. They found that experimenters (following advice given by Robinson, 1946, 1961, 1970) taught students to convert subheadings into questions irrespective of the criterion task. The researchers argued that it is realistic to expect the students to have knowledge of the criterion task and to use this knowledge to adjust their processing. Instruction, therefore, should include matching processing to the criterion task.

Anderson and Armbruster (1982) also believe there may be a three-way interaction between the material, the orienting task, and the criterion task variables. Instruction suggested by Robinson (1970), and used by most of the studies Anderson and Armbruster reviewed, presents the subheadings as reflecting the most important ideas of the material. Moreover, this instruction assumes that instructors will base their tests on the subheadings of the material used. Armbruster and Anderson's (1984) review of textbooks found that most had inadequate subheadings that failed to communicate either the important information or how that information was organized. They conclude that this factor should be considered in teaching students to use SQ3R and in future research into the study strategy.

To further these analyses of SQ3R, we will now look at the empirical literature. In our review, we were able to locate 25 reports citing 26 studies that explored SQ3R specifically (rather than its many variations): Beneke & Harris (1972), Briggs, Tosi, & Morley (1971), Butler (1983), Courtney (1965), DeLong (1948), Diggs (1972), Doctor et al. (1970), Driskell & Kelly (1980), Eanet (1978), Galloway (1983), Gurrola (1974), Hannah (1946), Harris & Ream (1972), Heerman (1972), Holmes (1972), Kremer, Aeschleman, & Petersen (1983), Martin (1983), McReynolds & Church (1973), Niple (1968), Robinson (1961), Scappaticci (1977), Snyder (1984), Stoodt & Balbo (1979), Willmore (1966), and Wooster (1953). Surprisingly, half of these reports were master's or doctoral theses, suggesting a serious paucity in the published literature. Only 11 of the studies reported significant improvement following use of the SQ3R study strategy. The intervening variables of the tetrahedral model may help explain this lack of positive effect.

Student Variables

From our review of these studies, we found that we could not separate the student variables from the orienting task variables. Virtually every study taught SQ3R; thus, their analyses may reflect the effect of instruction on students rather than the effect of the study strategy itself. From our analysis of this student/orienting task interaction, we found that varying amounts of instruction were needed for students with different levels of reading ability. Students with low ability seemed to need intensive and lengthy instruction for improved performance (Beneke & Harris, 1972; Briggs, Tosi, & Morley, 1971; Butler, 1983; Diggs, 1972; Driskell & Kelly, 1980; Martin, 1983; Stoodt & Balbo, 1979).

Only three studies (Galloway, 1983; Gurrola, 1974; Snyder, 1984) found no improvement among low-ability students after instruction. A closer examination of these three studies reveals that the interaction between students' reading ability and the length of instruction confounded the results, resulting in this lack of improvement. In these studies, students with low, medium, and high reading ability received less than 6 hours of instruction in SQ3R. Both a metaanalysis (Caverly, 1985) and empirical research (Orlando, 1980b) suggest that at least 10 hours of instruction is necessary for SQ3R to be effective for low-ability students. For medium-ability students, 7 to 10 hours are necessary, while for high-ability students, success has been demonstrated with less than 7 hours of instruction (Butler, 1983; Galloway, 1983; Gurrola, 1974; Martin, 1983).

Generally, teaching SQ3R was not sufficient to overcome students' lack of reading ability, although students at all levels seemed capable of learning how to use the strategy, given sufficient instruction. Moreover, there seems to be strong evidence in this literature that students' attitudes toward the amount of effort needed for SQ3R affect both whether they use the strategy beyond instruction and their subsequent improvement in performance (Butler, 1983; Briggs, Tosi, & Morley, 1971; Courtney, 1965; Doctor et al., 1970; Harris & Ream, 1972; Kremer, Aeschleman, & Petersen, 1983; McReynolds & Church, 1973; Niple, 1968; Scappaticci, 1977; Wooster, 1953).

No conclusions can be drawn regarding the effect of background knowledge on SQ3R. Only two studies considered this variable (Butler, 1983; Willmore, 1966), and both controlled it to remove any effect.

In summary, these conclusions can be drawn about the effect of the student variables on SQ3R:

1. Students must be taught how to use SQ3R.

2. Students with low reading ability must be taught for a longer period of time than those with medium ability, who, in turn, must be taught longer than those with high ability.

3. The effect of students' background knowledge on SQ3R cannot be determined since it was not considered in any of the research.

Material Variables

The material variables surrounding the use of SQ3R were not thoroughly examined in any of the research reviewed. A total of 24 pieces of text were used in these studies that examined SQ3R, most of which again were from the social sciences. Several other studies used the textbooks from students' current classes in an attempt to teach students how to transfer the SQ3R study strategy to their required reading material (Beneke & Harris, 1972; Briggs, Tosi, & Morley, 1971; Doctor et al., 1970; Harris & Ream, 1972; Kremer, Aeschleman, & Petersen, 1983; McReynolds & Church, 1973; Robinson, 1961). A few studies did not report what type of material was used (Courtney, 1965; DeLong, 1948; Eanet, 1978; Heerman, 1972). No conclusions can be drawn regarding the effectiveness of SQ3R in the different content areas college students study.

Few conclusions can be drawn about the readability of the material used by researchers, since only four reported the difficulty level of the material used in their study (Holmes, 1972; Martin, 1983; Snyder, 1984; Wooster, 1953). Three of these studies reported that material was written at the college level or higher. Several other studies, as just noted, attempted to have students transfer the SQ3R strategy to their required reading in their other classes. We can only assume these studies used college-level material.

Not unexpectedly, the material used in the studies examining SQ3R was considerably longer than the material found in the research on underlining or notetaking. This was probably because of the nature of the strategy, which requires material with an introduction, several subtitled sections, and a summary. Interestingly, the readability level of much of the material used in these studies was rather low for college-age students. Seemingly, the researchers conducting these studies were concerned with the effect of SQ3R and did not wish to confound this factor with passage difficulty. The only factor that might explain the lack of improved performance through SQ3R is the material/orienting task interaction.

Similarly, we can draw no conclusions based on the structure of the material, since virtually no experiment explored the effect of text structure on the use of SQ3R. This was a rather surprising finding, considering the extent of the literature on the effect of explicit structures on comprehension. Perhaps one explanation for this gap in the research is that the experimenters assumed the five organizational components (introduction, subheading, highlighted words, graphics, and summary) that students are induced to survey made up an explicit structure. Given the product perspective that we believe is inherent in Robinson's (1970) directions for the study strategy, this assumption is not unexpected. Much of the inconsistent results of the research on the SQ3R study strategy might be explained by the uncritical acceptance of this assumption by students and instructors.

In summary, we can draw the following conclusions about material variables on SQ3R:

1. Since research in this area is practically nonexistent, little can be said about the effect of material variables on SQ3R.

2. Future research needs to manipulate the content variable to examine whether SQ3R is equally effective in different content areas.

Caverly and Orlando

3. The material used in the research analyzed was generally at the college readability level, but only a few studies reported effects due to the material.

4. The material was generally longer than that used in research on other study strategies; this difference was probably due to the inherent nature of SQ3R.

5. No conclusion can be drawn regarding the effect of the structure of the material on the SQ3R study strategy.

Orienting Task Variables

One distinct orienting task variable is the opportunity for students to review after study. One might expect review to be an important factor, given its effect on underlining and note-taking, and given that it is presumably inherent in the last two steps of the SQ3R strategy (recite and review). Nevertheless, only four studies (Butler, 1983; Holmes, 1972; Willmore, 1966; Wooster, 1953) provided an opportunity for students to review before the criterion task, and the results were equivocal. With longer passages more likely to require the use of SQ3R, this failure to provide a review opportunity seems counter to the intention of the recite and review steps. This material/orienting task interaction might have much to do with the failure of the research to demonstrate improved performance when students use SQ3R.

A second orienting task variable is the importance of teaching students the SQ3R study strategy. As stated earlier, virtually every study taught this strategy, with the length of instruction ranging from 1 hour to 12 weeks. This instruction brought to light a distinct subject/orienting task interaction in that students with lower reading ability needed more instruction than those with higher reading ability.

In summary, these conclusions about the effect of the orienting task variables on SQ3R can be drawn:

1. The amount of instruction needed for SQ3R to be effective is directly related to the student's level of reading ability.

2. Lack of research makes it impossible to draw conclusions about the effect of reviewing before the criterion task.

Criterion Task Variables

The criterion task variables seem to have a distinct but inconsistent effect on SQ3R. In only 2 of the 13 experiments that used a recognition test as the criterion task was SQ3R found to be effective (Butler, 1983; Martin, 1983). Similarly, the 2 studies that used recall tasks (Gurrola, 1974; Stoodt & Balbo, 1979) had equivocal results. SQ3R was found to be effective, however, in 5 of the 8 experiments that used the students' GPA as the criterion (Beneke & Harris, 1972; Briggs, Tosi, & Morley, 1971; Driskell & Kelly, 1980; Harris & Ream, 1972; Heerman, 1972). This finding may suggest that recognition and recall tasks are not sensitive enough to identify performance differences with SQ3R. However, conclusions based on GPA must be made carefully since so many other factors can influence grades.

If we examine the interaction between the orienting task and the criterion task, we can see a reason for these inconsistent performance findings. For example, the amount of instruction given to low-ability students was often insufficient. With only one exception (Holmes, 1972), in the experiments in which students demonstrated no improvement on recognition or recall types of criterion tasks, less than 8 hours of instruction was provided. Therefore, it is difficult to draw conclusions about the effect of SQ3R on reading performance using these criterion task variables. One interpretation is that SQ3R does not affect reading comprehension and retention directly, but affects it indirectly through improving students' attitudes toward study. This improvement in students' attitudes about the amount of effort necessary to study college-level material would then be manifested in improvement in long term criterion measures such as GPA. Future research is needed to verify this hypothesis.

Another explanation for why SQ3R affects performance on GPA but not on recognition or recall tests is that the longer term measure allows more trial applications for learning this study strategy. That is, success on GPA measures could be related to our second criterion task variable, test administration delay. A recognition or recall criterion task tends to measure application of the study strategy after a single application. In most empirical studies, students apply SQ3R to a passage and then take a recognition or recall test either immediately or several days later. If the criterion task is semester GPA, however, students have the opportunity to apply SQ3R several times in a variety of study situations before their performance is measured. It may be, then, that a positive performance effect for SQ3R, shows up only after students have had a chance to apply the study strategy several times.

A test of this hypothesis is implicit in several experiments in which students who learned SQ3R demonstrated improved performance (as measured by GPA) after one semester (Briggs, Tosi, & Morley 1971; Driskell & Kelly, 1989; Stoodt & Balbo, 1979; Wooster, 1953), after two semesters (Heerman, 1972), and after three semesters (Beneke & Harris, 1972). As stated above, however, caution is advised in drawing global conclusions from these data since many other unmeasured intervening variables may have affected this improvement in GPA.

In summary, we can draw two conclusions about the effect of criterion task variables on SQ3R:

1. Successful performance following the use of SQ3R may require several applications of the strategy.

2. Long term performance gain may be a factor of the criterion measure.

Summary

A strong student/orienting task/criterion task interaction seems to be present in the use of SQ3R. Substantial, effective instruction is necessary for students with low or medium reading ability to succeed with this strategy. This instruction should include an attempt to build students' awareness of the effort required in using this strategy. Success is apparent only in long term measures such as GPA.

On the other hand, we know very little about the effect of students' background knowledge, or of the effect of material variables, on this study strategy.

Implications for Instruction

Based on this integrative review, we can conclude that under certain conditions, all five of these strategies help improve students' ability to study textbooks. These study strategies have the potential to improve students' acquisition of important material, develop deeper encoding of this information, encourage a more thorough integration of information into prior knowledge, develop cues for retention, and provide a permanent storage device for later review. Such strategies can direct students to understand and remember more of what they read. For this potential to be realized, however, students must be taught how to select a study strategy on the basis of their knowledge of these conditions. This finding directly supports the intent perspective of studying.

We suggest that the individual and combined effects of 10 of the 11 variables we used to examine the literature must be considered when teaching students to use these study strategies. The 1 variable that we cannot conclude has an effect on these study strategies is the content area of the material to which the strategies will be applied. The great majority of studies we reviewed did not manipulate this variable. Because of the predominate use of social science materials, our research review does not allow us to draw conclusions about the effects of these study strategies on other content areas.

We conclude that underlining and notetaking should not be taught to students who are developmentally unable to handle college-level material. Our review suggests that students with low reading ability will not profit from underlining or notetaking if the material is considered "hard" because of readability, length, or implicit structure; nor will students benefit if they are not allowed to review before the criterion task. This interaction seems to be the result of students' inability to recognize what is important in the text (i.e., the main or high structural ideas). There is some evidence, however, that once students with low reading ability have been taught how to find these main ideas and how to review what has been underlined or noted, they can learn to use underlining or notetaking effectively. Such instruction must center around a strategic approach to reading (Baker & Brown, 1984).

Students must be taught to recognize and take note of the explicit structure provided by the author to help in encoding and subsequent recall. If the structure is implicit, on the other hand, students must be taught how to engage their background knowledge to construct a personal structure to help in encoding and recall. Furthermore, students must be taught how to monitor the processing they engage in when underlining or notetaking in relationship to the demands of the criterion task. This strategic approach requires a time commitment on the part of the students, as well as criterion task knowledge, or knowledge of what the author and the instructor want them to understand. Given this commitment, both underlining and notetaking strategies can be said to be more effective (producing better performance on a criterion task) than reading or rereading, but they cannot necessarily be considered more efficient (i.e., less time consuming). Students must come to understand the trade-off between strategies that may produce better results and those that take less time to complete.

Outlining, mapping, and SQ3R all tend to be more effective for students with low and medium reading ability (after they have learned how to use these strategies) when the material is more difficult and when the opportunity for review is provided. Knowledge of the criterion task and whether the criterion task measures main ideas more than details also influences effectiveness. Readers of all ability levels, however, need to be taught how to use these three study strategies. They also need instruction in how to integrate these study strategies into their existing repertoire of strategies. All students must be taught to create their outlines, maps, or SQ3R questions on the basis of their perceptions of the criterion task. They must also be taught to review their outlines, maps, or answers to their questions before the test.

Finally, students must be taught to believe in and complete the extensive steps inherent in these study strategies—that is, the support strategies described by Dansereau (1985). Evidence suggests that unless students change their attitudes about these strategies, they will not be willing to continue the effort necessary for applying them outside of the empirical setting or developmental classroom. This is particularly true for SQ3R, which requires several applications with guided feedback to demonstrate improved performance. Therefore, students need to learn about the "cost-effectiveness" (more time but better performance) of study strategies like outlining, mapping, or SQ3R and be apprised of the metacognitive criteria they can use to evaluate their effective and efficient use of these strategies.

Future Research and Instructional Avenues

This review makes evident several specific research and instructional avenues. In particular, we recommend that the student/orienting task interaction present in these study strategies be explored further to verify the role of background knowledge in their successful use. Following the research of Nist and Hogrebe (1987) as well as Smith (1982) and Pugh-Smith (1985), background knowledge should be manipulated within the empirical or ethnographic research paradigm to see its effect on performance following the use of these study strategies.

In terms of research, other specific metacognitive strategies need to be developed and tested that monitor the progress of processing toward satisfying the intent for reading. Particularly promising is the recent work of Wade and Reynolds (1989) and Simpson, Stahl, and Hayes (1989). Also, it would seem warranted to continue this integrative review with the study strategies that are not directly addressed here. For example, a thorough exploration of rereading and summarizing is needed. Such an analysis has already begun, using a metaanalysis technique (Caverly, 1985) and other integrative criteria (Cook & Mayer, 1983; Thomas & Rohwer, 1986; Weinstein & Mayer, 1985).

In addition, other variables should be explored to determine their individual and combined effects on these study strategies. Additional student variables that might be considered include age, attitude, and academic aptitude. Another material variable that we believe influences the effectiveness of study strategies is the relevance of the material for the students. Other potentially important orienting task variables are metacognitive knowledge and length of instruction. Finally, criterion task variables that should be examined include intentional versus incidental types of recall, as well as what we call the significance of performance on criterion measures. Many of the studies in this review demonstrated statistically significant improvement with a 50-60 percent level of performance. This may satisfy an empirical paradigm, but it will not help a student pass a course. These integrative analyses should be continued in order to come to some consensus on the validity of each study strategy within the contextual constraints of the study situation.

College reading instructors need to explore pedagogical techniques for teaching students how to perceive these contextual constraints, how to choose a study strategy to match those constraints, how to monitor the application of a given study strategy within a given context, and how to adjust the strategy or change to a new one when the choice was inappropriate. In other words, college reading instructors need to teach their students metacognitive control of study strategies. Campione and Armbruster (1985) discuss initial attempts at this instruction. Wade and Reynolds (1989) and Simpson, Stahl, and Hayes (1989) present other instructional strategies applicable to college-age students. Nist and Mealey (Chapter 2, this volume) review two new attempts. A fifth avenue we have explored is using a decision-making model to teach students how to perceive contextual constraints and choose a strategy based on these constraints (Figure 3).

We use this model to teach our students that certain study strategies are more efficient (i.e., less time consuming) than other strategies, but not as effective in terms of improved performance. For example, underlining and rereading strategies take less time but also do less to increase performance on tests than a notetaking strategy, which in turn takes less time but

Figure 3
Demand Model for Choosing Study Strategies

Effective (Heavy teacher/material demands)		**Efficient** (Light teacher/material demands)
Outlining	Notetaking	Reading
Mapping	Summarizing	Rereading
SQ3R		Underlining

does less to improve test performance than outlining, mapping, or SQ3R. Presenting study strategies along this continuum seems to help students understand that different strategies have different strengths in different contexts. Our review supports the effectiveness dimension of this model; the efficiency dimension must be left to future empirical research or integrative and metaanalytic reviews.

After presenting the model to students, we teach them how to identify a particular strategy for each particular study situation. To help in this metacognitive decision, two criteria are taught to students. First, a given strategy might be chosen on the basis of the professor's demands (e.g., the role of the reading material in tests, lectures, or classroom discussions). Second, a strategy might be chosen on the basis of material demands (e.g., readability, length, background knowledge needed, ability level required). If the demands of the professor and the material are heavy, a strategy that is more effective (such as SQ3R or mapping) is appropriate. If the demands are light, a strategy that is less effective but more efficient (such as underlining) makes sense. If the demands are contrasting, a compromise strategy (such as notetaking) is appropriate. Students are taught how to identify such demands and how to use these criteria for selecting a demand-appropriate study strategy. Preliminary evidence based on student feedback is encouraging. Further research needs to be completed regarding the placement of each strategy along the dual continuum of effectiveness and efficiency.

A general conclusion that seems evident from this review of research is that most study strategies are effective, but no one study strategy is appropriate for all students in all study situations. This theoretical position has been argued elsewhere (Anderson & Armbruster, 1984; Elshout-Mohr, 1983; Ford, 1981; Laurillard, 1979; McKeachie, 1988; Schumacher, 1987) and has been verified here. To help their students deal with the variety of demands they face in higher education, college reading instructors should teach students to expand their repertoire of study strategies.

References and Suggested Readings

Adams, A., Carnine, D., & Gersten, S.L. (1982). Instructional strategies for studying content area texts in the intermediate grades. *Reading Research Quarterly, 18,* 27-55.

Adams, E.K. (1969). The graphical aid to comprehension. In G.B. Schick & M.M. May (Eds.), *Reading: Process and pedagogy* (pp. 12-22). Milwaukee, WI: National Reading Conference.

Alessi, S.M., Anderson, T.H., & Goetz, E.T. (1979). An investigation of lookbacks during studying. *Discourse Processes, 2,* 197-212.

*Anderson, J. R. (1976). *Language, memory, and thought.* Hillsdale, NJ: Erlbaum.

*Anderson, J.R. (1983). *The architecture of cognition.* Cambridge, MA: Harvard University Press.

*Anderson, R.C., & Pearson, P.D. (1984). A schema-theoretic view of basic processes in reading. In P.D. Pearson (Ed.), *Handbook of reading research* (pp. 255-292). New York: Longman.

Anderson, T.H. (1978). *Study skills and learning strategies* (Tech. Rep. No. 104). Champaign, IL: University of Illinois, Center for the Study of Reading.

Anderson, T.H. (1980). *Study strategies and adjunct aids.* In R.J. Spiro, B.C. Bruce, & W.F. Brewer (Eds.), *Theoretical issues in reading comprehension* (pp. 483-502). Hillsdale, NJ: Erlbaum.

Anderson, T.H., & Armbruster, B.B. (1980). *Studying* (Tech. Rep. No. 155). Champaign, IL: University of Illinois, Center for the Study of Reading.

*Anderson, T.H., & Armbruster, B.B. (1982). Reader and text: Studying strategies. In W. Otto & S. White (Eds.), *Reading expository material* (pp. 219-242). San Diego, CA: Academic Press.

Anderson, T.H., & Armbruster, B.B. (1984). Studying. In P.D. Pearson (Ed.), *Handbook of reading research* (pp. 657-679). New York: Longman.

Annis, L. (1979). Effect of cognitive style and learning passage organization on study technique effectiveness. *Journal of Educational Psychology, 71,* 620-626.

Annis, L.F., & Annis, D.B. (1982). A normative study of students' reported preferred study techniques. *Reading World, 21,* 201-207.

Annis, L.F., & Davis, J.K. (1978). Study techniques and cognitive style: Their effect on recall and recognition. *Journal of Educational Research, 71,* 175-178.

Arkes, N.R., Schumacher, G.M., & Gardner, E.T. (1976). Effects of orienting task on the retention of prose material. *Journal of Educational Psychology, 68,* 536-545.

Armbruster, B.B. (1979). *An investigation of the effectiveness of "mapping" texts as a studying strategy for middle school students.* Unpublished doctoral dissertation, University of Illinois, Champaign.

*Armbruster, B.B., & Anderson, T.H. (1984). *Producing "considerate" expository text, or easy reading is damned hard writing* (Reading Education Report No. 46). Champaign, IL: University of Illinois, Center for the Study of Reading.

Arnold, H.F. (1942). The comparative effectiveness of certain study techniques in the field of history. *Journal of Educational Psychology, 32,* 449-457.

Atkinson, R.C., & Shiffrin, R.M. (1968). Human memory: A proposed system and its control processes. In K.W. Spence & J.T. Spence (Eds.), *The psychology of learning and motivation: Advances in research and theory* (Vol. 2, pp. 89-195). San Diego, CA: Academic Press.

Baddeley, A.D. (1978). The troubles with levels: A reexamination of Craik and Lockhart's framework for memory research. *Psychological Review, 85,* 139-152.

Bahe, V.R. (1969). Reading study instruction and college achievement. *Reading Improvement, 6,* 57-61.

*Baker, L., & Brown, A. (1984). Metacognitive skills and reading. In P.D. Pearson (Ed.), *Handbook of reading research* (pp. 353-394). New York: Longman.

*Bartlett, F.C. (1932). *Remembering.* Cambridge, United Kingdom: Cambridge University.

Basile, D.D. (1978). Helping college students understand their textbooks. *Reading World, 17,* 289-294.

Bean, T., Smith, C., & Searfoss, L. (1980). *Study strategies for the content classroom.* Paper presented at the thirteenth annual conference of the California Reading Association, Newport Beach, CA.

Beneke, W.M., & Harris, M.B. (1972). Teaching self-control of study behavior. *Behavior Research and Therapy, 10,* 35-41.

Berg, P., & Rentle, V. (1966). Improving study skills. *Journal of Reading, 9,* 343-348.

Biggs, J.B. (1976). Dimensions of study behavior: Another look at ATI. *British Journal of Educational Psychology, 46,* 58-80.

Biggs, J.B. (1979). Individual differences in study processes and the quality of learning outcomes. *Higher Education, 8,* 381-394.

Biggs, J.B. (1980). The relationship between developmental level and the quality of school learning. In S. Modgil & C. Modgil (Eds.), *Toward a theory of psychological development.* Atlanta Highlands, NJ: Humanities Press.

Blanchard, J., & Mikkelson, V. (1987). Underlining performance outcomes in expository text. *Journal of Educational Research, 80,* 197-201.

Bower, G., Black, J.B., & Turner, T.J. (1979). Scripts in memory for text. *Cognitive Psychology, 11,* 177-220.

Brady, J., & Rickards, J.P. (1979). How personal evaluation affects the underlining and recall of prose. *Journal of Reading Behavior, 11,* 61-67.

*Bransford, J.D. (1979). *Human cognition: Learning, understanding, and remembering.* Belmont, CA: Wadsworth.

Bretzing, B.H., & Kulhavy, R.W. (1979). Notetaking and depth of processing. *Contemporary Educational Psychology, 4,* 145-154.

Bretzing, B.H., & Kulhavy, R.W. (1981). Notetaking and passage style. *Journal of Educational Psychology, 73,* 242-250.

*Breuker, J.A. (1984). A theoretical framework for spatial learning strategies. In C.D. Holley & D.F. Dansereau (Eds.), *Spatial learning strategies: Techniques, applications, and related issues* (pp. 21-43). San Diego, CA: Academic Press.

Briggs, R.D., Tosi, D.J., & Morley, R.M. (1971). Study habit modification and its effects on academic performance: A behavioral approach. *Journal of Educational Research, 64,* 347-350.

Brown, A.L. (1980). Metacognitive development in reading. In R.J. Spiro, B.C. Bruce, & W.F. Brewer (Eds.), *Theoretical issues in reading comprehension* (pp. 453-482). Hillsdale, NJ: Erlbaum.

Brown, A.L. (1982). Learning how to learn from reading. In J.A. Langer & M.T. Smith-Burke (Eds.), *Reader meets author/bridging the gap: A psycholinguistic and so-*

ciolinguistic perspective (pp. 26-54). Newark, DE: International Reading Association.

*Brown, A.L. (1985). Metacognition: The development of selective attention strategies for learning from text. In H. Singer & R.B. Ruddel (Eds.), *Theoretical models and processes of reading* (3rd ed., pp. 501-526). Newark, DE: International Reading Association.

*Brown, A.L., Campione, J.C., & Day, J.D. (1981). Learning to learn: On training students to learn from texts. *Educational Researcher, 10*, 14-21.

*Brown, A.L., & Palincsar, A.S. (1982). Inducing strategic learning from texts by means of informed self-control training. *Topics in Learning and Learning Disabilities, 2*, 1-17.

Brown, A.L., & Smiley, S.S. (1977). *The development of strategies for studying prose passages* (Tech. Rep. No. 66).Champaign, IL: University of Illinois, Center for the Study of Reading.

Browning, W.J. (1976). A critical review of research and expert opinion on the underlining study aid. In G. Miller & E. McNinch (Eds.), *Reflections and investigations on reading* (pp. 8-21). Clemson, SC: National Reading Conference.

Butler, T.H. (1983). *Effect of subject and training variables on the SQ3R study method.* Unpublished doctoral dissertation, Arizona State University, Tempe.

*Campione, J.C., & Armbruster, B.B. (1985). Acquiring information from texts: An analysis of four approaches. In J.W. Segal, S.F. Chapman, & R. Glaser (Eds.), *Thinking and learning skills: Vol. 1. Relating instruction to research* (pp. 317-359). Hillsdale, NJ: Erlbaum.

Camstra, B., & van Bruggen, J. (1984). Schematizing; The empirical evidence. In C.D. Holley & D.F. Dansereau (Eds.), *Spatial learning strategies: Techniques, applications, and related issues* (pp. 163-187). San Diego, CA: Academic Press.

*Carrier, C.A., & Titus, A. (1979). The effects of notetaking: A review of studies. *Contemporary Educational Psychology, 4*, 299-314.

Castaneda, S., Lopez, M., & Romero, M. (1987). The role of five induced learning strategies in scientific text comprehension. *Journal of Experimental Education, 55*, 125-130.

Caverly, D.C. (1982). *The effect of three study-reading strategies upon comprehension and recall.* Unpublished doctoral dissertation, Indiana University, Bloomington.

Caverly, D.C. (1985). *Textbook study strategies: A meta-analysis.* Paper presented at the annual meeting of the National Reading Conference, San Diego, CA.

Caverly, D.C., & Orlando, V.P. (1985). *How much do college students read their texts?* Paper presented at the annual meeting of the Western College Reading Learning Association, Colorado Springs, CO.

Charters, J.A. (1925). Methods of study used by college women. *Journal of Educational Research, 10*, 344-345.

Chiesi, H.L., Spilich, G.J., & Voss, J.F. (1979). Acquisition of domain-related information in relation to high and low domain knowledge. *Journal of Verbal Learning and Verbal Behavior, 18*, 257-273.

*Clymer, C. (1978). A national survey of learning assistance evaluation: Rationale, techniques, problems. (ED 155 603)

*Cook, L.K., & Mayer, R.E. (1983). Reading strategies training for meaningful learning from prose. In M. Pressey & J. Levin (Eds.), *Cognitive strategies research: Educational applications* (pp. 87-131). New York: Springer-Verlag.

Courtney, L. (1965). Organization produced. In H.L. Herber (Ed.), *Developing study skills in secondary schools* (pp. 77-97). Newark, DE: International Reading Association.

*Craik, F.I.M., & Lockhart, R.S. (1972). Levels of processing: A framework for memory research. *Journal of Verbal Learning and Verbal Behavior, 11*, 671-684.

*Craik, F.I.M., & Tulving, E. (1975). Depth of processing and the retention of words in episodic memory. *Journal of Experimental Psychology: General, 104*, 268-294.

Craik, J.M., & Martin, D.D. (1980). The effect of a presentation on how to underline a text in introductory psychology courses. *Journal of Reading, 213,* 404-407.

Crawford, R.C. (1938). *How to teach.* Los Angeles, CA: School Book Press.

Crewe, J.C. (1968). *The effect of study strategies on the retention of college text material.* Unpublished doctoral dissertation, University of Minnesota, Minneapolis.

Crewe, J., & Hultgren, D. (1969). What does research really say about study skills? In G.B. Schick & M.M. May (Eds.), *The psychology of reading behavior* (pp. 75-78). Milwaukee, WI: National Reading Conference.

*Dansereau, D.F. (1978). The development of a learning strategy curriculum. In H.F. O'Neil, Jr. (Ed.), *Learning strategies.* San Diego, CA: Academic Press.

Dansereau, D.F. (1980). Learning strategy research. Paper presented at the NIE-LRDC Conference on Thinking and Learning Skills, Pittsburgh, PA.

*Dansereau, D.F. (1985). Learning strategy research. In J.W. Segal, S.F. Chapman, & R. Glaser (Eds.), *Thinking and learning skills: Vol. 1. Relating instruction to research* (pp. 209-239). Hillsdale, NJ: Erlbaum.

Dansereau, D.F., Actkinson, T.R., Long, G.L., & McDonald, B. (1974). *Learning strategies: A review and synthesis of the current literature.* (ED 103 403)

Dansereau, D.F., Brooks, L.W., Holley, C.D., & Collins, K.W. (1983). Learning strategies training: Effects of sequencing. *Journal of Experimental Education, 51,* 102-108.

Dansereau, D.F., Collins, K.W., McDonald, B.A., Garland, J., Holley, C.D., Deikhoff, G., & Evans, S.H. (1979a). Development and evaluation of a learning strategy training program. *Journal of Educational Psychology, 71,* 64-73.

Dansereau, D.F., & Holley, C.D. (1981). *Development and evaluation of a text mapping strategy.* Paper presented at the International Symposium on Text Processing, Fribourg, Switzerland.

Dansereau, D.F., McDonald, B.A., Collins, K.W., Garland, J., Holley, C.D., Diekhoff, G., & Evans, S.H. (1979b). Evaluation of a learning strategy training program. In H.F. O'Neil & C.D. Speilberger (Eds.), *Cognitive and affective learning strategies* (pp. 3-43). San Diego, CA: Academic Press.

Dark, V.J., & Loftus, G.R. (1976). The role of rehearsal in long-term memory performance. *Journal of Verbal Learning and Verbal Behavior, 15,* 479-490.

Davis, J.K., & Annis, L. (1976). The effects of study techniques, study preference, and familiarity on later recall. *Journal of Experimental Education, 18,* 92-96.

*de Beaugrand, R. (1981). Design criteria for process models of reading. *Reading Research Quarterly, 16,* 162-313.

DeLong, G.H. (1948). *Relative effectiveness of six methods of teaching college students how to study.* Unpublished doctoral dissertation, Ohio State University, Columbus.

Diekhoff, G.M., Brown, P.J., & Dansereau, D.F. (1982). A prose learning strategy training program based upon network and depth of processing model. *Journal of Experimental Education, 50,* 180-184.

Diggs, V.M. (1972). *The relative effectiveness of the SQ3R method, a mechanized approach, and a combination method for teaching remedial reading to college freshmen.* Unpublished doctoral dissertation, West Virginia University, Morgantown.

Doctor, R.M., Aponte, J., Bury, A., & Welch, R. (1970). Group counseling vs. behavior therapy in the treatment of college underachievers. *Behavior Research & Therapy, 8,* 89-98.

Dooling, D.J., & Christiansen, R.E. (1977). Episodic and semantic aspects of memory for prose. *Journal of Experimental Psychology: Human Learning and Memory, 3,* 428-436.

*Dooling, D.J., & Lachman, R. (1971). Effects of comprehension on retention of prose. *Journal of Experimental Psychology, 88,* 216-222.

Dooling, D.J., & Mullett, R.L. (1973). Locus of thematic effects in retention of prose. *Journal of Experimental Psychology, 97,* 404-406.

Driskell, J.L., & Kelly, E.L. (1980). A guided notetaking and study skill system for use with university freshmen predicted to fail. *Journal of Reading, 23,* 327-331.

Dyer, J.W., Riley, J., & Yenkovich, F.R. (1979). An analysis of three study skills. *Journal of Educational Research, 73,* 3-7.

Eanet, M.G. (1978). An investigation of the REAP reading/study procedure: Its rationale and effectiveness. In P.D. Pearson & J. Hansen (Eds.), *Reading: Disciplined inquiry in process and practice* (pp. 229-232). Clemson, SC: National Reading Conference.

Eanet, M.G., & Manzo, A.V. (1976). REAP: A strategy for improving reading/writing/study skills. *Journal of Reading, 19,* 647-652.

Earp, N.W. (1959). *The effect of certain study conditions on the achievement of college freshmen.* Unpublished doctoral dissertation, University of Northern Colorado, Greeley.

Ebbinghaus, H. (1913). *Memory.* New York: Columbia University Press. (Original work published 1885.)

Elshout-Mohr, M. (1983). The research perspective of the study skill group of the COWO University of Amsterdam. *Higher Education, 12,* 49-60.

Entwistle, D.J. (1960). Evaluation of study skills courses: A review. *Journal of Educational Research, 53,* 243-251.

*Entwistle, N.J. (1978). Knowledge structures and styles of learning: A summary of Pask's recent research. *British Journal of Educational Psychology, 48,* 255-265.

Entwistle, N.J., Hanley, M., & Hounsell, D. (1978). Identifying distinctive approaches to studying. *Higher Education, 8,* 365-380.

Entwistle, N.J., Hanley, M., & Ratcliffe, G. (1979). Approaches to learning and levels of understanding. *British Educational Research Journal, 5,* 99-114.

Fairbanks, M.M. (1973). *An analytical study of the relationship of specified features of reported college reading improvement programs to program effect on academic achievement.* Unpublished doctoral dissertation, West Virginia University, Morgantown.

Fairbanks, M.M., & Costello, C. (1977). Measuring and evaluating changes in underlining and notetaking skills. In P.D. Pearson & J. Hansen (Eds.), *Reading: Theory, research, and practice* (pp. 21-25). Clemson, SC: National Reading Conference.

Fass, W., & Schumacher, G. (1978). Effect of motivation, subject activity, and readability on the retention of prose material. *Journal of Educational Psychology, 70,* 803-807.

*Ford, N. (1981). Recent approaches to the study and teaching of "effective learning" in higher education. *Review of Educational Research, 51,* 345-377.

Fowler, R.L., & Barker, A.S. (1974). Effectiveness of highlighting for retention of textual materials. *Journal of Applied Psychology, 59,* 358-384.

Fox, B.J., & Siedow, M.D. (1985). An investigation of the effects of notetaking on college students' recall of signalled and unsignalled text. *Journal of Research and Development in Education, 18,* 29-36.

Fox, L. (1962). Effecting the use of efficient study habits. *Journal of Mathematics, 1,* 75-86.

Friedman, M.P., & Wilson, R.W. (1975). Application of unobtrusive measures to the study of textbook usage by college students. *Journal of Educational Psychology, 60,* 659-662.

Galloway, J.S. (1983). *A comparison of the effectiveness of two study reading techniques: The SQ3R and the HM Study Skills Program Level 1 Mapping Technique.* Unpublished doctoral dissertation, University of South Carolina, Columbia.

*Gibbs, G., Morgan, A., & Taylor, E. (1982). A review of the research of Ference Marton and the Goteborg group: A phenomenological research perspective on learning. *Higher Education, 11,* 123-145.

Glynn, S.M. (1978). Capturing readers' attention by means of typographical cueing strategies. *Educational Technology, 18,* 7-12.

Goetz, E. (1984). The role of spatial strategies in processing and remembering text: An information processing approach. In D.C. Holley & D. F. Dansereau (Eds.), *Spatial learning strategies: Techniques, applications, and related issues* (pp. 47-71). San Diego, CA: Academic Press.

Good, C.V. (1926). Proficiency in outlining. *English Journal, 15,* 737-742.

Gurrola, S. (1974). *Determination of the relative effectiveness and efficiency of selected combinations of the SQ3R study method.* Unpublished doctoral dissertation, New Mexico State University, Las Cruces.

Gustafson, D.J., & Pederson, J. (1985). SQ3R: Surveying and questioning the relevant recent (and not so recent) research. Paper presented at the Great Lakes Regional Conference, Milwaukee, WI.

*Hakstain, A.R. (1971). The effects of type of examination anticipated on test preparation and performance. *Journal of Educational Research, 64,* 319-324.

Hale, G. (1983). Student predictions of prose forgetting and the effect of study strategies. *Journal of Educational Psychology, 75,* 708-715.

Hannah, D.C. (1946). *An analysis of students' work habits.* Unpublished master's thesis, Ohio State University, Columbus.

Harris, M.B., & Ream, F. (1972). A program to improve study habits of high school students. *Psychology in the Schools, 9,* 325-330.

*Harste, J.C., & Carey, R.F. (1979). Comprehension as setting. In J.C. Harste & R.F. Carey (Eds.), *Monograph on language and reading students: New perspectives on comprhension* (pp. 4-21). Bloomington, IN: University of Indiana School of Education.

Hartley, J., & Davies, I.K. (1978). Notetaking: A critical review. *Programmed Learning and Educational Technology, 15,* 207-224.

Heerman, J.E. (1972). *The effect of a reading improvement program upon academic achievement in college.* Unpublished doctoral dissertation, University of Connecticut, Storrs.

*Holley, C.D., & Dansereau, D.F. (1984). Networking: The technique and the empirical evidence. In C.D. Holley & D.F. Dansereau (Eds.), *Spatial learning strategies: Techniques, applications, and related issues* (pp. 81-106). San Diego, CA: Academic Press.

Holley, C.D., Dansereau, D.F., McDonald, B.A., Garland, J.C., & Collins, K.W. (1979). Evaluation of a hierarchical mapping technique as an aid to prose processing. *Contemporary Educational Psychology,4,* 227-237.

Holmes, J.T. (1972). *A comparison of two study-reading methods for college students.* Unpublished doctoral dissertation, University of Northern Colorado, Greeley.

Hoon, P.W. (1974). Efficacy of three common study methods. *Psychological Reports, 35,* 1057-1058.

Hyde, T.S. (1973). The differential effects of effort and orienting tasks on the recall and organization of highly associated words. *Journal of Experimental Psychology, 79,* 111-113.

Hyde, T.S., & Jenkins, J.J. (1969). Differential effects of incidental tasks on the organization of a list of highly associated words. *Journal of Experimental Psychology, 82,* 472-481.

Hyde, T.S., & Jenkins, J.J. (1973). Recall of words as a function of semantic, graphic, and syntactic orienting tasks. *Journal of Verbal Learning and Verbal Behavior, 12,* 471-480.

Idstein, P., & Jenkins, J.R. (1972). Underlining vs. repetitive reading. *Journal of Educational Research, 65,* 321-323.

Jackson, G.B. (1980). Methods for integrative review. *Review of Educational Research, 50,* 438-460.

Jacobowitz, T. (1988). Using theory to modify practice: An illustration with SQ3R. *Journal of Reading, 32,* 126-131.

Jacoby, L.L., & Bartz, W.H. (1972). Rehearsal and transfer to long term memory. *Journal of Verbal Learning and Verbal Behavior, 11,* 561-565.

James, W. (1890). *Principles of psychology.* New York: Holt.

*Jenkins, J.J. (1979). Four points to remember: A tetrahedral model and memory experiments. In L.S. Cermak & F.I.M. Craik (Eds.), *Levels of processing in human memory* (pp. 21-33). Hillsdale, NJ: Erlbaum.

Johns, J.C., & McNamara, L.P. (1980). The sq3r study technique: A forgotten research target. *Journal of Reading, 23,* 705-708.

Johnson, C.D., & Jenkins, J.J. (1971). Two more incidental tasks that differentially affect associative clustering in recall. *Journal of Experimental Psychology, 89,* 92-95.

*Jonassen, D.H. (1985). The electronic notebook: Integrating learning strategies in coursework to raise the levels of processing. In B.S. Alloway & G.M. Mills (Eds.), *Aspects of Educational Technology* (Vol. 17, pp. 42-54). London: Kogan Page.

*Kintsch, W., & van Dijk, T.A. (1978). Toward a model of text comprehension and production. *Psychological Review, 85,* 63-94.

Kohlers, P.A. (1975). Specificity of operations in sentence recognition. *Cognitive Psychology, 7,* 289-306.

Kohlers, P.A. (1976). Reading a year later. *Journal of Experimental Psychology: Human Learning and Memory, 2,* 554-565.

Kopfstein, R.W. (1982). *sq3r doesn't work—or does it?* (ED 216 327)

Kremer, J.F., Aeschleman, S.R., & Petersen, T.P. (1983). Enhancing compliance with study skill strategies: Techniques to improve self-monitoring. *Journal of College Student Personnel, 24,* 518-524.

*Kuhn, T.S. (1970). *The structure of scientific revolution* (2nd ed.). Chicago, IL: University of Chicago.

Kulhavy, R.W., Dyer, J.W., & Silver, L. (1975). The effects of notetaking and test expectancy on the learning of text material. *Journal of Educational Research, 68,* 363-365.

*Laurillard, D.M. (1979). The processes of student learning. *Higher Education, 8,* 395-409.

Laycock, S.R., & Russell, D.H. (1941). An analysis of thirty-eight how to study manuals. *School Review, 49,* 370-379.

Levin, J.R. (1986). Four cognitive principles of learning-strategy instruction. *Educational Psychologist, 21,* 3-17.

Lockhart, R.S., Craik, F.I.M., & Jacoby, L. (1976). Depth of processing, recognition, and recall. In J. Brown (Ed.), *Recall and recognition*. New York: John Wiley & Sons.

Long, G. (1977). The development and assessment of a cognitive process based learning strategy training program enhancing prose comprehension and retention. *Dissertation Abstracts International, 38.* (University Microfilms No. 77-14, 286)

Long, G.L., & Aldersley, S. (1982). Evaluation of a technique to enhance reading comprehension. *American Annals of the Deaf, 127,* 816-820.

Martin, J.A. (1983). *An investigation into self-questioning as a study technique for college developmental students.* Unpublished doctoral dissertation, University of Georgia, Athens.

*Marton, F., & Saljo, R. (1976a). On qualitative differences in learning: 1. Outcome and process. *British Journal of Educational Psychology, 46,* 4-11.

*Marton, F., & Saljo, R. (1976b). On qualitative differences in learning: 2. Outcome as a function of the learner's conception of the task. *British Journal of Educational Psychology, 46,* 115-127.

Mathews, C.O. (1938). Comparison of methods of study for immediate and delayed recall. *Journal of Educational Psychology, 44,* 184-192.

*Mayer, R.E. (1988a). Instructional variables that influence cognitive processes during reading. In B.K. Britton & S.M. Glynn (Eds.), *Executive control processes in reading* (pp. 201-216). Hillsdale, NJ: Erlbaum.

*Mayer, R.E. (1988b). Learning strategies: An overview. In C.E. Weinstein, E.T. Goetz, & P.A. Alexander (Eds.), *Learning and study strategies: Issues in assessment, instruc-*

tion, and evaluation (pp. 11-24). San Diego, CA: Academic Press.

McClusky, F.D., & Dolch, E.W. (1924). A study outline test. *School Review, 32,* 757-772.

McConkie, G.W. (1977). Learning from text. In L. Schulman (Ed.), *Review of research in education* (Vol. 5, pp. 3-48). Itasca, IL: Peacock.

*McKeachie, W.J. (1984). Spatial strategies: Critique and educational implications. In C.D. Holley & D.F. Dansereau (Eds.), *Spatial learning strategies: Techniques, applications, and related issues* (pp. 301-312). San Diego, CA: Academic Press.

*McKeachie, W.J. (1988). The need for study strategy training. In C.E. Weinstein, E.T. Goetz, & P.A. Alexander (Eds.), *Learning and study strategies: Issues in assessment, instruction, and evaluation* (pp. 3-9). San Diego, CA: Academic Press.

McKune, E.J. (1958). *An investigation of the study procedure of college freshmen.* Unpublished doctoral dissertaion, Colorado State College, Greeley.

McReynolds, W.T., & Church, A. (1973). Self-control, study skills development, and counseling approaches to the improvement of study behavior. *Behavior Research & Therapy, 11,* 233-235.

*Meyer, M.J.F. (1977). The structure of prose: Effects on learning and memory and implications for educational practice. In R.C. Anderson, R.J. Spiro, & W.E. Montague (Eds.), *Schooling and the acquisition of knowledge* (pp. 179-200). Hillsdale, NJ: Erlbaum.

Meyer, M.J.F. (1979). Organizational patterns in prose and their use in reading. In M.L. Kamil & A.J. Moe (Eds.), *Reading research: Studies and applications.* Clemson, SC: National Reading Conference.

*Meyer, M.J.F., Brandt, D.M., & Bluth, G.J. (1980). Use of top-level structures in text: Key for reading comprehension of ninth grade students. *Reading Research Quarterly, 16,* 72-109.

*Morris, C.D., Bransford, J.D., & Franks, J.J. (1977). Levels of processing versus transfer appropriate processing. *Journal of Verbal Learning and Verbal Behavior, 16,* 519-533.

Nelson, T.O. (1977). Repetition and depth of processing. *Journal of Verbal Learning and Verbal Behavior, 16,* 151-172.

Niles, O.S. (1963). Comprehension skills. *The Reading Teacher, 17,* 2-7.

Niple, M. (1968). *The relationship of different study methods to immediate and delayed comprehension.* Unpublished doctoral dissertation, Ohio State University, Columbus.

*Nist, S.L. (1985). Tetrahedral models of learning: Applications to college reading. *Journal of College Reading and Learning, 18,* 12-19.

Nist, S.L., & Hogrebe, M.C. (1987). The role of underlining and annotating in remembering textual information. *Reading Research and Instruction, 27,* 12-25.

Noall, M.S. (1962). Effectiveness of different methods of study. *Journal of Educational Research, 56,* 51-52.

Okey, J.J. (1979). *Achievement with two college textbook reading methods with considerations for locus of control influence.* Unpublished doctoral dissertation, West Virginia University, Morgantown.

*O'Neil, H.F. (1978). *Learning strategies.* San Diego, CA: Academic Press.

Orlando, V.P. (1978). *The relative effectiveness of a modified version of SQ3R on university students' study behavior.* Unpublished doctoral dissertation, Pennsylvania State University, University Park.

Orlando, V.P. (1979). Notetaking vs. notehaving: A comparison while studying from text. In M.L. Kamil & A.J. Moe (Eds.), *Reading research: Studies and application* (pp. 177-182). Clemson, SC: National Reading Conference.

Orlando, V.P. (1980a). A comparison of notetaking strategies while studying from text. In M.L. Kamil & A.J. Moe (Eds.), *Perspectives on reading: Research and instruction* (pp. 219-222). Clemson, SC: National Reading Conference.

Orlando, V.P. (1980b). Training students to use a modified version of SQ3R: An instructional strategy. *Reading World, 20,* 65-70.

Orlando, V.P. (1984). *Reflective judgment: Implications for teaching developmental reading students.* Paper presented at the annual meeting of the Western College Reading Association, San Jose, CA.

Orlando, V.P., & Hayward, K.G. (1978). A comparison of the effectiveness of three study techniques for college students. In P.D. Pearson & J. Hansen (Eds.), *Reading: Disciplined inquiry in process and practice* (pp. 242-245). Clemson, SC: National Reading Conference.

Palmatier, R.A. (1971). The last 2 R's: A research view. In D.M. Wark (Ed.), *College and adult reading* (pp. 120-130). Minneapolis, MN: North Central Reading Association.

*Paris, S. (1988). Models and metaphors of learning strategies. In C.E. Weinstein, E.T. Goetz, & P.A. Alexander (Eds.), *Learning and study strategies: Issues in assessment, instruction, and evaluation* (pp. 299-321). San Diego, CA: Academic Press.

Pask, G. (1976a). Conversational techniques in the study and practice of education. *British Journal of Educational Psychology, 46,* 12-25.

*Pask, G. (1976b). Styles and strategies of learning. *British Journal of Educational Psychology, 46,* 218-248.

Pathberg, J.P. (1972). Validation of reading strategies in secondary school. *Journal of Reading, 22,* 332-336.

*Perry, W.G. (1970). *Intellectual and ethical development in the college years: A schema.* New York: Holt, Rinehart & Winston.

*Pichert, J.W., & Anderson, R.C. (1977). Taking different perspectives on a story. *Journal of Educational Psychology, 69,* 309-315.

*Porter, N. (1876). *Books and reading.* New York: Scribner, Armstrong.

Postman, L. (1975). Verbal learning and memory. *Annual Review of Psychology, 16,* 291-335.

*Pugh-Smith, S. (1985). Comprehension and comprehension monitoring by experienced readers. *Journal of Reading, 28,* 292-300.

Radencich, M.C., & Schumm, J.S. (1984). A survey of college reading/study skill texts. *Reading World, 24,* 34-47.

*Rickards, J.P. (1980). Notetaking, underlining, inserted questions, and organizers in text: Research conclusions and educational implications. *Educational Technology, 20,* 5-11.

Rickards, J.P., & August, G.J. (1975). Generative underlining in prose recall. *Journal of Educational Psychology, 6,* 860-865.

Rickards, J.P., & Friedman, F. (1978). The encoding versus the external storage hypothesis in notetaking. *Contemporary Educational Psychology, 3,* 136-143.

*Rigney, J.W. (1978). Learning strategies: A theoretical perspective. In H.F. O'Neil, Jr., (Ed.), *Learning strategies* (pp. 165-205). San Diego, CA: Academic Press.

Robinson, F.P. (1946). *Effective study* (2nd ed). New York: Harper & Row.

Robinson, F.P. (1961). *Effective study* (3rd ed.). New York: Harper & Row.

*Robinson, F.P. (1970). *Effective study* (4th ed). New York: Harper & Row.

*Rohwer, W.D. (1984). An invitation to an educational psychology of studying. *American Psychologist, 19,* 1-14.

*Rosenblatt, L. (1978). *The reader, the text, and the poem.* Carbondale, IL: Southern Illinois University Press.

*Ryle, G. (1949). *The concept of mind.* London: Hutchinson University Library.

Salisbury, R. (1935). Some effects of training in outlining. *English Journal, 24,* 111-116.

Saljo, R. (1981). Learning approach and outcome: Some empirical observations. *Instructional Science, 10,* 47-65.

Sanders, V. (1979). *A meta-analysis: The relationship of program content and operation factors to measured effectiveness of college reading-study programs.* Unpublished doctoral dissertation, University of the Pacific, Forest Grove, CA.

Santa, C.M., Abrams, L., & Santa, J.L. (1979). Effects of notetaking and studying on the retention of prose. *Journal of Reading Behavior, 11,* 247-260.

Scappaticci, F.T. (1977). *A study of SQ3R and select and recite reading and study skills methods in college classes.* Unpublished doctoral dissertation, Lehigh University, Bethlehem, PA.

Schnell, T.R., & Rocchio, D.J. (1978). A comparison of underlining strategies for improving reading comprehension and retention. *Reading Horizons, 18,* 106-109.

Schultz, C.B., & DiVesta, F.J. (1972). Effects of passage organization and notetaking on the selection of clustering strategies and on recall of textual material. *Journal of Educational Psychology, 63,* 244-252.

*Schumacher, G.M. (1987). Executive control in studying. In B.K. Britton & S.M. Glynn (Eds.), *Executive control processes in reading* (pp. 107-144). Hillsdale, NJ: Erlbaum.

Shimmerlik, S.M., & Nolan, J.D. (1976). Reorganization and the recall of prose. *Journal of Educational Psychology, 68,* 779-786.

*Simpson, M.L. (1984). The status of study strategy instruction: Implications for classroom teachers. *Journal of Reading, 28,* 136-142.

Simpson, M.L., Stahl, N.A., & Hayes, C.G. (1989).PORPE: A research validation. *Journal of Reading, 33,* 22-28.

Slater, W.H., Graves, M.F., & Piche, G.L. (1985). Effect of structural organizers on ninth grade students' comprehension and recall of four patterns of expository text. *Reading Research Quarterly, 20,* 189-202.

Smart, K.L., & Bruning, J.L. (1973). *An examination of the practical impact of the Von Restorf effect.* (ED 102 502)

Smith, E.R., & Standal, T.C. (1981). Learning styles and study techniques. *Journal of Reading, 24,* 599-602.

*Smith, S.L. (1982). Learning strategies of mature college learners. *Journal of Reading, 26,* 5-12.

Snyder, V. (1984). *Effects of study techniques on developmental college students' retention of textbook chapters.* (ED 243 363)

Spencer, F. (1978). SQ3R: Several queries regarding relevant research. In J.L. Vaughn & P.J. Gaus (Eds.), *Research on reading in secondary schools.*

Spilich, G.J., Vesonder, G.T., Chiesi, H.L., & Voss, J.F. (1979). Text processing of domain-related information for individuals with high and low domain knowledge. *Journal of Verbal Learning and Verbal Behavior, 18,* 275-290.

*Spiro, R.J. (1977). Remembering information from text: The "state of the schema" approach. In R.C. Anderson, R.J. Spiro, & W.E. Montague (Eds.), *Schooling and the acquisition of knowledge* (pp. 137-166). Hillsdale, NJ: Erlbaum.

Spitzer, H.F. (1939). Studies in retention. *Journal of Educational Psychology, 30,* 641-656.

*Stahl, N.A. (1983). *A historical analysis of textbook study systems.* Unpublished doctoral dissertation, University of Pittsburgh, Pittsburgh, PA.

Stiles, H.L. (1963). Inservice training for the SQ3R reading-study method. *Journal of Developmental Reading, 6,* 126-130.

Stoodt, B.D., & Balbo, E. (1979). Integrating study skills instruction with content in a secondary classroom. *Reading World, 18,* 247-252.

Stordahl, J.B., & Christensen, C.M. (1956). The effect of study techniques on comprehension and retention. *Journal of Educational Research, 49,* 561-570.

*Sulin, R.A., & Dooling, D.J. (1974). Intrusion of a thematic idea in the retention of prose. *Journal of Experimental Psychology, 103,* 255-262.

Tadlock, D.F. (1978). SQ3R: Why it works, based on an information processing theory of learning. *Journal of Reading, 22,* 110-112.

*Tessmer, M., & Jonassen, D. (1988). Learning strategies: A new instructional technology. In D. Harris (Ed.), *World yearbook for education, 1988: Education for the new technologies* (pp. 29-47). New York: Kogan Page.

*Thomas, J.W., & Rohwer, W.D. (1986). Academic studying: The role of learning strategies. *Educational Psychologist, 21,* 19-41.

Till, R.E., & Jenkins, J.J. (1973). The effect of cued orienting tasks on the free recall of words. *Journal of Verbal Learning and Verbal Behavior, 12,* 489-498.

*Todd, J. (1854). *The student's manual.* New York: Baker & Taylor.

Todd, W.B., & Kessler, C.C. (1971). The impact of level of difficulty on four measures of recall of meaningful written material. *Journal of Educational Psychology, 62,* 229-234.

*Trillin, A.S., & Associates (1980). *Teaching basic skills in college.* San Francisco, CA: Jossey-Bass.

*Tulving, E. (1972). Episodic and semantic memory. In E. Tulving & W. Donaldson (Eds.), *Organization in memory* (pp. 381-403). San Diego, CA: Academic Press.

Tulving, E., & Thompson, D.M. (1973). Encoding specificity and retrieval processes in episodic memory. *Psychological Review, 80,* 352-373.

Vaughn, J, Stillman, P.L., & Sabers, D.L. (1978). *Construction of ideational scaffolding during reading.* (ED 165 109)

Wade, S.E., & Reynolds, R.E. (1989). Developing metacognitive awareness. *Journal of Reading, 33,* 6-14.

Walker, J.E. (1982). *Study strategies: Too many, too few...or just right.* Paper presented at the annual meeting of the Western College Reading Learning Association, Long Beach, CA.

Walsh, D.A., & Jenkins, J.J. (1973). Effects of orienting tasks on free recall in incidental learning: "Difficulty," "effort," and "process" explanations. *Journal of Verbal Learning and Verbal Behavior, 12,* 481-488.

*Wark, D.M. (1965). Survey Q3R: System or superstition? In D.M. Wark (Ed.), *College and adult reading* (pp. 161-168). Minneapolis, MN: North Central Reading Association.

*Watts, I. (1741). *The improvement of the mind, or a supplement to the art of logic.* Baltimore, MD: Baly & Burns.

Waugh, N.C., & Norman, D.A. (1965). Primary memory. *Psychological Review, 72,* 89-104.

Weatherly, J.J. (1978). *The effect of underlining and study time on the recall of written materials.* Unpublished doctoral dissertation, Georgia State University, Atlanta.

Weinstein, C.E. (1977). Elaboration skills as a learning strategy. In H. F. O'Neil & C.D. Spielberger (Eds.), *Cognitive and affective learning strategies* (pp. 31-55). San Diego, CA: Academic Press.

*Weinstein, C.E., & Mayer, R.E. (1985). The teaching of learning strategies. In M.C. Wittrock (Ed.), *Handbook of research on teaching* (pp. 315-327). New York: Macmillan.

Weinstein, C.E., & Underwood, V.L. (1985). Learning strategies: The how of learning. In J.W. Segal, S.F. Chapman, & R. Glaser (Eds.), *Thinking and learning skills: Vol. 1. Relating instruction to research* (pp. 241-258). Hillsdale, NJ: Erlbaum.

Weist, R.M. (1972). The role of rehearsal: Recopy or reconstruct. *Journal of Verbal Learning and Verbal Behavior, 11,* 440-450.

Wickelgren, W.A. (1973). The long and short of memory. *Psychological Bulletin, 80,* 425-438.

Willmore, D.J. (1966). *A comparison of four methods of studying a college textbook.* Unpublished doctoral dissertation, University of Minnesota, Minneapolis.

*Wittrock, M.C. (1988). A constructive review of learning strategies. In C.E. Weinstein, E.T. Goetz, & P.A. Alexander (Eds.), *Learning and study strategies: Issues in assessment, instruction, and evaluation* (pp. 287-298). San Diego, CA: Academic Press.

*Wittrock, M.C., Marks, C.B., & Doctorow, M. (1975). Reading as a generative process. *Journal of Educational Psychology, 67,* 484-489.

Wooster, G.F. (1953). *Teaching the SQ3R method of study: An investigation of the instructional approach.* Unpublished doctoral dissertation, Ohio State University, Columbus.

4

The Value of Taking Notes During Lectures

Thomas H. Anderson
Bonnie B. Armbruster

C ollege students typically spend 10 or more hours per week attending lectures. How can they make the most efficient use of that time? Is the time-honored suggestion to listen carefully and take good notes a sound one? If taking notes is helpful, how is it helpful? Seward (1910) answered some of these questions in about the same way many experts do today, by proposing two functions of notetaking:

Ask our friend, the average student, what is the use of taking notes, and he will answer without hesitation: Why, to preserve a record of what a lecturer has said, for the sake of future use, especially in reviewing for examinations (p. 1).

Our notes should, indeed, be useful for purposes of review yet that usefulness is not their chief value. They should be full, yet contain only what the mind has accepted as significant. The practical value of our notes will take care of itself as a matter of secondary importance if we devote ourselves wholly to their main purposes—to make us alert, clearheaded, and responsible as we listen to a lecture, and to serve as a ready test of the firmness of our grasp (p. 9).

These two purposes, identified by Seward 80 years ago, are still the hypothesized functions of notetaking. Today the functions are commonly labeled "external storage" and "encoding." The idea behind encoding is that the process of taking notes helps the notetaker learn and remember information; the external storage hypothesis postulates that the value of taking notes lies in preserving information for later use, such as review before an examination. Thus, the encoding and external storage functions offer two opportunities for learning information from a lecture: once while listening and recording notes and again while reviewing or studying the notes prior to an examination.

Recent theory and research in cognitive psychology suggest how taking notes on a lecture may affect learning at both the listening/encoding and reviewing/studying stages. In this chapter, we review the research on taking notes during lectures from a cognitive psychology perspective and draw implications for college instruction.

A Perspective from Cognitive Psychology

We have found the conceptual frameworks of levels of processing (Anderson, 1970, 1972; Craik & Lockhart, 1972) and the related transfer appropriate processing (Morris, Bransford, & Franks, 1977) to be particularly useful in interpreting the research literature on listening and notetaking. (Bretzing & Kulhavy, 1979, and Kiewra, 1985a, have also used the transfer appropriate processing framework to help conceptualize the effects of notetaking strategies.)

According to the concept of levels of processing, information is processed in a hierarchy of stages, from an analysis of surface, physical, or sensory features to a deeper semantic analysis involving the extraction of meaning. The level of analysis performed on incoming information determines what gets stored in memory. A deeper, semantic processing of information is assumed to be necessary for long term memory.

The idea of levels of processing is not without its critics. For example, Eysenck (1978) claims that no suitable criteria are available for indexing either the depth or the breadth of encoding. Lockhart and Craik (1978) agree that the definition of *depth* is somewhat circular and that the hypothesis cannot be classified as a theory, but they contend that it possesses considerable heuristic value. In this chapter, we build on the heuristic value of this model with no claims as to its theoretical purity.

The levels of processing framework suggests that what is learned from listening or reading is a function of two interacting factors:

1. The amount and type of cognitive effort given to processing the information. Different cognitive activities involve different levels of processing.

2. The nature of the input information. Many characteristics of the incoming information affect cognitive processing, including familiarity of content, concept load (number and density of ideas), and organization.

The conceptual framework of transfer appropriate processing (Morris, Bransford, & Franks, 1977) suggests another important factor influencing what is learned from listening or reading: the learner's purposes or goals.

According to the concept of transfer appropriate processing, particular types of processing are not inherently deep or shallow; their level depends on the learner's goals. Thus, the value of particular processing activities must be defined in relation to the particular goals of the learner. For example, if the learner's purpose is to attend to the "superficial" aspects of text—for instance, the number of multisyllabic words—deeper, more meaningful processing is not appropriate and may actually impede encoding of the target material. Transfer appropriate processing suggests that learners' knowledge or expectations about what they will do with the input information will guide the way they choose to process the information (Anderson & Armbruster, 1984).

Encoding Hypothesis Implications

We believe that the concepts of levels of processing and transfer appropriate processing have three main implications for the encoding hypothesis. First, theoretically the student could take notes at any level of processing. An example of notetaking while processing the information at a very superficial level is the verbatim script a secretary makes using shorthand or the script made by a court recorder during a trial. A somewhat deeper level of processing is involved in selectively noting information—for instance, identifying and recording main ideas that a speaker highlights. Finally, a deep, semantic level of processing is involved in recording notes that represent some meaningful transformation of the input information—for example, notes in which the listener paraphrases, draws inferences from, or elaborates on points made in lecture.

The second implication for the encoding hypothesis is that the level of processing will depend on characteristics of the lecture itself. Notetaking takes time and cognitive effort, both to process and to record the information. Deeper processing requires more time and effort than shallow processing; recording the notes takes a set amount of time and effort, regardless of the level of processing involved. Of course, there is a limit to the amount of time and effort students can or will spend on taking notes. Therefore, lecture characteristics that affect the time and effort involved in taking notes will also affect processing.

One such characteristic is the rate of presentation. The faster the lecture, the greater the restrictions on taking notes, especially when the notetaking involves processing at deeper levels. Another characteristic related to presentation rate is concept load. If the incoming information is dense, students have both a heavier cognitive processing load and more notes to record, both of which take time.

The third implication for the encoding hypothesis, suggested by the concept of transfer appropriate processing, is that students' purposes or goals will influence notetaking during a lecture. College students usually have some knowledge or expectation about what they should bring away from the lecture; for example, they may know what type of question is likely to appear on an upcoming examination. This knowledge or expectation establishes a purpose for taking notes and determines what students will note and what kind of cognitive processing they will engage in as they record notes.

These three implications provide a framework for interpreting the results of research related to the encoding hypothesis of notetaking.

Research Related to Encoding

Some of the research discussed in this section consists of experimental tests of the encoding function. The basic experimental procedure used to determine whether the process of taking notes facilitates learning is fairly simple. Subjects are randomly divided into at least two groups; those in one group take notes during a lecture, while the others listen to the lecture without taking notes. After the lecture, with no opportunity for reviewing notes, all students take the same criterion test. The idea is that if taking notes helps students process the information in a lecture, the notetaking group should score higher on the criterion test.

Our tally indicates that 10 experimental studies support the encoding hypothesis and 14 fail to do so (Table 1). Note that the entries in Table 1 differ in two respects from the entries in similar tables presented by Hartley (1983), Hartley and Davies (1978), and Kiewra (1985a). Unlike the summary tables of these other reviewers, ours does not include studies that investigated notetaking while reading or studies that gave students time to review (even mentally) before taking the criterion test. In addition, we sometimes reanalyzed the data reported in the original studies and drew different conclusions from those of the inves-

Table 1
Breakdown of Studies Testing the Encoding Hypothesis

Support for Encoding	No Support for Encoding
Taped Lectures	
Barnett, DiVesta, and Rogozinski, 1981 (audio)	Aiken, Thomas, and Shennum, 1975 (audio)
Berliner, 1969 (video)	Ash and Carlton, 1953 (film)
DiVesta and Gray, 1972 (audio)	Carter and Van Matre, 1975 (audio)
DiVesta and Gray, 1973 (2 studies) (audio)	Howe, 1970 (audio)
Maqsud, 1980 (audio)	McClendon, 1958 (audio)
Peper and Mayer, 1978 (1 study) (video)	Peper and Mayer, 1978 (2 studies) (video)
	Riley and Dyer, 1979 (audio)
Live Lectures	
Crawford, 1925a (Experiment 3)	Annis and Davis, 1975
Jones, 1923 (1 study)	Crawford, 1925a (Experiments 1 and 2)
Weiland and Kingsbury, 1979	Gilbert, 1975
	Jones, 1923 (2 studies)

tigators and/or reviewers. For example, we decided that only experiment 3 from Crawford (1925a) supported the encoding hypothesis, while experiments 1 and 2 failed to do so. (Crawford's other experiments do not fall within our guidelines for a test of the encoding hypothesis.)

It is noteworthy that among the nine studies in Table 1 that used live lectures, only three show support for the encoding hypothesis. Two of these studies are quite dated, and the more modern one failed to randomly assign individual students to treatment groups. Clearly, then, any effect of notetaking on encoding is difficult to demonstrate, especially in actual classroom settings. Nonetheless, it is possible to explain and interpret the results of several studies in terms of the implications we drew from the two processing models.

Qualitative Differences in Processing

Among the research related to the encoding hypothesis are two studies showing that students engage in qualitatively different kinds of processing when taking notes as opposed to when listening only. In the first of three experiments reported by Peper and Mayer (1978), subjects either listened only or listened and took notes during a 16-minute videotaped lecture on the Fortran computer language. They then took a test consisting of both generative items (which required subjects to write a computer program to solve a problem) and interpretive items (which were least similar to how the information was presented and thus required "far transfer" of knowledge). Results indicated a significant interaction between problem type and notetaking effectiveness: notetakers did better on interpretive items, and nonnotetakers did better on generative items. The second experiment essentially replicated the results of the first experiment, except with different lecture content. In the third experiment, subjects again listened to the Fortran lecture. Results on a free recall test revealed an interaction between notetaking and the types of items recalled. The notetakers remembered more about how a computer operates and included more intrusions, while the listen-only group recalled more technical symbols. The notetakers also produced more coherently patterned recalls, indicating that the learned information was structured differently. Thus the three experiments in the Peper and Mayer study demonstrate that notetaking *can* involve qualitative differences in cognitive processing during either input or recall.

A study reported by Howe (1976) provides additional evidence that notetaking entails different cognitive processing than does listening only. In this study, subjects were asked to take notes as they listened to an audiotaped excerpt from a novel. They then relinquished their notes for analysis. Results on a free recall test given one week later showed that noted items had a 0.34 probability of being recalled, while items not noted had only a 0.05 probability of being recalled. In other words, subjects were almost seven times more likely to recall information that appeared in their notes than information not recorded. Howe also developed the notion of "efficient" note-taking—the ratio of the number of meaningful ideas to the number of words used to record those ideas. The positive correlation between the efficient note index and the number of meaningful units recalled on the test was significant (0.53), thus indicating that what students chose to note was processed differently than other information.

A result similar to Howe's finding on efficient notetaking is reported by Maqsud (1980). In two experiments, college students classified as short or long notetakers either listened only or listened and took notes during a 2,200-word audiotaped lecture presented at 110 words a minute. Students who took brief notes recalled more information units than those who took detailed notes. Perhaps Maqsud's short notetakers are similar to Howe's efficient notetakers, with short, efficient notes reflecting deeper cognitive processing of the information. Short notetakers may parse and summarize a segment of lecture information, then search their memory to see if they know a word or phrase that represents that summary. If they do have such a label, they record it. On the other hand, long notetakers may be less likely to summarize and search memory, instead recording a more literal representation of the information.

Care must be exercised in interpreting Maqsud's results since the students were categorized into treatment groups based on their notetaking history in his course. This technique can confound important independent variables. For example, short notetakers may be more motivated and intelligent than long notetakers. Without random assignment to treatment groups, one cannot be sure whether some variables will be confounded, consequently affecting the criterion measure.

Lecture Effects

Other research related to the encoding hypothesis provides evidence that cognitive processing is affected by characteristics of the lecture, particularly presentation rate and information density.

We found some data on lecture presentation rates in a typical college course. Maddox and Hoole (1975) report the highest lecturing rate at 114 words a minute, while Fisher and Harris (1973) report the lowest rate at 44 words a minute. Nye (1978) refers to an in-between index of 84 words a minute. Obviously, the rate of presentation varies widely, depending both on speech rate and on how often and how long the lecturer pauses to entertain questions or discussion, writes on the chalkboard, or otherwise interrupts the presentation of the lecture material.

Evidence for the influence of presentation rate on the ability to process information from a lecture is found in a study by Aiken, Thomas, and Shennum (1975). Subjects listened to an audiotaped four-part lecture that was presented in one of three ways: once at a rate of 120 words a minute, once at 240 words a minute, or twice at 240 words a minute. Students either took notes during the lecture or listened only. The faster speed of 240 words a minute impeded recall, suggesting that a fast rate interferes with deeper cognitive processing. This study also provides evidence of the effect of information density on recall. Some subjects in the study listened to a low-density lecture (106 information units per 2,000 words), while others heard a high-density lecture (206 information units per 2,000 words). Subjects who listened to the low-density lecture recalled more information units, or facts, than did those who listened to the high-density lecture, suggesting that the dense content overloaded subjects' cognitive processing capabilities.

The Aiken, Thomas, and Shennum (1975) study also provides evidence on the effects of taking notes at different times. In the study, subjects who took notes did so either during the four lecture segments (parallel notetaking) or during breaks between lecture segments (spaced notetaking). Spaced notetakers recalled more information units than did parallel notetakers. We suggest that characteristics of the lecture precluded deeper processing by parallel notetakers. Remember that the slowest presentation rate in this study was 120 words a minute, well above the typical presentation rates reported by other researchers. Also, the density of information was quite high for some parallel notetakers. The requirement of taking notes while listening to dense, rapidly presented information could well have impeded deep cognitive processing of the information because the combination of listening and taking notes exceeded the students' cognitive capacity.

In studies by DiVesta and Gray (1972, 1973), one possible explanation that arises for this support for the encoding hypothesis of notetaking is that certain characteristics of the lecture were amenable to deeper processing by notetakers. In these studies, subjects listened to 5-minute audiotaped lectures presented at 100 words a minute. We argue this was probably little enough information presented at low enough speeds to allow deeper processing while subjects recorded notes.

In contrast to studies supporting the encoding hypothesis, nonsupportive studies had lecture conditions that were not conducive to deeper cognitive processing by notetakers. For example, in a study by Ash and Carlton (1953), college students viewed two 20-minute informational films. Some students took notes while viewing the films; others did not. Multiple choice and objective item tests were administered immediately after the films. For one film, the test scores of the two groups showed no statistically significant differences; for the other film, the notetakers scored significantly lower than the non-notetakers. We do not find these results surprising. Since films are characterized by concurrent streams of verbal and pictorial information, they often have a heavy information load. Therefore, it is likely that the requirement of taking notes while attending to a variety of information sources interfered with students' cognitive processing.

In a study by Peters (1972), college students either listened only or listened and took notes during an audiotaped lecture presented at two rates, 146 and 202 words a minute. On a 25-item multiple choice test (with a suspiciously low internal consistency reliability), subjects who did not take notes scored significantly higher than did subjects who took notes. Once again, we are not surprised at the results. The presentation rates of 146 and 202 words a minute are among the highest of any study we reviewed. Also, the lecture, on the topic of steel as an alloy, was probably dense with unfamiliar, difficult information. Given these factors, the additional requirement of taking notes is likely to have interfered with the cognitive processing of the notetakers.

Students' Purposes

In addition to the characteristics of the lecture itself, students' purposes or goals can influence how they take notes during a lecture. In the absence of specific information to the contrary, most college students assume that they will be tested on main ideas or important points and therefore try to record these ideas in their notes.

Research provides some evidence that this is so. Several researchers have analyzed student notes and compared the overlap with the lecture script and/or a set of "ideal" notes. (Ideal notes were compiled by the lecturer or a teaching assistant and were based on the lecturer's notes or script.) Such analyses show that, on average, students note a little more than one-half of the ideas from the lecture. One study showed that students recorded 60 percent of ideal notes (Locke, 1977), another showed 53 percent of relevant material (Crawford, 1925b), a third, 52 percent of ideal notes (Maddox & Hoole, 1975), and a fourth, 50 percent of ideal notes (Hartley & Cameron, 1967). Since it is difficult to determine from these studies how many of these ideal notes might be considered main points, we cannot tell how many main points students recorded in these studies. Nye (1978) analyzed students' notes differently and showed that they recorded 70 percent of the main points and 38 percent of minor points. On average, 50 percent of all lecture points were recorded—a value very consistent with those reported above. Thus, it appears that students typically record between 50 and 70 percent of the main ideas from a lecture.

Research also shows that certain conditions of the lecture situation can influence what students note. Maddox and Hoole (1975) reported that 70 to 96 percent of students were likely to note ideas when they were: (1) written on a chalkboard by the lecturer (a finding also reported by Locke, 1977), (2) dictated in the form of headings or subheadings, (3) read aloud as numbered points, (4) given strong signaling, or (5) repeated or restated. Maddox and Hoole also reported that students were *not* likely to note ideas when the lecturer: (1) was standing away from the lecture notes, (2) used ideas in a joke, or (3) used visual aids (an observation also made by Hartley & Cameron, 1967). Students were also unlikely to take notes when another student asked a question of the lecturer. Apparently, the students in the research studies cited above had learned that certain lecture conditions served as cues for what was likely or unlikely to appear on examinations; this expectation shaped their notetaking behavior.

One condition of the lecture situation that influences students' goals, and therefore their notetaking behavior, is specific directions about what to note or how to note it. One relevant study is reported by Barnett, DiVesta, and Rogozinski (1981). In this study, college students were told that they were in an experiment and would be tested later. Then they listened to an 1,800-word lecture on "The History of Roads in America" presented at 120 words a minute. Some students listened only, some listened and took notes, and some listened and were given notes. The students who took notes were told to listen carefully, identify key ideas, and place them in outline form. The notes that were given to students contained most of the important ideas from the lecture in outline form; these students were told not to take additional notes. Immediately after the lecture, some subjects engaged in a 20-minute "filler task" that required them to mentally manipulate objects in space. (Other students engaged in more relevant types of review activities, discussed later in this chapter; here we are concerned only with the filler task, no-review group.)

On a 20-item cued response test, the listening-only group obtained a mean score of 3.2 items correct, compared with the take-notes group mean of 8.2, a statistically significant difference. (The 5.9 mean of the group that was given notes did not differ significantly from the means of either the listening-only group or the take-notes group.) The 256 percent margin of superiority for notetakers over nonnotetakers is clear evidence that notetaking can facilitate cognitive processing. We think that notetaking was particularly effective in this study because the subjects were encouraged to take notes in a way that entailed relatively deep cognitive processing of the information; subjects could hardly take notes on main ideas organized into an outline without processing the information at a fairly deep level.

Finally, in a study by Kiewra and Fletcher (1984), undergraduate students were instructed to take factual, conceptual, or relational notes while listening to a taped lecture. Factual notes were described as those that record factual information or details, conceptual notes as those that summarize only main ideas, and relational notes as those that relate the main ideas to new situations. An analysis of their notes indicates that most students took conceptual notes irrespective of the instructions given. The group that was instructed to take only factual notes took more total notes (factual plus conceptual and relational) than the other two groups. Kiewra and Fletcher concluded that notetaking behavior was only moderately manipulated. Moderate manipulation seems like a reasonable outcome since these students had no notetaking training to change their natural inclination to record mostly main ideas (Nye, 1978).

From our review of the research testing the encoding hypothesis, we conclude that students can remember more about main points if they take notes on them than if they listen without taking notes. We suspect this is true only under certain conditions, however: (1) when the lecture situation (including such factors as speed of presentation and density of ideas) is such that taking notes does not interfere with cognitive processing, and (2) when students are able to take the kind of notes that entail deep processing of the input information, or at least processing appropriate to the criterion test.

External Storage Hypothesis Implications

The levels of processing and transfer appropriate processing models also have implications for the hypothesized ex-

Anderson and Armbruster

ternal storage function of notetaking. First, as with the encoding state, any level of processing could be taking place as students review notes before an examination. Students could do anything from skimming their notes (shallow processing) to meaningfully transforming their notes by outlining or elaborating them (deep processing).

A second implication for the external storage hypothesis is that the level of processing students use while studying notes is heavily influenced by characteristics of the notes. As the concept of transfer appropriate processing suggests, among the important characteristics of the notes is their ability to cue recall or reconstruction of information needed for the criterion test. In most cases, the ability to cue recall or reconstruction is probably a function of the degree of correspondence between the notes and the original lecture. The influence of the notes also varies with the time between taking notes and studying them: the greater the time elapsed, the greater the influence of the notes on learning outcomes. This relationship holds because information processed earlier is more likely to have been forgotten than information processed more recently.

A third implication for the external storage hypothesis is that the students' purposes or goals will influence how they choose to process their notes during review. Presumably, motivated college students will try to deeply process the information they know or expect will be on the upcoming examination. Their ability to do so will be constrained by the content of their notes (as discussed above) and the time available for study.

These implications provide a framework for interpreting the results of research related to the external storage hypothesis of notetaking.

Research Related to External Storage

In this section we discuss both correlational and experimental studies. The correlational studies were not specifically designed to test the external storage hypothesis; rather, their purpose was to investigate the general relationship between notetaking and some criterion measure without regard to whether learning occurred during either listening or review. In these naturalistic studies (Collingwood & Hughes, 1978; Crawford, 1925b; Locke, 1977), students took notes during a lecture and were tested later. The researchers did not determine whether students actually reviewed their notes; however, since the criterion tests were regular course examinations, it is likely that students did so. Also, the delay between the lecture and the criterion test in these studies makes the external storage function more plausible as an explanation of the results. The longer the delay between listening and testing, the less the effect of initial processing during the encoding stage because of how much students would have forgotten in the interim.

Researchers interested in experimentally testing the external storage hypothesis have usually tested it in conjunction with the encoding hypothesis. Therefore, a typical design includes groups that listen only and review provided notes, groups that take notes and review either their own or provided notes, and groups that take notes but do not review prior to the criterion test. Ideally, there should be a delay between the time of listening and the review (to decrease the effect of initial processing during the encoding stage), and the criterion test should immediately follow the review. Presumably, if the only or primary function of notetaking is external storage, the group that listens and reviews provided notes will outperform the other two groups on the criterion test.

Of the 15 studies we discuss in the next section, all provide some support for the external storage hypothesis. Obviously, researchers have found it easier to demonstrate the external storage hypothesis than the encoding hypothesis.

Congruence Between Notes and Tests

Several correlational studies we reviewed investigated the influence of note characteristics on learning outcomes. In general, these studies suggest that the greater the congruence between the information in the notes available for review and the information required on the criterion test, the better the learning outcomes.

Crawford (1925b) lectured in seven classes to a total of 211 students, who took notes in their usual manner. Between 2 and 35 days after the lectures, the students took announced quizzes on the lecture material. Most of the quizzes were essentially free recall tests of the lectures. After the quizzes, the students' notes were collected and analyzed. The points covered in the lectures were compared with those recorded in the notes and on the quizzes. Crawford found a significant positive correlation between the number of points recorded in the notes and the number recalled on the quiz. Furthermore, points noted correctly had a 0.50 correlation with correct quiz answers. Vaguely noted points tended to have a near zero or negative correlation with correct quiz answers. Points omitted from the notes had only a 0.14 probability of being answered correctly on the quiz.

In a naturalistic study completed more recently, Locke (1977) analyzed the notes taken during lectures and the course grades earned by 161 students in 12 courses. He found a significant positive correlation between completeness of lecture notes and course grades (although this relationship held only for the material not written on the chalkboard by the lecturer).

Kiewra (1985a) cites a naturalistic study in which the number of lecture notes taken over a 4-week period had a 0.61 correlation with performance on the course exam covering both lecture and reading material, and a 0.78 correlation with performance on items derived from the lecture only.

Other studies have compared the effectiveness of having students review their own notes with that of having them review supplied notes. In a naturalistic study by Collingwood and Hughes (1978), college students listened to three consecutive live lectures in their regular course in each of three notetaking conditions: taking notes, receiving full notes (a complete typed copy of the lecturer's notes, including diagrams), and receiving partial notes (an edited copy of the lecturer's notes, including headings, key points, unlabeled diagram outlines, tables, and references). Four weeks after the last lecture, students took a midterm exam including multiple choice items covering the lecture content. Students performed best when they had full notes and worst when they took their own notes, suggesting that the more complete the notes, the better the performance.

A naturalistic study by Powers and Powers (1978) with college students also presents some evidence in favor of the effectiveness of instructor-prepared notes. During the first half of the term, one experimental group received instructor-prepared notes, while the second experimental group served as a control. During the second half of the term, the roles were reversed. The instructor-prepared notes elaborated on content presented in the text. Multiple choice exams administered throughout the term tested these elaborated concepts. During the first half of the term, students who received notes and those who did not performed similarly, with no significant differences. During the second half of the term, however, students who received notes outperformed students who did not receive notes. Unfortunately, the authors did not provide enough information to permit speculation about why the provided notes were effective only in the second half of the term. The change could have been due to differences in course content, tests, instructor-prepared notes, or student attention.

In an experimental study by Annis and Davis (1975), college students were assigned to one of several notetaking and review conditions. Two weeks after listening to a 40-minute lecture on behavior modification, the students were given a 10-minute lecture review session followed by an examination consisting of objective and short-answer questions. A single factor analysis of variance revealed significant overall differences. Although posttest multiple comparisons were not performed, the students who reviewed mentally or not at all received the lowest means, and the students who reviewed notes received the highest means. These results support the value of notes as an external storage device. Furthermore, within the group that reviewed notes, the highest mean was obtained by students who reviewed their own and the lecturer's notes; this result suggests that the more complete the notes, the greater the potential for learning during review.

In the second of two experiments by Maqsud (1980), college students were assigned to one of four review conditions one week after listening to a taped lecture: some reviewed personal lecture notes, some reviewed a teacher-prepared handout described as "detailed but simplified and organized" (p. 292), some reviewed both personal notes and the teacher-prepared handout, and some reviewed mentally, without notes. Three hours after review, students were asked to recall as much as they could of the lecture. Those who reviewed personal notes and the teacher-prepared handout had the highest recall, followed by those who reviewed the teacher's handout, then those who reviewed personal notes, and finally those who reviewed mentally. The results support the value of reviewing notes over reviewing mentally and again suggest that the more information subjects have available at the time of review, the more they are likely to recall.

In three similar studies reported by Kiewra and his colleagues (Kiewra, 1985b, 1985c; Kiewra & Benton, 1985), college students listened to a 20-minute videotaped lecture with or without taking notes. (In the Kiewra, 1985b, study, a third group consisted of students who did not attend the lecture.) Two days after the lecture, notetakers reviewed their own notes while listeners (and nonattenders) reviewed notes provided by the instructor. The provided notes contained all the critical points of the lecture, including main ideas, supporting details, and examples. In all three studies, subjects who reviewed the instructor's notes scored significantly higher on factual multiple choice tests than did subjects who reviewed their own notes. Kiewra attributes this effect to the nature of the review materials, reporting that the instructor's notes were far more complete, detailed, and organized than were the students' notes.

While generally supporting the importance of the external storage function of notes, Fisher and Harris (1973) present some ambiguous results with respect to the idea of the more notes the better. In this study, college students listened to a live lecture presented at a rate of about 44 words a minute in one of five notetaking and review conditions. Immediately following the lecture, the students reviewed their notes or engaged in mental review for 10 minutes before completing a free recall test and an objective test. (Note that this situation does not represent an ideal test of the external storage hypothesis.) Three weeks later, the students took another objective test without review. Students who were allowed to review notes generally scored higher on all measures than did students who reviewed mentally. Those who reviewed their own notes outperformed those who reviewed the lecturer's notes, which may have been anything from a full transcript to a very sketchy outline. Since the lecture was presented at a very slow rate, students could have made quite complete notes on their own; it is possible that their notes were more complete than the lecturer's notes, thus providing support for the importance of congruence between note content and criterion test requirements. Finally, even if the lecturer's notes were more complete than their own notes, students may not have had time to review them adequately during the short review period.

Annis (1981) also reports results that seem to contradict the idea of the more notes the better. In this study, college students listened to a live lecture in a regular classroom context. One group of students received a full lecture transcript and were told not to take notes, one received partial notes consisting of headings and key points with space left for taking notes, and a third group was given blank paper and instructed to take notes. The criterion test consisted of multiple choice and short answer items on the regular midterm 2 weeks after the lecture. Students who took their own notes or received partial notes scored significantly higher than those who received full notes. However, the largest performance difference on the criterion test was on the short answer items, a fact that may help explain this apparently contradictory finding. Clearly, those students who wrote their own notes or filled in the partial notes were processing information in a more transfer appropriate way. The effect of this difference generally masked the effects of "the more notes the better" principle.

Transfer Appropriateness of Notes

The congruence between notes and test is only part of the answer to the value of review. In addition to having the right information available, students must process it in a transfer appropriate way—that is, the way they will need to use the information on the criterion test. A study by Carter and Van Matre (1975) suggests that opportunity for review is particularly helpful if subjects know what and how to review. Carter and Van Matre had college students listen to a 17-minute taped lecture in one of four studying conditions: they either took and reviewed notes, took notes and reviewed mentally, listened only and reviewed mentally, or listened only and engaged in a filler task. Free recall tests and alternate forms of a completion test consisting of verbatim and paraphrase items were administered immediately and after 1 week. Half the subjects reviewed prior to the delayed test and half did not.

The group that took and reviewed notes scored significantly higher than the group that took notes and reviewed mentally on all tests, a result that supports the external storage hypothesis. In addition, the group that took and reviewed notes scored higher on verbatim than on paraphrase items on the delayed test, while those in the other groups did not perform differently on the two types of items. Carter and Van Matre (1975) offer the explanation that over time, differences between verbatim and paraphrase performance tend to diminish, probably as a result of forgetting the superficially processed (verbatim) information. However, the students who were allowed to review their notes prior to the delayed test had a second opportunity to process the information. We know that subjects had the opportunity to review verbatim information, since the authors report that subjects' notes consisted largely of verbatim excerpts from the lecture. We suggest, too, that subjects probably expected a test similar to the one they already had, and thus had a reason to process the information in a way that was appropriate for answering verbatim questions. These explanations are also supported by the fact that students who were not permitted to review notes prior to the delayed test showed no significant differences in performance on verbatim and paraphrase tests.

Hartley and Marshall (1974) provide additional evidence that review is particularly helpful if subjects have the right information as well as some knowledge of how they will need to use it on the criterion test. In this naturalistic study, college students heard a lecture in a regular classroom context and took a recall test immediately afterwards. Then they were given 10 minutes to revise their notes, after which they took the same test again. The students were divided into good and poor notetakers on the basis of their relinquished notes. Although the good and poor notetakers scored similarly on the immediate test, the good notetakers improved more than did the poor notetakers on the second test. One possible explanation is that although all students had the same knowledge of the criterion test at the time of review, good notetakers were better able to use this knowledge during review because they had better information available in their notes.

Barnett, DiVesta, and Rogozinski (1981) report an experiment designed to test the effect of different types of processing during review. In the experiment discussed earlier in this chapter, the authors had observed that elaborating on notes (i.e., relating notes to prior knowledge) during review failed to improve test performance and in some cases even interfered with performance. They designed an experiment to test the hypothesis that students who elaborate on their notes learn qualitatively different kinds of information than students who simply review their notes. In this experiment, students either took notes or were provided with notes. During the review session, they either wrote down key ideas and details from the lecture or elaborated on their notes. Eight days later, the students completed an individualized test containing four types of completion items: items from the lecture itself, which were common to all students; items from the reviews or elaborations created by the individual; items randomly selected from a pool created for subjects who reviewed their notes; and items randomly selected from a pool created for subjects who elaborated

Anderson and Armbruster

on their notes. The researchers found that students who reviewed scored higher on the common items than those who
elaborated. They also found that, on average, students scored
about twice as high on items taken from their own protocols
than on items taken from the protocols of other subjects.

Barnett, DiVesta, and Rogozinski (1981) conclude that
elaboration during review interfered with performance on
items requiring accurate recall because subjects were not processing the information in a manner consistent with the way
they needed to use the information on the test. Subjects did
best when they were given test items congruent with the way
they had processed the information during review.

In the Kiewra and Benton (1985) study discussed previously, the authors also investigated the effect of different types
of processing during review. In this study, college students either took notes on or listened only to a 20-minute videotaped
lecture. Notes were collected after the lecture. Two days later,
notetakers received their own notes back while listeners received the instructor's notes. Both groups also received practice
questions designed to tap higher-order knowledge (application,
analysis, synthesis, and problem solving). Half the subjects were
given an answer key (feedback) for the questions. Subjects were
given 25 minutes to study the notes and answer the questions
before taking a multiple choice test consisting of factual and
higher-order items. When feedback accompanied the practice
questions, performance was facilitated on the factual items. The
authors speculate that the learning resulting from completing
the practice questions and receiving feedback provided an effective framework for organizing and for recalling associated
factual information. In other words, the activity that this experimental group engaged in during review was appropriate to the
demands of the criterion task.

From our review of the research testing the external storage hypothesis, we conclude that an important function of
notes is their availability for use in later review or study. The
bulk of the evidence shows that reviewing notes before a criterion test is likely to improve performance. Notes are helpful to

the extent that they contain the information that will be tested. In most cases, this probably translates as the more information the better. But what students do with their notes is also important. Students who engage in transfer appropriate processing (i.e., those who cognitively process the information in their notes in the same way they will need to use it on the criterion test) will fare the best.

A Notetaking System

We next take a critical look at advice given by Pauk (1984) about taking notes from lectures. Pauk has integrated 30 years of experience at the Cornell University Reading Research Center into the "Cornell System for Taking Notes." The critical features of this system are presented and discussed below.

Before the lecture:

- Take a few minutes to look over your notes on the previous lecture, to provide continuity with the lecture you are about to hear.

- Record your notes completely and clearly so they will still have meaning for you long after you have taken them.

- Strive to capture general ideas rather than illustrative details.

After the lecture:

- Consolidate your notes during your first free time after class by reading through them to clarify handwriting and meaning. Also underline or box in the words containing the main ideas.

- Restructure the notes by reading them and then jotting down key words and phrases that represent your reflections on them.

- Use the jottings as cues to help you recall and recite aloud the facts and ideas of the lecture in your own words.

Anderson and Armbruster

Pauk (1984) appears to be advocating the use of notetaking primarily as an external storage device: "Remember that your purpose is to record the lecturer's ideas for later study" (p. 122). We suspect, however, that he does not deny the potential benefits of encoding: "Notetaking does not interfere with listening and comprehension; in fact, it helps you listen" (p. 122). We disagree with one aspect of Pauk's advice in that research shows that there are some conditions in which notetaking can interfere with comprehension. Under those conditions in which one seemingly has to sacrifice either comprehension or notetaking, Pauk appears to recommend sacrificing comprehension: "Don't stop to ponder the ideas presented. By the time you have finished reflecting on idea number one, the lecturer will probably be on idea number four or five" (p. 123). In many lecture courses, however, we suspect that when students become confused, it would be wise for them to forgo notetaking and ask the lecturer to clarify the point rather than to faithfully persevere with the notetaking process. A successful clarification might help smooth out the encoding and notetaking processes for the remainder of the lecture.

We are not certain what level of detail Pauk advocates in notetaking. For example, in one place he suggests that students "strive to capture general ideas rather than illustrative details" (p. 128), while in another place his advice is to "make notes on main ideas and on subideas, examples, and details" (p. 122). Perhaps the best summary of Pauk's advice on this point is "make your notes complete and clear enough so that they will have meaning for you weeks and months later" (p. 125). In general we think Pauk's advice is consistent with our analysis of the research findings.

Conclusions

We raised a question at the beginning of this chapter: "Is the time-honored suggestion to listen carefully and take good notes a sound one?" From our review of the research, we conclude that the answer is yes, provided that the information in the notes is consistent with the criterion test and that enough time is provided for a review of that information.

Another question we raised was, "If taking notes is helpful, how is it helpful?" In general, the research supports the encoding and external storage functions of notetaking proposed by Seward (1910) more than three-quarters of a century ago. The process of taking notes can help the notetaker learn and remember information, and the notes themselves can preserve information for later use.

Drawing from cognitive psychology, particularly the concepts of levels of processing and transfer appropriate processing, we have been able to gain some insight into the conditions of effective notetaking. From our review of the research, we have concluded that students potentially benefit from the encoding function, as long as the lecture situation permits deeper processing while taking notes and students take the kind of notes that entail processing the information in the way they will need to use it on the criterion test. (We emphasize that the benefit is only potential because most of the live lecture research is not very convincing.) Also, students can benefit from reviewing notes when the notes contain the information that will be tested and when students process the information in a way similar to how it will be used on the criterion test.

Based on these conclusions, we offer the following recommendations for college instructors and students.

Instructors:

1. Lecture in a way that encourages processing the right information by presenting the material at a reasonable rate and by signaling important content (for example, by writing it on the chalkboard).

2. Design valid, reliable tests that assess students' understanding of important, relevant information. Then give students enough information about the tests to let them know how to take good notes and how to study them.

3. Encourage students to take notes in a way that entails

deep processing, and allow time for such processing. When lecturing on new and difficult topics, pause and direct students to write and think about what you are saying. Remember, cognition is time consuming.

4. Since students' notes typically include only about one-half of the lecturer's ideas, distribute lecture notes if it is important for students to know a comprehensive set of ideas.

5. Early in a course, collect students' notes after a lecture and review them. Use this exercise to determine how well your lectures are being understood and which students need assistance in notetaking skills. Give these students advice, refer them to a general source on how to develop notetaking skills (for example, Pauk, 1984), or refer them to a study skills center directed by the university or a private company.

Students:

1. Take complete notes as long as it does not interfere with listening and comprehending the information in the lecture.

2. If the speed of the lecture makes it impossible to record the most important ideas, note the names of the key concepts that pass by and later supplement your notes with information from the textbook, lecturer handouts, or notes from other students.

3. Try to take notes in a way that entails deep processing, or after the lecture revise your notes in such a way.

4. Find out as much as possible about the tests, and use this information as a guide for taking and studying notes.

5. Study your notes before the test in a transfer appropriate manner. If you anticipate multiple choice or short answer questions, practice asking and answer-

ing questions with a friend. If you anticipate an essay test, organize your notes around the major topics and commit that organization to memory. Try talking through the ideas from the organization with a friend.

Finally, we conclude with some lingering questions that beg for additional research on notetaking:

1. Under what conditions and to what extent is the Cornell or any other well-publicized notetaking system effective? How should such a system be modified to accommodate various content areas, study guides, examinations, and textbooks?

2. How and when should students be taught to take good notes? Is early elementary school too early? Is college too late?

3. Since taking notes is most effective when the notes are used as a means of externally storing ideas, what are the effects of the note providing services that are now prevalent on college campuses? Are there any advantages to using conferencing, or group notes, that can be generated on a network of computers?

4. How does a good, relevant textbook differ from a set of good, revelant notes? Is the students' objective in taking notes simply to create a personalized adjunct textbook?

5. What are the most effective ways of studying or reviewing a set of comprehensive notes? Is reciting notes a reasonable way to study for a test? Is generating questions from notes an effective review strategy?

6. Are findings in the recent novice-expert literature—for instance, that on writing (Scardamalia & Bereiter, 1985)—relevant to research on notetaking and studying? Do we gain any explanatory advantages by thinking about notetaking as just one strategy in a

Anderson and Armbruster

larger problem-solving effort (where the problem is to learn the material and do well on the test) rather than as a necessary procedure for improving comprehension?

References and Suggested Readings

Aiken, E.G., Thomas, G.S., & Shennum, W.A. (1975). Memory for a lecture: Effects of notes, lecture rate, and informational density. *Journal of Educational Psychology, 67*(3), 430-444.

Anderson, R.C. (1970). Control of student mediating processes during verbal learning and instruction. *Review of Educational Research, 40,* 349-369.

Anderson, R.C. (1972). How to construct achievement tests to assess comprehension. *Review of Educational Research, 42,* 145-170.

*Anderson, T.H., & Armbruster, B.B. (1984). Studying. In P.D. Pearson (Ed.), *Handbook of reading research* (pp. 657-679). New York: Longman.

Annis, L.F. (1981). Effect of preference for assigned lecture notes on student achievement. *Journal of Educational Research, 74,* 179-182.

Annis, L., & Davis, J.K. (1975). The effect of encoding and an external memory device on notetaking. *Journal of Experimental Education, 44,* 44-46.

Ash, P., & Carlton, B.J. (1953). The value of notetaking during film learning. *British Journal of Educational Psychology, 23,* 121-125.

Barnett, J.E., DiVesta, F.J., & Rogozinski, J.T. (1981). What is learned in notetaking? *Journal of Educational Psychology, 73*(2), 181-192.

Berliner, D.C. (1969). *Effects of test-like events and notetaking on learning from lecture instruction.* Paper presented to the American Psychological Association, Washington, DC.

Bretzing, B.H., & Kulhavy, R.W. (1979). Notetaking and depth of processing. *Contemporary Educational Psychology, 4,* 145-153.

Carter, J.F., & Van Matre, N.H. (1975). Notetaking versus note having. *Journal of Educational Psychology, 67*(6), 900-904.

Collingwood, V., & Hughes, D.C. (1978). Effects of three types of university lecture notes on student achievement. *Journal of Educational Psychology, 70*(2), 175-179.

Craik, F.I.M., & Lockhart, R.S. (1972). Levels of processing: A framework for memory research. *Journal of Verbal Learning and Verbal Behavior, 11,* 671-684.

*Crawford, C.C. (1925a). Some experimental studies of the results of college notetaking. *Journal of Educational Research, 12*(5), 379-386.

Crawford, C.C. (1925b). The correlation between college lecture notes and quiz papers. *Journal of Educational Research, 12*(4), 282-291.

DiVesta, F.J., & Gray, G.S. (1972). Listening and notetaking. *Journal of Educational Psychology, 63,* 8-14.

DiVesta, F.J., & Gray, G.S. (1973). Listening and notetaking II: Immediate and delayed recall as functions of variations in thematic continuity, notetaking, and length of listening-review intervals. *Journal of Educational Psychology, 64*(3), 278-287.

Eysenck, M.W. (1978). Levels of processing: A critique. *British Journal of Psychology, 69,* 157-169.

Fisher, J.L., & Harris, M.B. (1973). Effect of notetaking and review on recall. *Journal of Educational Psychology, 50*(6), 301-304.

Gilbert, T. (1975). The effects of dictated notes on the recall and comprehension of connected and disconnected verbal material. *British Journal of Educational Technology, 6*(1), 61-65.

*Hartley, J. (1983). Notetaking research: Resetting the scoreboard. *Bulletin of the British Psychology Society, 36*, 13-14.

Hartley, J., & Cameron, A. (1967). Some observations on the efficiency of lecturing. *Educational Review, 20*, 30-37.

*Hartley, J., & Davies, I.K. (1978). Notetaking: A critical review. *Programmed Learning and Educational Technology, 15*(3), 207-224.

Hartley, J., & Marshall, S. (1974). On notes and notetaking. *Universities Quarterly, 28*, 225-235.

Howe, M.J.A. (1970). Notetaking strategy, review and long-term retention of verbal information. *Journal of Educational Research, 63*, 285.

Howe, M.J.A. (1976). What is the value of taking notes? *Improving College and University Teaching, 24*, 22-24.

Jones, H.E. (1923). Experimental studies of college teaching. *Archives of Psychology, 68*.

*Kiewra, K.A. (1985a). Investigating notetaking and review: A depth of processing alternative. *Educational Psychologist, 20*, 23-32.

Kiewra, K.A. (1985b). Students' notetaking behaviors and the efficacy of providing the instructor's notes for review. *Contemporary Educational Psychology, 10*, 378-386.

Kiewra, K.A. (1985c). Learning from a lecture: An investigation of notetaking, review, and attendance at a lecture. *Human Learning, 4*, 73-77.

Kiewra, K.A., & Benton, S.L. (1985). The effects of higher-order review questions with feedback on achievement among learners who take notes or receive the instructor's notes. *Human Learning, 4*, 225-231.

Kiewra, K.A., & Fletcher, H.J. (1984). The relationship between levels of notetaking and achievement. *Human Learning, 3*, 272-280.

Locke, E.A. (1977). An empirical study of lecture notetaking among college students. *Journal of Educational Research, 71*, 93-99.

Lockhart, R.S., & Craik, F.I.M. (1978). Levels of processing: A reply to Eysenck. *British Journal of Psychology, 69*, 171-175.

Maddox, H., & Hoole, E. (1975). Performance decrement in the lecture. *Educational Review, 28*, 17-30.

Maqsud, M. (1980). Effects of personal lecture notes and teacher notes on recall of university students. *British Journal of Educational Psychology, 50*, 289-294.

McClendon, P.I. (1958). An experimental study of the relationship between the notetaking practices and listening comprehension of college freshmen during expository lectures. *Speech Monographs, 25*, 222-228.

Morris, C.D., Bransford, J.D., & Franks, J.J. (1977). Levels of processing versus transfer appropriate processing. *Journal of Verbal Learning and Verbal Behavior, 16*, 519-533.

Nye, P.A. (1978). Student variable in relation to notetaking during a lecture. *Programmed Learning and Educational Technology, 15*, 196-200.

*Pauk, W. (1984). *How to study in college*. Boston, MA: Houghton Mifflin.

*Peper, R.J., & Mayer, R.E. (1978). Note taking as a generative activity. *Journal of Educational Psychology, 70*(4), 514-522.

Peters, D.L. (1972). Effects of note taking and rate of presentation on short-term objective test performance. *Journal of Educational Psychology, 63*(3), 276-280.

Powers, S.M., & Powers, W.A. (1978). Instructor-prepared notes and achievement in introductory psychology. *Journal of Experimental Education, 47*, 37-41.

Riley, F.D., & Dyer, J. (1979). The effects of notetaking while reading or listening. *Reading World, 19*, 51-56.

Scardamalia, M., & Bereiter, C. (1985). Written composition. In M.C. Wittrock (Ed.), *Handbook of research on teaching* (Vol. 3). New York: Macmillan.

Seward, S.S., Jr. (1910). *Notetaking*. Boston, MA: Allyn & Bacon.

Weiland, A., & Kingsbury, S.J., (1979). Immediate and delayed recall of lecture material as a function of note taking. *Journal of Educational Research, 72*, 228-230.

5

External Factors That Influence Study

Victoria J. Risko
Marino C. Alvarez
Marilyn M. Fairbanks

ollege students are expected to be self-directed and
to use available resources effectively. Orienting students for successful academic achievement in college typically includes giving them advice on how to manage time to make studying effective, how to organize the study environment to make it conducive for learning, and how to use the library to complete class assignments. In this chapter we discuss time management, study environment, and library use as factors that influence students' study efforts. College instructors and authors of study skills texts often refer to these three areas as "how-to-study" behaviors. The goal of teaching students how to monitor their time and study environment and how to use library resources is to enhance their ability to make wise decisions about how and when to study. College students need to become proficient in controlling each of these factors in order to manage their own learning.

We decided to start our investigation of these three factors by examining study skills texts to identify what the authors recommend for enhancing college students' study habits with respect to our target factors. From an inspection of the *Subject Guide to Books in Print* (1988), we generated a list of 64 study skills texts published between 1981 and 1988. We eliminated 45 of these texts because they focused primarily on providing exercises for timed readings, fluency development, or practice in reading skills (e.g., vocabulary, word analysis), without providing substantial information about strategies to improve students' study habits.

The remaining 19 books exhibit characteristics of texts organized to develop reading or study strategies, as defined by Heinrichs and LaBranche (1986) in their classification of college reading texts. We conducted a content analysis of these 19 texts by coding information to determine the extent to which each of the three target areas was addressed; the nature of the information and suggestions given for each area so that a comparison between these ideas and relevant literature could be made; and the extent to which the authors of these study skills texts cited or explicitly related their suggestions to theoretical or research literature. Each of the 19 texts contained information about at least one of our areas, with corresponding suggestions and strategies that students could adopt to enhance their study efforts. Table 1 shows a summary of our survey results.

Our survey aided the development of this chapter in several ways. First, we were able to conclude that each study skills text reviewed addressed at least one target area, and usually two or all three of them. While we discuss the specific recommendations made by study skills authors elsewhere in this chapter, our review in general revealed a wide variance in the authors' inclusion of study skill areas within their texts.

Second, most of the authors do not relate their suggestions explicitly to supporting literature. Instead, they present their information informally and in a conversational style. Pauk's (1984) view that most college students who are learning how to develop better study habits are not interested in reading theory

Table 1
Relevant Areas Addressed in Current College Study Skills Texts

Text	Areas Addressed			Rationale Provided For Suggestions Given/Activities Included			
	Time Management	Study Environment	Library Use	Pragmatic Reasons	Theoretical Basis Established	Research Cited in Text	Research Reference List
Annis, 1983	X	X		Yes	Yes	Yes	Yes
Bradley, 1983		X		No	No	No	No
Brooks, 1984	X			Yes	Yes	No	No
Joffe, 1982	X		X	Yes	No	No	No
McWhorter, 1986a	X	X	X	Yes	No	Minimal	No
McWhorter, 1986b		X		Yes	No	No	No
McWhorter, 1987		X		Yes	No	Yes	Yes
Nist & Diehl, 1985	X	X		Yes	No	Minimal	No
Pauk, 1984	X	X	X	Yes	No	Minimal	No
Postman, Keckler, & Schneckner, 1985			X	Yes	No	No	No
Scales & Biggs, 1983	X	X		Yes	No	No	No
Schmelzer, Khristen, & Browning, 1984	X			Yes	No	Minimal	No
Shepherd, 1982	X	X	X	Yes	No	No	No
Shepherd, 1984	X			Yes	No	No	No
Shepherd, 1987	X	X	X	Yes	No	No	No
Sherman, 1984	X			Yes	No	No	No
Sotiriou, 1984	X	X		Yes	No	No	No
Walter & Siebert, 1984	X	X	X	Yes	No	Minimal	Minimal
Wood, 1986	X	X	X	Yes	No	Minimal	No

or research references seems prevalent in the texts we surveyed. The authors of these books present practical, readable suggestions based on their years of experience with college students. Most of the authors indicate that their suggestions are supported by a theoretical or research base, but they do not specify such relationships. One text (Cohen & Poppino, 1982), organized according to a theoretical framework, follows the Piagetian phases of exploration, invention, application, and recapitulation to illustrate how students can apply what they are learning. The remaining authors all present suggestions for applying their recommended strategies to content classes, although they do not indicate that they relied on a theoretical or empirical base to guide their recommendations.

We believe that this treatment of the related theoretical and empirical research may be disadvantageous to college students who have study problems. Presenting the findings from research so simply can encourage college students to overgeneralize an author's recommendations. For example, instead of stating that research indicates that music undermines study efforts, it would be more accurate and appropriate for study skills authors to describe how separate investigations have identified which conditions and for which tasks music may be distracting.

This chapter provides a review of the theoretical and empirical literature that relates to each of the three identified areas. Since the authors of study skills texts generally suggest, either explicitly or implicitly, that their recommendations have a theoretical or research basis, we were interested in determining how closely their suggestions did reflect the literature. For the most part, only literature relevant to college-age students is included. For each of our three areas, we organized our review to present (1) a brief review of what the authors of the 19 study skills texts recommend, (2) a review of the literature related to our target area and an interpretation of the correspondence between what is recommended and what is supported or proposed in the literature, and (3) a discussion of the issues addressed. We conclude with recommendations for research and instruction.

Time Management

Time management, the first of the three areas to be discussed, is often difficult for college students. The concept of how time can best be allocated to serve one's needs is often poorly understood, and the complaint "I need more time to study" is commonly used to explain poor study performance.

Suggestions from Study Skills Texts

The authors of the texts we reviewed had varied, yet similar, suggestions for students' use of time. Most authors of college study skills texts recommend devising a schedule as a way to regulate time. Some authors recommend developing a flexible schedule based on individual needs and circumstances (Nist & Diehl, 1985; Pauk, 1984; Shepherd, 1984, 1987; Wood, 1986), while others advocate a fixed time schedule (McWhorter, 1987; Sotiriou, 1984; Walter & Siebert, 1984).

Authors of college study skills texts often seem to make statements based on personal beliefs rather than on research. This tendency is illustrated in the mixed assortment of recommendations given under time management headings. Several authors organize their time management recommendations to contrast unhelpful and helpful time management habits. Most give advice focusing on what students should not do. "Absolutely no television...by far the greatest modern time waster" (Pauk, 1984, p. 53); don't "allow yourself to study more than the allotted time" (Walter & Siebert, 1984, p. 60).

The statements in these texts often need further clarification or elaboration. For example: "Always try to make your new subject as different as possible from the subject you have just finished [studying]. That way your mind can be assimilating one topic while you are reading about another" (Walter & Siebert, 1984, p. 61). The authors of this book should have explained more clearly how it is possible for students to be simultaneously concentrating on their reading and assimilating information about a different topic. Further, it is not clear how different the topics need to be for effective studying of each.

As indicated earlier, many authors refer vaguely to research to support their claims rather than stating specific sources for their information. Statements such as "Research studies have consistently showed that the most successful students stick to a very strict schedule of work and play" (Sotiriou, 1984, p. 11), for example, do not provide readers with enough information about the nature of the research that was conducted. Another example is authors' frequent assertion that "research studies" support the idea that exercise gives bodies more energy. And Walter and Siebert (1984), as well as Sotiriou, claim general research support for a relationship between memorization ability and amount of sleep.

While such well-intentioned advice appears logical and even may be supported in related literature, these suggestions tend to overgeneralize what needs to be done and to avoid answering specific questions about time management. For example, is a schedule good for everyone? How much flexibility should be allowed? When might extenuating circumstances allow one to deviate from a schedule? Does everyone need to eat a healthy breakfast? Is it imperative to stop studying at a given time? Questions such as these identify areas that need further investigation.

Time management seems to involve two main issues: the time needed for learning and the time spent on learning. A related issue that is seldom mentioned in the texts surveyed is the relationship between the type of task to be learned and the time needed for and spent on learning it. Authors of study skills texts focus instead on how to develop schedules to regulate time and how to adhere to these schedules. Our review of the related literature supports the need for further studies either to validate current advice given to college students or to suggest more precise procedures for using schedules to manage time.

Related Literature

Our goals for the literature review on time management were (1) to identify theoretical and/or empirical support for time use as a factor that contributes to effective study, and (2) to examine the relationship between time and other study variables. We have categorized the information we gathered into two groups: time variance according to student learning needs, and the nature of the learning tasks. As indicated by Carroll's (1963) earlier model of school learning, five factors affect student learning rates: aptitude, ability to understand, engaged time on task, allocated instructional time, and quality of instruction. Since these factors are interdependent, the study of time cannot preclude a closer investigation of the impact of these related factors on learning.

Time variance. Time variance, or the amount of time needed for learning, is highly idiosyncratic. Arlin (1984a, 1984b) and others (Atkinson, 1968; Carroll, 1967; Glazer, 1968; Washbourne, Vogel, & Gray, 1926) have demonstrated the need for time adjustment according to both the task assigned and students' learning needs. Describing the learning time of fast and slow learners, they indicated that the use of time for each group remained relatively constant regardless of task demands. In none of these studies did students use less than the allotted time, even when tasks may have required less time expenditure. It seems that students who want to use study time efficiently need to learn to discriminate between time allocated for learning and time needed for learning (Schmelzer et al., 1987).

Meaningful learning, defined as the process of linking new concepts with those already stored in memory, is dependent on the degree of associational background a learner has with these concepts (Johnson, 1975). Understanding concepts depends on the learner's conceptual organization, the clarity of ideas presented, and the relevance of learning the new material (Alvarez, 1983). However, as Frijda (1978) mentions, information as encounterd in a teaching and learning situation is unlikely to be presented in a form ideally matched to the learner's existing knowledge structure. Study skills texts need to acknowledge that use of time must be flexible and responsive to students' learning needs. Rather than advising students to adhere to a uniform allocation of time, these texts should make it clear that time demands will differ depending on factors such as prior knowledge, the context in which information is presented, and the nature of the learning task (Shuell, 1986).

Nature of the learning task. Most of the research on time management neglects to address how the type of learning task may affect the amount of time needed to learn. As Gettinger (1984) states, research is needed in both clarifying task conditions and determining the relationship between task demands and time allocation. Time becomes a more important variable when it is measured against the difficulty of the task to be learned. Both Carroll (1970) and Bloom (1974) have estimated that approximately 90 percent of students can master some school learning tasks within a 5:1 time ratio (that is, the slowest 5 percent of the students require about five times more time to complete the assignment correctly than the fastest 5 percent). This 5:1 ratio is used to provide an approximation of individual differences among students when completing tasks. However, as Lyon (1984) notes, there is a paucity of research investigating how this ratio may vary according to different task demands; for example, it is possible that the ratio increases with the difficulty of the task.

Lyon conducted one study that investigated how the nature of the learning task may affect time allocation (see also Lyon & Gettinger, 1985). Lyon studied the effect of learning tasks related to Bloom's (1956) taxonomy levels of knowledge, comprehension, and application. The results indicated that students need more time to learn tasks that are higher in the hierarchical order. Most students could learn literal knowledge tasks within the 5:1 ratio proposed by Bloom (1974) and Carroll (1970), but only one-third were able to complete learning tasks requiring application in a similar amount of time. Lyon (1984) concluded that junior high students who can handle literal knowledge tasks need to be taught independent study strategies for those tasks that require interpretive and applicative modes of comprehension. Although his subjects were seventh and eighth graders, the findings may well apply to college freshmen who are classified as remedial students. Obviously, this is an area that needs further research.

Risko, Alvarez, and Fairbanks

How a student manages time is personal and idiosyncratic. When the authors of study skills texts state that time needs to be managed, they are giving good and well-intentioned advice. However, when they make dogmatic statements about how this time must be scheduled, they go beyond sound reasoning. When this occurs, authors' recommendations become guided by what they would like to see happen rather than by what research says should happen. The idea that students need to manage time in a constrained manner in order to become successful learners needs to be substantiated before authors of college study skills texts make absolute statements about using scheduled time.

Implications

There are differences between the time needed for learning, the time spent on learning (time on task does not necessarily guarantee learning), the types of tasks students are asked to learn, and the quality and presentation of instruction. Research seems to be lacking on the type and level of tasks college students need to learn and the time needed to learn them (Carroll, 1989; Gettinger, 1984, 1985). It is one thing to know about independent learning/study strategies and another to have the inclination and ability to apply these strategies to different kinds of learning tasks.

McPartland and Karweit (1979) advocate a need for further research measuring the extent to which learning time can be reduced through appropriate types and amounts of instruction. Further research dealing with the quality of instruction and presentation of material needs to be conducted with college students of varying abilities. Researchers have studied the effects of teacher-assisted learning strategies on college students' performance. These strategies include the use of advance organizers (Ausubel, 1960, 1968), structured overviews or graphic organizers (Barron, 1969; Earle, 1969; Earle & Barron, 1973), concept maps and vee diagrams (Gowin, 1987; Novak & Gowin, 1984), thematic organizers (Alvarez & Risko, 1982, 1989), and case analyses (Christensen, 1987; Dewing, 1931; Gragg, 1954; Hunt, 1951; Lawrence, 1953) in single and varied contexts. More research needs to be conducted to determine whether these kinds of strategies can help college students better manage their time.

Another area that needs more study is procrastination and its effect on students' use of scheduled study time. Ottens (1982) has developed a Guaranteed Scheduling Technique designed to overcome procrastination tendencies in college students. Students using this technique record the amount of time spent on studies each day and work with counselors to assess how much they procrastinate and to help establish self-control and time management. Aside from this work, however, research in this area is scarce. Factors influencing procrastination that need further study include the nature and duration of an assignment, the ability to complete an assignment (knowing how), and the assignment's relevance. The effects of procrastination on the time spent on and needed for learning also need to be investigated.

Study Environment Management

Like time management, study environment management is an area over which students need to exercise some control. It seems logical that studying in an environment conducive to learning can be helpful even if students possess the knowledge, skills, and attitudes important for academic success. The specific elements that constitute an ideal study environment are difficult to define, however. In addition, the extent to which any set of study circumstances can be ideal for all students and all study situations is a complex issue.

Suggestions from Study Skills Texts

Authors of study skills texts make many suggestions about where and under what circumstances students should study. Their advice can be broken down into four categories: (1) establishing a place for study, (2) minimizing or eliminating distractions such as peers or music, (3) determining the optimal degree of comfort for studying, and (4) being ready to study.

Risko, Alvarez, and Fairbanks

Establishing a place for study. Study skills texts typically advise students to select a definite place (sometimes two places) to study and confine their studying to that place. Students are also usually advised not to engage in other activities in that designated place (Annis, 1983; McWhorter, 1986a, 1986b; Nist & Diehl, 1985; Pauk, 1984; Sherman, 1984; Sotiriou, 1984; Wood, 1986). Authors vary somewhat in the explanations given for this advice, but they usually refer to the conditioning principle that if certain behaviors occur in one place, that place becomes a cue or signal for that behavior to occur. Also, some authors indicate that designation of a study area is one way of controlling distractions—especially auditory ones, since familiar sounds are often unconsciously blocked out while new or less familiar sounds are more distracting.

Annis (1983) advises students to "bring your study behavior under what is called stimulus control" (p. 4). She stresses the possible self-reinforcement or reward value involved for the student who chooses to study in a place or places specifically reserved for study only. She admonishes students to "absolutely avoid incompatible activities such as leisure reading, daydreaming, or snacking" (p. 5). She also discusses the characteristics that should govern selection of the chosen study place, such as adequate heat and lighting and minimal distractions.

Bradley (1983) takes a somewhat modified approach to this selection of study places. While she advocates minimizing the number of places for study, she also suggests that at least one place of study be at home. She further indicates that studying in places where other activities take place, such as on the kitchen or dining room table, might not be as debilitating to study as many study skills instructors and authors suggest. She advises students, however, that they should be conscious of the possibility of disruptions in such locations because of associations with other activities, and suggests that they plan their study for times when others sharing the living quarters will be occupied elsewhere.

Controlling distractions. Study skills texts commonly advise students to study in places where visual and auditory distractions are minimal. They tell students to keep pictures and memorabilia out of sight, and to minimize the number of objects that suggest other activities. Walter and Siebert (1984) present a vivid scenario of how visual distractions can disrupt study. They describe a young woman attempting to study who is first distracted by photos that make her remember pleasant times in the past, then by her record albums, then by magazines that make her think of what she hasn't read, and finally by photos of friends that prompt her to abandon her study attempt in favor of phoning her friends.

With reference to auditory distractions, most authors suggest a quiet study environment, but several mention that students may vary in their tolerance to noise (McWhorter 1986a, 1986b; Pauk, 1984; Sherman, 1984). Pauk tells students who know they need silence while studying to seek a quiet place, even if it means walking several blocks to a library. Sherman asserts that complete quiet can actually distract some students, and advises students to keep a record of the times they are distracted when studying in order to determine their own problems and needs. McWhorter advises students to try several levels of noise (quiet, soft background music, louder music or other noises) to see what works best for them.

In discussing study distractions, textbook authors typically refer to peers as factors that may divert attention from study. A few authors deal with the issue more specifically. Sotiriou (1984) advises students to locate their dorm room or apartment desks as far away from friends as possible. If study conditions prove unsuitable at home, he suggests going to the library but cautions students to sit away from friends to avoid being distracted or interrupted by conversations irrelevant to the subject being studied. Walter and Siebert (1984) state that students who are frequently interrupted by noise, friends, or family should make a definite effort to change the behaviors of those around them. They advise students to avoid making rigid rules, instead asking friends or family what they think is reasonable, explaining exactly what is needed, and asking for cooperation. Similarly, Bradley (1983) expresses concern about possible interruptions when studying at home and seems to place a high priority on planning for productive study. Students who generate a creative plan for minimizing the amount of time and energy taken away from study and learning can lessen their chances of feeling victimized by those around them.

Some current study skills authors (Nist & Diehl, 1985; Pauk 1984; Sotiriou, 1984) advise students against studying with music in the background. Nist and Diehl argue that "you cannot study efficiently with a radio or television playing, because your attention will be divided" (p. 15). Pauk summarizes 13 studies (not specifically referenced in his text) pertaining to music and learning performance, conducted with students of varying ages and grade levels. Seven of the studies indicated that music was a definite distraction, five indicated no significant effect from music, and in one instance, the listening activity (listening to bell ringing) was found to facilitate performance. Pauk concludes that music is a potential distractor and advises students not to turn it on to avoid the risk of ineffective study.

Degree of comfort. The degree to which a student should be comfortable when studying is a point on which authors vary considerably. Nist and Diehl (1985) advocate a straight, hard-backed chair, while Pauk grumbles that "more ink and more words have been wasted extolling the virtues of a straight-backed, hard-seated hickory chair than on any other single piece of study equipment" (p. 61). Instead, Pauk advises students to choose a cushioned, comfortable chair. Sherman (1984) and McWhorter (1986a, 1986b) state that being either too comfortable or too uncomfortable could distract students from study. Most authors advise against studying in bed. Bradley (1983) goes so far as to tell students that the best way to treat insomnia is to go to bed with a textbook. Authors also advise that the room's lighting should be adequate and the temperature comfortable but not so warm as to induce sleepiness.

Readiness for study. Most authors advise students to have books, equipment, and other materials ready for study so they won't have to waste time by constantly leaving the study area to find additional materials. Sotiriou (1984) and Wood (1986) tell students to keep all of their books and study materials in one place, stating that keeping everything in a box will do if students do not have access to a desk or bookshelves of their own.

While most authors indicate that students should study in a designated place free from distractions, some acknowledge that not all students will react alike. The authors advise students to try out various environments, analyzing their study behavior to determine the environment that is best for them.

Related Literature

Theoretical and empirical literature related to study environment management has focused on the effects of stimulus control on students' study habits. One group of studies has concentrated on students' ability to exert rigid control over the variables in their place of study. Another set of studies has investigated more carefully the relationship between peer influence and study effectiveness. A third group focuses on the influence of music on students' ability to study.

Place variables. The advice of study skills texts to choose specified places designated for study only has been tested to a limited degree in a series of stimulus control studies. In the literature, these studies are evaluated and discussed in tandem with studies on other self-control strategies, such as self-monitoring, self-reward, or problem solving (see Chapter 6, this volume). According to Richards (1981), who prepared a review of self-control studies, stimulus control or environmental planning involves developing "an environment conducive to adaptive behavior" by manipulating cues associated with desirable and undesirable responses (p. 164).

Stimulus control directives are sometimes evaluated as part of an academic improvement package that includes study skills or other self-control strategies. This type of evaluation makes it difficult to determine the value of stimulus control in itself. For example, one summer school program for college student volunteers included 11 lessons encompassing both study behavior and self-control strategies (Beneke & Harris, 1972). In the one lesson devoted to stimulus control, students were instructed to extablish one or two places as a stimulus and to do all or most of their studying there. They were told to make sure their chosen place had good lighting, was free of distractions, and had no associations with behavior incompatible with studying. The total program of 11 lessons reportedly resulted in improved grade point average for three semesters following the study, but neither the contributions made by the stimulus control lesson nor the extent to which students followed it could be determined.

In a study with 106 college students, Richards et al. (1976) combined stimulus control with study behavior questionnaires and advice on study skills and compared this treatment with six different combinations of self-monitoring and study skills advice. In terms of grades, the group that received self-monitoring and study skills advice performed better than the group that received stimulus control and study skills advice; however, the stimulus control/study skills advice group performed better than the no-treatment control group. Since the study design did not include a control group of students who were given study skills advice only, it is impossible to determine whether the study skills advice or the stimulus control treatment was responsible for the superiority of this group over the control group.

Studies in which stimulus control was evaluated as a separate variable have not shown promising results (Richards, 1981). Richards (1975) reported a study that involved 101 students using a pyramid design and entailing combinations of self-control procedures as additions to study skills advice. Stimulus control was included in two of the subgroups, one in combination with self-monitoring and study skills advice, and the other combined with study skills advice alone. Results indicated that while self-monitoring was a helpful addition to study skills advice, stimulus control was not. Stimulus control, self-reinforcement, and a combination of the two formed the three experimental group treatments in a study by Ziesat, Rosenthan, and White (1978) involving college students who wanted to eliminate procrastination behaviors. Although students in the experimental groups reported increased time spent on study and those in the control groups did not, no improvement was found in overall grade point average. And according to Richards (1981), students showed a definite dislike for stimulus control procedures because these procedures were too different from their usual study practices. They also seemed to have problems carrying out the procedures independently and needed much direction from counselors.

Earlier in this discussion, we stated that most authors of study skills texts advise students to study in one or two pre-selected places, to use those places for study only, and to avoid distractions as much as possible. This advice was based on established conditioning principles, which theoretically should operate to increase student motivation by establishing a signal or "set" for study (Richards, 1981). Nonetheless, attempts to put such advice into operation through stimulus control procedures have not to date proved highly effective in enhancing academic performance.

Peer influence on study effectiveness. Two major areas have been empirically explored in terms of peer influence on study effectiveness: recognizing and coping with peer-related distractions, and determining the positive influences of peers on study performance. In the first area, the study problems and habits of adult college students (24 years of age or older) and students in the more typical college age range (18 to 21) were compared in a study that used self-report questionnaires and extensive interviews (Hogan & Hendrickson, 1984). Students in both age groups indicated "family/roommate" as a major study problem.

In a three-step study reported by Hefferman and Richards (1981), isolation from peers during study emerged as a possible effective way of managing some of the problems associated with peer influence during study. In the first step of the study, the investigators interviewed students who had reported overcoming previous problems in studying. The two methods that seemed the most helpful were planning schedules and studying away from peers. In the second step of the study, the senior author observed 4 successful and 2 unsuccessful students in their natural study environments and concluded that peer isolation, indicated as a modified stimulus control technique, was effective. In the third phase of the study, 45 college student volunteers who were seriously concerned about their poor study behaviors were randomly assigned to one of three groups: an experimental group in which students were encouraged to plan schedules and study away from peers; an experimental group in which a problem-solving technique and the broader, more formal stimulus control procedure discussed earlier were combined; and a no-treatment control group. Hefferman and Richards reported that the first group, which studied away from peers and planned schedules, scored better on examinations than either of the other two groups by a significant (although modest) margin. Although the authors considered the results promising, they advised caution in interpreting them because of the modest difference in performance, the necessity of relying on self-report measures in the initial phase of the study, and the possibility that students who successfully devise their own study strategies somehow may be different from those who have not been successful in such attempts.

Attempts to structure peer influence to improve study effectiveness and academic performance have included peer tutoring programs, collaborative study efforts, and residential hall arrangements. Fremouw and Feindler (1978) reported on a peer review study in which students requesting help with study skills were paired together as study partners; one member of each pair acted as a tutor to the other, after receiving training in study skills and self-control techniques from both psychology and study skills instructors. Results from interview data indicated that the students who had been trained as tutors showed as much improvement in study effectiveness as did those who met with graduate teaching assistants in an established study skills program, and more than a control group. It should be noted that because the peer tutors were trained by both psychology and study skills instructors, they invested more preparation time than the professional staff, who were trained only by the study skills instructors. Changes in grade performance across the groups were not significant.

The effects of positive peer influence on study habits, as measured by the Brown and Holtzman Survey of Study Habits and Attitudes (Brown & Holtzman, 1967), were investigated in a study involving 15 pairs of college roommates (Cappella, Hetzler, & MacKenzie, 1983). One randomly selected member of each pair was told the purpose of the study and was asked to spend 1 hour a day for 7 days modeling good study behavior and encouraging the roommate to study. At the end of the designated period, the students who had been encouraged by their roommates improved considerably on the Survey of Study Habits and Attitudes. The roommates themselves improved somewhat, but not significantly.

The effects of voluntary, semivoluntary, and nonvoluntary peer monitoring programs on college students' academic performance have also been investigated. In these studies, students in a particular college class are paired to study together for a designated minimum period of time each week. In one experiment (Fraser et al., 1977), students were assigned partners and asked to study together for at least one half hour per week outside of class. Both students received as a grade the average of their individual grades. The authors reported that the students who studied together received significantly higher grades than did those in control groups not assigned to study with a partner. However, students voiced many complaints, especially in the initial phases of the course, about being partly responsible for and affected by another student's performance.

In three later experiments, Beaman et al. (1977) attempted to maintain the advantage of mutual study while overcoming some of the problems associated with mutual grade assignment. In the first experiment, students were required to study with their assigned partner and report their study time each week, but grades were not averaged and no penalties existed for nonconformance. The researchers found that fewer than half of the students actually studied together for the required period of time each week. Those who did received significantly higher grades than students in the control group. In the second experiment, student participation was required. Instead of getting an averaged grade, participating students received points for reaching their required amount of study time with their partners. These students performed better on examinations than the control group, but the difference was not statistically significant. The authors reported, however, that several students admitted confidentially that they had falsified their time to receive the point, and student complaints about being required to study with an assigned partner continued throughout the semester. In the third experiment, grades were averaged for the partners, but participation was voluntary. Of the 108 class members, only 14 volunteered for peer monitoring, and they insisted on choosing their own study partners. Again, paired students received higher grades; the difference approached but did not reach statistical significance. The authors concluded that the peer monitoring idea showed promise, but that many details involving student reception and cooperation still needed to be addressed.

Another, more expansive, effort to harness peer influence in a positive manner has been the structuring of residence hall arrangements to group students on the basis of common elements. For example, in a number of studies, honor students have been grouped together (DeCoster, 1966, 1968; Duncan & Stoner, 1977). The grouped students showed some advantage in grade point average over control groups of honors students not assigned to group arrangements, but differences were significant only during some of the semesters in which the study was conducted. The grouping of students in residence halls by academic major (Snead & Caple, 1971; Taylor & Hanson, 1971) resulted in higher than predicted GPA for students in the first study and superiority over nonassigned students in the second.

Blimling and Hample (1979) evaluated the grouping of students on a more simple common element, the request for a more structured study environment. In this study, certain floors were designated as study floors and specific study hours were set during which study was optional, but quiet was required. Students who violated the quiet hours policy over an established limit were transferred to nonstudy floors. Students on study floors received higher grades; analysis indicated that the structured environment contributed about 0.05 points to quarter grades and about 0.02 to 0.03 points to cumulative grades. These differences were found to be significant in three of the six college quarters in which the data were collected. The authors regarded these results as an indication that even average students who want to improve their study can profit from a structured environment. Although causes cannot be completely known, the authors considered the plan's incorporation of positive peer influence to be a contributing factor to its success.

Though far from conclusive, research to date would indicate that the advice of study skills texts for students to study away from their peers (or family) may be more helpful than advice that students confine study to one or two places reserved solely for that activity. Literature on tutoring as a means of exerting a positive influence on students indicates that peer tutoring or modeling can effect some positive changes in study behavior; the extent to which such efforts may improve grade point average was less clear. Attempts to formalize collaborative study (a procedure students sometimes use on their own) within a classroom setting by assigning pairs of students to study together resulted in higher grades for paired students, but the difference was usually of marginal statistical significance. As noted earlier, students did not totally accept the procedure, citing concerns over being affected by someone else's work, dissatisfaction with being assigned to rather than choosing a study partner, and difficulties in getting together to meet the time commitments. Residence hall groupings based on such common factors as performing well academically, having the same major, or expressing a choice for a more structured study environment show potential benefits for grade point average.

Music and study effectiveness. Whether music interferes with study effectiveness is an issue of long standing. Traditionally, study skills text authors and college skills instructors have considered music a distraction and have advised studying without music or TV playing in the background. Because of the problems involved in directly observing studying in natural situations, the most relevant investigations into the music and studying issue have been those that deal with the effect of music on various cognitive and perceptual performance tasks.

Some studies have indicated that music detracts from task performance; others that music is a neutral factor; others that its effects are mixed; and still others that music boosts performance. When reviews of such studies have been included in study skills texts, the investigations are usually described briefly, without mention of the age or grade level of the students. We found 11 studies that met the two criteria established for inclusion in this review: undergraduate college student populations and tasks of a primarily cognitive nature. In 8 of these 11 studies, authors included no-music control groups in their investigations, allowing for an examination of evidence pertinent to the broader question: Is music a distraction, a neutral factor, a mixed factor, or a facilitator when it comes to college students' task performance? Three of the studies indicated that music had no significant effect (Smith & Morris, 1976, Wolf & Weiner, 1972; Wolfe, 1983). In three instances results were mixed, indicating differences related to music or student/music variables (Etaugh & Ptasnik, 1982; Freeburne & Fleischer, 1952; Henderson, Crews, & Barlow, 1945). One study indicated performance superiority for the music listening group (Blanchard, 1979). In just one study (Fendrick, 1973) was music found to be detrimental to task performance for all participating students.

These mixed results can perhaps be better understood by considering the many different variables involved in each study. Tasks, for example, varied from study to study. Out of the 11 studies included in this review, 6 involved reading comprehension or other reading tasks (Etaugh & Michals, 1975; Etaugh & Ptasnik, 1982; Fendrick, 1973; Freeburn & Fleischer, 1952; Henderson, Crews & Barlow, 1945; Hilliard & Tolin, 1979).

Two studies involved taking regular course examinations (Blanchard, 1979; Smith & Morris, 1976), and two others involved simple mathematical tasks (Wolf & Weiner, 1972; Wolfe, 1983). In the remaining study (Belsham & Harman, 1977), students examined a photo using a printed questionnaire and then completed a recall task on photo details.

Studies also varied in number of students involved, proportion of male and female students, length of the testing period, and types of questions asked (beyond the broad question concerning the overall effect of music on performance). The questions asked fell into three categories: Does type of music (classical, jazz, rock and roll) make a difference? Do student factors related to music (student preferences, familiarity with music, frequency of listening) affect results? Does the volume of music matter, and is music different from other noises (speeches, industrial noise) in its effect on performance?

Three studies explored the effect of classical versus other types of music. Blanchard (1979) found that students listening to rock and roll, jazz, or classical music during an extended course examination performed better than students who did not listen to music during the exam. No differences were found between the experimental groups. In addition, when blood pressure and pulse rates (which were taken before, during, and after the test) were compared, experimental group students returned to pretest levels faster than did control group students. No significant differences among the groups were found on the reading comprehension task; however, the group listening to jazz read faster.

Henderson, Crews, and Barlow (1945) compared the effects of classical and popular music and quiet conditions. They found no significant differences on the vocabulary section of the Nelson-Denny Reading Test (Nelson, Denny, & Brown, 1938), but popular music served as a distraction on the comprehension portion of the test. The authors indicated that the task difficulty of the comprehension test could have been a factor. It should be noted that all of the students in this sample were female; also, although it was not specifically stated, it appears from the titles that the classical music was purely instrumental while the popular music was vocal.

Two other factors concerning type of music were addressed in the literature: the effects of vocal versus nonvocal music and the effects of stimulative versus sedative music. Belsham and Harman (1977), testing the relative distractiveness of vocal and nonvocal music, found vocal music to be more distracting. They concluded that investigators should designate whether vocal or nonvocal music is used in experiments. The authors who compared the relative effects of stimulative and sedative music (classified on the basis of an existing scale) were primarily interested in how music affected emotionality and worry during a course examination. The stimulative music tended to keep emotion and worry levels up, as indicated by student reports at intervals throughout the exam, but the type of music played during various sections of the test had no apparent effect on exam performance.

Variables tested relating to both the student and the music included student experience in listening to music and student familiarity with the music played. The frequency with which students listened to music was examined in two studies. Etaugh and Michals (1975) found males to be less distracted than females by music of their preference; however, a questionnaire indicated that the males in the sample listened to music more frequently than the females. When that variable was included in the analysis, it appeared that the difference in distraction level should be attributed to frequency of listening rather than primarily to sex differences. Etaugh and Ptasnik (1982) further tested for this variable with a balanced sample of males and females and found that students who listened to music frequently were not distracted (according to their performance) during a reading comprehension task; however, students who reported that they infrequently listened to music while reading performed significantly better in the quiet condition. Hilliard and Tolin (1979) tested whether familiarity with the music affected student performance. They found that students who had heard the music in a pretest session performed better while completing a section of the Sequential Test of Educational Progress (1969) than did students who listened to unfamiliar music.

Wolf (1983) tested the relative effects of the same music played at three different volumes: 60-70 decibels, 70-80 decibels, and 80-90 decibels. No differences were found in students' ability to solve simple arithmetic problems, but a student questionnaire administered after the test indicated that a majority of the students who listened to the loudest music found it both annoying and distracting; this was not true for the other two loudness conditions. Wolf and Weiner (1972) compared students' ability to solve simple arithmetic problems in a quiet condition, while listening to a speech recorded from television, while listening to industrial noise (a recording of a buzz saw), and while listening to rock and roll music. Students who listened to rock and roll performed significantly better than students who heard the buzz saw. No significant differences were found among the other groups.

These studies, all of which involved college undergraduate students in primarily cognitive tasks, do not lend support to the inflexible position taken by many authors of study skills texts that music is universally distracting to the performance of intellectual tasks. Assuming these results transfer to more natural study tasks, study skills authors would be better able to justify discussing the various variables that may make listening to music during study distracting and then encouraging students to make their own decisions.

Research indicates several factors that may affect how distracting music is. The two studies that investigated frequency of listening to music indicated that students who listened to music infrequently found music distracting when they were reading or studying, while students who listened to music frequently did not. Findings from one direct and one indirect study indicate that vocal music may be more distracting than nonvocal music, presumably because words are more apt to catch the conscious attention of the person reading or studying. In a study investigating the role of familiar and unfamiliar music on cognitive task performance, students were less distracted when music was familiar than when it was unfamiliar. Although music volume did not affect performance in the one study that investigated this factor, the fact that students cited loud music as annoying and potentially distracting is worth considering. Finally, the study that investigated the effects of music versus other noises found that music was less distracting than industrial noise. While absolute conclusions are not warranted, the results of these studies indicate that music may indeed be a nondistracting background factor for many students in some reading/study situations.

Implications

An analysis of the literature pertinent to the study environment raises questions concerning some of the advice given by study skills texts, and possibly by study skills instructors as well. Other suggestions found more support in the literature. With reference to student control of study environment, the available literature on stimulus control did not support the suggested practice of studying totally or mainly in one, or at most two, places and reserving those areas for study only. The practice did not seem to contribute substantially to improved study or academic success, and students resisted such contrived control over their study environment as being too unnatural. The findings did support the advice of some texts to study away from friends or family, as well as the idea of planning schedules with specific times designated for studying.

With reference to music and studying, a review of all studies in which college students comprised the populations did not lend support to an unqualified statement that listening to music while studying interferes with the learning process. While the finding that students who listen to music frequently are less distracted by music than those who do not lends support to the theory that unfamiliar noises are more distracting than familiar ones, it also seems to suggest that some students require a greater degree of quiet than do others. Research seems to support the suggestion that students should monitor their distractions by writing down times when their thoughts were interrupted and then analyzing the results and making necessary changes. Research also supports the notion that students should choose and use music so that it stays in the background, not commanding their conscious attention. On this basis, support could be given for listening to familiar instrumental music while studying, and for keeping the music at a reasonable volume.

Attention must be drawn to a major problem that has impeded research in the area of study environment. Ideally, conclusions about students' study behavior should be based on substantive observations of students studying in their natural settings. However, possibly because such observation would contaminate the naturalness of the environment, this has not been the usual practice. Therefore, many of the findings reported were based on performance of cognitive tasks of varying natures. Even within the group of tasks involving reading comprehension, variance in task could cause variance in performance. For example, completing a standardized test in which the reading material is always before the student does not require precisely the same skills as reading something and taking a test afterward; neither task is completely analogous to study. Also, more attention to characteristics that may affect the findings, such as volume and type of music, would be helpful.

The possibility of maximizing the positive aspects of peer influence through such practices as peer tutoring or collaborative study shows some promise for research and practice for college reading instruction. Students who are well trained in study skills strategies and management may be able to help others, especially in improving study habits and behaviors. When students were required to study together, course examination grades showed at least marginal improvement, although students often objected to such practices as averaging their grades with those of their study partner or requiring them to study with assigned partners. Students who want to study with others may profit from study skills training in this area; this possibility merits further investigation.

Risko, Alvarez, and Fairbanks

Finally, it should be noted that since study environment is so closely related to such other study variables as time management, memory and concentration, knowledge of learning strategies, and motivation and interest, research that involves several of these variables might be more profitable than studies relating strictly to an isolated aspect of study environment. Also, investigations of such self-control measures as self-monitoring and problem solving are needed. Controlling variables in the study environment to accommodate individual learning preferences and promote maximum learning from a study situation may be a key element of success for college students with at least minimal motivation, academic competency, and learning skills.

Library Use

The library is a major resource and service agency for both students and faculty. Those who use the library wisely find it offers a diversified knowledge base that can extend learning experiences. For some, it provides a way to access information quickly and efficiently; for others, it is a place that is more perplexing than helpful and therefore becomes a study hall or reading room (Moran, 1984). Lyle (1963) reported that 50 percent of all students using libraries in a university setting were using their own textbooks exclusively, compared with 16 percent who were using the varied library materials for independent study.

Rather than using the library as a study hall, students need to learn how to use it as a resource to help in their studying. The former tendency may result from students not knowing how to use library aids (e.g., card catalog, indexes) to access information in general, or it may result from students' limited prior knowledge of information relevant to their academic goal (Alvarez et al., 1984). The latter would indicate that students may be less certain about what information needs to be retrieved from the library than about how it can be accessed. Often students are more focused on writing the assigned papers than on the process of collecting appropriate information for those papers.

In our review of study skills texts and the related literature, we found disparate ideas. First, only 33 percent of the authors we reviewed provide information about library use. These authors limit their suggestions to how students can use reference tools to obtain material in the library. Our review of the literature relating to library use by college students addresses a broader issue. We present information on how the library is currently used and technological advances that will change the learning needs of college students in their use of the library. This information could provide direction for expanding discussions on library use by both authors of study skills texts and instructors of study skills classes.

Suggestions from Study Skills Texts

Some authors of study skills textbooks provide exercises that are designed to give students practice in finding information (Joffe, 1982; Postman, Keckler, & Schneckner, 1985; Shepherd, 1987). Often these exercises require students to use reference materials such as card catalogs, indexes, abstracts, government documents, newspapers, and encyclopedias to find information on specific topics. Typically, these topics are chosen without consideration of students' interests, assignments for other courses, or long term projects. For these exercises, the search for materials often becomes the goal rather than a means of accomplishing the broader goals of finding and integrating information across sources.

Related Literature

An important consideration in this review is why students may be having difficulty when given library assignments. Students' limited prior knowledge of the library, narrow topic assignments, and limited preparation for assignments are some of the factors that contribute to students' inability to use the library effectively. We have organized the relevant literature as follows: students' use of the library, instructors' expectations,

Risko, Alvarez, and Fairbanks

distinction between library and research skills, students' preparation, and databases and workstations.

Students' use of the library. According to Sellen and Jirouch (1984), students seem to prefer textbooks, encyclopedias, or dictionaries when gathering information for a report. Students make minimum use of varied library reference sources unless compelled by the assignment. The college students in this study tended to rely on high school library skills such as use of encyclopedias. They seemed to lack both the knowledge and the skills needed to access and use other sources. College juniors and seniors performed much the same as freshmen and sophomores in their general use of library sources.

Even when students have libraries in their residence halls, there is evidence that they don't make full use of the available resources. Oltmans and Schuh (1985) found that students prioritized their use of residence hall libraries as follows: first, for current periodicals and leisure reading; second, for class-related materials; third, for listening to records and tapes; and fourth, for reviewing art prints. Given the findings of Sellen and Jirouch (1984), it is not surprising that these authors also describe a limited scope in students' use of library materials.

Instructors' expectations. Faculty may have different perceptions of students' ability and use of library resources. Instructors who are unaware of students' lack of library skills may give directives their students don't understand (e.g., "Use the library for this assignment"). Faculty members responding to Sellen & Jirouch's (1984) questionnaire all said they preferred students to use a wide variety of resources (periodicals, indexes, abstracts) when writing papers and for class preparation. Instructors in natural science and engineering favored use of indexes and abstracts more heavily than their colleagues in other disciplines, but that was the only major difference in preference. Sellen & Jirouch further indicated that faculty from most disciplines expected students to use periodicals that reflect both a historical and a current perspective rather than just current periodicals, and regarded encyclopedias and dictionaries as inappropriate sources of information.

Library assignments need to be carefully planned if they are to be effective in developing students' use of the library. Instructors need to become knowledgeable about their library's collection and to alert students to the library services available to them. In a study conducted by Hofman (1981), instructors were found to have limited knowledge of their library's collections, services, and materials. Despite information sources such as library study guides, self-guided tape tours, and student handbooks, instructors often sent students to the library with course assignments requiring them to use reference materials not in the collection. Assignments that don't provide students with information about how to use the library effectively can lead to student frustration and poor performance.

Getting students to use the library involves more than giving simple assignments without course-related relevance and putting books on the library reserve list. It demands a cooperative endeavor between faculty and librarians (Barnes, 1988; Carlson & Miller, 1984; Gwinn, 1978; Lyle, 1963; Morris, 1980) to help students learn to choose appropriate reference materials.

Distinction between library and research skills. Confused use of the terms library skills and research skills—often used interchangeably in study skills texts—may create further disparity between instructors' expectations and students' performance in the library. Stoan (1984), acknowledging the importance of distinguishing these two terms for students, defined research skills as those needed to search for knowledge and library skills as those needed to search for information. More specifically, he described research skills as encompassing in-depth knowledge about a specific subject area, knowledge of research methods associated with the discipline, the ability to gather and test primary data (which usually come from outside the library), and the ability to think in a particular subject area. Stoan described library skills as a set of mechanical skills that are generic across disciplines. The authors of study skills texts seem to focus on enhancing library skills rather than research skills.

Risko, Alvarez, and Fairbanks

While undergraduate students are not expected to use the same rescarch skills as experienced researchers, our review of the literature suggests that authors of study skills texts could rely on the strategies used by researchers to broaden students' use of library resources. Both Rambler (1982) and Stoan (1984) acknowledge that research methodology evolves from a well-developed knowledge base of a subject area and that students' ability to integrate information across courses is a process that begins at the undergraduate level and proceeds through graduate study. Undergraduate education focuses primarily on acquainting students with the basic knowledge of a discipline and on teaching them how to search independently for related information through use of texts, reserve book lists, and relevant additional readings.

Alerting students to informal methods used by researchers to obtain information may be useful. Studies conducted at Bath University of Technology (1971), and by Hernon (1982), McBride and Stenstrom (1980-1981), Stenstrom and McBride (1979), Van Styvendael (1977), and Wood and Bower (1969) indicate that footnotes, personal recommendations from scholars, personal bibliographic files, serendipitous discovery, browsing, and similar methods that involve no formal use of indexes or abstracts account for the great majority of citations obtained by scholars. For instance, 94 percent of the researchers who responded to a questionnaire at Bath University of Technology said that references in books and periodicals were useful to them in locating materials for research. In contrast, fewer than 15 percent of respondents used indexes or abstracts—a finding consistent with those of a study with college faculty conducted by Stenstrom and McBride. These authors reported that faculty relied primarily on footnotes in journals and books as sources for additional references. In a later study with psychology and educational psychology faculty, McBride and Stenstrom reported that fewer than 20 percent of either group made even minimal use of abstracts or references in periodicals or bibliographies to identify sources. The informal reference sources favored by these scholars are easily accessible and understood, and may thus be good resources for undergraduate students.

Students' preparation. Some investigators have found that community college libraries do not recognize the special needs of their students with academic problems (Breivik, 1977a; Shaughnessy, 1975; Truett, 1983); thus, the students who need library skills the most appear to be receiving the least amount of instruction (Lolly & Watkins, 1979). If we expect students with academic problems to use both library and basic research reference tools, we need to help them learn how to use these tools. Lolly and Watkins (1979) note that although community colleges require academic courses at the developmental level, they do little to prepare students to use library resources. Truett (1983) found that although more than 90 percent of the colleges surveyed offered a developmental education program for their students, fewer than 28 percent of the colleges had library services to support these programs. For example, only one community college library reported having a bilingual handbook written in English and Spanish, even though most of the colleges surveyed were in cities with an above average Hispanic population. Instruction in library use was also found lacking. The type of instruction most prevalent in the surveyed community colleges was the traditional orientation lecture tour. Truett described this instruction as the least effective method of helping students use the library because it included no course-related instruction.

Bibliographic instruction (instruction in how to use catalogs to search for chapter titles) is better received and understood when it is related to the research needs of specific courses (Carlson & Miller, 1984). In one investigation, course-related library instruction conducted with developmental students resulted in academic gains as measured by reading comprehension tests and student-written term papers (Breivik, 1977a). The effectiveness of integrating coursework and related library instruction has been supported by several other investigations (Breivik, 1977b, 1987; Wagner, 1973).

Josey (1971) suggests that varied library services should be made available to students with academic problems. These services should include special library counseling, instruction specific to course assignments, and selective dissemination of information utilizing honors students and service-oriented volunteer groups.

Databases and workstations. Libraries are in transition from manual to electronic systems (Henry et al., 1988; Moran, 1984), but this technological advance is not acknowledged by most authors of study skills tests. Computerized systems have made interlibrary loans, library acquisitions, searches for references, and circulation much easier. Even notetaking changed with the availability of photocopying machines in the library. Authors of study skills texts need to include such information to improve college students' use of the library's technological resources.

Perhaps the first direct experience students and faculty will have with computerized library systems is with the library's card catalog system. Online catalog systems are beginning to replace the 3 × 5 card catalogs used in most academic libraries. These computerized systems provide the user with a fast method of accessing all of the library's holdings.

Using a computer terminal to interact with the database of catalog information, students can send and receive messages instantaneously, requesting subject information as well as titles or authors of books, journals, and documents. Searching for references on the computer can save hours over a manual search.

Other technological advances are in the works. Morgan (1984) states that library loans in the future will be accessed through such methods as digital telefacsimile for the delivery of documents. Already, libraries are linked through computer networks. According to Moran, more than 2,000 library databases or computerized information files are available, and these are increasing at a rate of 20 to 30 percent a year. Some of these databases include the Washington Library Network (WLN), Online Computer Library Center (OCLC), Research Library Information Network (RLIN), and Bibliographic Retrieval Service (BRS). Some bibliographic databases, such as BRS, have introduced an "Afterdark" service to encourage individuals who have a personal computer, modem, and phone to access and use these files in the evening hours. Special evening rates for database access, as well as menu-driven software packages, are available to further encourage use of these services (Rice, 1985).

Databases are being considered as viable alternatives for reducing the escalating costs of library acquisitions. Stueart (1982) reports that an experimental plan called Adonis has been developed by several periodical publishers to issue 10 to 15 journals in an electronic format. According to Stueart, this type of format is evolving to accommodate the increasing number of periodicals produced each year. Library subscriptions have increased dramatically because of the burgeoning number of journals available, resulting in higher expenses. Libraries may be forced to reduce their ownership of journals or other materials in favor of information available on databases. Stueart has warned that libraries' increased reliance on electronically transmitted publications may limit access to information by those students who are unfamiliar with electronic information retrieval. Clearly, study skills texts must address this area.

Another area that authors of study skills texts do not address is the use of outside workstations to access library resources. In the near future, scholars and student researchers may have library reference tools available to them at special workstations located in dorms or classroom buildings, which will preclude the need to go to the library. Ohio State University, for example, has a Telephone Center where students can check the location and availability of a book or journal in the library's collection, have it charged out to them, and even have it mailed to their offices or dormitory rooms (Lawrence, 1980).

Other universities are preparing their physical facilities to deal with accessing databases directly by creating workstations for faculty and students. Tucker (1983-1984), for example, reports that Brown University has begun installing 10,000 workstations across the campus to serve the needs of both faculty and students. These workstations will be able to access the library's catalog and other bibliographic and nonbibliographic databases.

Implications

Advice offered by authors of study skills texts does not represent a comprehensive view of the library skills students may need to manage their study efforts. Exercises to practice the use of library resources need to be made relevant to students' course assignments so they can learn how to search for and use information from varied sources for class preparation and when writing papers. Also, students should be advised to take advantage of tutoring or orientation programs offered through their school library program.

There is a difference between library skills (searching for information) and research skills (searching for knowledge). Many undergraduate students are concerned only with library skills. The need for research skills increases as students become more interested in and knowledgeable about a given discipline. Authors of study skills texts and instructors of college study classes need to provide a comprehensive approach to their suggestions for library use. Needed are suggestions that not only orient students to library resources but also specify methods of conducting library research.

Many undergraduate students do not fully utilize the library's reference sources because their knowledge is limited. These students seem to rely on the same library reference sources they used in high school. Unfortunately, this narrow list of sources (e.g., dictionaries, encyclopedias) seems to be what is primarily advocated in college study skills textbooks. Even though these authors also advocate indexes and abstracts, without specific instruction in the use of these materials, students from disadvantaged educational backgrounds will probably fall back on more familiar sources. Professors frequently hand out library assignments with little or no support for students who have limited library skills.

Authors of study skill texts should alert students to informal methods of gathering information as one way to improve their library and research skills. Informal methods (e.g., making use of footnotes and reference lists, keeping personal bibliographic files) may prove beneficial not only in maximizing students' use of reference materials but also in helping them see the value of setting up their own index of information.

Advances in technology have affected how library information can be accessed. Now that databases are replacing card catalogs and printed indexes, they need to be explained by authors of study skills texts, college instructors, and librarians. Workstations also need to be discussed in study skills texts and developmental studies courses if college students with academic problems are going to be able to rely on these resources to help them study.

Conclusions

Two major conclusions can be made from our review of time management, study environment, and library use. First, there is both pragmatic and theoretical/empirical support for giving students information and exercises to help them prepare to manage their study efforts. Students should be taught how to analyze and monitor the amount of time needed for study, how to analyze and control the study environment, and how to make effective use of reference materials. Second, specific directives (e.g., "Study with music but not television") commonly found within study skills texts receive mixed support in the literature. More research is needed to determine the appropriateness of each of these directives and to assess how use of time, study environment, and library resources may differ according to specific student and course needs.

The following suggestions are offered for authors of study skills texts, instructors of reading and study skills courses, and researchers. Study skills texts could be extended to describe how students can monitor their use of time and regulate factors such as music and peer influence that may impede their study efforts. These texts should also help students establish strategies to correct their problems. Information and exercises related to library use should present course-related illustrations to help students transfer the use of specific library skills and resources to classes in which they are currently enrolled. Without using the technical language of published research, authors could provide a more comprehensive view of the topics they discuss so that students can understand the conditions and reasons for the advice that is given. Instructor manuals that accompany students' texts should include a summary of the theoretical and empirical research on which the text was based.

Corresponding to these suggestions, instructors of college reading and study skills courses should provide opportunities for students to study and monitor (1) their use of time during study, (2) the environmental factors that influence their study, and (3) their use of library skills for course assignments. Class discussions and individual conferences should be provided to help students select and implement problem-solving strategies. Instructors need to be knowledgeable about the library resources available to their students and coordinate their instruction with instructional programs offered through the library.

Several areas within this topic require further research. For instance, the amount of time needed to study effectively and across different tasks should be studied. Given that multiple factors have an impact on college students' study environments, research is also needed to investigate the synergistic effects of these factors on study habits. Also, investigators need to identify effective strategies for enhancing students' knowledge and flexible use of library resources.

References and Suggested Readings

Alvarez, M.C. (1983). Using a thematic preorganizer and guided instruction as aids to concept learning. *Reading Horizons, 24*(1), 51-58.

Alvarez, M.C., & Risko, V.J. (1982, October). *Using a thematic organizer to enhance conceptual understanding of verse and prose.* Paper presented at the Twenty-Sixth College Reading Association Annual Conference, Philadelphia, PA.

Alvarez, M.C., & Risko, V.J. (1989). Using a thematic organizer to facilitate transfer learning with college developmental studies students. *Reading Research and Instruction, 28,* 1-15.

Alvarez, M.C., Risko, V.J., Cooper, J., & Hall, A. (1984). A comparison study of background knowledge of college undergraduates enrolled in teacher education classes with developmental reading classes. In G.H. McNinch (Ed.), *Fourth yearbook of the American reading forum* (pp. 105-110). Athens, GA: American Reading Forum.

Annis, L.F. (1983). *Study techniques.* Dubuque, IA: W.C. Brown.

Arlin, M. (1984a). Time, equality, and mastery learning. *Review of Educational Research, 54,* 65-86.

Arlin, M. (1984b). Time variability in mastery learning. *American Educational Research Journal, 21,* 103-120.

Atkinson, R.C. (1968). Computer-based instruction and the learning process. *American Psychologist, 23,* 225-239.

Ausubel, D.P. (1960). The use of advance organizers in the learning and retention of meaningful verbal material. *Journal of Educational Psychology, 51,* 267-272.

Ausubel, D.P. (1968). *Educational psychology: A cognitive view.* Orlando, FL: Holt, Rinehart & Winston.

Barnes, J.W. (1968). *Practical and effective point-of-use library guides from the Oscar A. Silverman undergraduate library.* (ED 297 744)

Barron, R.F. (1969). The use of vocabulary as an advance organizer. In H.L. Herber & P.L. Sanders (Eds.), *Research in reading in the content areas: First year report* (pp. 29-39). Syracuse, NY: Syracuse University, Reading and Language Arts Center.

Beaman, A.L., Diener, E., Fraser, S.C., & Endresen, K.L. (1977). Effects of voluntary and semivoluntary peer-monitoring programs on academic performance. *Journal of Educational Psychology, 69,* 109-114.

Belsham, R.L., & Harman, D.W. (1977). Effect of vocal vs. nonvocal music on visual recall. *Perceptual and Motor Skills, 44,* 857-858.

Beneke, W.M., & Harris, M.B. (1972). Teaching self-control of study behavior. *Behavior Research and Therapy, 10,* 35-41.

Blanchard, B.E. (1979). The effect of music on pulse rate, blood pressure, and final exam scores of university students. *Journal of School Health, 49,* 470-472.

Blimling, G.S., & Hample, D. (1979). Structuring the peer environment in residence halls to increase academic performance in average-ability students. *Journal of College Student Personnel, 20,* 310-316.

Bloom, B.S. (1956) *Taxonomy of educational objectives (cognitive domain).* New York: McKay.

Bloom, B.S. (1974). Time and learning. *American Psychologist, 29,* 682-688.

Bradley, A. (1983). *Take note of college study skills.* Glenview, IL: Scott, Foresman.

Breivik, P.S. (1977a). *Open admissions and the academic library.* Chicago IL: American Library Association.

Breivik, P.S. (1977b). Resources: The fourth R. *Community College Frontiers, 5,* 46-50.

Breivik, P.S. (1987). The role of libraries in the search for educational excellence. *School Library Media Quarterly, 16,* 45-46.

Brooks, C.C. (1984). *Setting objectives for college reading and study skills* (2nd ed.). Dubuque, IA: Eddie Bowers.

Brown, W.F., & Holtzman, W.H. (1967). *Survey of study habits and attitudes: Manual.* New York: Psychological Corporation.

Cappella, B.J., Hetzler, J.T., & MacKenzie, C. (1983). The effects of positive peer influence on study habits. *Reading Improvement, 20,* 299-302.

Carlson, D., & Miller, R.H. (1984). Librarian and teaching faculty: Partners in bibliographic instruction. *College & Research Libraries, 45,* 483-491.

Carroll, J.B. (1963). A model of school learning. *Teachers College Record, 64,* 723-733.

Carroll, J.B. (1967). *A study of a model of school learning.* Cambridge, MA: Harvard University, Center for Research and Development of Educational Differences.

Carroll, J.B. (1970). Problems of measurement related to the concept of learning for mastery. *Educational Horizons, 48,* 71-88.

Carroll, J.B. (1989). The Carroll model: A 25-year retrospective and prospective view. *Educational Researcher, 18,* 26-31.

Christensen, C.R. (1987). *Teaching and the case method.* Boston, MA: Harvard Business School Press.

Cohen, E.L., & Poppino, M.A. (1982). *Discovering college reading, thinking, and study skills: A Piagetian approach* (pp. 3-8, 75-86). Orlando, FL: Holt, Rinehart & Winston.

DeCoster, D.A. (1966). Housing assignments for high ability students. *Journal of Col-*

lege Student Personnel, 7, 19-20.

DeCoster, D. A. (1968). Effects of homogeneous housing assignments for high ability students. *Journal of College Student Personnel, 9*, 75-78.

Dewing, A.S. (1931). An introduction to the use of cases. In C.E. Fraser (Ed.), *The case method of instruction.* New York: McGraw-Hill.

Duncan, M.C., & Stoner, K.L. (1977). The academic achievement of residents living in a scholar resident hall. *Journal of College and University Housing, 6*, 7-10.

Earle, R.A. (1969). Use of the structured overview in mathematics classes. In H.L. Herber & P.L. Sanders (Eds.), *Research in reading in the content areas: First year report* (pp. 49-58). Syracuse, NY: Syracuse University, Reading and Language Arts Center.

Earle, R.A., & Barron, R.F. (1973). An approach for teaching vocabulary in content subjects. In H.L. Herber & R.F. Barron (Eds.), *Research in reading in the content areas: Second year report* (pp. 84-100). Syracuse, NY: Syracuse University, Reading and Language Arts Center.

Etaugh, C., & Michals, D. (1975). Effects on reading comprehension of preferred music and frequency of studying to music. *Perceptual and Motor Skills, 31*, 553-554.

Etaugh, C., & Ptasnik, P. (1982). Effects of studying to music and poststudy relaxation on reading comprehension. *Perceptual and Motor Skills, 55*, 141-142.

Fendrick, P. (1973). The influence of music distraction upon reading efficiency. *Journal of Educational Research, 31*, 264-271.

Fraser, S.C., Beaman, A.L., Diener, E., & Kelem, R.T. (1977). Two, three, or four heads are better than one: Modification of college performance by peer monitoring. *Journal of Educational Psychology, 69*, 101-108.

Freeburne, C.M., & Fleischer, M.S. (1952). The effect of music distraction upon reading rate and comprehension. *Journal of Educational Psychology, 43*, 101-109.

Fremouw, W., & Feindler, E, (1978). Peer versus professional models for study skills training. *Journal of Counseling Psychology, 25*, 276-288.

Frijda, N. (1978). Memory processes and instruction. In A.M. Lesgold, J.W. Pellegrino, S.D. Fokkema, & R. Glaser (Eds.), *Cognitive psychology and instruction.* New York: Plenum.

*Gal'Perin, P.Y., & Danilova, V.L. (1980). Training students to think systematically in the process of solving minor creative problems. *Voprosy Psihologii, 1*, 31-38.

*Gettinger, M. (1984). Achievement as a function of time spent on learning and time needed for learning. *American Educational Research Journal, 21*, 617-628.

Gettinger, M. (1985). Time allocated and time spent relative to time needed for learning as determinants of achievement. *Journal of Educational Psychology, 77*, 3-11.

Glazer, R. (1968). Adapting the elementary school curriculum to individual performance. *Proceedings of the 1967 conference on testing problems.* Princeton, NJ: Educational Testing Service.

Gowin, D.B., (1987). *Educating.* Ithaca, NY: Cornell University Press.

*Gragg, C.I. (1954). Because wisdom can't be told. In M.P. McNair (Ed.), *The case method at the Harvard Business School.* New York: McGraw-Hill.

Gwinn, N.E. (1978). The faculty-library connection. *Change, 10*, 19-21.

*Hefferman, T., & Richards, C.S. (1981). Self-control of study behavior: Identification and evaluation of natural methods. *Journal of Counseling Psychology, 28*, 361-364.

Heinrichs, A.S., & LaBranche, S.P. (1986). Content analysis of 47 college learning skills textbooks. *Reading Research and Instruction, 25*(4), 277-287.

Henderson, M.T., Crews, A., & Barlow, J. (1945). A study of the effects of music distraction on reading efficiency. *Journal of Applied Psychology, 29*, 313-317.

Henry, M., Dodson, S., Magnuson, B., Anderson, K., & Barrett, M. (1988). Electronic library instruction program. (ED 302 260)

Hernon, P. (1982). Use of microformated government publications, *Microfilm Review,*

11, 241-242.

Hilliard, O.M., & Tolin, P. (1979). Effect of familiarity with background music on performance of simple and difficult reading comprehension tasks. *Perceptual and Motor Skills, 49,* 713-714.

*Hofman, L.A. (1981). Educate the educator: A possible solution to an academic librarian's dilemma. *Journal of Academic Librarianship, 7,* 161-163.

Hogan, T.P., & Hendrickson, E. (1984). The study habits of adult college students. *Life Long Learning, 8,* 7-11, 20-27.

Hunt, P. (1951). The case method of instruction. *Harvard Educational Review, 21*(3), 175-192.

Information requirements of research in the social studies. (1971). Bath, England: Bath University of Technology.

Joffe, I.L. (1982). *Achieving success in college.* Belmont, CA: Wadsworth.

Johnson, R.E. (1975). Meaning in complex learning. *Review of Educational Research, 45,* 425-459.

Josey, E.G. (1971). The role of the academic library in serving disadvantaged students. *Library Trends, 20,* 432-444.

Lawrence, G.H. (1980). The computer as an instructional device: New directions for library user education. *Library Trends, 29,* 139-152.

Lawrence P. (1953). The preparation of case material. In K.R. Andrews (Ed.), *The case method of teaching human relations and administration.* Cambridge, MA: Harvard University Press.

Lolly, J., & Watkins, R. (1979). Welcome to the library. *Journal of Developmental and Remedial Education, 3,* 25-26.

Lyle, G.R. (1963). *The president, the professor, and the college library.* New York: H.W. Wilson.

Lyon, M.A. (1984, April). Learning rate differences for knowledge, comprehension, and application tasks. (ED 252 303)

Lyon, M.A., & Gettinger, M. (1985). Differences in student performance on knowledge, comprehension, and application tasks: Implications for school learning. *Journal of Educational Psychology, 77,* 12-19.

McBride, R.B., & Stenstrom, P. (1980-1981). Psychology journal usage. *Behavioral and Social Sciences Librarian, 2,* 1-12.

McPartland, J.D., & Karweit, N. (1979). Research on educational effects. In H.J. Walberg (Ed.), *Educational environments and effects: Evaluation, policy, and productivity.* Berkeley, CA: McCutchan.

McWhorter, K.T. (1968a). *College reading and study skills* (3rd ed.). Boston, MA: Little, Brown.

McWhorter, K.T. (1987). *Efficient and flexible reading* (2nd ed.). Boston, MA: Little, Brown.

Moran, B.B. (1984). *Academic librarians: The changing knowledge centers of colleges and universities.* Washington, DC: ASHE ERIC Higher Education Report No. 8.

Morris, J.M. (1980). A philosophical defense of a credit course. In C. Oberman-Soroka (Ed.), *Proceedings from the Southeastern Conference on Approaches to Bibliographic Instruction.* Charleston, SC: College of Charleston Library Associates.

Nelson, M.J., Denny, E.C., & Brown, J.I. (1938). *The Nelson-Denny Reading Test.* Boston, MA: Houghton Mifflin.

Nist, S.L., & Diehl, W. (1985). *Developing textbook thinking.* Lexington, MA: D.C. Heath.

Novak. J.D., & Gowin, D.B. (1984). *Learning how to learn.* New York: Cambridge University Press.

Oltmans, G., & Schuh, J.H. (1985). Purposes and uses of residence hall libraries. *College and Research Libraries, 46,* 172-177.

Ottens, A.J. (1982). A guaranteed scheduling technique to manage students' procrastination. *College Students Journal, 16,* 371-376.

Pauk, W. (1984). *How to study in college* (3rd ed.). Boston, MA: Houghton Mifflin.

Postman, R.D., Keckler, B., & Schneckner, P. (1985). *College reading and study skills.* New York: Macmillan.

Rambler, L.K. (1982). Syllabus study: Key to a responsive academic library. *Journal of Academic Librarianship, 8,* 155-159.

Resnick, J., & Page, R. (1984). *Reading and reasoning.* New York: Macmillan.

Rice, B.A. (1985). Evaluation of online databases and their uses in collection evaluation. *Library Trends, 22,* 297-325.

Richards, C.S. (1975). Behavior modification of studying through study skills advice and self-control procedures. *Journal of Counseling Psychology, 22,* 431-436.

Richards, C.S. (1981). Improving college students' study behaviors through self-control techniques: A brief review. *Behavioral Counseling Quarterly, 1,* 159-175.

Richards, C.S., McReynolds, W.T., Holt, S., & Sexton, T. (1976). Effects of information feedback and self-administered consequences on self-monitoring study behavior. *Journal of Counseling Psychology, 23,* 316-321.

Scales, A.M. & Biggs, S.A. (1983). *Reading to achieve: Strategies for adult/college learners.* Columbus, OH: Merrill.

Schmelzer, R.V., Khristen, W.L. & Browning, W.G. (1984). *Reading and study skills: Book one.* Dubuque, IA: Kendall/Hunt.

Schmelzer, R.V., Schmelzer, C.D., Figler, R.A., & Brozo, W.G. (1987). Using the critical incident technique to determine reasons for success and failure of university students. *Journal of College Student Personnel, 28,* 261-265.

Sellen, M.K., & Jirouch, J. (1984). Perceptions of library use by faculty and students: A comparison. *College & Research Libraries, 45,* 259-267.

Sequential Test of Educational Progress (1969). New York: Educational Testing Service.

Shaughnessy, T.W. (1975). Library services to educationally disadvantaged students. *College & Research Libraries, 36,* 443-448.

Shepherd, J.F. (1982). *The Houghton Mifflin study skills handbook.* Boston, MA: Houghton Mifflin.

Shepherd, J.F. (1984). *RSVP reading, study, and vocabulary program* (2nd ed.). Boston, MA: Houghton Mifflin.

Shepherd, J.F. (1987). *College study skills* (3rd ed.). Boston, MA: Houghton Mifflin.

Sherman, T.M. (1984). *Proven strategies for successful learning.* Columbus, OH: Merrill.

*Shuell, T.J. (1986). Cognitive conceptions of learning. *Review of Educational Research, 56, 4,* 411-436.

Smith, C., & Morris, L. (1976). Effects of stimulative and sedative music on cognitive and emotional components of anxiety. *Psychological Reports, 38,* 1187-1193.

Snead, R.F., & Caple, R.B. (1971). Some effects of environment on university housing. *Journal of College Student Personnel, 12*(3), 189-192.

Sotiriou, P.E. (1984). *Integrating college study skills: Reasoning in reading, listening, and writing.* Belmont, CA: Wadsworth.

Stenstrom, P., & McBride, R.B. (1979). Serial use of social science faculty: A survey. *College & Research Libraries, 40,* 429.

Stoan, S.K. (1984). Research and library skills: An analysis and interpretation. *College & Research Libraries, 45,* 99-109.

Stueart, R.D. (1982). Libraries: A new role? In E. Seigel (Ed.), *Books, libraries, and electronics: Essays on the future of written communication.* White Plains, NY: Knowledge Industry.

Subject Guide to Books in Print. (1988). New York: R.R. Bowker.

Taylor, R.G., & Hanson, G.R. (1971). Environmental impact on achievement and study habits. *Journal of College Student Personnel, 12,* 445-454.

Truett, C. (1983). Services to developmental education students in the community college: Does the library have a role? *College & Research Libraries, 44,* 20-28.

Tucker, J.S. (Ed.). (1983-1984). *Computers on campus: Working papers.* Current Series in Higher Education No. 2. Washington, DC: American Association for Higher Education. (ED 240 947)

Van Styvendael, J.H. (1977). University scientists as seekers of information: Sources of reference to periodical literature. *Journal of Librarianship, 9,* 271-272.

Wagner, W.C. (1973). On integrating libraries and classrooms. *Learning Today, 6,* 48-62.

Walter, T., & Siebert, A. (1984). *Student success* (3rd ed.) Orlando, FL: Holt, Rinehart & Winston.

Washburne, C.W., Vogel, M., & Gray, W.A. (1926). Results of practical experiments in fitting schools to individuals. *Journal of Educational Research* (supplementary monograph).

Wolf, R.H., & Weiner, F.F. (1972). Effects of four noise conditions on arithmetic performance. *Perceptual and Motor Skills, 35,* 928-930.

Wolfe, D.E. (1983). Effects of music loudness on task performance and self-report of college-age students. *Journal of Research in Music Education, 31,* 191-201.

Wood, D.N., & Bower, C.A. (1969). The use of social science periodical literature. *Journal of Documentation, 25,* 115-117.

Wood, N.V. (1986). *College reading and study skills.* Orlando, FL: Holt, Rinehart & Winston.

Ziesat, H.A., Rosenthal, T.I., & White, G.M. (1978). Behavioral self-control in treating procrastination of studying. *Psychological Reports, 42,* 59-69.

6

Internal Factors That Influence Study

Victoria J. Risko
Marilyn M. Fairbanks
Marino C. Alvarez

C ollege instructors, authors of college reading and
study skills texts, and researchers suggest that the
goal of reading and study skills classes is to prepare students to
use strategies that will boost their level of motivation and change
the way they select, organize, and remember new knowledge.
Adult learners and college students often fail to use effective
study strategies either because they are insufficiently informed
about these strategies or because they are unable to monitor the
strategies they use (Johnston, 1985; Palmer & Goetz, 1988; Simpson, 1984). In this chapter we discuss three factors—motivation,
memory, and attention—since the goal of instruction for college
students is to increase their control of each of these in order to
establish effective study habits.

For this analysis, we began with the same 64 current
study skills texts we examined for the preceding chapter. This

time we eliminated 40 of the 64 texts because they provided no substantial information about the strategic management of motivation, memory, or attention. Again, we completed a content analysis of the remaining texts to determine the extent to which each of the three target areas was addressed, the nature of the information and suggestions provided for each area, and the extent to which authors of study skills texts cited or explicitly related their suggestions to theoretical or research literature. Each of the 24 texts contained information about at least one of our target areas. Table 1 summarizes the results of our analysis.

As in our previous analysis, each study skills textbook we reviewed discussed at least one target area, and usually two or all three. We again found that most authors do not relate their suggestions explicitly to supporting literature. Instead, they tend to provide pragmatic reasons for their suggestions, stating their case simply and in a generalized manner without reflecting on differing perspectives presented in the literature.

In this chapter, we provide a review of the theoretical and empirical literature that relates to each of the three target factors. We examine whether the suggestions in the textbooks under review reflect research findings and then discuss related literature. For the most part, we have limited our discussion to the literature on college-age students. For each of the target areas, we organized our review to present: (1) a brief review of what authors of the 24 study skills texts recommend, (2) a review of literature related to the designated factor and an interpretation of the correspondence between what is recommended and what is supported or proposed in the literature, and (3) a discussion of the issues addressed. We conclude with recommendations for research and instruction.

Motivational Variables

In our work with college students in both voluntary and required study skills program settings, we have found wide variation in students' motivation to achieve academic improvement and success. Some students seemed eager to try new ideas or adapt ideas they had tried and abandoned in the past, and were delighted when they received a good test grade or saved time with one of our suggested study strategies. Others seemed just as dedicated to proving that nothing we could suggest could possibly help them. We tried everything we could think of to improve students' academic motivation. What seemed to work the best for us was stressing college "survival" skills early in the program and encouraging students to exert enough effort to achieve at least a little success. We found that with many students, a little success spurred desire for more success and could sometimes help turn around a predisposition to failure, or at least help a fair student become a good or excellent student.

In our experience, poor academic achievement in high school often contributes to poor study skills in college. Further, students who experience academic problems in college seem to lack clear-cut goals and to have a poor self-concept, often accompanied by the attitude that failure is more a matter of bad luck than of their own efforts. Often, these students seem to have concluded that it is better to fail by not trying than by making an unsuccessful effort. Similarly, Fischer and Mandl (1984) and Palmer and Goetz (1988) note that poor readers who have trouble with comprehension are more likely to be predisposed toward expecting failure and to "react affectively rather than effectively" (p. 53).

The complex relationships between motivational variables and study behaviors have been addressed by a number of investigators. Biggs (1979) has hypothesized that the best academic results for a student will occur when the student's basic motivation and strategy match. He proposes three motivational modes: utility, represented by the student who is attending college for nonacademic reasons; learning, characterized by the student who is truly devoted to intellectual growth; and achievement, descriptive of the student who places priority on high grades and organizes accordingly. Biggs suggests a corresponding study strategy for each mode. Other investigators (Entwistle, 1981; Hattie & Watkins, 1981; Watkins, 1982;

Table 1
Relevant Areas Addressed in Current College Study Skills Texts

Text	Areas Addressed			Rationale Provided for Suggestions Given/Activities Included			
	Attitude/ Motivation	Memory	Concen- tration	Pragmatic Reasons	Theoretical Basis Established	Research Cited in Text	Research Reference List
Annis, 1983	X	X		Yes	Yes	Yes	Yes
Bradley, 1983			X	No	No	No	No
Brooks, 1984	X			Yes	Yes	No	No
Cohen & Poppino, 1982		X		Yes	Yes	Yes	No
Joffe, 1982	X	X	X	Yes	No	No	No
Joffe, 1988		X	X	Yes	No	No	No
Kolzow & Lehmann, 1986		X		Yes	No	No	No
McWhorter, 1986a	X	X	X	Yes	No	Minimal	No
McWhorter, 1986b	X	X	X	Yes	No	No.	No
McWhorter, 1987		X	X	Yes	No	Yes	Yes
Nist & Diehl, 1985	X	X		Yes	No	Minimal	No
Pauk, 1984	X	X	X	Yes	No	Minimal	No

Risko, Fairbanks, and Alvarez

Table 1 (continued)

Postman, Keckler, & Schneckner, 1985			X	Yes	No	No	No
Resnick & Page, 1984		X		Yes	No	No	No
Schmelzer, Khristen, & Browning, 1984		X	X	Yes	No	Minimal	No
Shepherd, 1982		X	X	Yes	No	No	No
Shepherd, 1984	X	X	X	Yes	No	No	No
Shepherd, 1987		X	X	Yes	No	No	No
Sherman, 1984	X	X	X	Yes	No	No	No
Smith, 1981		X	X	Yes	No	Minimal	No
Sotiriou, 1984		X		Yes	No	No	No
Walter & Siebert, 1984	X	X	X	Yes	No	Minimal	Minimal
Wood, 1984	X	X	X	Yes	No	No	Minimal
Wood, 1986	X	X	X	Yes	No	Minimal	No

Watkins & Hattie, 1980) have attempted to verify this theory and have indicated partial support, with the utility factor noted as the least defensible.

Half of the study skills texts we reviewed dealt directly with the problem of motivation. For example, Nist and Diehl (1985) call motivation one of the most important keys to successful learning and studying, while Walter and Siebert (1984) assert that motivation and learning how to study are the most important variables in whether students will finish college.

The ideas and suggestions in these books that relate to the role of motivation in students' academic performance seemed to fall into four interrelated categories:

- assuming responsibility for academic achievement or improvement,
- developing positive attitudes toward self and surroundings,
- setting goals, and
- managing stress and anxiety.

In the review of the research literature, we found two types of studies pertinent to these four groups of variables: studies investigating the relationship of motivational variables (and sometimes other factors) to academic success, and studies concerned with improving academic performance by manipulating motivational variables. In the discussion that follows, we examine each of the four categories, summarizing in turn the suggestions made in study skills texts and the available empirical studies of both types.

Suggestions from Study Skills Texts

Assuming responsibility. Walter & Siebert (1984) and McWhorter (1986a, 1986b) stress the importance of students' accepting total responsibility for learning and taking a positive rather than a passive attitude. They advise students not to expect teachers to be entertainers whose job is to get their attention but instead to accept an active role in finding useful information available in every class. They also indicate that being responsible for oneself means accepting both successes and failures, and viewing failures as a signal for the need to change. Sherman (1984) advises students to gain control of their learning by using good study skills; however, few authors offer suggestions for self-directed strategies students can adopt.

Instead of simply giving advice about self-responsibility, at least two authors attempt to build the concept into the book's approach. Cohen and Poppino (1982) designed their book around what they term a Piagetian/schema or discovery approach. For each of the skills introduced, they direct the student first to approach a learning problem and figure out solutions (exploration), then to state the solution as a principle or formula (invention), then to field test the solution (application), and finally to restate the problem and their decisions (recapitulation). Brooks (1984) organized his text to encourage students to examine and build on their background knowledge and then make their own study skills decisions in a motivationally oriented psycholinguistic approach.

Developing positive attitudes. Student attitudes, which are firmly linked to other motivational factors, can have a powerful impact on the success of students' study habits. Walter and Siebert (1984) stress five major points about this topic (some of which other study skills authors also address). First, they try to impress on students the importance of believing in their ability to achieve academic success. This point is echoed by Sherman (1984) and Nist and Diehl (1985), who tell students they should accept their admission to college as evidence of their potential for academic success, but that they have to consciously supply the motivation to achieve.

Second, Walter and Siebert (1984) stress the importance of students' belief that they are in control of their own lives. The authors include an attitude survey to help students determine the extent to which they feel in control of their lives, and explain that students who read texts with the belief that they can learn and gain from them are more apt to be internally rather than externally oriented. Third, they emphasize the need to avoid negative thinking and the games losers play, such as attributing success or failure to luck, or making excuses for not doing what they knew would bring academic success.

Fourth, Walter and Siebert (1984) as well as Wood (1986) advise students to replace negative thinking with positive thinking, or self-talk, and to imagine themselves in rewarding and successful situations. Last, the authors tell students to cultivate a positive approach toward academic surroundings—for instance, to expect to learn something from every lecture.

Setting goals. As with the other motivational variables, goal setting is a factor students can learn to control. Walter and Siebert (1984) and Wood (1986) emphasize setting reasonable goals and then judging one's success by the extent to which those goals are met. Sherman (1984) also addresses the importance of goal setting as a motivational strategy, viewing it as a way of dealing with anxiety. Both Wood (1986a, 1986b) and McWhorter (1986) advise students to reward themselves when goals are met. Further, Wood asks students to consider the consequences of not meeting established goals. Other study skills texts do not address this issue in any depth.

Managing stress and anxiety. Stress, a complex motivational variable, often is difficult to assess and to channel productively. Pauk (1984) differentiates between stress and tension, describing stress as a bodily response to demands placed on it and tension as the "wrong" response. In attempting to help students deal with tension, Pauk offers four general suggestions for dealing with stress: (1) avoid stressful situations, (2) be overprepared for academic work, (3) learn to relax without feeling guilty, and (4) avoid procrastination. He lists 11 specific ways of releasing tension, including talking it out and escaping temporarily, and recommends relaxation methods such as controlled breathing techniques. Sherman (1984) and Wood (1986) both note that some stress is natural and can even be helpful, but that stress sometimes becomes too great and turns into worry and nervous anxiety. Wood advises students to determine what is causing their anxiety and to set constructive ways of eliminating or minimizing the contributing problem.

Related Literature

Assuming responsibility. We reviewed the literature to investigate possible relationships between academic performance and a number of factors considered closely associated with assuming responsibility for academic achievement. These factors include locus of control, students' attributions of success or failure, academic job involvement, self-monitoring, self-reinforcement, and problem solving.

Locus of control. Locus of control refers to personal perceptions of what accounts for the successes or failures in your life. This construct can be measured by the Internal/External Locus of Control Scale developed by Rotter (1966). Individuals with a high internal locus of control (as measured by the scale) attribute their successes or failures to the consequences of their own actions. Conversely, individuals with a high external locus of control attribute their successes or failures to outside forces (family, peers, enemies, fate).

The notion that a high internal locus of control will correlate with high academic achievement is based on the assumption that a person who believes that successes and failures are due to the results of his or her own behavior will be more likely to exhibit initiative and persistence in meeting achievement goals, (Rotter, 1966). Keller, Sutterer, and Goldman (1978), however, think that evidence casts doubt on the veracity of this assumed relationship. They cite separate reviews by Phares (1976) and Lefcourt (1976) in which the authors examined numerous studies, found mixed results, and came to different conclusions. Phares concluded that internal locus of control does tend to correlate with academic performance, while Lefcourt concluded that the studies are often inconsistent and contain odd results.

Studies not included in these two reviews also show mixed results. Keller, Sutterer, and Goldman (1978) cite three studies (Allen, Giat, & Cherney, 1974; Daniels & Stevens, 1976; Parent et al., 1975) investigating the relationship between perceived locus of control, course structure, and achievement in which students with a high external locus of control performed better under highly structured conditions than those with a high internal locus of control. A study by Johnson and Croft (1975), however, found no differences in achievement attributable to locus of control or structure. Similarly, Keller et al. (1978) found no relationship between locus of control (as measured by the Rotter Scale) and academic success in a study involving 463 university students. Traub (1982), also using the Rotter Scale, found that course grades of female freshmen correlated significantly with locus of control but that course grades of male freshmen did not. The correlation was moderate, however, even for females. The metaanalyses conducted by Findley and Cooper (1983) and Hansford and Hattie (1982) revealed that students' perceptions of themselves and their control over learning showed consistent relationships with educational accomplishments.

Some researchers attribute the inconsistencies in the locus of control results to differences in instruments used, the methods employed, or the selection of subjects. There are also two conflicting theoretically based viewpoints about the causes of these inconsistencies. Rotter (1966), taking a social theory viewpoint, maintains that locus of control is more operational in novel situations. He notes that while some students may encounter novel situations in their academic endeavors, most academic situations in college are very similar to those students have met before. Therefore, he would not expect completely consistent results.

The alternative viewpoint is that the inconsistencies may be due to a confounding factor in the locus of control concept itself. Heider (1958) suggests consideration of four related factors to which a behavior can be attributed: task difficulty and ability (considered to be stable factors), and effort and luck (considered to be unstable factors). Weiner et al. (1971) maintain that internality as measured by the locus of control concept centers on one stable factor (ability) and one unstable factor (effort), thus producing the inconsistencies noted in the literature. Weiner and others (Frieze & Weiner, 1971; McMahan, 1973; Weiner et al., 1972) further maintain that the unstable factors are more closely associated with affective responses, such as happiness over success or despondency over failure, while the more cognitively oriented stable factors are more closely associated with performance.

In several studies designed to control the confounding factor, these researchers found that academic performance had a stronger relationship to stable factors (ability, task difficulty) than to unstable factors (effort, luck). These studies also indicated the expected positive relationship between locus of control and affective responses. In a later study conducted with students in a psychology class, Keller, Sutterer, and Goldman (1978) used Rotter's scale as a locus of control measure, the Survey of Study Habits and Attitudes Inventory (SSHA) (Brown & Holzman, 1967) as a measure of study habits and attitudes, and rate of progress and final grade point average as performance measures. All the locus of control measures were more highly correlated with the SSHA attitude scales than with the study habits scales. Locus of control was not found to be a significant predictor of either performance measure.

Attributions. Some theorists (Johnston & Winograd, 1985) and investigators (DeBoer, 1983) have extended Weiner et al.'s (1972) idea that "attributions" for failure or success are linked to academic achievement. Weiner et al. referred to attribution theory, which describes motivations for human behavior, as the search for a causal understanding of failures. DeBoer devised a survey form that included the 4 factors used by Weiner as well as 7 others (quality of instruction, quality of high school preparation, social distractions, desire to achieve high grades, ability to work hard and long on difficult tasks, standards set by the instructor, and ability to concentrate while studying). The survey, which was sent to 650 college freshmen, asked students to rate the relative importance of the 11 factors and to predict expected course grades. Respondents were designated "high success" students if they met or exceeded grade predictions and "low success" students if they did not. Those later designated high success students rated 8 of the 11 factors as having more of an effect on their performance than did the low success students. The two groups showed no significant differences on their rating of the other 3 factors (quality of high school preparation, social distractions, and course difficulty). DeBoer notes that his findings are basically in agreement with the theory proposed by Weiner et al. (1971), and concludes that the association between long term expectancy and stable success factors does affect academic motivation. Further research in this area seems warranted.

Academic job involvement. Several investigators have adapted instruments developed for business and industry to academic settings to measure the degree to which a job situation affects a student's academic success. Batlis (1978) and Edwards and Waters (1980) found positive relationships between academic job involvement (i.e., students' degree of involvement in class assignments and class situations) and course performance. Edwards and Waters (1982) investigated a possible relationship between academic job involvement and attrition in a two-year follow-up of 135 students on whom data were gathered in their freshman year. No significant relationship was found, however. They conclude that attrition may reflect a much wider range of variables than does academic achievement in a particular course.

Self-monitoring. Since self-monitoring strategies encourage students to channel their academic achievement responsibility to improve academic performance, and since these strategies have also been found to enhance motivation, they seem pertinent to this discussion. Two elements are considered essential in self-monitoring: systematic self-observation and subsequent recording of these observations (Nelson, 1977; Richards, 1977). Self-monitoring can be applied to numerous situations, such as observing and recording the number of pages read or the amount of notes taken in studying a subject for a particular period of time, observing and recording distractions encountered in a particular study situation, or observing and recording instances of success or failure in taking effective notes from a lecturer (Kirschenbaum & Perri, 1982).

Richards (1981) has directed a number of controlled studies investigating self-monitoring. He has concluded that research results on self-monitoring indicate progress beyond the "promising" stage, and that this strategy is an effective way of helping students improve their academic performance. Numerous controlled studies involving groups of college students support this view (Groveman, Richards, & Caple, 1977; Richards et al., 1976). In addition to the group successes, Richards (1981) reports that he and his colleagues have found self-monitoring to be an important discriminant of successful self-management by students coping with study problems on their own, citing studies by Hefferman and Richards (1981) and Perri and Richards (1977) among others. He notes that two remaining concerns are to gain an understanding of why the procedure works and to determine the factors that may contribute to long term effects on student behavior.

Investigators outside of the Richards group have reported mixed results in studies in which self-monitoring—either alone or combined with study skills strategies such as stimulus control, self-reinforcement, or goal setting—was an independent variable. In a number of studies including self-monitoring of such procrastination behaviors as neglecting to turn work in on time, delaying studying, or arriving late to class, self-monitoring was reported to improve both academic behaviors and achievement (Jackson & Van Zoost, 1972; Kirschenbaum & Perri, 1982; Sieveking et al., 1971). However, other researchers (Bristol & Sloane, 1974; Green, 1982; Greiner & Karoly, 1976) found that self-monitoring, either alone or combined with study skills strategies, did not help students decrease procrastination behaviors or improve grades.

In a study in which a variety of self-monitoring techniques were used, Johnson and White (1971) compared grade point averages of 97 college students in three groups: those assigned to monitor their study behaviors, those who monitored their dating behavior, and those in a control group who conducted no self-monitoring. The students who engaged in self-monitoring of study behaviors received higher grades than either of the other two groups, but only superiority over the control group was statistically significant. In a study conducted by Morgan (1981), self-monitoring of specific study behaviors chosen and formulated by the students was effective in improving both the target behaviors and course grades.

Some experimental efforts have been directed toward determining factors that may increase the effects of self-monitoring on academic behaviors and performance. Mahoney et al. (1973) found that students on a continuous self-monitoring schedule during review for the Graduate Record Examination (GRE) studied longer and performed better on the exam's quantitative problems than did students on an intermittent self-monitoring schedule. Richards et al. (1976), investigating the relationship between how much students know about their own study behaviors and the impact of self-monitoring, found that students who had the least prior information about their own study behaviors gained the most from using the self-monitoring strategy. The number of self-monitoring methods used was found to be a contributing factor in a study by Mount and Tirrell (1977). Some theorists, such as Bandura (1982) and Mc-Combs (1988), suggest that to assume self-management of their learning students need to perceive themselves as competent in their ability to apply appropriate cognitive and affective strategies. They note that increasing students' ability to monitor their behavior while enhancing their perceptions of being in control of their own learning can enhance both motivation and achievement.

Although few study skills authors advise students to self-monitor their study behavior, research suggests that this strategy may help improve academic performance. The relative ease of using the strategy, plus the fact that students have used it successfully as a self-administered technique as well as in group and individual counseling settings (Richards, 1981), would seem to warrant its inclusion in study skills texts and in college reading/study skills classes.

Self-reinforcement. Self-reinforcement, like self-monitoring, is a strategy that students can assume themselves. With this technique, students reward themselves in some way after a desired response (Jones, Nelson, & Kazdin, 1977; Mahoney & Arnkoff, 1978). In his discussion of self-control studies,

Richards (1981) concludes that self-reinforcement does not improve study behavior or academic performance more than self-monitoring alone, citing two studies that specifically illustrate this point (Richards et al., 1976; Van Zoost & Jackson, 1974). Richards also contends that self-reinforcement needs careful handling by a counselor for students to take it seriously.

Two other studies indicate that self-reinforcement, in conjunction with other self-control or related techniques, may enhance academic behaviors or achievement. In a study with 96 college students, Greiner and Karoly (1976) found that students trained in a combination of self-reinforcement, self-monitoring, planning, and study methods performed better than students trained in study methods alone. However, groups who were trained only in self-reinforcement and self-monitoring, or in self-monitoring alone, did not significantly outperform students trained in study methods alone. Only the students trained in the combination of all four strategies displayed superior performance. A later study (Green, 1982) also presented a somewhat encouraging picture. Green evaluated the effectiveness of self-monitoring alone or self-monitoring plus self-reinforcement in improving procrastination behaviors displayed by six academically disadvantaged minority college students. Although self-reinforcement alone had no significant effect, self-monitoring plus self-reinforcement decreased procrastination and improved academic behaviors.

While none of the studies discussed here indicates that self-reinforcement alone is an effective strategy, self-reinforcement combined with other strategies proved effective in two out of four of them. Further research is needed to determine under what conditions self-reinforcement may improve academic behaviors and performance.

Problem solving. Problem solving is an important and complex part of assuming self-responsibility. In this section we address several aspects of this issue, including theoretical views on the nature of the problem-solving process; steps or stages involved in problem solving; factors related to successful problem solving, traits of successful and unsuccessful problem solvers; indications that problem solving can be learned; and the use of problem-solving strategies in programs designed to enhance the academic behaviors and achievement of college students.

Pitt (1983) sees problem solving as having two main theoretical perspectives: an information processing model and a Piagetian model. Arguing that these viewpoints are complementary rather than mutually exclusive, Pitt has created her own model to reconcile the two. Looking at the issue from a somewhat different perspective, Heppner (1978) has identified a range of views about the problem-solving process, varying from the learning approaches typified by the cited works of such investigators as Gagne (1964) and Skinner (1974), to the traditional cognitive gestalt approaches exemplified by Koehler (1925) and Maier (1970), to the computer simulation and mathematical models described by Newell and Simon (1972).

Although problem solving is viewed from many different vantage points, there seems to be considerable agreement on the steps or stages involved in the problem-solving process. Pitt (1983) lists these five steps, which researchers seem to agree on almost universally: (1) recognition of the problem, (2) analysis of contributing factors, (3) consideration of possible solutions, (4) choice of optimal solution, and (5) evaluation of feedback to determine results. These steps closely approximate the five problem-solving stages involved in the utility model introduced by D'Zurilla and Goldfried (1971).

In an analytical review of the research on problem solving, Heppner (1978) discusses the characteristics and research findings associated with each of the five stages proposed by D'Zurilla and Goldfried (1971). In the initial stage, general orientation, Heppner indicates a need to accept the existence of problems as a normal part of living, to accept the presence of particular problems, and ideally to feel competent to solve problems. The suggested procedures for helping someone use problem-solving strategies include showing short videotapes of people in the process of solving problems, encouraging verbalization of problems, and sharing information on successful problem-solving instances. With reference to the second stage, referred to as problem identification and verification, Heppner suggests encouraging behaviors typical of good problem solvers, such as gathering information about the problem, operationalizing vague elements, and identifying relationships among environmental events related to the problem. Heppner's analysis of the third stage of the problem solving, generation of alternatives, is that it is not as simple as it might seem. He notes that students may need help in overcoming the tendency to reduce the number of alternatives by exhibiting bias against certain possibilities or by not being creative enough to see novel solutions. Brainstorming and reorganizing ideas were strategies suggested as being helpful.

The fourth stage, decision making, involves selecting one of a set of alternatives. Here Heppner (1978) reports D'Zurilla and Goldfried's (1971) contention that making good decisions entails choosing an alternative with both high probability and high desirability, being consistent with personal goals, being willing to assume personal responsibility for decisions, and reaching a solution that has minimum negative aspects. The fifth stage, verification and evaluation, involves testing the plan of action and matching the outcome of the response to some standard. Heppner suggests that in evaluating responses, individuals should use techniques such as self-monitoring and self-reinforcement to encourage continuation of the behaviors necessary for dealing successfully with the identified problem. Although Heppner's review was not limited to college students or to the solving of academic problems, his analysis of D'Zurilla and Goldfried's stages of problem solving can be used in dealing with academic and personal problems that may impede study.

A number of investigators have examined the differences between effective and ineffective problem solvers. Nezu (1985) administered the Problem Solving Inventory (Heppner & Petersen, 1982)—along with depression, anxiety, problem identification, and locus of control measures—to 213 undergraduate students. Self-appraised effective problem solvers reported less depression, fewer trait and state problems, and less distress associated with these problems than did self-appraised poor problem solvers. These findings are consistent with those of Heppner, Reeder, and Larson (1983), who found that self-appraised effective problem solvers had better self-concepts, displayed more consistency in their self-perceptions and were less critical of themselves than self-perceived ineffective problem solvers. This study also found that effective problem solvers had fewer dysfunctional thoughts, fewer irrational beliefs, and less blameful coping styles.

Attempts to train students to use problem-solving strategies more effectively also have been reported in the literature. Gal'Perin and Danilova (1980) reported on the effectiveness of training students in an analytical process that involved studying the problem situation in general and then the various associated hypotheses. They reported that 16 university students trained to study in this way replaced their tendency to collect necessary information in an unconscious and unorganized way and learned to make decisions intuitively with an approach that included a systematic, conscious, and well-organized analysis of the problem, the formulation and verification of possible solutions, and a more divergent and productive thinking process.

Nezu and D'Zurilla (1981) investigated the effects of training students in a method of defining and formulating socially oriented problems on their ability to choose effective solutions for such problems. This method was based on the utility model of decision making formulated by D'Zurilla and Goldfried (1971). The researchers confirmed their hypothesis that students trained in this decision-making method would make significantly better decisions about problems presented. Finally, Lochhead (1982) asserts that students can be taught to become effective problem solvers without being programmed to execute specific problem-solving techniques. He offers evidence to support his system, which emphasizes training in the art of inventing and selecting appropriate strategies.

Of particular relevance here are the investigations linking training in problem-solving strategies with improvement in college students' academic performance. In a case study of three college students learning genetics, Baird and White (1982) reported that increasing students' awareness of the nature of the learning process and training them in procedures for enhancing self-evaluation and decision making helps them improve learning. Richards and Perri (1978) investigated two means of prolonging the effectiveness of self-control treatments intended to improve college students' academic performance: behavioral problem solving and faded counselor contact. The results indicated that training in problem solving was an effective treatment maintenance strategy, but that brief fading of counselor contact was not. Hunter et al. (1982) reported on a successful program called Stress on Analytical Reasoning (SOAR), which was designed to enhance the problem-solving and academic abilities of prefreshmen during a summer program. Stowbridge (1983) described an introductory course in computer programming that emphasized the problem-solving processes taught to college freshmen to improve their ability to learn other college subjects. Results indicated that the course was successful in improving academic performance.

Although more controlled research is needed on the use of problem-solving techniques for dealing with college students' academic and related problems, currently available research has shown promising results. The studies reviewed here indicate that effectiveness in problem solving is related to personality traits associated with academic success, and that problem-solving strategies can help college students improve academic performance.

Our review of the literature related to locus of control, attributions, and academic job involvement suggests that more research in these areas is needed before specific recommendations can be made to authors of study skills texts. It does seem appropriate, however, to recommend that such authors could elaborate on their general advice for developing positive attitudes by helping students identify situations in which success has been attained (e.g., graduating from high school, being accepted to college). Building such a recognized history of success may contribute to the stability of students' academic expectations and motivation.

In this section we reviewed three strategies for assuming responsibility for academic achievement: self-monitoring, self-reinforcement, and problem solving. These techniques, along with stimulus control (discussed in Chapter 5 of this volume), have been used to motivate college students to put suggested study strategies into actual practice. These techniques have also been used to help college students change behaviors that interfere with academic progress and success. Self-monitoring has been used with some success both in group counseling sessions and in self-help situations in which students were given handouts describing its use. While self-monitoring and problem solving have been successful in programs in which they were the sole behavioral component, self-reinforcement has shown success only in combination with other behavioral strategies. Tailoring combinations of behavioral strategies to suit the needs of individual students may be especially effective in motivating students to apply study strategies or to overcome interfering habits. Although, as Richards (1981) notes, it is difficult to get students to continue using learned behaviors that enhance academic success, problem solving has shown some promise as a maintenance strategy.

In view of these findings, including more of these strategies in study skills texts would seem warranted. Also, their careful implementation into college reading and study skills programs seems justified.

Developing positive attitudes. Several researchers have found positive relationships between general achievement in college and self-concept (Bailey, 1971; DeLisle, 1953; Griffore & Samuels, 1978; Simpson & Boyle, 1975). However, other investigators have failed to find a significant relationship (Badgett, 1968; Boshier & Hamic, 1968; Iglinsky & Wiant, 1971). Badgett, Hope, and Kerley (1971) investigated the possibility that self-concept may be more positively related to some academic areas than to others. They found a positive relationship between self-concept and academic aptitude among students in the colleges of architecture, liberal arts, and sciences, but an inverse relationship among students in the colleges of agriculture, business, engineering, and veterinary medicine. In a more recent study, Robinson and Cooper (1984) found a positive relationship between self-concept and academic success among freshmen pursuing technological careers.

A number of methods have been used in an attempt to change attitudes and increase student motivation with the hope of improving academic performance. We review selected treatment studies associated with two methods: extrinsic rewards and contingency contracting.

Extrinsic rewards. Bebeau and Sullivan (1982) conducted a study to determine university education juniors' preference for various academic incentives. Their results showed that release from final exams and positive comments from the instructor were the preferred incentives. Jackson and Van Zoost (1972) randomly assigned 47 university freshmen to a self-administered reinforcement group, an external reinforcement group, or to one of two control groups. Both treatment groups were given the opportunity to earn back a $10 deposit they had made. Both types of reinforcement were found to benefit study habits, but neither produced a significant gain in academic performance.

Interrelationships between various types of extrinsic motivation and instructor variables have also been examined. For example, Marsh (1984) conducted a study in which 416 college students viewed one of several videotaped lectures and then completed an objective examination based on the lecture. The lectures varied in the amount of test content covered and the degree of lecturer expressiveness. Some groups were told before the lecture that they would receive money for correct responses (incentive to learn and perform), some were given this information after the lecture (incentive to perform), and others were not given an incentive. Marsh found that better student performance was associated with incentives, content coverage, and lecturer expressiveness, although the effects of instructor expressiveness varied with the incentives. When no outside incentive was given, the effects of lecture expressiveness were significant; however, when extrinsic motivation was provided, instructor expressiveness had no significant effect. Perry and Dickens (1984) found similar results in a separate study. Overall, the findings of these studies suggest that extrinsic rewards can enhance academic performance, particularly when associated with other forms of reinforcement.

Contingency contracting. In a study in which some students had short term contracts for curriculum mastery, some had long term contracts, and some none at all, students operating with contracts had higher final exam scores than students in the self-paced groups (Brooke & Ruthven, 1984). Changes in study habits and attitudes also tended to favor contract group students.

Since the enrollment of college students with academic problems in study skills or related courses is not voluntary, and since the nature of the relationship between locus of control and academic achievement is far from clear, study skills instructors must work with students whose attitudes vary widely. As Paris, Lipson, and Wixson (1983) note, students' independent learning is often a combination of "both skill and will" (p. 305). Therefore, extrinsic reinforcement and contingency contracting strategies seem worth consideration by authors of study skills texts and college instructors. Further research and analysis are warranted.

Setting goals. Supporters of the expectancy theory, as postulated by Vroom (1964, 1965) and later modified by others, argue that an individual's short term goals affect performance and are related to long term goals. Malloch and Michael (1981) state that self-efficacy (expectancy) may provide a simple method of measuring and quantifying motivation and thus may also prove useful in predicting academic success. In a study conducted by these two investigators, 71 college students were asked to predict their grade point average for a particular semester (considered a short term goal). They were also asked to indicate the relative importance to them of such alternative long term goals as material success and lasting friendships. The researchers concluded that the expectancy (short term goal) measure contributed more to the predictability of GPA than an ability measure (American College Testing assessment) alone.

In a study designed to investigate the congruence of self-efficacy and locus of control, Minor and Roberts (1984) asked students to predict their ability to solve anagrams. When directions for the task were given, some subjects were told that their ability to solve the problems would depend on their verbal ability (skill directions), while others were told that verbal ability would not be a determining factor (chance directions). The researchers reasoned that internally oriented students would perform better with skill directions and externally oriented students with chance directions. No significant differences were found, but the order of results was as expected.

A number of studies have investigated the relationships among factors pertinent to career goals, academic motivation, and performance. Chase and Keene (1981) found a positive relationship between time of declaration of major and academic performance. Students who declared their majors early tended to achieve at a higher level than their academic indicators (Scholastic Aptitude Test and high school grades) would have predicted. On the other hand, students who delayed their declaration of major beyond the second year of college tended to achieve below their predicted levels. Super (1977) postulated that students are more likely to succeed in college if they explore career choices, if they have facility in decision making, if they seek occupational direction congruent with their interests, and if they estimate their interests accurately. And according to Altmaier, Rapaport, and Seeman (1983), probationary students listed uncertainty over career goals as one of the major factors interfering with their academic performance.

Using recently developed measures of career maturity, Healy et al. (1984) investigated the relationship between career indicators and college grade point averages for two groups of students: 182 community college students taking either a health science or a psychology course, and 126 freshmen in an academic advancement program for disadvantaged students. Students' perceptions of their decision-making abilities correlated significantly with GPA for both groups of students. The authors pointed out that it was impossible to determine the extent to which basic motivation to achieve in college affected career indicators, or vice versa, but they noted that students might well profit from attempts to move forward on their career-setting goals and other aspects of career maturity.

A somewhat more generalized goal-related factor is goal instability, defined as a lack of the mature, self-directed system of values and goals that guide individuals toward accomplishments and self-expression (Scott & Robbins, 1985). These investigators found a moderate correlation between goal instability scores and several measures of academic achievement in a study involving 72 undergraduate students enrolled in learning skills classes.

The positive influence of setting relevant goals on the performance of a task has been well documented in the literature, as indicated in an extensive review spanning the period from 1969 to 1980 (Locke et al., 1981). The authors found that the beneficial effects of goal setting on task performance was one of the most robust and replicable findings in the psychological literature. According to the authors, these benefits accrue because goals direct the individual's attention to the task, mobilize energies and efforts, promote persistence, and encourage the development of strategies relevant to goal attainment. Goals are indicated as most likely to benefit performance when they are challenging without being unattainable, when they are specific, when they are accepted or chosen by the individual, when their outcomes are of high value, and when the time needed for their attainment seems reasonable. Students often fail to achieve not because they lack ability but because they don't use goal-directed strategies efficiently (Winograd, 1984).

Studies using goal setting with college students have tended to be designed either to use goal setting to improve course grades or to determine whether goal setting affects the learning of particular academically oriented tasks. Studies examining the effects of goal setting on academic achievement (as

Risko, Fairbanks, and Alvarez

reflected by course performance) have varied considerably in experimental design and have shown mixed results. Locke and Bryan (1968), for example, investigated the relationship of goal level to academic performance by asking college students to indicate the grade point averages they hoped for, expected, and would try for, both in their easiest and most difficult courses. The researchers found that students who set difficult goals more often failed to meet their goals but also achieved higher-level course performance.

Mercier and Ladouceur (1983) investigated the relative value of five different self-control treatments, including setting proximal goals, setting distal goals, and increasing study time, on improving grades. The treatment group that involved both self-monitoring and distal goals spent more time studying than either the group that used self-monitoring alone or the groups that received no treatment. No significant improvement was found in grades, however. Warner (1984) examined the effects of goal setting on test performance in an education course that involved 167 undergraduate students. Students in the experimental group completed a "goal card" one week before each of three course exams, noting their anticipated grade on the tests. Analysis of the data indicated no significant differences between goal-setting conditions and task difficulty.

Morgan (1985) conducted a study with 240 education students to determine the relative influence on course grades of three treatment packages designed for private study: self-monitoring of subgoals, self-monitoring of distal goals, and self-monitoring of time. In the subgoal group, students were given training in goals setting. They were then asked to set their own specific process and product goals and modes of evaluation for study sessions in the target courses, and to record both their goals and their progress evaluations. In the distal goals group, students had the same training but set only one product goal for each session relevant to notes they took using a recommended format. Students in the time monitoring group set targets for the amount of time they wanted to study and kept records of time actually spent. The group that monitored time spent studying did in fact spend more time studying. However, the group that set definite process-oriented subgoals for each study session outperformed both of the other groups on final examinations. This group also indicated the highest degree of interest in the course.

This seems of special interest for a number of reasons. First, the study design took into consideration several of the principles that Locke et al. (1980) associate with high effects for goal setting. Second, students in the subgoal and distal groups set their own goals. Third, the subgoals used were process oriented, relating to specific study tasks connected with the chapter being read.

Research on the effects of goal setting on improving academic performance is a relatively recent development, and results are mixed. Further research is indicated, with careful consideration given to the types of goals that may prove most effective in boosting academic performance.

To summarize, studies focusing on the relationships of career goals and goal instability on performance indicated that students who set career goals early or who have an overall sense of goal and value direction tend to perform better. It is difficult to determine the extent to which poor motivation causes a delay in setting career goals, or the extent to which not having career goals adversely affects motivation.

Studies focusing on goal setting as a strategy for improving academic performance vary in the type of goals set and other aspects of design, and show mixed results; further research is indicated.

The study skills texts that address the issue of goal setting explicitly are the exception rather than the rule. This should certainly change. Since goal setting can be done relatively easily and with little interruption in other activities, using this strategy along with self-monitoring or other self-management strategies seems worth the effort, especially if evaluation procedures are included.

Managing stress and anxiety. In a review of the empirical literature related to anxiety and college-age students, Head and Lindsey (1982) examine numerous studies and draw the following conclusions regarding the relationship between anxiety and academic performance:

- a high anxiety level impedes performance, at least for poor and average students;
- sometimes anxiety can be helpful for students of high intelligence;
- females tend to show a higher correlation between anxiety and performance than males and also tend to have higher levels of anxiety;
- task difficulty has a definite effect on anxiety; and
- certain instructional variables affect anxiety and thus performance.

A number of studies have found a significant relationship between self-perceived problem-solving ability and anxiety (Gross & Mastenbrook, 1980; Hentschel & Ternes 1984; Nezu, 1985). These studies indicate that students who perceive themselves as poor problem solvers tend to be more anxious about life in general and about academic pursuits in particular.

Much literature has focused on reducing anxiety in order to improve performance. In their review, Head and Lindsey (1982) distill the numerous recommendations made for reducing anxiety down to three approaches that research findings suggest are reasonably successful: using behavior modification techniques; conducting group or individual counseling sessions, and developing students' studying and test taking skills. Each of these approaches could be discussed in study skills texts as reasonable ways to manage stress and anxiety; other than Pauk (1984) and Wood (1986), the authors of the texts we reviewed offered few suggestions in this area. Test anxiety is addressed more fully by Wark and Flippo (Chapter 7, this volume).

Implications

Three types of strategies regarding motivation seem worthy of special note. Research on problem solving and self-monitoring seems to indicate that these strategies are worth serious consideration for inclusion in study skills programs. Since they are process-oriented, they can be used to implement rather than replace other matters of concern, such as the teaching of reading comprehension. Goal setting also is of special interest. The theory that goal setting may be closely related to the motivational construct has some support, and this strategy seems worthy of further research and instructional attention.

Some concerns might be raised about strategies emerging from the counseling literature being recommended for use by reading and study skills instructors without special training. However, the strategies that seem to show the most promise (self-monitoring and problem solving) are not new and have not been confined to counseling environments. Richards (1981) points out that the idea of self-monitoring is at least 400 years old and has been used in many situations. Also, we recommend that study skill instructors avail themselves of opportunities for training in these procedures, either through coursework, independent study, or other means. A review of training manuals for self-control techniques is currently available (Glasgow & Rosen, 1978).

The need for further research is apparent, and study skills instructors, especially those who work with required or credited programs that produce stable populations, are in a good position to conduct such research. Research using various components of both study strategies and self-control or related strategies seems desirable.

Memory and Attention

Our review of the theoretical and empirical literature on memory and attention has led us to identify three assumptions that seem to have influenced suggestions from study skills texts, questions for empirical research, or both. First, variables such as assuming self-responsibility, developing a positive self-concept, establishing personal goals for learning, and managing stress and the learning environment not only enhance motivation but also influence the activation and maintenance of attention and memory. As Pauk (1984) states in his study skills text, memory is boosted by attention, and attention is dependent on interest. Whether tasks require rote memorization or complex learning, interest, memory, and attention affect each other as information is processed (Weinstein & Mayer, 1986). Since many of these factors have been discussed elsewhere in the chapter, we will emphasize here only those factors not previously dealt with.

The second assumption we identified is that memory and attention are interactive, and activating them successfully depends on many of the same learning strategies. Authors of study skills texts, however, typically have dichotomized learning strategies, suggesting that each strategy is designed exclusively for the attainment of either memory or attention. They do not address the idea that these strategies may improve both memory and attention simultaneously. For example, one author may recommend the use of reflective pauses during reading as a way to focus attention while another may recommend the same technique as a way to store information in long term memory.

The confusion over whether a specific study strategy enhances memory or attention probably relates to a changing theoretical base. Theories of how memory operates and what constitutes attention are under constant revision. In examining models of information processing, such as the one proposed by Cook and Mayer (1983), it is apparent that it is not easy to identify behaviors that are strictly memory or attention oriented. According to the Cook and Mayer model, for instance, attention and memory interact at every level of information processing. These levels include *selection* (the student actively attends to specific information, allowing this information to transfer into working memory), *construction* (the student actively makes connections between ideas being processed in working memory), *integration* (the student relates prior knowledge held in long term memory to new information in working memory), and *acquisition* (the student actively transfers the information from working memory to long term memory). In this section we discuss specific study strategies as helpful for either memory or attention with the understanding that their functions are not mutually exclusive.

The third assumption that relates to this review is that the strategies for aiding memory and attention (the *process* of learning) are often the same as those for improving comprehension (the *product* of learning). Because some authors of study skills texts or empirical literature view comprehension as easier to measure than memory or attention, they often assume that if students are comprehending they are also attending and remembering. This, however, is not an assumption that guided our review or the presentation of information in this section of the chapter. We agree with Baker and Brown (1984) and Kintsch (1986) that reading to comprehend and reading to remember involve different tasks. While comprehension is desirable for studying, to remember information a student must employ purposeful use of memory-facilitating activities (Baker & Brown; Weinstein, 1987). For this review, only theoretical literature and empirical research related explicitly to how strategies enhance memory and attention are discussed.

Managing Memory: Suggestions from Study Skills Texts

Most authors of the study skill texts we reviewed (88 percent) make suggestions about ways to improve students' memory. These authors usually preface their suggestions to enhance memory with a description of long and short term memory. They note that cognitive psychologists describe memory as the process of retaining information in the brain and then retrieving it when it is needed. Consistent with our definition, these authors describe memory as an active and selective process requiring the use of strategies for the reconstruction, storage, and retrieval of information. The suggestions these texts offer for enhancing memory seem to relate directly to four interrelated areas: mnemonics, classification, summarization, and elaboration.

In their study skills text, Postman, Keckler, and Schneckner (1985) define mnemonics as "memory words," or words, phrases, jingles, or acronyms used to aid memory for specific information. Mnemonics (also called "memory tricks" by McWhorter, 1987, and Sherman, 1984) are recommended to help students rehearse information that has no inherent, meaningful organization (Nist & Diehl, 1985; Sotiriou, 1984) or lists of factual information (McWhorter, 1987; Wood, 1986).

Even though mnemonics are recommended by most authors of study skill texts, all authors who discussed memory provided additional suggestions. To enhance memory of text ideas, students are encouraged to use text information meaningfully by summarizing, classifying, and elaborating on the text. The authors present various activities to develop each of these strategies. For example, students are advised to rewrite ideas from their texts in their own words (McWhorter, 1986a, 1986b; Postman, Keckler, & Schneckner, 1985; Sherman, 1984); attach details to main ideas and choose specific details to be remembered (Joffe, 1988; McWhorter, 1986a, 1986b, 1987; Pauk, 1984; Postman, Keckler, & Schneckner, 1985; Sotiriou, 1984; Wood, 1986), rely on prior knowledge to aid understanding of new information (Joffe, 1988; McWhorter, 1984, 1987; Pauk, 1984; Wood, 1986); devise or make use of associations or analogies among units of information (Pauk, 1984; Sherman, 1984; Sotiriou, 1984); and discover text organization (McWhorter, 1987; Sherman, 1984; Wood, 1984).

Managing Memory: Related Literature

Mnemonics. Numerous researchers (Bellezza, 1981; Levin, 1981) attribute the ability to remember information, at least in part, to the use of deliberate mnemonic strategies. In a survey by Carlson et al. (1976), college students using mnemonics to learn a list of words had a higher GPA than students who did not generate mnemonics to aid recall. Experiments in which students were induced to use organizational mnemonics (those that relate apparently unrelated information) and encoding mnemonics (those that transform information into another framework) revealed superior recall of information. Mnemonic devices producing such favorable results included the organizational method of loci, in which students assign units of information to visual images of specified locations (Groninger, 1971; Ross & Lawrence, 1968); peg words, in which units of information are assigned to images of concrete objects and remembered in serial order (Bugelski, 1968; Morris & Reid, 1970; Wood, 1967); and links, in which units of information are linked to one another through visual images (Delin, 1969). Using an organizational mnemonic to create meaningful associations through construction of simple stories (Bower & Clark, 1969) or to develop hierarchical relationships to remember lists of unassociated words (Wittrock & Carter, 1975) also was found to improve college students' retention of information.

Encoding mnemonics, such as keyword devices and visual imagery, have also been used to facilitate memory. The literature provides at least some support for the use of keywords to induce visual images of representative and meaningful words. This strategy was found to help college students memorize definitions of unfamiliar words (Sweeney & Bellezza, 1982) and foreign language vocabulary (Atkinson, 1975; Atkinson & Raugh, 1975; Raugh & Atkinson, 1975); however, its usefulness for college foreign language learners described as "good students" was not substantiated in a study conducted by Hall, Wilson, and Patterson (1981). The keyword method as defined by Levin (1981) and others requires the learner to establish a keyword that has an acoustic link to the word or words being memorized and to form an imagery link between the keyword and the meaning of the information to be learned. Visual images that create a context or situation for new information may produce recall of related information. Roediger (1980), for instance, found that images created by a group of college students to encourage serialized recall worked better than the formation of separate images for each item of information to be learned. In an earlier study, Bower (1972) also found that simultaneous formation of two separate images produces weaker associations than composite, interacting images.

While authors of study skills texts do not distinguish different levels of mnemonic learning, their suggestions for study strategies can be categorized into at least two levels: simple repetition and meaningful organization of information to be remembered. Support for different levels of learning through mnemonics is found in the literature. For example, Weinstein and Mayer (1986) categorize mnenomics as either rehearsal (i.e, repetition, such as the use of peg words) or elaborative (i.e., meaningful organization, such as the keyword method).

Although mnemonics are commonly associated with rote learning, Bellezza (1981) distinguishes mnemonic learning from learning by rote or learning by assimilation. He acknowledges that a simple verbal rehearsal (rote learning) may influence memorization of factual information, but he argues that it is the least efficient way of enhancing memory. According to Bellezza's framework, mnemonics provide organization (described as "cognitive cueing structures") of the information so it can be remembered. The cognitive cueing structures can take the form of rhymes, visual images, or stories and serve as signals to aid retrieval of information from memory. According to Bellezza, mnemonics are also different from assimilative learning, which he describes as the ability to remember information through associations with prior knowledge. According to this model, then, a mnemonic can be used to provide a meaningful classification system, such as the loci or keyword methods, and is used when prior knowledge is not activated to provide a strategy for remembering. The authors of study skills texts seem to follow this model.

The use of deliberate mnemonic strategies can produce superior recall of certain types of information, particularly lists of words or meaningful words for which images can be induced. As one strategy for learning, mnemonics may have an important effect on students' memory and attention power. Because of its limitations for more complex learning, however, mnemonics should be used in combination with other learning strategies (for instance, classification of thematic information).

Classification. Classifying information according to meaningful clusters is a common theme of study skills texts and is seen as important in improving memory. In general, students are advised to follow one or more of three strategies to organize information according to (1) major and supporting ideas, (2) the author's text structure, and (3) clusters or networks to illustrate relationships among superordinate and subordinate information.

The first of these strategies, preservation of meaning in memory, appears to require the ability to understand the central concepts and to selectively omit less relevant information (Gomulicki, 1956). The suggestion that students organize information around main ideas and supporting details is supported by the empirical literature. In their study with college students, Reder and Anderson (1980) conclude that subordinate information can be retrieved from memory only if the higher-level information is retrieved first. Additionally, understanding the theme or major concept of a passage and its relation to supporting details while selectively omitting less relevant details has been found to have a positive influence on memory of text ideas (Alvarez & Risko, 1982, 1989; Bransford & Johnson, 1972; Dooling & Christiansen, 1977; Gomulicki, 1956; Pompi & Lachman, 1967; Sulin & Dooling, 1974).

The usefulness of the second strategy, reliance on text organization to aid recall of information, has been established for some age groups (Frase, 1969, 1975; Montague & Carter, 1973; Myers, Pezdek, & Coulson, 1973), but its effect on college students' recall is not well-grounded in the empirical literature. Research presents us with evidence that children as young as 5 years old can rely on top-level information to aid memory (Christie & Schumacher, 1976). Identifying and using the author's structure has been found to aid the retention of elementary and middle school students (Bartlett, 1978; Taylor & Beach, 1984). Ideas that are functionally important according to an author's text organization are often recalled more easily than lower-order information (Meyer, 1975; Rumelhart & Ortony, 1977; Thorndyke, 1977). Further, explicit instruction on how to use top-level information was found to be helpful for retrieval of information by middle school students (Bartlett, 1978; Taylor, 1982).

Alerting students to text patterns to facilitate memory was not supported by Horowitz (1982). There is some evidence that college students are insensitive to text structure (Cooper et al., 1979), but further research with college students needs to be conducted to establish more precisely whether eliciting or inducing sensitivity to text structure across texts of varying organizational patterns will affect memory of text ideas.

The third strategy, making maps or networks to illustrate relationships among text ideas, is recommended (Weinstein, 1987), and has been found to aid college students' memory (Dansereau et al., 1979; Diekhoff, Brown, & Dansereau, 1982). Concept maps, as developed by Novak and Gowin (1984), are diagrams that visually represent a set of "concept meanings embedded in a framework of propositions" (p.15). Research by Novak and Gowin and their colleagues revealed that teaching college students how to construct concept maps has a powerful effect on retention of information (Cardemone, 1975; Minemier, 1983; Novak & Gowin, 1984). Concept maps provide students with a strategy to identify the hierarchical arrangement of concepts within texts and a way to cross-link relationships among text ideas.

Strategies such as identifying a text's central information, relying on text structure, and generating maps or conceptual frameworks seem to have potential for helping college students organize and classify text ideas. Although more research is needed to determine the effects of these procedures on students' learning and achievement, explicitly alerting students to important text ideas seems important for enhancing memory. Once students are able to classify and interrelate information to be remembered, they should be better able to summarize and synthesize this information.

Summarization. Summarizing is another strategy commonly recommended in study skills texts. It is seen as an activity that may encourage readers to allocate their attention more effectively so that memory of important information increases (Barclay, 1973; Honeck, 1973; Ross & DiVesta, 1976; Tierney & Cunningham, 1984; Weinstein, 1987). Corresponding to the rationale for classifying text information, the authors of study skills texts describe summarization as a way to help students reduce text information into meaningful units.

The use of a strategy such as summarization to reduce information to "gist" as a method to enhance memory is supported across a number of studies. For example, Welborn and English (1937), after a review of 83 experiments, concluded that memory for gist was more durable than memory for exact wording of information. Even with repeated practice, memory for gist rather than for verbatim information seemed to aid retention better (Howe, 1970); in addition, it was less resistant to interference from form change, such as a shift from passive to active voice (Sachs, 1967). Anderson (1980) and Howe and Singer (1975), however, found that rereading was a more effective strategy than summarizing for aiding college students' memory.

In their review of empirical research on the effects of summarization on learning, Anderson and Armbruster (1984) conclude that summarization is more likely to influence retention of information if students are taught how to summarize and if the information that is summarized relates to the criterion task. Brown, Campione, and Day (1981) report an example of this finding. Working with low-ability community college students, Day studied the effectiveness of summarization training with and without explicit cues intended for facilitating self-monitoring. She concluded that students with more learning problems required more explicit training in summarization. Providing such explicit training until the students could follow the rules of summarization seemed to improve their ability to recall main ideas and delete less important information. Brown & Campione (1978) found that junior college students were unable to adequately abbreviate text. Providing college students, who may not possess adequate summarization skills, with instruction in how to summarize—rather than just telling them to do so without instruction—may be what is needed in study skills texts for college students. Providing students with strategies for independent use of information in a meaningful way may further help students remember important ideas.

Elaboration. Advising students to use information meaningfully to increase memory and learning encompasses the concept of elaboration, or integrating prior knowledge into new information (Mayer, 1982, 1984; Weinstein, 1987; Weinstein & Mayer, 1986). While strategies such as mnemonics may enhance the "work space for problem-solving" function of working memory (Schiffrin & Schneider, 1977), long term memory is better enhanced by more meaning-oriented strategies (Bovy, 1981; Craik & Watkins, 1973). We know from research, even with very young children, that memory increases substantially when the material is meaningful, but "meaningful" is a relative term. Learning and memory are context sensitive (Jenkins, 1979), varying with the characteristics of the students, the text, the criterion task, and the learning content (Caverly & Orlando, this volume).

The advice of study skills texts to associate text information with prior knowledge has support in both the theoretical and empirical literature. Elaborating, or establishing connections between prior knowledge and to-be-learned information, plays a major role in knowledge acquisition (Schallert, 1982; Weinstein & Mayer, 1986). According to Wittrock's (1981, 1986) model of generative learning, students' ability to generate relationships between text information and prior knowledge is directly related to learning and memory. Several researchers have concluded that prior knowledge has a powerful effect on the learning of college students. Wittrock and Carter (1975) found that college students who were asked to generate meaningful associations among hierarchically arranged words significantly increased their retention of those words. In studies conducted with college students and adults, Anderson et al. (1977) and Snyder and Uranowitz (1978) concluded that the reader's perspective influences the amount and nature of recall, and that prior knowledge encourages inferences about text ideas.

In another series of experiments, Dansereau and his colleagues (Dansereau et al., 1979; Diekhoff, Brown, & Dansereau, 1982) found that encouraging students to use elaborative strategies aided memory of text ideas. In the treatment group, students working in pairs summarized what they read and then provided corrective feedback on each other's summaries. The researchers named this strategy MURDER, which stands for **M**ood (positive mindset for reading), **U**nderstand, **R**ecall, **D**etect (check for errors), **E**laborate, and **R**eview. The MURDER strategy involves learners in identifying, defining, and elaborating on key concepts and encourages them to self-monitor this knowledge. In these studies, the treatment group received significantly higher scores on recall tests than did students who were not trained.

Managing Attention: Suggestions from Study Skills Texts

Terms such as attention, concentration, intentional learning, and active participation are often used interchangeably by authors of study skills texts. For this chapter, we use the term *attention* to represent this area of study. Study skills texts generally describe attention as a limited capacity requiring an ability to focus on one thing while eliminating thoughts of other things (Joffe, 1988). In order to elicit and maintain attention, these authors recommend direct, purposeful, and selective action on the learner's part.

Among the strategies these authors suggest to aid attention are:

- establishing a study environment conducive to learning, with good lighting, appropriate equipment, and minimal external distraction (Pauk, 1984; Smith, 1981);

- setting goals, such as time goals, or establishing monitoring sheets on which goals or tasks are listed (Joffe, 1988; McWhorter, 1986a, 1986b, 1987; Shepherd, 1987; Smith, 1981).

- using the "humble pencil technique"—studying with a pencil in hand and summarizing, underlining, or writing down key words (Joffe, 1988; McWhorter, 1986; Pauk, 1984);

Risko, Fairbanks, and Alvarez

- having a positive attitude (McWhorter, 1987; Pauk, 1984);
- using study questions (Sherman, 1984);
- being an active reader by using reflective pauses, making notes, and self-checking (Sherman, 1984);
- rewarding personal study effort (Joffe, 1988; McWhorter, 1986a, 1986b; Shepherd, 1987); and
- relating new information to current knowledge (Sherman, 1984).

Some of these strategies have been discussed previously. Only those strategies that have not been discussed elsewhere in this or the previous chapter will be addressed here. These remaining strategies seem to relate to the effect of goal setting on attention, the "pencil in hand" strategies, or self-monitoring. We will also present suggestions from our review of related literature (e.g., use of text overviews or advance organizers), even though these suggestions do not correspond to recommendations made by authors of study skills texts.

Managing Attention: Related Literature

Several investigators (Anderson, Spiro, & Montague, 1977; Weinstein & Mayer, 1986; Wittrock, 1986) support the use of certain learning strategies to facilitate selective attention, which is defined as the ability to make active choices about information to be learned. Rather than relying on concepts such as practice, reinforcement, or review to explain how concentrated efforts encourage learning, some researchers have proposed and investigated models of attention (Wittrock, 1986). Research on how strategies can help students focus on certain kinds of information has provided us with insights about the effects of selective attention on memory and achievement.

Goal-setting activities. The use of cues, encouraged by college instructors and authors of content texts, has helped students direct their attention to important concepts. Cueing strategies such as inserted questions (Andre, 1979; Reynolds &

Anderson, 1980; Rickards, 1976), prereading objectives (Borer, 1981; Duchastel, 1979; Duell, 1974; Levin & Pressley, 1981; Melton, 1978), pretests (Hartley & Davies, 1981), guiding questions (Page, 1988), and postreading response criteria (Alexander, 1986) have been shown to help upper elementary, secondary, and college students to focus directly on criterion-relevant information (Baker, 1974; Bovy, 1981; Kaplan & Simmons, 1974). Such findings are consistent with attentional models of learning (Wittrock & Lumsdaine, 1977) in which theorists have speculated that when attention is focused on task-relevant information students will attend more closely to this information.

Researchers have attempted to monitor such attention focusing to determine more precisely how college students' attention is allocated. For example, McConkie, Rayner, and Wilson (1973) found that when college students constrained by time were encouraged to pace their reading, they directed their attention to the more task-relevant information and did not learn incidental information as well. Britton, Muth, and Glynn (1986) also found that students making an extra cognitive effort allocated attention to important information when processing time was limited. Manipulating the rate of text presentation by computer control, Allessi, Anderson, and Goetz (1979) found that focusing attention on important information through text look-backs related closely to performance on criterion texts.

Across a series of studies in which prereading goals (Anderson & Biddle, 1975; Rothkopf & Billington 1979) and text inserted questions (Britton et al., 1978) were presented to college students, researchers concluded that students were better able to answer questions on target information and to increase their inspection time and cognitive effort when they focused on task-relevant information. In a study by Alexander (1986), prereading directions encouraged college students to stay with a task to redo all or part of postreading questions. As Anderson and Armbruster (1984, p. 663) note, this increased focusing may produce a "burst of processing energy or a quantum leap in cognitive effort" that influences learning; the generation of deliberate behavior is probably stimulated by orienting tasks, such as prereading goals. Consistent with the theory of encoding specificity (which states that retrieval of information is influenced by cues received during acquisition), if learners have complex, meaning-oriented goals, they will focus their attention on a search for meaning relevant to those goals—in other words, they will engage in transfer-appropriate processing (Morris, Bransford, & Franks, 1977).

"Pencil in hand" strategies. A second set of factors that have been studied are those incorporated in what Weinstein and Mayer (1986) describe as complex rehearsal tasks. These include such strategies as copying material, taking selective verbatim notes, outlining, and underlining. In general, these strategies are supported by researchers because they allow time for the learner to select and practice specific information-gathering techniques. As indicated by Brennan et al. (1986), however, college students seem to prefer relying on underlining as a study strategy and excluding other options.

Studies conducted with college students seem to support the notion that such strategies may be beneficial because they aid the learner in directing attention to specific information. For example, Weinstein and Mayer (1986) argue that if a rehearsal strategy such as underlining is effective—as indicated by Blanchard & Mikkelson (1987), Fowler and Barker (1974), Rickards and August (1975), and Schnell and Rocchio (1975)— it seems to be because the learner is allocating more attention to acquire information. However, Weinstein and Mayer argue that there is little evidence that these rehearsal strategies help learners establish internal connections between text ideas or relate text information to prior knowledge (Caverly & Orlando, this volume).

The effectiveness of notetaking, another rehearsal strategy, on college students' learning has also received both support (Bretzing & Kulhavy, 1979) and notes of caution (Anderson, 1980; Poppleton & Austwick, 1964). Anderson and Armbruster (1984) conclude that notetaking can be effective in aiding study efforts if it encourages more attention to text ideas that are needed for criterion tasks. Mayer (1988) indicates that learning strategies aimed at focusing attention may be most useful when the goal of the learning task is to retain specific information rather than to determine which information is important to be learned.

Self-monitoring strategies. The authors of some study skills texts also suggest that students engage in activities that involve self-monitoring, (e.g., reflective pauses, self-questioning), but these authors do not provide explicit directions for doing so. Encouraging students to make active and conscious decisions about learning is recommended to enhance memory, attention, and motivation. There is some evidence that college students usually do not monitor their comprehension and that even when they do, they are inconsistent about it (Baker & Anderson, 1982; Brennan et al., 1986). Brennan and her colleagues found college students' self-reporting of strategic use to be different from actual use during observed study sessions.

College students who do monitor their study behavior—defined as self-observation—have consistently achieved higher grades than students who are not self-monitors (Groveman, Richards, & Caple, 1977; Johnson & White, 1971; Richards et al., 1976; Richards & Perri, 1978; Richards, Perri, & Gortney, 1976). Diekhoff, Brown, & Dansereau (1982) have established positive effects on information retention through their cooperative learning model (MURDER), which requires each student to monitor his or her processing of text information by listening and providing feedback to peers.

Self-questioning strategies have been found to be effective for college students. Duell (1978) found that students who developed multiple choice items from instructional objectives outperformed their peers who studied with a list of objectives. A similar finding was reported by Frase and Schwartz (1975) in a study in which college students who read a text and wrote questions performed better than their peers who simply read the text.

Advance organizers. Most authors of study skills texts do not explicitly direct students to use text-embedded overviews or advance organizers (Ausubel, 1960, 1968) to aid selective attention, even though they consider these strategies important in other aspects of studying. Although college students may not spontaneously use prereading strategies (Brenann et al., 1986), the use of previews or advance organizers has been found to help them focus their attention on important ideas, allowing them to elaborate and improve their retention (Mayer, 1979; Reigeluth, 1979). In a study conducted with college students, Goetz et al. (1983) found that the reader's perspective affected the allocation of attention, with more attention given to sentences relevant to the learner's prior knowledge or orienting framework. As suggested by Cirilo and Foss (1980) and Reynolds and Shirey (1988), attention is allocated to information deemed important according to the learning context or goals of the reader. Students can use strategies such as overviews, analogies, and narrative advance organizers to help them activate their prior knowledge and to focus their attention on relevant and important information.

Implications

There is a considerable amount of correspondence between what authors of study skills books suggest and what has been reported in the theoretical and empirical literature in regard to memory and attention. Both memory and attention are thought of as active and selective processes that can be enhanced by specific study strategies. The effectiveness of such strategies as mnemonics, classification, summarization, meaningful use of information, goal setting, and text overview with selected groups of students has been amply supported. Still needed are more explicit directions for the use and implementation of these strategies.

Although, for the most part, trends in research and the suggestions made by the authors of college study skills texts are congruent, it is difficult to determine whether the strategies recommended in the study skills texts are the most appropriate ones for students in college study skills programs. While researchers have reported positive effects of specific study strategies on memory and attention, this research has been conducted with college students enrolled in undergraduate psychology courses. Typically, researchers have not identified these students as having academic problems. Authors of study skills texts have relied on this literature, however, and have applied the findings of studies with mixed populations (students with both high and low levels of achievement) to a limited portion of that population (students with academic problems). Research is needed on the effects of target strategies on low achievers' learning and performance. Also, because study skills texts do not place much emphasis on self-monitoring of attention and memory strategies, it is not known whether students who know about these but do not use them will benefit from this approach. Finally, there is a need for research on the differential effects of strategies to determine what may work better for certain students and certain materials in specific learning contexts.

Conclusions

From our content analysis of college reading and study skills texts and our study of corresponding literature, three major conclusions can be made about motivation, memory, and attention. First, there is both pragmatic and theoretical/empirical support for teaching college students to control their own study efforts. Among the strategies strongly supported in the literature are those that help students establish self-reinforcing schedules and generate questions about the material they are studying. Students need to be encouraged to be self-disciplined and to make decisions about what is important for them to learn and to remember. The strategies discussed here are suggested to help students become aware of the processes of learning applicable to different learning contexts. The major discrepancy between the study skills texts and the literature is the amount of explicit information presented. Authors of study skills texts advise students to manage and govern their own learning, but for the most part they are not precise about how

Risko, Fairbanks, and Alvarez

students can acquire independent learning strategies and apply them to novel contexts (i.e., their content classes).

Our second conclusion is that students need to be encouraged to develop organizational strategies such as relying on text structure, relating subordinate details to central concepts, relating new information to prior knowledge structures, being selective about the information to be learned, and generating concept maps or networks. Such strategies are designed to help students reduce large masses of information into meaningful chunks or units. Authors of study skills texts and empiricists suggest that organizational aids help students to better manage and focus their study time.

Third, our review suggests that some recommendations within study skills texts may require a multidisciplinary approach. For example, while some study skills authors suggest ways for students to reduce their own stress level and to cope with anxiety, others suggest that counselors be brought in to train students in such strategies. Further study is needed to determine the extent and the range of optimal multidisciplinary resources.

These suggestions are offered for authors of reading and study skills texts, instructors of classes for college students with academic problems, and researchers. As an extension of what is currently found in reading and study skills texts, authors of such texts could include explicit information about the processes through which students can progress in self-monitoring and problem-solving strategies (Brown, Campione, & Day, 1981). In general, the authors of study skills texts explain neither the importance of nor the process for students taking responsibility for their own learning through the use of self-monitoring strategies such as self-observation, self-questioning, and goal setting. The relationship of such strategies to motivational attainment and the activation of attention and memory strategies needs to be explained to college students. The benefits and limitations of mnemonics as a rehearsal strategy should be explained in a context that illustrates how other strategies, such as goal setting, classification of thematic information, and reliance on text structure cues, can be developed to increase attention on and memory of complex information presented in texts. Procedures to identify and solve problems should be included and applied to content areas.

Instructors of college reading and study skills courses should provide well-balanced programs including strategies to promote motivation, self-monitoring, and problem solving. They should give students opportunities to learn how to apply self-monitoring and problem-solving strategies to their learning contexts. Instead of having students complete exercises within continued study skills learning situations or contrived texts, instructors should encourage them to apply study strategies to the learning tasks and texts in their classes. Instructors can serve as coaches and consultants to help students apply study strategies to their content classes (Schallert, Alexander, & Goetz, 1988). Strategies that respond simultaneously to multiple factors that affect learning should be emphasized. For example, Memory and Yoder (1988) provide a study strategy to improve concentration that also helps students monitor their concentration efforts, set goals for study, eliminate distractions, maintain an interest in the content being studied, and provide rewards for personal study. Gill and Bear (1988) suggest that variations of a directed reading-thinking activity can aid students' memory of text ideas as well as self-monitoring. Methods to record and evaluate the use of strategies should be practiced during in-class discussion, individual conferences, or both.

Our review suggests that additional research is needed in our target areas. Specifically, we see a need for systematic research investigating how strategies currently popular in study skills texts affect the learning of college students enrolled in reading and study skills classes. Cioffi's (1986) research provides a description of strategy clusters that high-achieving college students use when studying (e.g., use of imagery and paraphrasing to focus on target concepts) and suggests a line of study that may influence effective remedial interventions. Too much research has focused on the products of studying rather than on strategic behaviors that influence study efforts

(Alexander, 1986; Rothkopf & Bisbicos, 1967). Theoretical frameworks (Kirschenbaum & Perri, 1982) to examine the interaction of various task-related strategies (Alexander, 1986) and to determine the most useful research approaches to academic intervention for college students with academic difficulties need to be explored. Examining the effects of training on students' perception of competence and strategic behavior (Palmer & Goetz, 1988) could identify effective intervention strategies to modify study efforts.

References and Suggested Readings

Alexander, P.A. (1986). College students' use of task-related information during studying. *Reading Research and Instruction, 25*(2), 91-101.

Allen, G.J., Giat, L., & Cherney, R.J. (1974). Locus of control, test anxiety, and student performance in a personalized instruction course. *Journal of Educational Psychology, 66,* 968-973.

Allessi, S.M., Anderson, J.H., & Goetz, E.T. (1979). An investigation of lookbacks during studying. *Discourse Processes, 2,* 197-212.

Altmaier, E.M., Rapaport, R.J., & Seeman, D. (1983). A needs assessment of liberal arts students on academic probation. *Journal of College Student Personnel, 24,* 266-267

Alvarez, M.C., & Risko, V.J. (1982, October). *Using a thematic organizer to enhance conceptual understanding of verse and prose.* Paper presented at the Twenty-Sixth College Reading Association Conference, Philadelphia, PA.

Alvarez, M.C., & Risko, V.J. (1989). Using a thematic organizer to facilitate transfer learning with college developmental studies students. *Reading Research and Instruction, 28,* 1-15.

Anderson, R.C., & Biddle, W.B. (1975). On asking people questions about what they are reading. In G.H. Bower (Ed.), *The psychology of learning and motivation* (Vol. 9, pp. 89-132). San Diego, CA: Academic Press.

Anderson, R.C., Reynolds, R.E., Schallert, D.L., & Goetz, E.G. (1977). Frameworks for comprehending discourse. *American Educational Research Journal, 14,* 367-381.

Anderson, R.C., Spiro, R.J., & Montague, W.E. (Eds.). (1977). *Schooling and the acquisition of knowledge.* Hillsdale, NJ: Erlbaum.

Anderson, T.H. (1980). Study strategies and adjunct aids. In R.J. Spiro, B.C. Bruce, & W.F. Brewer (Eds.), *Theoretical issues in reading comprehension: Perspectives from cognitive psychology, artificial intelligence, linguistics, and education.* Hillsdale, NJ: Erlbaum.

*Anderson, T.H., & Armbruster, B.B. (1984). Studying. In P.D. Pearson (Ed.), *Handbook of reading research* (pp. 657-679). New York: Longman.

Andre, T. (1979). Does answering higher-level questions while reading facilitate productive learning? *Review of Educational Research, 49,* 280-318.

Annis, L.F. (1983). *Study techniques.* Dubuque, IA: William C. Brown.

Atkinson, R.C. (1975). Mnemotechnics in second-language learning. *American Psychologist, 30,* 821-828.

Atkinson, R.C., & Raugh, M.R. (1975). An application of the mnemonic keyboard method to the acquisition of a Russian vocabulary. *Journal of Experimental Psychology: Human Learning and Memory, 1,* 126-133.

Ausubel, D.P. (1960). The use of advance organizers in the learning and retention of meaningful verbal material. *Journal of Educational Psychology, 51,* 267-272.

Ausubel, D.P. (1968). *Educational psychology: A cognitive view.* Orlando, FL: Holt, Rinehart & Winston.

Badgett, J.L., Jr. (1968). *The relationship between self-concept and certain academic, vocational, biographical, and personality variables of entering male freshmen at a major land grant university.* Washington, DC: Office of Education, Bureau of Research.

Badgett, J.L. Jr., Hope, L.H., & Kerley, S. (1971). The relationship between self-concept and academic aptitude of entering male college freshmen. *Psychology, 8,* 43-47.

Bailey, R.C. (1971). Self-concept differences in low and high achieving students. *Journal of Clinical Psychology, 27,* 188-191.

Baird, J.R., & White, R.T. (1982). Promoting self-control of learning. *Instructional Science, 11,* 227-247.

Baker, J.R. (1974). Immediate and delayed retention effects of interspersing questions and written instructional passages. *Journal of Educational Psychology, 66,* 96-98.

Baker, L., & Anderson, R.I. (1982). Effects of inconsistent information on text processing: Evidence for comprehension monitoring. *Reading Research Quarterly, 17,* 281-294.

*Baker, L., & Brown, A.L. (1984). Metacognitive skills and reading. In P.D. Pearson (Ed.), *Handbook of reading research* (pp. 353-394). New York: Longman.

Bandura, A. (1982). Self-efficacy mechanism in human agency. *American Psychologist, 33,* 344-358.

Barclay, J.R. (1973). The role of comprehension in remembering sentences. *Cognitive Psychology, 4,* 229-254.

Bartlett, B.J. (1978). *Top-level structure as an organizational strategy for recall of classroom text.* Unpublished doctoral dissertation, Arizona State University, Tempe, AZ.

Batlis, N. (1978). Job involvement as a predictor of academic performance. *Educational and Psychological Measurement, 38,* 1177-1180.

Bebeau, M.J., & Sullivan, H.J. (1982). Educational technology research: Learning incentives preferred by university students. *Educational Technology, 22*(8), 32-35.

Bellezza, F.S. (1981). Mnemonic devices: Classification, characteristics, and criteria. *Review of Educational Research, 51,* 247-275.

Biggs, J.B. (1979). Individual differences in study processes and the quality of learning outcomes. *Higher Education, 8,* 381-394.

*Blanchard, J., & Mikkelson, V. (1987, March/April). Underlining performance outcomes in expository text. *Journal of Educational Research, 2,* 197-201.

Borer, G.S. (1981). Effect of advance organizers and behavioral objectives on the reading of sixth graders with selective attention deficits. *Abstracts International, 42,* 1052A. (University Microfilms No.81-19, 760)

Boshier, R., & Hamic, P.N. (1968). Academic success and self-concept. *Psychological Reports, 22,* 1191-1192.

Bovy, R.C. (1981). Successful instructional methods: A cognitive information processing approach. *Educational Communication and Technology Journal, 29*(4), 203-217.

Bower, G.H. (1972). Mental imagery and associative learning. In L.W. Gregg (Ed.), *Cognition in learning and memory.* New York: John Wiley & Sons.

Bower, G.H., & Clark, M.C. (1969). Narrative stories as mediators for serial learning. *Psychonomic Science, 14,* 181-182.

Bradley, A. (1983). *Take note of college study skills.* Glenview, IL: Scott, Foresman.

Bransford, J.D., & Johnson, M.K. (1972). Contextual prerequisites for understanding: Some investigations of comprehension and recall. *Journal of Verbal Learning and Verbal Behavior, 8,* 229-309.

Brennan, S., Winograd, P.N., Bridge, C.A., & Hiebert, E.H. (1986). A comparison of observer reports and self-reports of study practices used by college students. In J.A. Niles and R.V. Lalik (Eds.), *Solving problems in literacy: Learners, teachers, and researchers* (pp. 353-365). Rochester, NY: National Reading Conference.

Bretzing, B.H., & Kulhavy, R.W. (1979). Notetaking and depth of processing. *Contemporary Educational Psychology, 4,* 145-153.

Bristol, M.M., & Sloane, H.N., Jr. (1974). Effects of contingency contracting on study rate and test performance. *Journal of Applied Behavior Analysis, 7,* 271-285.

Britton, B., Muth, K.D., & Glynn, S. (1986). Effects of text organization on memory: Text of a cognitive effort hypothesis with limited exposure time. *Discourse Processes, 9*(4), 475-487.

Britton, B.K., Piha, A., Davis, J., & Wehausen, E. (1978). Reading and cognitive capacity usage: Adjunct question effects. *Memory and Cognition, 6,* 266-273.

Brooke, R.R., & Ruthven, A.J. (1984). The effects of contingency contracting on student performance in a PSI class. *Teaching of Psychology, 11*(2), 87-89.

Brooks, C.C. (1984). *Setting objectives for college reading and study skills* (2nd ed.). Dubuque, IA: Eddie Bowers.

*Brown, A.L., & Campione, J.C. (1978). The effects of knowledge and experience in the formation of retrieval plans for studying from texts. In M.M. Grunesberg, P.E. Morris, & R.N. Sukes (Eds.), *Practical aspects of memory* (pp. 378-384). San Diego, CA: Academic Press.

*Brown, A.L., Campione, J.C., & Day, J.D. (1981). Learning to learn: On training students to learn from texts. *Educational Researcher, 10*(2), 14-21.

Brown, W.F., & Holtzman, W.H. (1967). *Survey of study habits and attitudes: Manual.* New York: Psychological Corporation.

Bugelski, B.R. (1968). Images as mediators in one-trial pair-associate learning, 2: Self-timing in successive lists. *Journal of Experimental Psychology, 77,* 328-331.

Cardemone, P.F. (1975). *Concept mapping: A technique of analyzing a discipline and its use in the curriculum and instruction in a portion of a college level mathematics skills course.* Unpublished master's thesis, Cornell University, Ithaca, NY.

Carlson, R.F., Kincaid, J.P., Lance, S., & Hodgson, T. (1976). Spontaneous use of mnemonics and grade point average. *Journal of Psychology, 92,* 117-122.

Chase, C.I., & Keene, J.M. (1981). Major declaration and academic motivation. *Journal of College Student Personnel, 22,* 496-502.

Christie, D.J., & Schumacher, G.M. (1976). Some conditions surrounding the effectiveness of advance organizers for children's retention of orally presented prose. *Journal of Reading Behavior, 8,* 299-309.

Cioffi, G. (1986). Relationships among comprehension strategies reported by college students. *Reading Research and Instruction, 25*(3), 220-231.

Cirilo, R.K., & Foss, D.J. (1980). Text structure and reading time for sentences. *Journal of Verbal Learning and Verbal Behavior, 11,* 671-684.

Cohen, E.L., & Poppino, M.A. (1982). *Discovering college reading, thinking, and study skills: A Piagetian approach* (pp. 3-8, 75-86). Orlando, FL: Holt, Rinehart & Winston.

Cook, L.K., & Mayer, R.E. (1983). Reading strategies training for meaningful learning from prose. In M. Pressley & J. Levin (Eds.), *Cognitive strategies training and research* (pp. 87-131). New York: Springer-Verlag.

Cooper, C., Cherry, B., Gerber, R., Fleischer, S., Copley, B., & Sartisky, M. (1979). *Writing abilities of regularly admitted freshmen at SUNY, Buffalo.* Buffalo, NY: Center and Graduate Program in English Education.

Craik, F.I.M., & Watkins, M.J. (1973). The role of rehearsal in short-term memory. *Journal of Verbal Learning and Verbal Behavior, 12,* 599-607.

Daniels, R.L., & Stevens, V.P. (1976). The interaction between the internal-external locus of control and two methods of college instruction. *American Educational Research Journal, 13,* 103-113.

Dansereau, D., Collins, K., McDonald, B., Hailey, C., Garland, J., Diekoff, G., & Evans, S. (1979). Development and evaluation of a learning strategy training program. *Journal of Educational Psychology, 71,* 64-73.

DeBoer, G.E. (1983). The importance of freshman students' perceptions of the factors responsible for first-term academic performance. *Journal of College Student Personnel, 24,* 344-349.

Delin, P.S. (1969). The learning to criterion of a serial list with and without mnemonic instructions. *Psychonomic Science, 16,* 169-170.

DeLisle, F.H. (1953). A study of the relationship of the self-concept of adjustment in a selected group of college women. *Dissertation Abstracts International, 13,* 719.

Diekhoff, G.M., Brown, P.J., & Dansereau, D.F. (1982). A prose learning strategy training program based on network and depth of processing models. *Journal of Experimental Educational Education, 50,* 180-184.

Dooling D.J., & Christiansen, R.E. (1977). Episodic and semantic aspects of memory for prose. *Journal of Experimental Psychology: Human Learning and Memory, 3,* 428-436.

Duchastel, P.C. (1979). Learning objectives and the organization of prose. *Journal of Educational Psychology, 71,* 100-106.

Duell, O.K. (1974). Effect of types of objectives, level of test questions, and judged importance of tested materials upon posttest performance. *Journal of Educational Psychology, 66,* 225-232.

Duell, O.K. (1978). Overt and covert use of objectives of different cognitive levels. *Contemporary Journal of Educational Psychology, 3,* 239-245.

D'Zurilla, T.J., & Goldfried, M.R. (1971). Problem solving and behavior modification. *Journal of Abnormal Psychology, 78,* 107-126.

Edwards, J.E., & Waters, L.K. (1980). Relationships of academic job involvement to biographical data, personal characteristics, and academic performance. *Educational and Psychological Measurement, 40,* 547-551.

Edwards, J.E., & Waters, L.K. (1982). Involvement, ability, performance, and satisfaction as predictors of college attrition. *Educational and Psychological Measurement, 42,* 1149-1152.

Entwistle, N. (1988). Motivational factors in students' approaches to learning. In R.R. Schmeck (Ed.), *Learning strategies and learning styles* (pp. 21-51). New York: Plenum.

Findley, M., & Cooper, H. (1983). Locus of control and academic achievement: A literature review. *Journal of Personality and Social Psychology, 44,* 419-427.

Fischer, P.M., & Mandl, H. (1984). Learners, text variables, and the control of text comprehension and recall. In H. Mandl & T. Trabasso (Eds.), *Learning and comprehension of text* (pp. 213-254). Hillsdale, NJ: Erlbaum.

Fowler, R.L., & Barker, A.S. (1974). Effectiveness of highlighting for retention of text material. *Journal of Applied Psychology, 59,* 358-364.

Frase, L.T. (1969). Paragraph organization of written materials. The influence of conceptual clustering upon level of organization. *Journal of Education Psychology, 60,* 394-401.

Frase, L.T. (1975). Prose processing. In G.H. Bower (Ed.), *The Psychology of Learning and Motivation* (Vol. 9, pp. 1-47). San Diego, CA: Academic Press.

Frase, L.T., & Schwartz, B.J. (1975). The effect of question production and answering on prose recall. *Journal of Education Psychology, 67,* 628-635.

Frieze, I., & Weiner, B. (1971). Cue utilization and attributional judgments for success and failure. *Journal of Personality and Social Psychology, 29,* 591-606.

Gagne, R.M. (1964). Problem solving. In A.W. Metton (Ed.), *Categories of human learning.* San Diego, CA: Academic Press.

Gal'Perin, P.Y., & Danilova, V.L. (1980). Training students to think systematically in the process of solving minor creative problems. *Voprosy Psihologii, 1,* 31-38.

Gill, J.T., & Bear, D.R. (1988). No book, whole book, and chapter DRTAS. *Journal of Reading, 31*(5), 444-449.

Glasgow, R.E., & Rosen, G.M. (1978). Behavioral bibliotherapy: A review of self-help behavior therapy manuals. *Psychological Bulletin, 85,* 1-23.

*Goetz, E.T., Schallert, D.L., Reynolds, R.E., & Radin, D.I. (1983). Reading in perspective: What real cops and burglars look for in a story. *Journal of Educational Psychology, 75,* 500-510.

Gomulicki, B.R. (1956). Recall as an abstract process. *Acta Psychologica, 12,* 77-94.

Green, L. (1982). Minority students' self-control of procrastination. *Journal of Counseling Psychology, 29,* 636-644.

Greiner, J.M., & Karoly, P. (1976). Effects of self-control training on study activity and academic performance: An analysis of self-monitoring, self-reward, and systematic-planning components. *Journal of Counseling Psychology, 23,* 495-502.

Griffore, R.J., & Samuels, D.D. (1978). Self-concept of ability and college students' academic achievement. *Psychological Reports, 43,* 37-38.

Groninger, L.D. (1971). Mnemonic imagery and forgetting. *Psychonomic Science, 23,* 161-163.

Gross, T.F., & Mastenbrook, M. (1980). Examination of the effects of state anxiety on problem-solving efficiency under high and low memory conditions. *Journal of Educational Psychology, 72,* 605-608.

Groveman, A.M., Richards, C.S., & Caple, R.B. (1975). Literature review, treatment manuals, and bibliography for study skills counseling and behavioral self-control approaches to improving study behavior. *JSAS Catalog of Selected Documents in Psychology, 5,* 342-343.

*Groveman, A.M., Richards, C.S., & Caple, R.B. (1977). Effects of study skills counseling versus behavioral self-control techniques in the treatment of academic performance. *Psychological Reports, 11,* 186.

Hall, J.W., Wilson, K.P., & Patterson, R.J. (1981). Mnemotechnics: Some limitations of the mnemonic keyword method for the study of foreign language vocabulary *Journal of Educational Psychology, 73,* 345-357.

*Hansford, B., & Hattie, J. (1982). The relationship between self and achievement performance measures. *Review of Educational Research, 52,* 123-142.

*Hartley, J., & Davies, I.K. (1981). Preinstructional strategies: The role of pretests, behavioral objectives, overviews, and advance organizers. *Review of Educational Research, 46,* 239-265.

Hattie, J., & Watkins, D. (1981). Australian and Filipino investigations of the internal structure of Biggs' new study process questionnaire. *British Journal of Educational Psychology, 51,* 241-244.

Head, L.Q., & Lindsey, J.D. (1982). Anxiety and the university student: A brief review of the professional literature. *College Student Journal, 16,* 176-182.

Healy, C.C., Mourton, D.L., Anderson, E.C., & Robinson, E. (1984). Career maturity and the achievement of community college students and disadvantaged university students. *Journal of College Student Personnel, 25,* 347-352.

Hefferman, T., & Richards, C.S. (1981). Self-control of study behavior: Identification and evaluation of natural methods. *Journal of Counseling Psychology, 28,* 361-364.

Heider, F. (1958). *The psychology of interpersonal relations.* New York: John Wiley & Sons.

Hentschel, U., & Ternes, G. (1984). Moderating effects of trait anxiety on electrodermal reactions in different learning conditions. *Psychological Reports, 54,* 803-809.

Heppner, P.P. (1978). A review of the problem-solving literature and its relationship to the counseling process. *Journal of Counseling Psychology, 25*(5), 366-375.

Heppner, P.P., & Petersen, C.H. (1982). The development and implications of a personal problem-solving inventory. *Journal of Counseling Psychology, 29,* 66-75.

*Heppner, P.P., Reeder, B.L., & Larson, L.M. (1983). Cognitive variables associated with personal problem-solving appraisal: Implications for counseling. *Journal of Counseling Psychology, 30,* 537-545.

Honeck, R.P. (1973). Interpretive vs. structural effects on semantic memory. *Journal of Verbal Learning and Verbal Behavior, 12*(4), 448-455.

Horowitz, R. (1982). The limitations of contrasted rhetorical predicates on reader recall of expository English prose. *Dissertation Abstracts International, 43,* 1089-A. (University Microfilms No. 82-21,289).

Howe, M.J.A. (1970). Using students' notes to examine the role of the individual learner in acquiring meaningful subject matter. *Journal of Educational Research, 64,* 61-63.

Howe, M.J.A., & Singer, L. (1975). Presentation variables and students' activities in meaningful learning. *British Journal of Educational Psychology, 45,* 52-61.

Hunter, J., Jones, L., Vincent, H., & Carmichael, J. (1982). Project SOAR: Teaching cognitive skills in a precollege program. *Journal of Learning Skills, 1,* 24-26.

Iglinsky, C.L., & Wiant, H.A. (1971). Nonintellectual factors in academic success. *Improving College and University Teaching, 19,* 197-198.

Jackson, B.T., & Van Zoost, B.L. (1972). Changing study behaviors through reinforcement contingencies. *Journal of Counseling Psychology, 19,* 192-195.

Jenkins, J.J. (1979). Four points to remember: A tetrahedral model of memory experiments. In L.S. Cermak & F.I.M. Craik (Eds.), *Level of processing in human memory* (pp. 429-446). Hillsdale, NJ: Erlbaum.

Joffe, I.L. (1982). *Achieving success in college.* Belmont, CA: Wadsworth.

Joffe, I.L. (1988). *Opportunity for skillful reading* (5th ed.). Belmont, CA: Wadsworth.

Johnson, S.M., & White, G. (1971). Self-observation as an agent of behavioral change. *Behavior Therapy, 2,* 488-497.

Johnson, W.G., & Croft, R.G.F. (1975). Locus of control and participation in a personalized system of instruction course. *Journal of Educational Psychology, 67,* 416-421.

Johnston, P. (1985). Understanding reading failure: A case study approach. *Harvard Educational Review, 55,* 153-177.

Johnston, P., & Winograd, P. (1985). Passive failure in reading. *Journal of Reading Behavior. 17*(4), 279-300.

Jones, R.T., Nelson, R.E., & Kazdin, A.E. (1977). The role of external variables in self-reinforcement: A review. *Behavior Modification, 1,* 147-178.

Kaplan R., & Simmons, F.G. (1974). Effects of instructional objectives used as orienting stimuli or as summary/review upon prose learning. *Journal of Educational Psychology, 614*-622.

Keller, J.M., Sutterer, J.R., & Goldman, J.A. (1978). Locus of control in relation to academic attitudes and performance in a personalized system of instruction course. *Journal of Educational Psychology, 70,* 414-421.

Kintsch, W. (1986). Learning from text. *Cognition and Instruction 3*(2), 87-108.

Kirschenbaum, D.S., & Perri, M.G. (1982). Improving academic competence in adults: A review of recent research. *Journal of Counseling Psychology, 29,* 76-94.

Koehler, W. (1925). *The mentality of apes.* (E. Winter, Trans.). Orlando, FL: Harcourt Brace Jovanovich.

Kolzow, L.V., & Lehmann, J. (1986). *Fundamentals of college reading: Strategies for success.* Englewood Cliffs, NJ: Prentice Hall.

Lefcourt, H.M. (1976). *Locus of control: Current trends in theory and research.* Hillsdale, NJ: Erlbaum.

Levin, J.R. (1981). The mnemonic 80s: Keywords in the classroom. *Educational Psychologist, 16,* 65-82.

Levin, J.R., & Pressley, M. (1981). Improving children's prose comprehension: Selected strategies that seem to succeed. In C.M. Santa & B.L. Hayes (Eds.), *Children's prose comprehension: Research and practice* (pp. 44-77). Newark, DE: International Reading Association.

Lochhead, J. (1982). An anarchistic approach to teaching problem solving. *Journal of Learning Skills, 1*(2), 3-12.

Locke, E.A., & Bryan, J.F. (1968). Goal-setting as a determinant of the effect of knowledge of score on performance. *American Journal of Psychology, 81,* 398-406.

Locke, E.A., Shaw, K.N., Saari, L.M., & Latham, G.P. (1981). Goal setting and task performance: 1969-1980. *Psychological Bulletin, 90,* 125-152.

Mahoney, M.J., & Arnkoff, D.B. (1978) Cognitive and self-control therapies. In S.L. Garfield, & A.E. Begin (Eds.), *Handbook of psychotherapy and behavior change: An empirical analysis* (2nd ed, pp. 689-722). New York: John Wiley & Sons.

Mahoney, M.J., Moore, B.S., Wade, T.C., & Moura, N.G.M. (1973). Effects of continuous and intermittent self-monitoring on academic behavior. *Journal of Consulting and Clinical Psychology, 41,* 65-69.

Maier, N.R.F. (1970). *Problem solving and creativity.* Belmont, CA: Brooks/Cole.

Malloch, D.C., & Michael, W.B. (1981). Predicting student grade point average at a community college from scholastic aptitude tests and from measures representing three constructs in Vroom's expectancy theory model of motivation. *Journal of Educational and Psychological Measurement, 41,* 1127-1131.

Marsh, H.W. (1984). Experimental manipulation of university student motivation and its effects on examination performance. *British Journal of Educational Psychology, 54,* 206-213.

*Mayer, R. (1988). Learning strategies: An overview. In C. Weinstein, E. Goetz, & P. Alexander (Eds.), *Learning and study strategies: Issues in assessment, instruction, and evaluation* (pp. 11-22). San Diego: Academic Press.

Mayer, R.E. (1979). Can advance organizers influence meaningful learning? *Review of Educational Research, 49,* 371-383.

Mayer, R.E. (1982). Instructional variables in text processing. In A. Flammer & W. Kintsch (Eds.), *Discourse processing.* Amsterdam: North-Holland.

Mayer, R.E. (1984). Aids to prose comprehension. *Educational Psychologist, 19,* 30-40.

*McCombs, B. (1988). Motivational skills training: Combining metacognitive, cognitive, and affective learning strategies. In C. Weinstein, E. Goetz, & P. Alexander (Eds.), *Learning and study strategies: Issues in assessment, instruction, and evaluation* (pp. 141-169). San Diego CA: Academic Press.

McConkie, G.W., Rayner, K., & Wilson, S. (1973). Experimental manipulation of reading strategies. *Journal of Educational Psychology, 65,* 1-8.

McMahan, I.D. (1973). Relationships between casual attributions and expectancy of success. *Journal of Personality and Social Psychology, 28,* 108-113.

McWhorter, K.T. (1986a). *College reading and study skills* (3rd ed.). Boston, MA: Little, Brown.

McWhorter, K.T. (1986b). *Guide to college reading.* Boston, MA: Little, Brown.

McWhorter, K.T. (1987). *Efficient and flexible reading* (2nd ed.). Boston, MA: Little, Brown.

Melton, R.F. (1978). Resolution of conflicting claims concerning the effect of behavioral objectives on student learning. *Review of Educational Research, 48,* 291-302.

*Memory, D.M., & Yoder, C.Y. (1988). Improving concentration in content classrooms. *Journal of Reading, 31*(5), 426-435.

Mercier, P., & Ladouceur, R. (1983). Modification of study time and grades through self-control procedures *Canadian Journal of Behavioral Science, 15*(1), 70-81.

Meyer, B.J.F. (1975). *The organization of prose and its effects on memory.* Amsterdam: North-Holland.

Minemier, L. (1983). *Concept mapping: An educational tool and its use in a college level mathematics skills course.* Unpublished master's thesis, Cornell University, Ithaca, NY.

Minor, S.W., & Roberts, A.M. (1984). Effects of congruence between locus of control and task instructions on self-efficacy. *Psychological Reports, 54*(1), 39-42.

Montague, W., & Carter, J. (1973). Vividness and imagery in recalling connected discourse. *Journal of Educational Psychology, 64,* 72-75.

Morgan, M. (1981). Self-derived objectives in private study. *Journal of Educational Research, 74,* 327-332.

Morgan, M. (1985). Self-monitoring of attained subgoals in private study. *Journal of Educational Psychology, 77,* 623-630.

Morris, C.D., Bransford, J.D., & Franks, J.J. (1977). Levels of processing versus transfer appropriate processing. *Journal of Verbal Learning and Verbal Behavior, 16,* 519-533.

Morris, P.E., & Reid, R.L. (1970). The repeated use of mnemonic imagery. *Psychonomic Science, 20,* 337-338.

Mount, M.K., & Tirrell, F.J. (1977). Improving examination scores through self-monitoring. *Journal of Educational Research, 71,* 70-73.

Myers, J.L., Pezdek, K., & Coulson, D. (1973). Effects of prose organization upon free recall. *Journal of Educational Psychology, 65,* 313-320.

Nelson, R.O. (1977). Methodological issues in assessment via self-monitoring. In J.D. Cone & H.P. Hawkins (Eds.), *Behavioral assessment: New directions in clinical psychology* (pp. 217-240). New York: Brunner/Mazel.

Newell, A., & Simon, H.A. (1972). *Human problem solving.* Englewood Cliffs, NJ: Prentice Hall.

Nezu, A.M. (1985). Differences in psychological distress between effective and ineffective problem solvers. *Journal of Counseling Psychology, 32,* 135-138.

Nezu, A., & D'Zurilla, T.J. (1981). Effects of problem definition and formulation on decision making in the social problem-solving process. *Behavior Therapy, 12,* 100-106.

Nist, S.L., & Diehl, W. (1985). *Developing textbook thinking.* Lexington, MA: D.C. Heath.

Novak, J.D., & Gowin, D.B. (1984). *Learning how to learn.* New York: Cambridge University Press.

Page, H.W. (1988). Literature across the college curriculum. *Journal of Reading, 31,* 520-531.

*Palmer, D., & Goetz, E. (1988). Selection and use of study strategies: The role of the studiers' beliefs about self and strategies. In C. Weinstein, E. Goetz, & P. Alexander (Eds.), *Learning and study strategies: Issues in assessment, instruction, and evaluation* (pp. 25-40). San Diego, CA: Academic Press.

Parent, J., Forward, J., Center, R., & Mobling, J. (1975). Interactive effects of teaching strategy and locus of control on student performance and satisfaction. *Journal of Educational Psychology, 67,* 764-769.

*Paris, S.G., Lipson, M.Y., & Wixson, K.K. (1983). Becoming a strategic reader. *Contemporary Educational Psychology, 8,* 293-316.

Pauk, W. (1984). *How to study in college* (3rd ed.). Boston, MA: Houghton Mifflin.

Perri, M.G., & Richards, C.S. (1977). An investigation of naturally occurring episodes of self-controlled behaviors. *Journal of Counseling Psychology, 24,* 178-182.

Perry, R.P., & Dickens, W.J. (1984). Perceived control in the college classroom: Response-contingency training and instructor expressiveness—effects on student achievement and causal attribution. *Journal of Educational Psychology, 76,* 966-981.

Phares, E.J. (1976). *Locus of control in personality.* Morristown, NJ: General Learning Press.

Pitt, R.B. (1983). Development of a general problem-solving schema in adolescence and early adulthood. *Journal of Experimental Psychology, 112,* 547-584.

Pompi, K.F., & Lachman, R. (1967). Surrogate processes in the short-term retention of connected discourse. *Journal of Experimental Psychology, 75*(2), 143-150.

Poppleton, P.K., & Austwick, K. (1964). A comparison of programmed learning and notetaking at two age levels. *British Journal of Educational Psychology, 34,* 43-50.

Postman, R.D., Keckler, B., & Schneckner, P. (1985). *College reading and study skills.* New York: Macmillan.

Raugh, M.R., & Atkinson, R.C. (1975). A mnemonic method for learning a second-language vocabulary. *Journal of Educational Psychology, 67,* 1-16.

*Reder, L.M., & Anderson, J.R. (1980). A comparison of texts and their summaries: Memorial consequences. *Journal of Verbal Learning and Verbal Behavior, 19,* 121-134.

Reigeluth, C.M. (1979). In search of a better way to organize instruction: The elaboration theory. *Journal of Instructional Development, 2*(3), 8-15.

Resnick, J., & Page, R. (1984). *Reading and reasoning.* New York: Macmillan.

Reynolds, R.E., & Anderson, R.C. (1980). *The influence of questions during reading on allocation of attention* (Tech. Rep. No. 183). Urbana, IL: University of Illinois, Center for the Study of Reading.

*Reynolds, R., & Shirey, L. (1988). The role of attention in studying and learning. In C. Weinstein, E. Goetz, & P. Alexander (Eds.), *Learning and study strategies: Issues in assessment, instruction, and evaluation* (pp. 77-100). San Diego CA: Academic Press.

Richards, C.S. (1977). Assessment and behavior modification via self-monitoring: An overview and a bibliography. *JSAS Catalog of Selected Documents in Psychology, 7,* 15.

Richards, C.S. (1981). Improving college students' study behaviors through self-control techniques: A brief review. *Behaviors Counseling Quarterly, 1,* 159-175.

Richards, C.S., McReynolds, W.T., Holt, S., & Sexton, T. (1976). Effects of information feedback and self-administered consequences on self-monitoring study behavior. *Journal of Counseling Psychology, 23,* 316-321.

Richards, C.S., & Perri, M.G. (1978). Do self-control treatments last? An evaluation of behavioral problem solving and faded counselor contact as treatment maintenance strategies. *Journal of Counseling Psychology, 25,* 376-383.

Richards, C.S., Peri, M.G., & Gortney, C. (1976). Increasing the maintenance of self-control treatments through faded counselor contact and high information feedback. *Journal of Counseling Psychology, 23,* 405-406.

Rickards, J.P. (1976). Adjunct postquestions in text: A critical review of methods and processes. *Review of Educational Research, 49*(2), 181-196.

Rickards, J.P., & August, G.J. (1975). Generative underlining strategies in prose recall. *Journal of Education Psychology, 67,* 860-865.

Robinson, D.A.G., & Cooper, S.E. (1984). The influence of self-concept on academic success in technological careers. *Journal of College Student Personnel, 25,* 145-149.

Roediger, H.L. (1980). The effectiveness of four mnemonics in ordering recall. *Journal of Experimental Psychology: Human Learning and Memory, 6*(5), 558-567.

Ross, J., & Lawrence, K.A. (1968). Some observations on memory artifice. *Psychonomic Science, 13,* 107-108.

Ross, S.M., & DiVesta, F.J. (1976). Oral summary as a review strategy enhancing recall of textual material. *Journal of Educational Psychology, 68,* 689-695

Rothkopf, E.Z., & Billington, M.J. (1979). Goal-guided learning from text: Inferring a descriptive processing model from inspection times and eye movements. *Journal of Educational Psychology, 71,* 310-327.

Rothkopf, E.Z, & Bisbicos, E.E. (1967). Selective facilitative effects of interspersed questions on learning from written prose. *Journal of Educational Psychology,* 58-61.

Rotter, J.B. (1966). Generalized expectancies for internal versus external control of reinforcement. *Psychological Monographs, 80* (609).

Internal Factors That Influence Study

Rumelhart, D.E., & Ortony, A. (1977). The representation of knowledge in memory. In R.C. Anderson, R.J. Spiro, & W.E. Montague (Eds.), *Schooling and the acquisition of knowledge*. Hillsdale, NJ: Erlbaum.

Sachs, J.D.S. (1967). Recognition memory for syntactic and semantic aspects of connected discourse. *Perception & Psychophysics, 2,* 437-442.

Schallert, D. (1982). The significance of knowledge: A synthesis of research related to schema theory. In W. Otto & S. White (Eds.), *Reading expository material* (pp. 13-48). San Diego, CA: Academic Press.

*Schallert, D., Alexander, P., & Goetz, E. (1988). Implicit instruction of strategies for learning from text. In C. Weinstein, E. Goetz, P. Alexander (Eds.), *Learning and study strategies: Issues in assessment, instruction, and evaluation* (pp. 193-214). San Diego, CA: Academic Press.

Schiffrin, R.M., & Schneider, W. (1977). Controlled and automatic human information processing, 2: Perceptual learning, automatic attending, and a general theory. *Psychological Review, 84,* 127-190.

Schmelzer, R.V., Khristen, W.L., & Browning, W.G. (1984). *Reading and study skills: Book one.* Dubuque, IA: Kendall/Hunt.

Schnell, T.R., & Rocchio, D. (1975). A comparison of underlining strategies for improving reading comprehension and retention. In G.H. McNinch & W.D. Miller (Eds.), *Reading: Convention and inquiry* (pp. 279-283). Clemson, SC: National Reading Conference.

Scott, K.J., & Robbins, S.B. (1985). Goal instability: Implications for academic performance among students in learning skills courses. *Journal of College Student Personnel, 26,* 129-133.

Shepherd, J.F. (1982). *The Houghton Mifflin study skills handbook.* Boston, MA: Houghton Mifflin.

Shepherd, J.F. (1984). *R.S.V.P.: Reading, study and vocabulary program* (2nd ed.). Boston, MA: Houghton Mifflin.

Shepherd, J.F. (1987). *College study skills* (3rd ed.). Boston, MA: Houghton Mifflin.

Sherman, T.M. (1984). *Proven strategies for successful learning.* Columbus, OH: Merrill.

Sieveking, N.A., Campbell, M.L., Raleigh, W.J., & Savitsky, J. (1971). Mass intervention by mail for an academic impediment. *Journal of Counseling Psychology, 18,* 601-602.

Simpson, C., & Boyle, D. (1975). Esteem construct generality and academic performance. *Educational and Psychological Measurement, 34,* 897-904.

Simpson, M.L. (1984). The status of study strategy instruction: Implications for classroom teachers. *Journal of Reading, 28,* 136-142.

Skinner, B.F. (1974). *About behaviorism.* New York: Knopf.

Smith, B.D. (1981). *Bridging the gap: College reading.* Glenview, IL: Scott, Foresman.

Snyder, M., & Uranowitz, S.W. (1978). Reconstructing the past: Some cognitive consequences of person perception. *Journal of Personality and Social Psychology, 3(9),* 941-950.

Sotiriou, P.E. (1984). *Integrating college study skills: Reasoning in reading, in listening, and in writing.* Belmont, CA: Wadsworth.

Stowbridge, M.D. (1983). Becoming a better student with computer games. *Journal of Learning Skills, 2,* 35-43.

Subject Guide to Books in Print. (1987-1988). New York: R.R. Bowker.

Sulin, R.A., & Dooling, D.J. (1974). Intrusion of a thematic idea in retention of prose. *Journal of Experimental Psychology, 103,* 255-262.

Super, D.E. (1977). Vocational maturity in mid-career. *Vocational Guidance Quarterly, 25,* 294-302.

Sweeney, C.A., & Bellezza, F.S. (1982). Use of keyword mnemonic in learning English vocabulary. *Human Learning, 1,* 155-163.

Taylor, B.M. (1982). Text structure and children's comprehension and memory for expository material. *Journal of Psychology, 74,* 322-340.

Taylor, B.M., & Beach, R.W. (1984). The effects of text structure instruction on middle-grade students' comprehension and production of expository text. *Reading Research Quarterly, 29*(2), 134-146.

Thorndyke, P.W. (1977). Cognitive structures in comprehension and memory of narrative discourse. *Cognitive Psychology, 9,* 77-110.

Tierney, R.J., & Cunningham, J.W. (1984). Research on teaching reading comprehension. In P.D. Pearson (Ed.), *Handbook on reading research* (pp. 609-655). New York: Longman.

Traub, G.S. (1982). Relationship between locus of control and grade point average in freshman college students. *Psychological Reports, 50*(3), 1294.

Van Zoost, B.L., & Jackson, B.T. (1974). Effects of self-monitoring and self-administered reinforcement on study behaviors. *Journal of Educational Research, 67,* 216-218.

Vroom, V.H. (1964). *Work and motivation.* New York: John Wiley & Sons.

Vroom, V.H. (1965). *Motivation in management.* New York: American Foundation for Management Research Study.

Walter, T., & Siebert, A. (1984). *Student success* (3rd ed.). Orlando, FL: Holt, Rinehart & Winston.

Warner, D.A. (1984). Effects of goal setting on classroom test performance of college undergraduates. *Journal of Instructional Psychology, 11*(4), 187-194.

*Watkins, D. (1982). Academic achievement and the congruence of study motivation and strategy. *British Journal of Educational Psychology, 52,* 260-263.

Watkins, D., & Hattie, J. (1980). An investigation of the internal structure of the Biggs study process questionnaire. *Educational and Psychological Measurement, 40,* 1125-1130.

Weiner, B., Frieze, I., Kukla, A., Reed, A., Rest, S., & Rosenbaum, L.M. (1971). *Perceiving the causes of success and failure.* Morristown, NJ: General Learning Press.

Weiner, B., Heckhausen, H., Meyer, W., & Cook, R.E. (1972). Causal ascriptions and achievement behavior: A conceptual analysis of effort and reanalysis of locus of control. *Journal of Personality and Social Psychology, 21,* 239-248.

*Weinstein, C.E. (1987). Fostering learning autonomy through the use of learning strategies. *Journal of Reading, 30,* 590-595.

Weinstein, C.E., & Mayer, R.E. (1986). The teaching of learning strategies. In M.C. Wittrock (Ed.), *Handbook of research on teaching* (3rd ed, pp. 315-327). New York: Macmillan.

Welborn, E.L., & English, H.B. (1937). Logical learning and retention: A general review of experiments with meaningful verbal materials. *Psychological Bulletin, 34,* 1-20.

Winograd, P. (1984). Strategic difficulties in summarizing texts. *Reading Research Quarterly, 19,* 404-425.

Wittrock, M.C. (1981). Reading comprehension. In F.J. Pirozzalo & M.C. Wittrock (Eds.), *Neuropsychological and cognitive processes of reading.* San Diego, CA: Academic Press.

Wittrock, M.C. (1986). Students' thought processes. In M.C. Wittrock (Ed.), *Handbook of research on teaching* (3rd ed., pp. 297-314). New York: Macmillan.

Wittrock, M.C., & Carter, J. (1975). Generative processing of hierarchically organized words. *American Journal of Psychology, 88,* 489-501.

Wittrock, M.C., & Lumsdaine, A.A. (1977). Instructional psychology. *Annual Review of Psychology, 28,* 417-459.

Wood, G. (1967). Mnemonic systems in recall. *Journal of Educational Psychology, 58,* 1-27.

Wood, N.V. (1984). *Improving reading.* New York: Holt, Rhinehart & Winston.

Wood, N.V. (1986). *College reading and study skills.* Orlando, FL: Holt, Rinehart & Winston.

7

Preparing for and Taking Tests

David M. Wark
Rona F. Flippo

I n this chapter we review the techniques of preparing for and taking tests at the college level. We open with an introduction to useful skills and follow with an extensive review of the literature on test coaching and test wiseness for objective examinations, strategies for taking those tests, and the treatment of test anxiety. A section on implications for practice contains suggestions on how instructors can teach strategies for preparing for and taking tests and how students can apply them. Finally, we include a brief summary of implications for future research.

The Learnable Skill of Preparing for a Test

Tests are a fact of life for anyone moving through the educational system or up a career ladder. Students must perform acceptably on tests to pass their courses and receive credit. Students expecting to receive financial aid must have appropriate grades and test scores to qualify. Admission to graduate school depends largely on test grades. Some occupations require tests to advance, or simply to remain employed in a current position. Many professionals must pass tests to qualify or be certified in their fields. Considering all the ways test scores can affect lives, knowing the techniques of preparing for and taking a test can be very useful. That information, along with methods of teaching it, should be part of every reading and study skills instructor's professional toolkit.

The research literature supports the idea that special instruction in preparing for and taking a test can lead to higher scores. Studies show positive effects among various populations for a variety of approaches. Marshall (1981), for instance, cites reports from some 20 institutions of higher education. Across that range, nearly 41 percent of the students leave before the start of their second year, and 50 percent leave before graduation. Some of these dropouts and transfers are, of course, due to financial, social, personal, and developmental concerns. But the author cites studies showing that retention is improved when supportive services like instruction in study and test taking skills are made available to students. Other researchers have found similar results. Arroyo (1981) showed that Chicano college students' test and class performance, as well as their study skills, improved when they were taught to use better study and test taking procedures through a self-monitoring and modeling approach. Evans (1977) produced the same type of gain working with black students using a combination of anxiety reduction and basic problem-solving methods.

Further, the literature shows clearly that even major tests are amenable to test practice and training. To name only a few, scores on the Scholastic Aptitude Test (SAT) (Slack & Porter, 1980), the Graduate Record Examination (GRE) (Evans, 1977; Swinton & Powers, 1983), the National Board of Medical Examiners (NBME) (Scott et al., 1980), and the Georgia Regents' Competency Exam (Naugle & McGuire, 1978) have increased after use of a variety of training approaches.

The literature covers many distinct topics under the broad categories of test preparation and test taking, including philosophical orientations, specific drills for coaching students to take certain tests, special skills such as reducing test anxiety, and test wiseness strategies. In this chapter we review the research and application literature relevant to these areas for the postsecondary and college student. Some of the studies reviewed were conducted with younger student populations. We include those when findings or implications are useful to postsecondary and college students or to reading and study skills specialists working with that population.

Instruction in test preparation and test taking can make a difference in some students' scores. The literature shows that students from different populations, preparing for tests that differentiate at both high and low levels of competence, may improve their scores using a number of training programs. This chapter explains and extends these results.

Coaching

Coaching is a controversial area in test preparation, partly because the term is poorly defined. Both Anastasi (1981) and Messick (1981) acknowledge that the word has no agreed upon meaning in the measurement field. A coaching program can have any combination of strategies or exercises in test familiarization, drill and practice, motivational encouragement, taking tests with specific item formats, subject matter review, or cognitive skill development. Other components may be special modules such as test wiseness or test anxiety reduction. The duration of a coaching program may be from 1 hour to 9 hours or more (Samson, 1985).

Because the operational definition of coaching is so varied, it evokes a range of reactions and raises a variety of issues. For the purposes of this chapter we use a widely permissive definition and include studies that involve any test preparation or test taking technique in addition to formal instruction in the knowledge content of a test.

One of the issues raised by coaching is actually a problem of social policy. The argument is that students from economically disadvantaged schools or families will not be able to afford expensive coaching courses (Nairn, 1980). Consequently, decisions based on the results of the tests when some students have had coaching and some have not are inherently unfair. The same argument is offered when the examinees are not uniformly told of the kinds of special preparation they should undertake (Cait, 1980; Green, 1981). Referring specifically to the SAT, Anastasi (1981) says that individuals who have deficient educational backgrounds are more likely to reap benefits from special coaching than those who have had "superior educational opportunities" and already are prepared to do well on tests.

Another and more technical debate focuses on the problem of transfer. What is transferred from the coaching to the test taking, and ultimately to the performance being assessed or predicted? Anastasi believes that the closer the resemblance between the test content and the coaching material is, the greater the improvement in test scores will be. However, the more restricted the instruction is to specific test content, the less valid the score will be in extending to criterion performance. In essence, the argument is that coaching reduces the validity of the test.

A third issue is that of maximal student development. Green suggested that certain types of coaching should, in fact, become long term teaching strategies. The notion is that comprehension and reasoning skills should be taught at the elementary and secondary levels and that school programs should integrate the development of thought with the development of knowledge. Schools also should prepare students in ways that reduce anxiety over being evaluated, and not simply familiarize them with test formats and test taking skills.

Note that the social policy, transfer of training, and student development arguments make a common assumption: coaching does have a real, observable effect. If not, there would be no reason to fear that many minority students are disadvantaged by their inability to afford coaching classes. Similarly, if coaching were not associated with gains in certain important test scores, there would be no need to debate whether the gain signified an increase in some basic underlying aptitude or whether the schools should take the responsibility of coaching scholarship. These arguments do not settle the debate. In fact, they raise a basic question: How effective is coaching?

The effects of coaching. Consider first the SAT. Anastasi (1981) reports that the College Board, concerned about ill-advised commercial coaching, has conducted studies covering a wide variety of methods. The samples included white and minority students from both urban and rural areas and from public and private schools. The general conclusion was that intensive drill on test items similar to those on the SAT do not produce greater gains in test scores than those earned by students who retake the SAT after a year of regular high school instruction. A second conclusion was that the results of short term drills, which can raise performance on some test items, are not retained in the operational form of the test. But some scholars would conclude that coaching was effective if an intensive short program produced the same gain as a year's regular study.

Coffman (1980), writing from a perspective of 17 years of experience at the Educational Testing Service, recalls thousands of studies on the SAT and concludes that while it is difficult to differentiate teaching from coaching, "there is some evidence...that systematic instruction in problem-solving skills of the sorts represented by SAT items may improve not only test performance but also the underlying skills the test is designed to assess" (p. 11).

Many studies of other instruments support the idea that test preparation has a positive effect on the academic retention of various populations of postsecondary students. Arroyo (1981) states that Chicano college students have a higher dropout rate than do Anglo-Americans at all levels and notes that one factor thought to contribute to this high dropout rate is poor academic performance due to lack of learned skills or educational preparation. Arroyo tried to improve the test performance and increase the class participation of Chicano college students by teaching them productive studying skills in preparation for testing. Arroyo's coaching procedures were based on self-monitoring and self-reinforcement, along with shaping instructions and reinforcement from a Chicano program director. The results were impressive: students increased the time spent studying and improved in both test results and class performance.

Swinton and Powers (1983) studied university students to see the effects of special preparation on GRE analytical scores and item types. They coached students by offering familiarization with the test. Their results showed that scores may improve on the GRE Aptitude Test following short term interventions based on practice on items similar to those found on the test. The authors contend that if the techniques learned in coaching are retained, students may improve performance both on the GRE itself and in graduate school.

Evans (1977) conducted another study dealing with the GRE, using a special course designed to aid black and Chicano volunteer subjects in preparing for the exam. Students received four sessions focusing specifically on instruction in the basic mathematics required for the test, including strategies for dealing with the various types of questions found on the GRE. In addition, the course included a short one-session discussion of the GRE and its uses that was designed to reduce anxiety. Students in the program showed a small but consistent increase in GRE Quantitative scores. The increase was found early in the program, and there was no evidence that the program's effectiveness varied either by sex or by ethnic group.

Other studies that indicate positive results from coaching involve the National Board of Medical Examiners. The NBME is a standardized test of considerable importance. A passing grade on Part 1 is required for graduation from a majority of the medical schools in the United States. Weber and Hamer (1982) found that students in medical schools that offered or recommended a review course for Part 1 earned higher scores than students from schools that did not. The difference was slight but statistically significant. Scott et al. (1980), over a 3-year period, followed 55 second-year medical students who purchased a commercial test-coaching service. The students scored significantly higher on the exam than students who had not received coaching but who had comparable basic science grade point averages. While the participants did not think the commercial course offered a shortcut to passing the test, they saw the coaching as a well-organized, condensed review program that helped them focus on the most important concepts.

Naugle and McGuire (1978) documented that Georgia Institute of Technology students who attended a workshop to prepare for the Georgia Regents' Competency Test achieved a 10 percent greater passing rate than a sample of students who did not attend the workshop. The workshop had a dual purpose: to increase motivation by pointing out that those who failed the test once and made no special preparation for the second time generally failed again and would be refused a diploma, and to teach the students how to apply writing skills on the exam. The coaching was designed, in part, to produce effects by appealing to individual pride and self-interest.

Two recent metaanalyses look at the effect of coaching on achievement test scores. Samson (1985) summarized 24 studies involving elementary and secondary students. Bangert-Drowns, Kulik, and Kulik (1983) reviewed 25 studies, mostly of secondary and college students. Thirteen studies were common to the two papers. Both reports came to surprisingly similar conclusions.

Samson (1985) found that across all types of treatments the average effect size of coaching was .33. (In other words, among all students involved in any type of treatment the average gain was .33 standard deviation.) Thus, the average coached student moved from the 50th percentile to the 63rd. Bangert-Drowns et al. (1983) found similar results. Across all variables, the average effect size was .25, representing a gain from the 50th to the 60th percentile. Both analyses concur in the main finding that coaching is associated with significant gains in test scores.

Both research studies also found the same two secondary relationships. The first is that length of treatment made an important difference in the effectiveness of a coaching program. In the Samson (1985) study, coaching raised the average score from the 50th to the 57th percentile after 1-2 hours, to the 64th percentile after 3-9 hours, and back to the 62nd percentile after more than 9 hours. In the Bangert-Drowns et al. (1983) summary, the increases were to the 61st percentile after 1-2 hours, the 59th percentile after 3-6 hours, and the 64th percentile after 7 or 8 hours. Apparently, a program of between 6 and 9 hours is most effective. The general effect of coaching seems to be slightly greater for the younger students in the Samson study. That makes some sense, since the older students already have learned how to take tests. But the results of both studies agree that coaching can be effective.

The other secondary effect was type of treatment. For Samson (1985), general test taking skills such as following directions, making good use of time, and using answer sheets correctly made up the effective program content. Those skills would be very appropriate for younger students who did not have much practice with objective testing formats. In the Bangert-Drowns et al. (1983) study, the effective treatments focused not on simple test taking mechanics but on "intensive, concentrated 'cramming' on sample test questions." The greatest gain was found in a single program that included 15.3 hours of instruction in recognizing and using the psycholinguistic cue system in the flow of language (McPhail, 1977).

These two reports also had some consistent negative findings. Both metaanalyses showed that reducing test anxiety and increasing motivation did not significantly increase scores in these samples. Perhaps the results would have been different if the authors had been able to categorize the subjects by level of anxiety, motivation for school, risk taking, or some other individual differences.

Conclusions. Coaching does seem to work. Studies of commercial and other coaching courses have implications for review programs sponsored by educational institutions. The courses should be consistent with the school's curriculum and should provide a framework for review of the basic material taught. This type of review would be a learning and thinking experience rather than simply a crash course or cramming strategy to pass an exam. In addition to the content review, coaching should cover specific techniques for the types of items to be encountered. Anxiety reduction or motivation enhancement should be part of the curriculum if appropriate.

Test Wiseness

Test wiseness, like coaching, is a meaningful but often misunderstood concept of psychological measurement. In fact, the notion of test wiseness is often used as ammunition in the battle over the value of objective testing. The varied and vocal opponents of objective testing have claimed that high-scoring students may be second rate and superficial, performing well because they are merely clever or cynically test wise (Hoffman, 1962).

Other, more temporate scholars, analyzing the problems of test preparation and test taking, have suggested that lack of test wiseness simply may be a source of measurement error. Millman, Bishop, and Ebel (1965), who have done extensive work in the field, say that "test wiseness is defined as a subject's capacity to utilize the characteristics and formats of the test and/or the test taking situation to receive a high score. Test wiseness is logically independent of the examinee's knowledge of the subject matter for which the items are supposedly measures" (p. 707). Millman et al. and Sarnacki (1979) present reviews of the concept and the taxonomy of test wiseness.

Test wiseness is a collection of skills and possibly traits that enable certain students to score well, more or less independent of their knowledge of the information being tested. How can that happen? Test wise students develop test taking strategies which they transfer to similar tests. They know how to take advantage of clues left in questions by some item writers. They know that if they change their answers after some reflection, they will generally improve their scores. They never leave questions blank when there is no penalty for guessing.

Some readers will vigorously question the propriety of teaching test wiseness. Should professionals committed to strengthening the skills of learning engage in such a seemingly inappropriate endeavor? If, as Millman, Bishop, and Ebel (1985) suggest, lack of test wiseness is a source of measurement error, the answer seems to be yes. In fact, teaching all students to be test wise should increase test validity. Scores would better reflect the underlying knowledge or skill being tested rather than sensitivity to irrelevant aspects of the test. Should reading and study skills professionals teach their colleagues how to write items that cannot be answered by test wiseness? Again yes. To the extent that items are focused, and all the alternatives are plausible, test validity will be increased. Therefore, it seems to be a good idea to teach both students and instructors to be test wise.

Strategies of high-scoring students. Some researchers have attempted to determine the various strategies used by high-scoring test takers. Although Paul and Rosenkoetter (1980) found no significant relationship between completion time and test scores, they did find that better students generally finish examinations faster. There were exceptions, however. Some poorer students finished early, and some high scorers took extra time to contemplate answers. High scorers seemingly have two strategies: know the material well enough to go through the test very quickly; or go through the test slowly, checking, changing, and verifying each answer. Either seems to be an effective approach.

In an effort to determine what test taking strategies are used by A students compared with those used by C and F students, McClain (1983) asked volunteers taking a multiple choice exam in an introductory psychology course to verbalize their test taking procedures while taking the exam. She found that, unlike the C or F students, the A students consistently considered all alternative answers and read the answers in the order in which they were presented in the test. They also anticipated answers to more questions than did the lower-scoring students. In addition, they were more likely to analyze and eliminate incorrect alternatives to help determine the correct answer. The A students also skipped more questions they were unsure of (coming back to them later) than did the c and f students. On a later exam, some of the c and f students who reported using the strategies characteristic of the a students reported an improvement in their exam scores.

At least some test taking strategies develop with age. Slakter, Koehler, and Hampton (1970) reported that fifth graders were able to recognize and ignore absurd options in test items. This is a fundamental strategy, one whose appearance demonstrates a developing sense of test wiseness. In the same study they looked at another basic strategy, eliminating two options that mean the same thing. Being able to recognize a similarity is developmentally and conceptually more advanced than recognizing an absurdity. Not surprisingly, these authors found that the similar option strategy did not appear until the eighth grade. In a study of strategies for taking essay tests, Cirino-Gerena (1981) distributed a questionnaire. Higher-scoring students reported using the following strategies: quoting books and articles, rephrasing arguments several times, rephrasing the questions, and including some irrelevant material in the answer. The most common strategy used by all students, however, was that of expressing opinions similar to those of the teacher.

Huck (1978) was interested in what effect the knowledge of an item's difficulty would have on students' strategy. His hypothesis was that students might read certain items more carefully if they were aware of how difficult those items had been for previous test takers. The study revealed that knowing the difficulty of an item had a significant and positive effect on test scores. It is not clear, however, how the students used that information to improve their scores.

A fascinating use of prior knowledge has come to light with reading tests. Chang (1979) found that a significant number of the undergraduate students he tested were able to correctly answer questions about passages on a standardized reading comprehension test without seeing the text. Some authors would say that the questions could be answered independently of the passages. Chang, on the other hand, attributed the

Wark and Flippo

students' success to test wiseness. Blanton and Wood (1984) designed a specific four-stage model to teach students what to look for when taking reading comprehension tests, making the assumption that students could be taught to use test wiseness strategies.

Other researchers have made the same assumption. Sarnacki (1981) urged that medical students taking the NBME be taught a strategy for Type K items. These are multiple choice items in which options represent different combinations of possible answers. In the student vernacular, this is the "all of the above, none of the above" format. Sarnacki observed that Type K items are particularly sensitive to one strategy. Regardless of the number of alternatives, each must be evaluated separately as true or false. Thus, a five-choice item could have anywhere from zero to five correct answers. The student's best strategy is to decide whether each single statement is true or false and then select the most correct option (e.g., all of the above, one of the above). But this format is so complex as to be unreliable. Sarnacki suggests that either the use of Type K items be restricted or that students be taught this strategy to equalize their chances of doing well.

Some empirical attempts have been made to teach test wiseness strategies. Flippo and Borthwick (1982) taught test wiseness strategies to their undergraduate education students as part of a teacher training program. Each of their trainees later taught test wiseness as part of their student teaching. At the completion of the treatment activities, they gave each class of children a unit test they had developed. The results showed no significant difference between experimental and control groups' performance. Focusing on an older population, Bergman (1980) tried to teach junior college students to be test wise. His treatment group of nonproficient readers was enrolled in a reading and study skills improvement class. The control groups either practiced taking tests or received no extra instruction or practice. Bergman found no significant difference in scores on multiple choice and open-ended questions for those receiving instruction. It may be that the time devoted to test wiseness instruction in each of these studies was too short. Perhaps coaching over a longer period of time would have proved more successful. Moreover, strategy effects may be too small to be measurable by tests with the reliability typical of student teacher exams such as were used in the Flippo and Borthwick study.

In summary, the identification of test taking strategies has been more successful than the attempts to teach them. Good test takers instruct themselves in a variety of strategies, at least some of which require a certain level of cognitive development. While the idea of teaching test taking strategies is intuitively acceptable, a few researchers have reported success. Perhaps the techniques take a long time to learn. It is also possible that individual differences such as personality, anxiety level, and intelligence affect how test wiseness information will be used. Few studies control for these possible effects.

Recognizing cues. Another proposed test wiseness skill is the ability to make use of cues in the stems or the alternative answers by test writers (Millman, Bishop, & Ebel, 1965). Some test constructors may, for example, write a stem and the correct answer, and generate two good foils. Stumped for a good third foil, such a teacher takes the easy way out by restating one of the false foils. But a test wise student spots the ruse and rejects both similar alternatives. Or perhaps the correct answer is the most complete, and hence the longest. These and other cues can take a variety of forms, and can be found in a variety of test types, including multiple choice, true/false, matching, and fill-in-the-blank.

There is an interesting body of literature investigating the effects of using cues to correct answers. An illustrative example is the work of Huntley and Plake (1981), who investigated cues provided by grammatical consistency or inconsistency between the stem and the set of alternatives. They focused on singular/plural agreement and vowel/consonant clues. A stem might contain a plural noun that could give a clue to the correct answer if any of the alternatives did not have agreement in number. A stem ending in ''a'' or ''an'' might also provide a clue to the correct choice depending on whether the alternatives began with vowels or consonants. The authors found that there was some cueing with these patterns and recommended that test makers write multiple choice items to avoid grammatical aids.

Other cues have to do with the position or length of the correct answer. Inexperienced test writers have a tendency to hide the correct alternative in the B or C position of a multiple choice alternative set, perhaps thinking that the correct choice will stand out in the A or D position and be too obvious. Jones and Kaufman (1975) looked at the position and length of alternatives on objective tests to determine their effects on responses. They found that the students involved in their research project were more likely to pick out a correct response because of its B or C position than because of its length in relation to the other choices. Both cues had an effect, however; apparently some students are alert for the possibility of such cues.

A study by Flynn and Anderson (1977) investigated four types of cues and their effects on students' scores on tests measuring mental ability and achievement. The four cues were (1) options that were opposites, so that if one were correct, the other would be incorrect (e.g., "the war started in 1812" versus "the war ended in 1812"); (2) longer correct options; (3) use of specific determiners; and (4) resemblance between the correct option and an aspect of the stem. The undergraduate subjects were given a pretest of test wiseness and classified as either test wise or test naive. Then instruction was given for recognizing the four cues. The students showed no gains on the ability and achievement tests, although the students who were classified as test wise did score higher than those classified as test naive. Perhaps those students who were originally labeled test wise used test taking strategies other than the ones measured, or were brighter or better guessers. It is also possible that the target cues were not present in the ability and achievement tests. In any case, it seems that the more test wise students were more effective in applying some strategies to various testing situations.

Two studies focused on technical wording as a cue. In one, Strang (1977) used familiar and unfamiliar choices that were either technically or nontechnically worded. He asked students, in a somewhat artificial situation, to guess on each item. He found that nontechnically worded options were chosen more often than technically worded items regardless of familiarity. In the second study, Strang (1980) used questions that required students either to recall or to interpret familiar content from their child growth and development course. The items contained different combinations of technically and nontechnically worded options. The students had more difficulty with recall items in which the incorrect option was technically worded. Strang suggested that this difficulty might spring from students' tendency to memorize technical terms when studying for multiple choice tests. They would thus use technical words as cues to a correct choice.

Smith (1982) made a subtle contribution to the test wiseness cues research with the notion of convergence. He points out one of the principles of objective item construction: every distractor must be plausible. If it isn't, it contributes nothing to the value of the item as measurement. Smith offers the following example of implausibility:

Who was the seventeenth President of the United States?
a. Andrew Johnson
b. 6 3/8
c. 1812
d. A Crazy Day for Sally

Clearly, foils need to be plausible if the item is to discriminate between students who know the content of the test domain and those who do not. However, the requirement that foils be plausibly related to the stem creates a problem. Many test writers generate a stem first, and then the correct answer. To build a set of plausible foils, they consider how the correct answer relates to the stem. To use Smith (1982) again, suppose "Abraham Lincoln" is the correct answer to a history question. Most likely, the question has something to do with either American presidents or personalities from the Civil War era. So a plausible set of alternatives might include those two dimensions. Alternatively, it could include people from Illinois or men with beards. Using the first possibility, a set of alternatives might be:

a. Abraham Lincoln
b. Stephen Douglas
c. Robert E. Lee
d. James Monroe

Smith suggests that test wise students look for the dimensions that underlie the alternatives. In this case, the dimensions are:

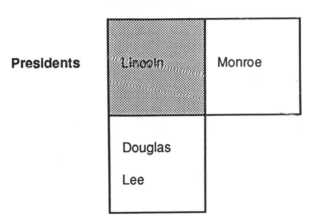

**Civil War
Personalities**

Presidents   Lincoln   Monroe

Douglas

Lee

Lincoln is the only alternative on which the two dimensions converge.

Smith (1982) reports a number of experimental studies to test the use of the convergence cue. Leary and Smith (1981) gave graduate students in education some instruction in recognizing dimensions and selecting the convergence point. Then they gave students items from the abstract reasoning section of the Differential Aptitude Test, the verbal section of the SAT, and the Otis Quick Score Mental Ability Test. They asked the students to find correct answers without seeing the stems. Subjects scored significantly better than chance on all three tests. It appears that convergence can be a usable cue.

Next, Smith (1982) randomly divided a group of high school students and gave the experimental group 2 hours of instruction in finding the convergence point. The control group had 2 hours of general test taking instruction. Both groups had previously taken the Preliminary Scholastic Aptitude Test (PSAT) and took the SAT after the experiment. The mean for the experiment group, adjusted for the PSAT covariate, was 39 points higher on the verbal subscale. Smith believes that convergence training is the explanation of the findings.

Test wiseness does seem to be due, in part, to sensitivity to certain cues in the items. Some of the cues are obvious to those who are familiar with the grammatical conventions of the language. The cue effect of familiar technical words is another example. Other cues, like position and length of the correct answer, seem to be the result of repeated exposure to the various forms of objective test items. The cues based on the logical relationships between alternatives are probably of a different sort, and may depend on the test takers' general intellectual ability or other characteristics. With that possibility in mind, it is interesting that studies have achieved positive results in teaching sophisticated cue use. While it is hard to cleanly separate cues from strategy, it does seem that the cue approach to teaching test wiseness is more effective.

Changing answers. There is a false but persistent notion in the test taking field that a student's first answer is likely to be correct. The implication is that one should stay with the first choice, since changing answers is likely to lead to a lower score. Contrary to this belief, research indicates that changing answers produces higher test scores (Edwards & Marshall, 1977; Lynch & Smith, 1975; McMorris & Leonard, 1976; Mueller & Schwedel, 1975; Smith, Coop, & Kinnard, 1979). These studies confirm earlier research findings that changing answers is, in fact, a mark of test wiseness. The research on this point is remarkably consistent.

To begin, it should be clear that answer changing is not a random event. Lynch and Smith (1975) found a significant correlation between the difficulty of an item and the number of students who changed the answer to that item. They suggested that other items on the test may have helped the students reconsider their answers for the more difficult items. It seems possible that changes produce higher scores because later items help students recall information they did not remember the first time through. Two studies looked into the answer-changing patterns of males and females (Mueller & Schwedel, 1975; Penfield & Mercer, 1980). Neither found a significant difference in score gains as a function of the sex of the test taker. For the most part, higher-scoring students gained more points by changing answers than their lower-scoring colleagues (Mueller & Schwedel; Penfield & Mercer). Only one study (Smith et al., 1979) found that the lower-scoring group benefited more from their answer changes. In general, the higher-scoring students made more changes (Lynch & Smith; Mueller & Schwedel; Penfield & Mercer).

McMorris & Leonard (1976) looked into the effect of anxiety on answer-changing behavior and found that low-anxiety students tended to change more answers, and to gain more from those changes, than did high-anxiety students. But both groups did gain.

In writing about the answer-changing research, Wilson (1979) cited many of the same findings already discussed. She reiterated the main concern of most of those researchers: that students should know the true effects of answer changes (Edwards & Marshall, 1977; Lynch & Smith, 1975; Mueller & Schwedel, 1975; Smith et al., 1979). It seems that changing answers is a good test strategy when, after some reflection or a review of previous responses, the student thinks changing is a wise idea. In general, the low-anxiety, high-scoring students both make more changes and benefit more, in spite of contrary belief.

Retesting. A final area of research delves into the effects of simply repeating a test in the original or parallel form. The second score will reflect a number of effects: regression to the mean, measurement error, and the increased information gained by study between tests. But part of the difference will be due to a type of test wiseness. An instructor may give several tests during a course, and students may begin to see a pattern in the types of questions asked. Besides giving students some direction for future test preparation, this may help them develop a certain amount of test wiseness. Can the effects be generalized? The research on retesting starts with the premise that the actual taking of the test helps students develop certain strategies for taking similar tests at a later time. Some of the retesting research involves typical classroom exams. Other studies cover the effects of repeated testing on standardized measures of intelligence, personality, or job admission.

Studying classroom tests, Cates (1982) investigated whether retesting would improve mastery and retention in undergraduate courses. The study sample included 142 students from five different sections of educational psychology taught over a 3-year period. Of the 202 retests taken to improve an original score, 139 (or 68.8 percent) showed improved performance. The mean gains in tested performance ranged from 1.2 percentage points to 6.3 percentage points. The author notes that the students frequently took retests 2 to 4 weeks after the original test date, suggesting that distributing test practice may be an effective strategy in increasing knowledge of the subject material. However, the gains are rather modest.

Allowing that retesting can produce some gains, are the gains specific to the content of the retested items, or do they constitute a type of general test wiseness? Bondy (1978) found that reviewing specific questions from a multiple choice test improved students' performance on a retest involving those specific items. However, the students who had reviewed those questions scored no better on reworded items than did students who had not reviewed the questions and answers. Simple retesting does not seem to be very effective if the item wording is changed.

A study done by Tips and others (1978) indicates that retesting may improve test scores. The study was done with 55 college students who were enrolled in a noncredit reading improvement course. The purpose of the study was to record the effects of an instructional unit on taking analogy tests. The results showed that college students can improve analogy test performance with instruction on a test preparation strategy. However, the instruction may be no more effective than the practice effects of retesting.

For classroom testing, it seems, the results are not very exciting. Simple testing and retesting, without some explicit test wiseness instruction, have little to recommend them. What about the effect of simple retesting on more standardized tests? Various types of tests have been studied in the research. Catron and Thompson (1979) looked into gains on the Weschler Adult Intelligence Scale Using four test-retest intervals, they found that regardless of the time between the original test and the retest, the gains on the performance IQ section were greater than the gains on the verbal IQ section. The researchers believe that the experience of taking a test alters the results of any similar tests taken afterwards. One would not expect retesting to alter basic traits. Hess and Neville (1977) studied retest effects on personality tests using the Personality Research Form. Their results led to the conclusion that what subjects learn or think about after seeing their test results affects future scores on a personality test. Thus the intervening event, not the retesting, is what is powerful.

But still the question remains: Can retesting affect scores on basic characteristics? Wing (1980) did a study using a multiple abilities test battery in use nationwide since 1974 as an entrance criterion for federal professional and administrative occupations. The major concern of the study was to see whether practice would aid test repeaters. During the first 3 years, alternate forms of the test battery were administered on 17 occasions to 600,000 subjects, with a little less than 3 percent of these subjects taking the test battery two or more times.

The findings are that score gains depended on age, gender, and the number of previous testings. Older test takers averaged lower gains than younger test takers. Wing also found a difference in subtest gains by sex. Compared with scores for males, the average gains for females were higher in inductive reasoning, the same in verbal ability and deductive reasoning, and lower in judgment and numerical items. Applicants with lower initial scores repeated the test more often. Higher final scores were recorded by those who repeated the battery the most times. It seems unlikely that scores on these tests could be improved by study of the content. The improvement is probably at least partly due to test wiseness gained from simple retesting.

Naugle and McGuire (1978) make an interesting and pertinent observation: Several students, when interviewed, said they did not prepare for the Georgia Regents' Competency Exam because it cost nothing to take and because failures were not recorded on their records. Therefore, they could continue to retake the test until they passed it. The data support this idea. In the summer of 1978, 25 percent of all students taking the Regents' Exam were repeaters, and many passed with no additional help since taking it the first time. It seems that familiarity with the test, due to repeated retesting, aided them in passing the test.

In summary, it seems that retesting, without any explicit content tutoring, can have positive effects on certain scores. However, the studies which show effects allow for repeated retesting. Perhaps the gain is due in part to regression upward toward the mean, and in part to a test-specific type of test wiseness.

Conclusions. The literature on test wiseness seems to support several conclusions. Some strategies have been identified for helping on essay and multiple choice tests, especially Type K items. Avoiding absurd options and rejecting options that mean the same thing are common strategies. Probably one part of any strategy is recognizing the presence of certain cues in the test items, such as grammatical agreement, length, convergence, and technical wording. Students who are test wise can recognize these cues and may implicitly use them when the situation allows it. Almost all students, regardless of level of anxiety and test wiseness, can improve their scores by changing answers as they work. And simple retesting, even without any formal review of content, has a small but positive impact on scores.

Test Anxiety

One of the major problems students face in taking tests is test anxiety. Test anxious students often earn lower scores on classroom tests than their ability would predict. The highly anxious student may have done a creditable job of preparation, using all the appropriate study techniques. Up to the moment of the exam, the student may be able to summarize and report content and demonstrate other necessary skills. But in the actual test situation, when it counts, this student fails to perform.

The typical test anxious student may show distress in one or more of the following ways: physiologically (excessive perspiration, muscular tension, accelerated heartbeat), intellectually (forgetting, incorrect response fixation), or emotionally (worry, self-degeneration). After the exam has been turned in, the test anxious student reports a rush of recall, after it is too late to change answers. Gaudry and Spielberger (1971) suggest that as many as 20 percent of a given college sample may suffer from severe and debilitating test anxiety.

Test anxiety, as a scientific concept, is approximately 40 years old (Mandler & Sarason, 1952). In their initial investigations, Mandler and Sarason asked students about their feelings and performance while being evaluated. Questions covered increases in heart rate, perspiration, feelings of uneasiness, and worry. From the responses, the authors computed a score of testing-produced anxiety. They found that students who had high levels of anxiety worked slower and showed more overt signs of anxiety on a block design test that was presented as a measure of academic aptitude. After completing six trials, the students were randomly told they scored either very high, about average, or very low. They were then asked to complete another six trials.

Specific findings from the second trial were linked to level of test anxiety. On the second series, the high-anxiety students showed depressed scores, regardless of their previous performance. It seems that these students collapsed under the pressure of further evaluation. For the low-anxiety students, however, further testing led to an improved performance. They were energized and worked faster. The effect was particularly strong for those low-anxiety students who were told they had done very poorly on the earlier test.

To account for those effects, Mandler and Sarason (1952) hypothesized two mechanisms that produced the anxiety-related deficit. In the psychological language of the day, they talked of two learned drives—one for task performance and the other for anxiety. In an evaluation situation, both drives operate. The "learned task drive" elicits useful and score-enhancing feelings of competence, accurate recall, and rapid, skilled performance. The "learned anxiety drive," in part, brought on the same effect. But the anxiety drive also elicited task-interfering feelings of inadequacy, memory blocking, helplessness, and excessive questioning. In the high-anxiety student, these two drives conflict and produce lower scores.

All of these feelings and thoughts, positive and negative, presumably were learned in the past, as the student was growing up and being evaluated by parents and teachers. Later, in a college testing situation, all the old learning came back when stimulated by evaluation. The net effect, which was predicted and then validated by research, is that as the test becomes more important and negative evaluation becomes more damaging, learned anxiety drive becomes stronger and has more destructive effects. Highly anxious students may flunk because of their anxiety, not because they do not know the material.

Since the classic work by Mandler and Sarason (1952), the investigation of test anxiety has blossomed. Reviews by Allen (1971), Allen, Elias, and Zlotlow (1980), Tryon (1980), and Wildemouth (1977) attest to the theoretical and empirical

Wark and Flippo

growth of the field. A recent metaanalysis (Hembree, 1988) covered 562 high-quality studies. A volume edited by Sarason (1980) details work on a variety of special fields including the development of test anxiety in children, the physiological base of test anxiety, a variety of intervention models, and the impact of test anxiety on math and on computer-based learning environments. Much of the research has been aimed at understanding the dynamics of test anxiety treatment, reducing subjective discomfort, and improving academic performance. In this section we focus specifically on those treatment techniques that have been shown to improve grades among college students.

Measurement and theories. As a prelude to a survey of treatment techniques, we present a brief overview of the measures and theories of test anxiety. The first instrument for measuring test anxiety, the Test Anxiety Questionnaire (Mandler & Sarason, 1952), contained 42 questions. Participants were asked to record their responses to each item by placing a mark on a horizontal line. The more discomfort they felt, the further to the right they made their checkmark. To score an item, the experimenter measured the number of centimeters from the left edge of the line to the check—a very unwieldy procedure. A more usable instrument was the Test Anxiety Scale (Sarason, 1978), a 37-item instrument covering most of the same experiences but in a much more convenient true-false scoring format. An earlier 16-item true-false Test Anxiety Scale (Sarason & Ganzer, 1962) is an excellent instrument for screening a large class. Wark and Bennett (1981) have normed the scale for high, medium, and low achievement students.

Several significant trends have arisen in the development of test anxiety measures. One such development grew out of the work of Liebert and Morris (1967). They hypothesized that test anxiety had two components: (1) physiological and emotional arousal, such as increases in heart rate, perspiration, and muscular tension (the common overt symptoms of anxiety); and (2) worried thoughts about the negative consequences of failure, about doing poorly, and about lack of skills (conscious, internal talk that interfered with competent performance).

When they did a factor analysis of the Test Anxiety Questionnaire, Liebert and Morris did indeed find these two factors, which they distilled into a short 10-item test called the Worry-Emotionality Questionnaire (Morris & Liebert, 1970). The two factors have very different effects on test taking.

Emotionality, or excessive physiological arousal, may or may not be detrimental to student performance. Some level of arousal is absolutely necessary for a student to learn, retain, and perform. The optimal level of arousal for any given task depends on a person's history, physiology, and state of health. If emotionality goes beyond that optimal level, performance may begin to deteriorate. But emotionality is not a universally negative variable.

Worry, the other factor, is seen as always being detrimental to test performance. The high-anxiety student has internal responses that interfere with optimal test performance. Hollandsworth et al. (1979) have cleverly documented the kinds of internal statements made during a test by high- and low-anxiety students. Calm people recall themselves saying things like "I was thinking this was pretty easy," "I was just thinking about the questions mostly," or "I always love doing things like these little designs." Their comments contrast strongly with those recalled by anxious students: "I decided how dumb I was," or "My mother would say. . .don't set bad examples because I'm watching you." These internal statements may reduce performance by interfering with task relevant thoughts, and may also increase emotionality.

Another important theory about variables affecting test anxiety was put forward by Wine (1971), who noted the importance of how students direct their attention. According to her analysis, calm students pay most attention to test items. Anxious students, on the other hand, attend to their internal states, their physiological arousal, and especially their negative self-talk. In essence, high-anxiety students are focusing their attention internally rather than externally to the examination. Wine was able to reduce test anxiety effects by showing students how to attend to the test, and not to their internal states.

We have only touched on the trends in test anxiety measurement here, summarizing the points that have implications for practice. The literature in this field is both extensive and quite technical. Interested readers should consult Sarason (1980) or Gaudry and Spielberger (1971).

In summary, there are three general approaches to test anxiety. The physiological or behavioral approach stresses the disruptive effects of arousal and emotionality. Treatment is geared toward helping students relax and desensitizing them to their presumed phobic fear of tests and evaluations. The second approach flows from the worry or cognitive component of test taking. Students are taught how to change the way they think and talk about themselves in a test situation. The third approach involves teaching test anxious students to focus on the exam, to use good test taking skills, and to ignore, for a while, the internal distractions of tension.

Reducing emotionality. The most common technique for reducing emotionality and physiological arousal is relaxation and desensitization (Wolpe, 1969). In varying numbers of sessions, students are first taught how to use deep muscle relaxation (Jacobson, 1938). In that relaxed state, they are asked to imagine themselves in increasingly difficult situations. Students might be asked to imagine themselves studying a week before the exam, and to hold that scene in mind until they are quite comfortable with it. Then they would be asked to imagine studying the night before the exam, and to get comfortable with that idea. Succeeding mental images would involve the morning of the exam, walking to the exam, receiving the test, and taking the exam. Desensitization can be more effective than simple relaxation or no treatment at all (Aponte & Aponte, 1971). The desensitization may be done in massive doses rather than spread out over several days (Dawly & Wenrich, 1973). Or the students may be exposed only to the most feared items in the hierarchy; for instance, "Imagine that you have just received your test booklet and you can not recall the answer to a single question." The technique of asking a relaxed student to imagine the most anxiety-provoking situation is called *implosion* (Cornish & Dilley, 1973).

In general, simple relaxation, systematic desensitization, and implosion techniques have not been shown to be strikingly effective in reducing test anxiety. In her review, Tryon (1980) stated that systematic desensitization and/or implosion resulted in significant academic improvement for participants relative to no-treatment controls in only 7 of 17 studies. Another review (Allen et al., 1980) showed improvement in 22 percent of the reviewed studies. In general, it is fair to say that systematic desensitization worked in about 30 percent of the recorded studies, and those studies tended to be methodologically flawed in that they often did not contain a credible placebo procedure to control for nonspecific treatment effects.

One theoretically important refinement in the emotionality control research has demonstrated a high percentage of grade improvements. Instead of leaving control with the therapist, students are given more responsibility. Subjects are taught specific techniques to adjust their own level of relaxation. They might practice saying the word *calm* and pairing it with a relaxed state. Then, in a test situation when they say the word *calm* to themselves, the cue helps them relax and reduce the effects of anxiety (Russell & Sippich, 1974). Subjects also have been taught to control their own desensitization with good results (Denny & Rupert, 1977). Giving subjects control over relaxation seems desirable. Tryon (1980) reports that four of the five studies in which subjects had conscious control over relaxation led to significant grade improvements (Deffenbacher, Mathis, & Michaels, 1979; Delprato & DeKraker, 1976).

Reducing worry. The generally higher effectiveness of client controlled desensitization leads naturally to a discussion of the research on cognitive interventions. These procedures, flowing from interpretations by Wine (1971), deal with the worry component of test anxiety. Hollandsworth et al. (1979) documented the kinds of things high-anxiety students say to themselves during a test situation. Cognitive therapy techniques were developed to counter those negative, worrisome thoughts. Cognitive therapy techniques go beyond desensitization. Clients are taught to use coping imagery in which they imagine themselves reducing their tension, solving their problems, and being successful. Note the difference between emotion oriented and worry oriented therapy. With desensitization for emotionality, the clients relax and imagine themselves being comfortable in progressively more difficult situations. The therapist is generally in charge, and the focus is on the emotional or physical component of test anxiety. In a cognitive therapy approach for worry, clients imagine themselves actively taking steps to reduce the negative effects of anxiety. They might imagine themselves taking slow, deep breaths, becoming calm, and giving themselves successful instructions. In a cognitive approach to alleviate test panic, students would see themselves start to check the time, skim over the entire test, skip difficult items, and recall material from a chapter that contains the answer to a question. In essence, clients are taught to imagine themselves going through a therapeutically effective checklist of activities.

The results of the earliest studies of cognitive therapy on test anxiety were very encouraging. Meichenbaum (1972) taught test anxious students to be acutely aware of their negative self-verbalization and instruction. He also modified the standard desensitization procedures so that instead of just imagining themselves relaxing, students were taught to give themselves support statements and instruction in relaxation. The students in Meichenbaum's cognitive modification group made significant gains in grades. Holroyd (1976) found essentially the same result. His cognitive therapy group received training to be more aware of their negative internal self-talk and to prompt themselves to react well in stressful situations.

In her review, Tryon (1980) found that of four cognitive intervention studies monitoring academic performance, two showed significant grade improvement from cognitive therapy work. In review of later test anxiety studies, Lent (1984) looked for grade change effects as a result of cognitive therapy. Of seven methodologically acceptable studies using some sort of cognitive intervention, he found only two that showed improvement in GPA. And both of those studies (Kirkland &

Hollandsworth, 1980; Decker & Russell, 1981) used a treatment that involved study skills training as well as cognitive therapy. In fact, in the Decker and Russell study, cognitive restructuring and anxiety reduction were less effective than study skills counseling in improving grades. It would appear that cognitive restructuring to attack the worry component is not a great deal more effective than the desensitization techniques used to attack emotionality when grade change is the target of interest. That leads to another possible area, the use of study skills training as a technique for attacking test anxiety.

Improving study skills. Reducing test anxiety by improving study skills is not an either/or approach. The literature illustrates the effectiveness of a combination of treatments. Allen (1971), working with a group of anxious, high-achieving college students (mean pretreatment GPA, 3.5), found that the most effective treatment involved systematic desensitization combined with study skills training. The skills content was based on the classic SQ3R text study strategy (Robinson, 1946). In addition, students were taught behavioral techniques for monitoring time, charting rate, and giving self-reinforcement. The students in the combination group improved their course examination percentile by 24 percent. Similar results were reported by Mitchell and Ng (1972). They found the greatest impact from combining techniques. Each of the nine sessions they offered the mixed treatment group covered relaxation, desensitization, and skills work. Finally, Mitchell, Hall, and Piatkowska (1975) found that a combination of study skills instruction and systematic desensitization was more effective than either study skills plus relaxation training or intensive study skills instruction alone. On a 2-year follow up, 73 percent of the students given desensitization plus study skills training were still in college, while only 25 percent of the relaxation group were still enrolled.

Later research has uncovered refinements to the general conclusion that a combination of techniques is effective. Brown and Nelson (1983) studied a sample of high-anxiety college students, all of whom scored above the 67th percentile on the Test

Anxiety Survey (Sarason, 1978). Part of the group consisted of low achievers (GPA less than 2.7) and part consisted of high achievers (GPA greater than 3.3). The two subgroups differed in important ways. The high achievers knew more about good study skills. In addition, they were better able to stop their own negative self-descriptions during an examination. In a sense, they could handle their anxiety. The low achievers, on the other hand, lacked both information on study skills and the ability to counter their negative thinking. Naveh-Benjamin, McKeachie, and Lin (1987) also found two categories of test anxious students. Both types had trouble recalling material for an exam, but one type had good study skills and the ability to encode and organize materials in a way that matched the lecturer's structure, while the other type had trouble with encoding.

Covington and Omelich (1987) also studied types of highly anxious students and the ways they studied. The authors investigated the presence of anxiety blockage on both easy test items calling for recognition and difficult items measuring the ability to make generalizations or inferences. They found that high-anxiety students who used good study habits suffered some interference, but only on difficult items. Using a path analytic technique to partition the causal determinants of blockage, they estimated that the causal effects on test performance due to anxiety (7.34 percent) were greater than the effects due to study skills (1.05 percent). (The main determinant of test performance was intellectual ability, at 91.6 percent.)

Thus, Brown and Nelson (1983), Covington and Omelich (1987), and Naveh-Benjamin et al. (1987) all agree that there are subcategories of high-anxiety students. In terms of treatment, some may need study skills assistance, some may need cognitive control training, and some may need both.

There is one contrary finding regarding study skills treatment. In a second study, Allen (1973) gave a group of high-anxiety students training in deep muscle relaxation with and without behavioral study skills counseling. Again the skills counseling was based on SQ3R, augmented by behavioral self-control techniques. Surprisingly, Allen found no differences between the two groups. Students in both groups improved their exam scores and their GPAs more than the nontreated control group. For those highly anxious students, simply learning to relax and reduce arousal seemed to be as important as learning new study skills.

What can be said about the use of study counseling as a way to reduce test anxiety? Clearly, a behavioral approach to study skills improvement is an important variable in reducing test anxiety and raising grades (Hembree, 1988). Tryon (1980) concludes that packages that include study skills plus some other kind of intervention always show better results than no-treatment control groups. Deciding which type of student needs which type of treatment is a worthwhile subject of research.

Other treatment techniques. Several other methods for reducing test anxiety have been investigated. For the most part, they do not flow from any of the three previously discussed approaches. Rather, they seem to come from other aspects of psychological research. Observation learning from a model student is one example. Horne and Matson (1977) had a group of high-anxiety students listen to a series of tapes purporting to be group sessions of test anxious patients. Over the course of a 10-week treatment, students heard three tapes, in which the model students expressed progressively less concern about test panic. During the sessions in which no tapes were played, counselors verbally reinforced the subjects' nonanxious self-reports. Students in other groups were treated by desensitization, flooding (asking students to imagine test failure), or study skills counseling. Horne and Matson found that modeling, desensitization, and study skills training were more effective than flooding in producing grade improvements and reducing anxiety. On the other hand, McCordick et al. (1979), comparing modeling with cognitive treatment and study skills, found that no treatment in their study was effective in improving grades. As these researchers admit, "the ideal treatment for test anxiety is still elusive" (p. 420).

Working from a general anxiety theory stance, Bushnell (1978) investigated several ingenious approaches to reducing test anxiety. If, he speculated, high-anxiety students are sensitive to any stimulation that increases concern for evaluation, why not try reducing such stimulation? He had high-anxiety students take mid-quarter exams either in a large lecture hall where they saw other students or in a language lab where they were screened off from one another. He found that grades were significantly higher in the lab for both high- and low-anxiety students. For the high-anxiety students, the difference was marked. He also found that among mildly anxious students, those who sat next to highly anxious students earned lower scores than those who did not, regardless of test setting.

Clearly, the research raises some interesting questions. Is the positive effect of the lab setting due to a reduction of visual distraction, or to the novelty of taking a test in a special place? The fact that the marginally anxious students were affected by the presence of anxious students, even in the lab, suggests that more than just visual separation is responsible for the test score gains. While all the questions have not been answered, the data certainly do suggest interesting ways to reduce the effects of test anxiety.

In another facet of this field, there is fascinating and consistent literature on the impact of allowing students to express their feelings about a test. McKeachie, Pollie, and Speisman (1955) presented tests with a special answer sheet that had space to comment about any item. The students who received sheets with a comment section earned higher scores than the students who used conventional answer sheets. Smith and Rockett (1958) replicated the study but extended the effect. They used three groups of students, one given standard answer sheets, one given sheets that allowed for comments, and one that contained the message, "Please comment on anything unusual about each question." They found that the three types of answer sheets were associated with successively better test scores by high-anxiety students, and successively worse scores by low-anxiety students. Why does an invitation to comment about a test reduce anxiety effects for anxious students? Perhaps because the moment or two taken to write out any feelings about the item reduces some of the worry about the test. Students may feel that they have explained their answers, so they can stop worrying. Perhaps they feel that with the explanation, graders will give them the benefit of the doubt. Unfortunately, for the low-anxiety students, the invitation to comment seemed to lower motivation and drive.

Conclusions. What can we conclude about test anxiety? The most restrictive position, best exemplified by Kirkland and Hollandsworth (1980), is that educators would be better off scrapping the concept entirely. They believe that as far as test performance and grades are concerned, inadequate performance simply indicates ineffective test taking. Their conclusions are based on studies conducted with simple anagram tasks. Training in academic test taking skills did seem to be more effective than either relaxation to reduce emotionality or meditation to reduce worry. But while anagram tasks are good research tools, they are not real world learning tasks.

What about more realistic measures? When performance is measured in GPA change, the Kirkland and Hollandsworth (1980) study showed that meditation was just as effective as study skills instruction, although relaxation was not as effective. These findings fit with the more liberal conclusion in the general literature that treatment involving systematic desensitization, or study skills training plus some cognitive intervention, is effective in producing grade changes (Denney, 1980; Hembree, 1988; Tryon, 1980).

That conclusion may change in time. Psychological techniques, like pest control chemicals, seem to lose their impact through successive generations. But for now, the real problem of test anxiety seems to be best treated by teaching students better ways to study and take tests as well as methods for exerting active self-control over their own process of preparing for and taking exams. Of course, instructors can make some environmental changes to reduce test anxiety effects. Bushnell

(1978), McKeachie et al. (1955), and Smith and Rockett (1958) point the way to techniques that deserve more consideration. Teachers who do their best to reduce tension, project hope and kindness, and model efficiency rather than panic are also exercising good preventive counseling. The real challenge is to find and manipulate ways to separate and individualize programs so that activities that are effective for high-anxiety students do not penalize low-anxiety ones.

Implications for Practice

We have reviewed three aspects of the process of preparing for and taking examinations. Certain findings seem to be clear. First, test coaching is not a waste of time. Students of a wide range of abilities have been shown to profit from certain kinds of coaching programs. The consensus from measurement experts is that the more disadvantaged and deficient a student's background, the greater the impact of test coaching. Yet the data also suggest that medical students as well as educationally impoverished minority high school students show positive effects from coaching.

Test wiseness strategies present a more complex situation that is harder to summarize. High-scoring students report using some strategies to good effect. A presumed mechanism accounts for at least part of the test wiseness effect: a student's sensitivity to the various cues to the correct answer left by unpracticed item writers. Test wise students apparently use these cues to gain an advantage. To some extent, then, the strategies take advantage of certain errors in item construction and measurement. In addition, the test wise student, when taking an exam, seems to use a large body of accepted techniques of time use, skipping, and so on. Test wise students also seem to take risks and make guesses. Both the sensitivity to cues and the test taking techniques appear to be teachable. It is not yet clear whether a teacher can impart the judgment or wisdom to know which strategy to apply in a given instance, or the willingness to use it.

Finally, we reviewed the status of test anxiety as an aspect of test preparation and test taking. Test anxiety has been identified and studied for more than three decades. In that period, research on the identification and treatment of the test anxious student has moved apace. It is now possible to teach students how to avoid the personal effects of anxiety, and to teach instructors how to arrange testing to reduce the likelihood that anxiety will affect test scores.

How might reading and study skills professionals use the information presented here? Perhaps by incorporating it into work with an individual student, or by creating a test preparation unit in a class, or by developing a systematic program that is open to a wide audience. In any case, the actual form of the program will depend on the nature of the students, the needs of the institution, and the resources available. What follows is a set of suggested components for any program. Some of the suggestions are strongly supported by research evidence. Others are based on our own clinical and teaching experience.

Study Skills

Most test preparation programs assume that students know how to study and, in fact, have done so. If there is any reason to think otherwise, the program must have a study skills component. The literature on study skills instruction and on specific techniques for reading and studying textbook material is summarized elsewhere in this volume. Without reiterating here, we can say that certain specific study skills seem appropriate for the special process of test preparation. Preparation for an exam should include instruction in the following areas:

- Time scheduling
  Setting personal priorities
  Setting aside time for review and practice
- Spaced vs. massed review
  Massed sessions for reading and integration
  Spaced time for new material and motor learning

- Memory
    Imagery and association techniques
    Mnemonic systems
    Effects of recitation on retention.
- Effects of stressors on test performance
    Sleep loss
    Drugs
    Test anxiety

Content Review

The review of successful test preparation programs is consistent on one point. Good programs are not simple content cram courses. They must be planned as an integrated package of experiences. In most cases, the presentation team is an interdisciplinary one. A reading and study skills specialist will present the study skills material and the test wiseness strategies. Depending on staff make-up, either the study skills specialist or a psychologist will help students learn techniques to reduce test anxiety. But there must also be a subject matter expert (SME) on the team.

The SME must be knowledgeable both in the content area of the test and in the techniques of teaching the subject. Such a person must know where students typically have trouble. If it is with the conceptual aspect, the SME must be prepared to offer important ideas at a more basic level. If the problem is computational, there must be drill and guidance to make the applications clear. If the problems are perceptual, the SME must teach the necessary discriminations that a competent student should demonstrate. The study skills specialist may be the expert in memory techniques or in planning spaced versus massed reviews or group study sessions to go over facts, but the SME has to limit and define those concepts and facts.

Test Practice and Test Taking

The collection of suggestions for taking exams is vast. This chapter has reviewed the impact and value of many of them. Which techniques to teach in a particular situation is a decision for the reading and study skills specialist. However, the following categories do seem to be generally valuable:

- Use of time
  Read all directions
  Plan time for review at the end
  Skip difficult items and go back to them
  Change any answer if it seems appropriate to do so
- Guessing
  If there is no penalty for wrong answers, guess
  Even if there is a penalty, if one or more alternatives can be eliminated, guess

Beyond these general rules, instructors can find a body of more or less validated strategies that apply to specific item types. There is, for example, a set of strategies for the various objective items in general, for Type K items, for matching items, and for analogies (Flippo, 1988). A similar body of suggestions exists for approaching and answering essay questions. Some of the suggestions are conventional: write neatly (Marshall & Powers, 1969; Raygor & Wark, 1980); and avoid spelling, grammar, and punctuation errors, which can result in lower scores (Scannell & Marshall, 1966). Note, however, that within certain limits, the lower the legibility of an answer, the higher the grade (Chase, 1983). Other suggestions are more complex, involving an attempt to train students in patterns of precise thinking and organization. This discussion is not the place for those details. However, some excellent sources on this topic are available. They should be consulted for management procedures (Flippo, 1984) and specific examples to illustrate techniques. The works by Boyd (1988), Ellis (1985), Flippo (1988), Millman and Pauk (1969), Pauk (1984), Raygor and Wark (1980), and Sherman and Wildman (1982) are all appropriate for postsecondary and college students.

Test Anxiety

What can we conclude about the most effective ways to reduce test anxiety and increase grades for college students? The research literature has some clear suggestions (see especially Hembree, 1988). A good program will include as many as possible of the following specific components:

1. Self-controlled systematic desensitization. Teach deep muscle relaxation, using the script in Wolpe (1969) or any of various commercial audiotapes. While they are relaxed, have students imagine themselves going through the steps of study, and finally going into the exam. Have the students tell themselves to be calm while imagining being in the exam room. Have them direct themselves through the test wiseness steps they know. Relaxation and desensitization are important, but the major benefit probably comes from calm students giving themselves instructions.

2. Cognitive self-instruction training. Teach students to be aware of any negative internal self-talk and to counter it with self-support. Have students practice a self-instructional script that contains instructions to relax, to give reminders of material studied, to use test wiseness strategies, to focus on exam items, and to give gentle self-support.

3. Behavior self-control techniques. Have students select a specific place for study and write precise goals for time and number of pages to read or problems to solve. Keep a chart of the number of hours spent in study and the goals met. Contract for rewards to be taken only when the goals are met. The payoff may be tangible or just supportive self-statements.

4. Study skills instruction. This intervention is important for students who are anxious and who lack good study skills. Teach the student to do a prestudy Sur-

vey, ask Questions about the content, Read for the answers to the questions, Recite the answers from memory, and Review all the previous questions and answers. This widely accepted plan was developed by Robinson (1946); however, there are many acceptable variations to SQ3R. Always be cautious in teaching the Question step, no matter what it is called. Students will learn the answers to their questions, even if they are wrong (Wark, 1965).

5. Test wiseness instruction. Anxious students should be taught a checklist of steps to recall during a test (e.g., plan time, eliminate similar options, look for associations, look for specific determiners). But note that the literature gives no support for test wiseness training as an isolated treatment. Instruction in test wiseness seems to work only when combined with other interventions.

Some institutions may be planning a structured program to combat test anxiety. The suggestions discussed earlier should enable study skills teachers with some background in psychology to set up an effective antianxiety program. For those readers who want more details, two articles in the literature review (Mitchell & Ng, 1972; Mitchell et al., 1975) give complete descriptions of their treatment groups. Wark et al. (1981) give details of an effective treatment program for students who are anxious when doing study-type reading and get low scores on their reading comprehension.

Some teachers may want to screen a class to pick out the students who are at risk for test anxiety. Those students identified by the screening can be referred for group or individual attention. For such screening purposes, the best instrument is probably the Anxiety Scale developed by Sarason and Ganzer (1962). Wark and Bennett (1981) recommend using a cutoff score of 11 or above as a sign of test anxiety. Either article can be consulted for a copy of the items, which may be used without permission.

Evaluating an individual for test anxiety is essentially a clinical activity. Test anxiety and study skills tests are helpful in this evaluation. Each gives some additional information that can lead to a diagnosis. Part of the process should be obtaining a history of school experiences and conducting a specific probe of recent anxiety experiences in test taking.

Implications for Future Research

Suggestions for further research in test preparation and test taking were implicit in many of the sources reviewed for this article. From an informal summary across the sources, two specific areas of concern seem to emerge. One is best characterized as a broad educational focus. Anastasi (1981) notes that current research is focusing on the development of widely applicable intellectual skills, work habits, and problem-solving strategies. The types of programs developed from this research would provide education rather than coaching or short term cramming to pass certain test items (Flippo & Borthwick, 1982). Cheek, Flippo, and Lindsey (1989) suggest that test wiseness training should begin in the elementary grades.

In the same tradition, Coffman (1980) says there is some evidence that instruction in item-oriented problem solving may improve the underlying skills a test is designed to assess. Further research could develop systematic methods to improve not only test performance but also latent skills. This research should provide information about the detailed nature of these "deeper" abilities, along with the conditions under which they may be expected to improve. One result of this research thrust could be tailored instruction to teach significant thinking skills that go beyond the strategies of test preparation and test taking.

If this broad type of suggested research can be called molecular, the second trend in the literature is more atomic. The assumption is that instruction can be given to help students simply become more test wise. Rickards and August (1975) suggest that research is needed on better ways to teach such pretest strategies as underlining, organizing, and notetaking. But what is the psychological basis for using these techniques? Weinstein and others (1980) look for research to refine our understanding of the covert processes involved in using cognitive strategies for learning and retention. Bondy (1978) suggests that further research be directed toward manipulating the variables within review sessions that are beneficial to students and efficient for instructors.

The results of the molecular and the atomic approach to test research will be similar: the difference is in the hypotheses and methods used. If continued research can provide better strategies for test preparation, perhaps some of the negative aspects of testing can be reduced. More important, test wiseness research may lead to new and important methods of teaching and learning. Tests will always be a fact of life for anyone moving up the educational ladder. But it is interesting to consider how learning might change if much of the negative aspect of testing could be removed.

References and Suggested Readings

Allen, G.J. (1971). Effectiveness of study counseling and desensitization in alleviating test anxiety in college students. *Journal of Abnormal Psychology, 77,* 282-289.

Allen, G.J. (1973). Treatment of test anxiety by group-administered and self-administered relaxation and study counseling. *Behavior Therapy, 4,* 349-360.

Allen, G.J., Elias, M.J., & Zlotlow, S.F. (1980). Behavioral interventions for alleviating test anxiety: A methodological overview of current therapeutic practices. In I.G. Sarason (Ed.), *Test anxiety: Theory, research, and application.* Hillsdale, NJ: Erlbaum.

Anastasi, A. (1981). Diverse effects of training on tests of academic intelligence. In W.B. Schrader (Ed.), *New directions for testing and measurement.* San Francisco, CA: Jossey-Bass.

Aponte, J.F., & Aponte, C.F. (1971). Group preprogrammed systematic desensitization without the simultaneous presentation of aversive scenes with relaxation training. *Behaviors Research and Therapy, 9,* 337-346.

Arroyo, S.G. (1981). Effects of a multifaceted study skills program on class performance of Chicano college students. *Hispanic Journal of Behavior Sciences, 3*(2), 161-175.

Bangert-Drowns, R.L., Kulik, J.K., & Kulik, C.C. (1983). Effects of coaching programs on achievement test performance. *Review of Educational Research, 53,* 571-585.

Bergman, I. (1980). The effects of providing test-taking instruction for various types of examinations to a selected sample of junior college students. (ED 180-566)

Blanton, W.E., & Wood, K.D. (1984). Direct instructions in reading comprehension test-taking skill. *Reading World, 24,* 10-19.

Bondy, A.S. (1978). Effects of reviewing multiple-choice tests on specific versus general learning. *Teaching of Psychology, 5*(3), 144-146.

Boyd, R.T.C. (1988). Improving your test-taking skills. Washington, DC: American Institutes for Research.

Brown, S., & Nelson, T.L. (1983). Beyond the uniformity myth: A comparison of academically successful and unsuccessful test-anxious students. *Journal of Counseling Psychology, 30*(3), 367-374.

Bushnell, D.D. (1978). Altering test environments for reducing test anxiety and for improving academic performance. (ED 161 946)

Cait, N. (1980). The implications of coaching for ability testing. (ED 131 598)

Cates, W.M. (1982). The efficacy of retesting in relation to improved test performance of college undergraduates. *Journal of Educational Research, 75*(4), 230-236.

Catron, D., & Thompson, C. (1979, April). Test-retest gains in WAIS scores after four retest intervals. *Journal of Clinical Psychology, 8*(3), 174-175.

Chang, T. (1979). Test wiseness and passage-dependency in standardized reading comprehension test items. *Dissertation Abstracts International, 39*(4-12), 7-8.

Chase, C.I. (1983). Essay test scores and reading difficulty. *Journal of Educational Measurement, 20*(3), 293-297.

Cheek, E.H., Flippo, R.F., & Lindsey, J.D. (1989). *Reading for success in elementary schools*. Fort Worth, TX: Holt, Rinehart & Winston.

Cirino-Grena, G. (1981, February). Strategies in answering essay tests. *Teaching of Psychology, 8*(1), 53-54.

Coffman, W.E. (1980). The Scholastic Aptitude Test: A historical perspective. *College Board Review, 117*, A8-A11.

Cornish, R.D., & Dilley, J.S. (1973). Comparison of three methods of reducing test anxiety: Systematic desensitization, implosive therapy, and study counseling. *Journal of Counseling Psychology, 20*, 499-503.

Covington, M.V., & Omelich, C.L. (1987). I knew it cold before the exam: A test of the anxiety-blockage hypothesis. *Journal of Educational Psychology, 79*(4), 393-400.

Dawley, H.H., & Wenrich, W.W. (1973). Massed groups desensitization in reduction of test anxiety. *Psychological Reports, 33*, 359-363.

Decker, T.W., & Russell, R.K. (1981). Comparison of cue-controlled relaxation and cognitive restructuring versus study skills counseling in treatment of test-anxious college underachievers. *Psychological Reports, 49*, 459-469.

Deffenbacher, J.L., Mathis, J., & Michaels, A.C. (1979). Two self-control procedures in the reduction of targeted and nontargeted anxieties. *Journal of Counseling Psychology, 26*, 120-127.

Delprato, D.J., & DeKraker, T. (1976). Metronome-conditioned hypnotic-relaxation in the treatment of test anxiety. *Behavior Therapy, 7*, 379-381.

Denny D.R. (1980). Self-control approaches to the treatment of test anxiety. In I.G. Sarason (Ed.), *Test anxiety: Theory, research, and applications* (pp. 209-243). Hillsdale, NJ: Erlbaum.

Denny, D.R., & Rupert, P.A. (1977). Desensitization and self-control in the treatment of test anxiety. *Journal of Counseling Psychology, 45*, 272-280.

Edwards, K.A., & Marshall, C. (1977, December). First impressions on tests: Some new findings. *Teaching of Psychology, 4*(4), 193-195.

*Ellis, D.B. (1985). *Becoming a master student* (5th ed). Rapid City, SD: College Survival.

Evans, F.R. (1977). The GRE-Q coaching/instruction study. (ED 179 859)

*Flippo, R.F. (1988). *TestWise: Strategies for success in taking tests*. Carthage, IL: Fearon Teacher Aids/Simon & Schuster.

Flippo, R.F. (1984). A test bank for your secondary/college reading lab. *Journal of Reading, 27*(8), 732-733.

*Flippo, R.F., & Borthwick, P. (1982). Should testwiseness curriculum be a part of undergraduate teacher education? In G.H. McNinch (Ed.), *Reading in the disciplines* (pp. 117-120). Athens, GA: American Reading Forum.

Preparing for and Taking Tests

Flynn, J., & Anderson, B. (1977, Summer). The effects of test item cue sensitivity on IQ and achievement test performance. *Educational Research Quarterly, 2*(2), 32-39.

*Gaudry, E., & Spielberger, C.D. (1971). *Anxiety and educational achievement.* Sidney, Australia: John Wiley & Sons.

Green, B.F. (1981). Issues in testing: Coaching, disclosure, and ethnic bias. In W.B. Schrader (Ed.), *New directions for testing and measurement.* San Francisco, CA: Jossey-Bass.

Hembree, R. (1988). Correlates, causes, effects, and treatment of test anxiety. *Review of Educational Research, 58(1),* 47-77.

Hess, A., & Neville, D. (1977, April). Test wiseness: Some evidence for the effect of personality testing on subsequent test results. *Journal of Personality Assessment, 41*(2), 170-177.

Hoffman, B. (1962). *The tyranny of testing.* New York: Collier.

Hollandsworth, J.G., Galazeski, R.C., Kirkland, K., Jones, G.E. & Van Norman, L.R. (1979). An analysis of the nature and effects of test anxiety: Cognitive, behavior, and physiological components. *Cognitive Therapy and Research, 3*(2), 165-180.

Holroyd, K.A. (1976). Cognition and desensitization in group treatment of test anxiety. *Journal of Consulting and Clinical Psychology, 44,* 991-1001.

Horne, A.M., & Matson, J.L. (1977). A comparison of modeling, desensitization, flooding, study skills, and control groups for reducing test anxiety. *Behavior Therapy, 8,* 1-8.

Huck, S. (1978, Spring). Test performance under the condition of known item difficulty. *Journal of Educational Measurement, 15*(1), 53-58.

Huntley, R., & Plake, B. (1981). An investigation of study sensitivity to cues in a grammatically consistent stem and set of alternatives. (ED 218-310)

Jacobson, E. (1938). *Progressive relaxation.* Chicago, IL: University of Chicago Press.

Jones, P., & Kaufman, G. (1975, Winter). The differential formation of response sets by specific determiners. *Educational and Psychological Measurement, 35*(4), 821-833.

Kirkland, K., & Hollandsworth, J.G., Jr. (1980). Effective test taking: Skills-acquisition versus anxiety-reduction techniques. *Journal of Consulting and Clinical Psychology, 48,* 431-439.

Leary, L., & Smith, J.K. (1981). *The susceptibility of standardized tests to the convergence strategy of test wiseness.* Paper presented at the Annual Meeting of the Eastern Educational Research Association, Philadelphia, PA.

Lent, R. (1984). The treatment of test anxiety: An updated review. Unpublished research. Minneapolis, MN: University Counseling Services.

Liebert, R.M., & Morris, L.W. (1967). Cognitive and emotional components of test anxiety: A distinction and some initial data. *Psychological Reports, 20,* 975-978.

Lynch, D., & Smith, B. (1975, January). Item response changes: Effects on test scores. *Measurement and Evaluation in Guidance, 7*(4), 220-224.

Mandler, G., & Sarason, S.B. (1952). A study of anxiety of learning. *Journal of Abnormal and Social Psychology, 47,* 166-173.

Marshall, J.C., & Powers, J.M. (1969). Writing neatness, composition errors, and essay grades. *Journal of Educational Measurement, 6,* 97-101.

Marshall, J.S. (1981). A model for improving the retention and academic achievement of nontraditional students at Livingston College, Rutgers University. (ED 203 831)

McClain, L. (1983, April). Behavior during examinations: A comparison of A, C, and F students. *Teaching of Psychology, 10*(2), 69-71.

McCordick, S.M., Kaplan, R.M., Finn, M.E., & Smith, S.H. (1979). Cognitive behavior modification and modeling for test anxiety. *Journal of Consulting and Clinical Psychology, 47*(2), 419-420.

McKeachie, J.J., Pollie, D., & Speisman, J. (1955). Relieving anxiety in classroom examination. *Journal of Abnormal and Social Psychology, 51,* 93-98.

McMorris, R., & Leonard, G. (1976). Item response changes and cognitive style. (ED 129 918)

McPhail, I.P. (1977). A psycholinguistic approach to training urban high school students in test taking strategies. *Dissertation Abstracts International, 37,* 5667A.

Miechenbaum, D.H. (1972). Cognitive modification of test-anxious college students. *Journal of Consulting and Clinical Psychology, 39,* 370-380.

Messick, S. (1981). The controversy over coaching: Issues of effectiveness and equity. In W.B. Schrader (Ed.), *New directions for testing and measurement.* San Francisco, CA: Jossey-Bass.

Millman, J.C., Bishop, C.H., & Ebel, R. (1965). An analysis of test wiseness. *Educational and Psychological Measurement, 25,* 707-727.

*Millman, J., & Pauk, W. (1969). *How to take tests.* New York: McGraw-Hill.

*Mitchell, K.R., Hall, R.F., & Piatkowska, O.E. (1975). A program for the treatment of failing college students. *Behavior Therapy, 6,* 324-336.

*Mitchell, K.R., & Ng, K.T. (1972). Effects of group counseling and behavior therapy on the academic achievement of test-anxious students. *Journal of Counseling Psychology, 19,* 491-497.

Morris, L.W., & Liebert, R.M. (1970). Relationship of cognitive and emotional components of test anxiety to physiological arousal and academic performance. *Journal of Consulting and Clinical Psychology, 35,* 332-337.

Mueller, D., & Schwedel, A. (1975, Winter). Some correlates of net gain resulting from answer changing on objective achievement test items. *Journal of Educational Measurement, 12*(4), 251-254.

Nairn, A. (1980). *The reign of ETS: The corporation that makes up minds.* Washington, DC: Learning Research Project.

Naugle, H., & McQulic, P. (1979) The preparatory workshop: A partial solution to an English compulsory exam failure rate. (ED 163 489)

Naveh-Benjamin, M., McKeachie, W., & Lin, Y. (1987). Two types of test anxious students: Support for an information processing model. *Journal of Educational Psychology, 79*(2), 131-136.

*Pauk, W. (1984). *How to study in college* (3rd ed.). Boston, MA: Houghton Mifflin.

Paul, C., & Rosenkoetter, J. (1980, Spring). Relationship between completion time and test score. *Southern Journal of Educational Research, 12*(2), 151-157.

Penfield, D., & Mercer, M. (1980, Spring). Answer changing and statistics. *Educational Research Quarterly, 5*(5), 50-57.

*Raygor, A.L., & Wark, D.M. (1980). *Systems for study* (2nd ed.). New York: McGraw-Hill.

Rickards, J.P., & August, J.G. (1975). Generative underlining strategies in prose recall. *Journal of Educational Psychology, 67*(8), 860-865.

Robinson, F.P., (1946). *Effective study.* New York: Harper & Row.

Russell, R.K., & Sippich, J.F. (1974). Treatment of test anxiety by cue controlled relaxation. *Behavior Therapy, 5,* 673-676.

Samson, G.E. (1985). Effects of training in test-taking skills on achievement test performance. *Journal of Educational Research, 78,* 261-266.

Sarason, I. (1978). The test anxiety scale: Concept and research. In C.D. Spielberger & I.G. Sarason (Eds.), *Stress and anxiety* (Vol. 5). Washington, DC: Hemisphere.

*Sarason, I.G. (Ed.). (1980). *Test anxiety: Theory, research, and applications.* Hillsdale, NJ: Erlbaum.

*Sarason, I.G., & Ganzer, V.J.(1962). Anxiety, reinforcement, and experimental instruction in a free verbal situation. *Journal of Abnormal and Social Psychology, 65,* 300-307.

Sarnacki, R. (1979). An examination of test wiseness in the cognitive test domain. *Review of Educational Research, 49*(2), 252-279.

Sarnacki, R. (1981, June). The effects of test wiseness in medical education. *Evaluation and the Health Professions, 4*(2), 207-221.

Scannell, D.P., & Marshall, J.C. (1966). The effect of selected composition errors on grades assigned to essay examinations. *American Educational Research Journal, 3,* 125-130.

Scott, C., Palmisano, P., Cunningham, R., Cannon, N., & Brown, S. (1980). The effects of commercial coaching for the NBME Part 1 examination. *Journal of Medical Education, 55*(9), 733-742.

*Sherman, T.M., & Wildman, T.M. (1982). *Proven strategies for successful test taking.* Columbus, OH: Merrill.

Slack, W. V. & Porter, D. (1980). The Scholastic Aptitude Test: A critical appraisal. *Harvard Educational Review, 50,* 154-175.

Slakter, M.J., Koehler, R.A., & Hampton, S.H. (1970). Grade level, sex, and selected aspects of test wiseness. *Journal of Educational Measurement, 7,* 119-122.

Smith, J. (1982, Fall). Converging on correct answers: A peculiarity of multiple-choice items. *Journal of Educational Measurement, 19*(3), 211-220.

Smith, M., Coop, R., & Kinnard, P.W. (1979, Fall). The effect of item type on the consequences of changing answers on multiple-choice tests. *Journal of Educational Measurement, 16*(3), 203-208.

Smith, W.F., & Rockett, F.C. (1958). Test performance as a function of anxiety, instructor, and instructions. *Journal of Educational Research, 52,* 138-141.

Strang, H. (1977, Fall). The effects of technical and unfamiliar options on guessing on multiple-choice test items. *Journal of Educational Measurement, 14*(3), 253-260.

Strang, H. (1980, May-June). The effects of technically worded options on multiple-choice test performance. *Journal of Educational Research, 73*(5), 262-265.

Swinton, S.S., & Powers, D.E. (1983). A study of the effects of special preparation of GRE analytical scores and item types. *Journal of Educational Psychology, 75*(1), 104-115.

Tips, M., & Others (1978). The effects of instruction in verbal reasoning strategies (analogies) in a college reading improvement course. (ED 173 763)

Tryon, G.S. (1980). The measurement and treatment of test anxiety. *Review of Educational Research, 2,* 343-372.

Wark, D.M. (1965). Survey Q3R; System or superstition? D. Wark (Ed.), *College and adult reading,* 3-4. Minneapolis, MN: North Central Reading Association.

*Wark, D.M. & Bennett, J.M. (1981). The measurement of test anxiety in a reading center. *Reading World, 20,* 215-222.

Wark, D.M., Bennett, J.M., Emerson, N.M., & Ottenheimer, H. (1981). Reducing test anxiety effects on reading comprehension of college students. In G. H. McNinch (Ed.), *Comprehension: Process and product* (pp. 60-62). Athens, GA: American Reading Forum.

Weber, D.J., & Hamer, R.M. (1982). The effects of review courses upon student performance on a standardized medical college examination. *Evaluation and the Health Professions, 5*(3), 35-43.

Weinstein, C.E., & Others (1980). The effects of selected instructional variables on the acquisition of cognitive learning strategies. (ED 206 929)

Wildemouth, B. (1977). *Test anxiety: An extensive bibliography.* Princeton, NJ: Educational Testing Service.

Wilson, P. (1979). Answer-changing behavior on objective tests: What is our responsibility? (ED 199 638)

Wine, J. (1971). Test anxiety and direction of attention. *Psychological Bulletin, 76,* 92-104.

Wing, H. (1980, September). Age, sex, and repetition effects with an abilities test battery. *Applied Psychological Measurement, 4*(2), 141-155. (ED 194 582)

*Wolpe, J. (1969). *Practice of behavior therapy,* New York: Pergamon.

Author Index

Author Index

Author Index   343

Subject Index

Note: An "f" following a page number indicates that the reference may be found in a figure; a "t," that it may be found in a table.